PRAISE FOR *JEWISH VEGANISM AND VEGETARIANISM*

"Whether looking at the pages of the Talmud, vegetarian poems written in Yiddish, lyrics written by Jewish punk rockers, or into a pot of vegan matzo ball soup, this book explores the many ways in which Jews have questioned the ethics of eating animals. Labendz and Yanklowitz achieve their stated goal of exploring 'what distinguishes Jewish veganism and vegetarianism as Jewish.' You do not have to be a vegetarian or a vegan (or Jewish!) in order to learn from, and indeed grapple with, the many questions, dilemmas, and readings that the contributors raise."
— Jordan D. Rosenblum, author of *The Jewish Dietary Laws in the Ancient World*

"*Jewish Veganism and Vegetarianism* offers theological, pragmatic, ethical, environmental, and other ways to view non-meat eating as a viable, healthy, and holy Judaic strategy to consume the world. Anyone who eats or thinks about eating should take this volume seriously."
— Rabbi Jonathan K. Crane, author of *Eating Ethically: Religion and Science for a Better Diet*

JEWISH VEGANISM AND VEGETARIANISM

JEWISH VEGANISM and VEGETARIANISM

STUDIES AND NEW DIRECTIONS

Edited by Jacob Ari Labendz
and Shmuly Yanklowitz

Cover: Marc Chagall, *The Cattle Dealer*, 1912, oil on canvas

Published by State University of New York Press, Albany

© 2019 State University of New York

All rights reserved

Printed in the United States of America

No part of this book may be used or reproduced in any manner whatsoever without written permission. No part of this book may be stored in a retrieval system or transmitted in any form or by any means including electronic, electrostatic, magnetic tape, mechanical, photocopying, recording, or otherwise without the prior permission in writing of the publisher.

For information, contact State University of New York Press, Albany, NY
www.sunypress.edu

Library of Congress Cataloging-in-Publication Data

Names: Labendz, Jacob Ari, 1977- editor. | Yanklowitz, Shmuly, 1981- editor.
Title: Jewish veganism and vegetarianism : studies and new directions / edited by Jacob Ari Labendz and Shmuly Yanklowitz.
Description: Albany, New York : State University of New York Press, [2019] | Includes bibliographical references and index.
Identifiers: LCCN 2018027702 | ISBN 9781438473611 (hardcover : alk. paper) | ISBN 9781438473628 (e-book) | ISBN 9781438473604 (pbk : alk. paper)
Subjects: LCSH: Vegetarianism—Religious aspects—Judaism. | Veganism—Moral and ethical aspects. | Jewish ethics.
Classification: LCC BM538.V43 J49 2019 | DDC 296.3/693—dc23 LC record available at https://lccn.loc.gov/2018027702

10 9 8 7 6 5 4 3 2

CONTENTS

Illustrations vii

Introduction: Considering Jewish Veganism and Vegetarianism ix
Jacob Ari Labendz and Shmuly Yanklowitz

PART ONE: STUDIES

1 The Slipperiness of Animal Suffering: Revisiting the Talmud's Classic Treatment 3
Beth A. Berkowitz

2 Vegetarianism as Jewish Culture and Politics in Interwar Europe 23
Nick Underwood

3 "I am a Vegetarian": The Vegetarianism of Melech Ravitch 49
Irad Ben Isaak

4 Farm Animal Welfare in Jewish Art and Literature 67
Hadas Marcus

5 Vegetarianism and Veganism among Jewish Punks 95
Michael Croland

6 Opening the Tent: Jewish Veganism as an Expression of an Ecological Form of Judaism 117
Adrienne Krone

7 A Linguistic Appraisal: Jewish Perceptions of Animal Suffering 131
Victoria Greenstone and Shlomi Shmuel

PART TWO: NEW DIRECTIONS

8 Veganism and Covenantalism: Contrasting and Overlapping Moralities 161
David Mevorach Seidenberg

9 Musar and Jewish Veganism 195
Geoffrey D. Claussen

10 The Vegetarian Teachings of Rav Kook   217
    Richard H. Schwartz and David Sears

11 Relevant and Irrelevant Distinctions: Speciesism, Judaism, and Veganism   233
    Alan D. Krinsky

12 A Morally Generative Tension: Conflicting Jewish Commitments to Humans and Animals   251
    Shmuly Yanklowitz

13 Linking Judaism and Veganism in Darkness and in Light   267
    Sherry F. Colb

14 Jewish Veganism as an Embodied Practice: A Vegan Agenda for Cultural Jews   289
    Jacob Ari Labendz

    Report: Jewish Vegan and Vegetarian Movements in North America   315
    Sarah Chandler and Jeffrey Cohan

    Afterword   325
    Aaron S. Gross

    Contributors   331

    Index   337

ILLUSTRATIONS

Figure 4.1　Rembrandt, *Slaughtered Ox*　82

Figure 4.2　Chaim Soutine, *The Beef*　83

Figure 4.3　Chaim Soutine, *Butcher's Meat Rack*　84

Figure 4.4　Chaim Soutine, *Still Life with Herrings*　85

Figure 4.5　Chaim Soutine, *Still Life with Chicken*　86

Figure 4.6　Marc Chagall, *Butcher*　88

Figure 4.7　Marc Chagall, *The Cattle Dealer*　89

Figure 4.8　Camille Pissarro, *The Cowherd*　90

Figure 4.9　Camille Pissarro, *Cowherd, Pointoise*　90

Figure 4.10　Camille Pissarro, *Autumn, Montfoucault Pond*　91

Figure 7.1　Secondary coding categories and metacategories　145

Figure 7.2　Visual representation of hypothesis regarding Jewish understanding of animal suffering　147

Table 7.1　"Comparisons to humans" code results by language　139

Table 7.2　Sample responses of "comparisons to humans" code　139

Table 7.3　Demographics of respondents with "agency" codes in English survey　142

Table 7.4　Demographics of respondents with "agency" codes in Hebrew survey　142

Table 7.5　Demographics of respondents with "comparisons to humans" codes in English survey　143

Table 7.6　Demographics of respondents with "comparisons to humans" codes in Hebrew survey　143

Table 7.7　Selected examples of secondary coding with response excerpts, codes, and metacategories　146

INTRODUCTION
Considering Jewish Veganism and Vegetarianism

JACOB ARI LABENDZ AND SHMULY YANKLOWITZ

JEWISH VEGANISM AND VEGETARIANISM

This volume reflects the studied intuition that Jewish veganism and vegetarianism have come of age. Jewish vegans and vegetarians have formed organizations and online forums to advocate within their communities and beyond and to develop, debate, and promote animal-product- and meat-free Jewish cultures.[1] One finds no shortage of Jewish vegan and vegetarian cookbooks, blogs, and other resources. Articles appear frequently in the Jewish press and have crossed over into mainstream publications, such as the *New York Times* and the *Wall Street Journal*.[2] Jewish communities across denominations and around the world are renegotiating their food practices and implementing policies to reflect their new or renewed ethical commitments.[3] By some counts, up to 5 percent of the Israeli population has gone vegan. This includes Jews of all backgrounds, from secular Jews to *Haredim*, as well as Muslim, Christian, and nonreligious Palestinians, and others. Even the Israeli Defense Forces have had to accommodate the demands of vegan soldiers.[4] Jewish people have also counted among the most prominent vegan activists, such as Mayim Bialik, a founding member and senior leadership consultant at the Shamayim V'Aretz Institute, and Academy Award-winning actor Natalie Portman.

This collection of essays by scholars, rabbis, activists, and community leaders explores the history, contours, and scope of veganism and vegetarianism among Jews and presents compelling new directions in Jewish thought, ethics, and foodways. As ever more Jews adopt vegan and vegetarian lifestyles, and thereby join movements that transcend the porous boundaries of Jewish communities, this volume asks what distinguishes Jewish veganism and vegetarianism as Jewish. It offers opportunities to meditate on the varied intellectual, cultural, and religious roots of these movements across centuries and continents. *Jewish Veganism and Vegetarianism* asks how Judaism, broadly considered, has inspired Jews to embrace such practices and how those lifestyles in turn have enriched and helped define Jewishness. This collection of essays tests the boundaries of Jewish veganism and vegetarianism and calls attention to divisions within those dynamic movements, along with some of the resistance they have faced.

Studies of Jewish veganism and vegetarianism, such as those that fill this volume, offer insights into Jewish culture and history that go beyond culinary and dietary spheres. We have learned from the growing field of food studies that examining how and what groups eat, as well as how they conceptualize their foods, can open vistas into their cultures and social worlds. Attention to how and why foodways change can help us mark, characterize, and account for broader sociocultural transformations. This is because foodways—cultures of food production and consumption—are central to how groups work. The provision of food rests at the foundation of society, economies, and politics. Anthropologist Mary Douglas has shown that how groups think about, distribute, and consume food can simultaneously reflect and produce their values and social structures.[5] Studies of foodways can thus inform how we consider a broader range of issues related to Jewish life. The essays that follow situate Jewish veganism and vegetarianism in discussions of food politics, animal rights and welfare, social justice, environmentalism, Jewish identity, cultures of (Holocaust) memory, nationalism, and religion.

WHAT'S JEWISH ABOUT VEGANISM? WHAT'S VEGAN ABOUT JEWISHNESS?

> Behold I give to you all the vegetation that sprouts seed which is upon the face of all the earth, and every tree in which the fruit of the tree sprouts seed, for you it shall be as food. And to all the animals of the earth and to all the birds of the sky and to all that creeps on the earth, in which there is life, [I give] all the green vegetation for food.
>
> —Genesis 1:29–30

> And the wolf will dwell with the sheep, and the leopard will lie down with the kid, and the calf and the young lion and the fatling together, with a young lad leading them. And the cow and the bear shall graze, together their young shall lie down, and the lion shall eat straw like the ox.
>
> —Isaiah 11:6–7

> The wolf and the lamb will graze together, and the lion shall eat straw like the ox ... they shall not do evil and they shall not destroy in all my holy mountain, says the Lord.
>
> —Isaiah 65:25

Historian Gary A. Rendsburg teaches that the Tanakh, the Jewish Bible, presents a world and human ideal "characterized by peace, harmony, and vegetarianism."[6] As demonstrated by the quotes from Genesis and Isaiah reproduced in his work and above, not only do humans in the Garden of Eden and in the Days of the Messiah survive on vegetables alone, so too do all animals, including those known as omnivores and carnivores. Of course, the Tanakh also makes clear that the foodways and rituals of ancient Israel depended on animal agriculture and meat consumption. Rendsburg thus argues further that the restrictions on such practices—which evolved into the laws of *kashrut*—reflect a divine concession or a compromise with God:

> humans are unable to live up to the vegetarian ideal set forth at creation; God compromises and allows humanity to eat meat. But Israel wishes to adhere to that ideal, even in a compromised fashion, and therefore Israel consumes only those animals that themselves have not killed other animals.[7]

Rendsburg is sure to account for cases where this compromise does not hold as well as it might, such as the permission granted to consume fish-eating fowl. He also draws specific attention to the Israelite taboo against consuming blood.

In the two millennia since the end of Judean ritual animal sacrifice in Jerusalem (and beyond), one can point to instances of vegetarianism and perhaps even veganism among Jews, as well as a general, if often subordinated, concern for the welfare of animals. Yet only in this century and the last may one speak of mass movements among Jews that eschewed meat consumption, let alone ones that approximated contemporary veganism. These phenomena reflect the boundedness of Jewish cultures and traditions to the wider contexts in which they have unfolded. The essays in this volume by Nick Underwood, Irad Ben Isaak, and Hadas Marcus analyze the emergence of these new vegetarian trends and their meanings.

At the 2017 meeting of the Society of Jewish Ethics, David Mevorach Seidenberg, a contributor to this volume, provocatively asked whether contemporary Jews have grafted veganism and vegetarianism artificially onto the Jewish tradition—perhaps in ironic opposition to the Torah's taboo against hybridization—or if Jewish veganism and vegetarianism represent natural outgrowths of Judaism as an ever-evolving tradition.[8] One would indeed be amiss if they were to argue that biblical or rabbinic Judaism promoted either veganism or vegetarianism. To be sure, none of the contributors in this volume make such a case, even if some argue that the proper normative application of Jewish law and values today should lead one to adopt veganism or vegetarianism.

This discussion raises complex questions about the authenticity of Jewish veganism and vegetarianism with which our authors wrestle implicitly and explicitly. Seidenberg, in the same comments, recognized the potential for Jewish veganism and vegetarianism to be profoundly effective and powerful movements. However, he also warned against the tendencies to make "superficial" cases for them. Simply collecting all the textual sources that could support these positions and then declaring veganism or vegetarianism to be authentic or essential to the Jewish tradition, he contends, does not make this claim true (nor does it establish a firm foundation for the movements in question).

One might counter, perhaps, with historian David Biale's argument regarding the character of Jewish communities from antiquity until the present: "it was precisely in their profound engagement with the cultures of their environment that the Jews constructed their distinctive identities."[9] He later continues,

> Jewish self-definition was, then, bound up in a tangled web with the non-Jewish environment in which the Jews lived, at once conditioned by how non-Jews saw the Jews and by how the Jews adopted and resisted the majority culture's definition of them. For all that Jews had their own autonomous traditions, their very identities throughout their history were inseparable from that of their Canaanite, Persian, Greek, Roman, Christian, and Muslim neighbors.... Viewed in this light, Jewish identity cannot be considered immutable, the fixed product of either ancient ethnic or religious origins, but rather to have changed as the cultural context changed.[10]

This suggests that Jewish veganism and vegetarianism may be yet another case of Jews and Jewish communities adopting (and contributing to) concepts and practices from the broader cultures in which they have existed and participated, while also making them distinctively their own (and thereby distinguishing themselves). Biale warns, however, that

> such a definition would be missing a crucial aspect of Jewish culture: the continuity of both textual and folk traditions throughout Jewish history and throughout the many lands inhabited by Jews. The multiplicity of Jewish cultures always rested on the Bible and . . . on the Talmud and other rabbinic literature.[11]

Roberta Rosenthall Kwall echoes such concerns in her provocative book, *The Myth of the Cultural Jew: Cultural and Law in Jewish Tradition*.[12] She argues that too profound a departure from systems of Jewish law and tradition—inseparable in her account from Jewish culture and socialization—threatens the undoing of Jewish particularity and historical continuity.

What, then, should we make of Jewish veganism and vegetarianism—if we may speak of such things? As activists in the field, we, Jacob and Shmuly, believe strongly that Jewish veganism is a significant, complex, and meaningful development in the history of Jewish culture, religion, and practice. We embarked on this publication unabashedly dedicated to presenting Jewish veganism as a phenomenon unto itself and worthy of study, reflection, and adoption. Without reservation, we hope for this volume to advance our common cause and help construct Jewish veganism as a part of our world. Although we have remained committed to the standards of academic research and publishing, we also conceive of this volume as an act of structural activism. Its existence helps present Jewish veganism as "a thing," and a thing of beauty at that.

NOTES ON PURPOSE AND SCOPE

We hope for *Jewish Veganism and Vegetarianism* to stand out as a unique collection because it includes works of scholarship in the fields of history, literary and religious studies, and the social sciences, alongside more normative contributions to Jewish philosophy, culture, and religious thought—chapters that some may consider valuable primary sources in their own rights. We intend for this volume to gesture toward the breadth of contemporary discussions around Jewish veganism and vegetarianism and to serve as a resource for developing them further across disciplinary, professional, and denominational lines. These goals are reflected in the biographies of our contributors, whose backgrounds, professions, and perspectives attest (not exhaustively) to the diversity within Jewish vegan and vegetarian communities and to the complexity, appeal, and significance of the phenomena we seek to explore. Not only do our authors contribute individually to their respective fields of study, but the tensions between their ideas promise to open additional avenues of thought and research.

With the transnational scope of *Jewish Veganism and Vegetarianism*, which reaches into North America, Europe, and Israel, we sought to contribute to conversations about Judaism and Jewishness in a globalizing world. This proved challenging. Our authors hail primarily from North America and write recognizably from that perspective—even if some contributed studies of European and Israeli phenomena. A fuller collection could have included comparative considerations of how the contexts of Jewish self-rule and hegemony—situated in contemporary Israel—continue to shape and produce competing Jewish vegan and vegetarian cultures and also a varied vegan politics among non-Jews.[13] It could have explored how the veganisms of Orthodox Jews in Israel can differ from those of non-Orthodox Jews there, and how Israeli veganisms relate to and depart from the veganisms of Jews elsewhere in the world.[14] Despite our many inquiries, we remain curious as to whether one may speak today of a specific European-Jewish vegan culture or cultures. More attention to Sephardi and Mizrahi frameworks would have further enriched this collection.

In its particularity, this book may complement the works of other minority vegan and vegetarian communities. Black vegans and vegans of color, as well as vegetarians, have produced cultures and texts that continue to create, enrich, challenge, and focus the tenets of veganism and vegetarianism and how those movements are perceived.[15] The lived experiences of Black Jews and Jews of color show that our communities are not mutually exclusive. We regret that *Jewish Veganism and Vegetarianism*, despite our efforts to the contrary, does not include chapters written explicitly from these perspectives or on related topics. We acknowledge that featuring such texts in a volume of this sort can function as a form of tokenism, if minority voices are included for the sake of representation alone, if they are prevented from influencing those frameworks perceived to be normative and treated as dominant.

It would be impossible (and wrong) to distill the contributions of Black vegans and vegans of color into a single paragraph or imagine their movements as fully separate from the veganisms found in predominantly white communities. Activists and scholars debate a wide range of issues related to animal welfare and rights; social, racial, and environmental justice; and human health in varied conversations, often pertaining to specific contexts and communities. A predominant commitment within many of these movements, however—one shared by ecofeminism[16]—has been to locate veganism within a broader, intersectional struggle against all hierarchy and oppression. (Adopting an intersectional approach does not entail collapsing the distinctions between species or oppressions, because differences fundamentally matter. It offers, instead, a moral and political framework for analysis, forging alliances, and taking action.) Intersectional veganism can assume context-specific and varied forms in our complexly racialized, classed, and gendered world and lead to the fusion of veganism with spheres of activism and politics often considered to fall beyond the normative scope of its concerns. For some, this means that veganisms that are insufficiently integrated into antiracist activism should be considered incomplete. This, in turn, can produce tensions among vegans of all faiths and ethnicities divided on issues such as Israeli politics and issues of race in the United States.

Introduction

In the introduction to *Veganism in an Oppressive World*, Julia Feliz Brueck writes, "diversity is not enough; truly listening and creating change through dialogue and implementing changes is vital."[17] Brueck quotes Aph Ko and Syl Ko's instructions to vegans who do not belong to communities of color:

> Challenge yourself not just to provide an ear for folks to talk into, but to slacken your attachment to your own beliefs and preferred strategies . . . and allow yourself to actually be influenced by the ideas of marginalized folk.[18]

Listening to marginalized voices entails a willingness to change one's own frameworks and approach. It also demands of those vegans and vegetarians who seek to ally with communities to which they do not belong that they adopt strategies appropriate to those specific communities.[19] This applies even across the racialized boundaries within the Jewish world.

Editing this volume has taught us much about the character and scope of the varied Jewish conversations around veganism and vegetarianism. In addition to many wonderful and surprising lessons, we came to recognize challenges that must be met in the future. Some of the chapters in this book wrestle with the intersection of veganism and racialized understandings of Judaism. Others discuss the relationship of veganism to broader issues in human politics and society. We look forward to engaging in deeper and transformational conversations in the years to come, inspired by the chapters in this volume and other perspectives on Jewish veganism and vegetarianism; discussions that respond to and embrace as inextricably Jewish the conceptions of veganism and vegetarianism promoted by Black Jews and Jews of color and perhaps by non-Jews as well.

ORGANIZATION OF THE BOOK

Jewish Veganism and Vegetarianism comprises two sections. The first, "Studies," includes seven chapters whose authors present Jewish veganism and vegetarianism in their historical, literary, and sociological contexts, from the time of the Talmud to the present day, in North America, Europe, and Israel, and among rabbis, chefs, artists, activists, punks, and farmers, just to name a few. Seven chapters also compose the second section, "New Directions." Submitted by authors from a wide range of backgrounds and professions, the contributions reflect contemporary currents in Jewish vegan and vegetarian thought. They manifest much of the cultural, theological, and ideological diversity among Jews invested in such conversations and seek to introduce readers to some of the more prominent debates and concerns within their movements. Some authors wrestle with Jewish law and tradition, while others seek to explore and embellish Jewish identities and politics. The volume concludes with a report on the history of Jewish vegan and vegetarian organizations in North America by activists Sarah Chandler and Jeffrey Cohan, and with an afterword by Aaron S. Gross.[20]

Studies

In chapter 1, Beth A. Berkowitz examines concern for animal suffering in the Talmud, where she finds it always in competition with and often "eclipsed" by other legal and moral considerations. She argues that attention to Talmudic discussions reveals how easily one may be distracted from the obligation to treat animals well. The next two chapters focus on vegetarianism among Central and Eastern European Jews in the early decades of the twentieth century. Nick Underwood shows that Jewish communities, and especially women, responded to the pressures of interwar Poland and early Nazi Germany by forging Jewish vegetarian cultures to express new national identities and politics of resistance. Not only does Underwood differentiate between the practices and ideologies in these two locations, he also contrasts them with movements in the United States and Western Europe. Irad Ben Isaak analyzes the interwar "vegetarian poems" of Melech Ravitch, a prominent figure of Yiddish literature. He locates the poet's vegetarianism—which reportedly influenced Isaac Bashevis Singer—at the intersection of Jewish culture and Austrian modernism. Ben Isaak argues further for the relative idiosyncrasy of Ravitch and the personal experiences that led him to avoid and criticize the eating of animals.

Hadas Marcus bridges past and present in chapter 4 by seeking the foundations of modern Jewish vegetarianism and veganism in the artistic and literary production of the nineteenth and twentieth centuries. Through the interdisciplinary lens of ecocriticism, she explores the widely accepted metaphorical interpretations of the animals who appear in these works. Marcus concludes, however, that such readings tend to occlude how Jewish artists have struggled with actual issues related to animal welfare and thereby have left lasting traces on Jewish culture.

The final three chapters in part one address aspects of Jewish veganism and vegetarianism today. In chapter 5, Michael Croland calls attention to the prevalence—even the expectation—of vegetarianism and veganism among Jewish punks, with a primary focus on musicians. He points to a commonality between the Jewish and punk values that have inspired some to eschew animal-product consumption, and further shows how some punks have used their veganism or vegetarianism and Jewishness to craft their public images.

In chapter 6, Adrienne Krone adopts Shaul Magid's concept of "postethnic Judaism" to study contemporary North American Jewish farming movements.[21] She argues that participants forge new Jewish and vegan identities by deploying veganism and Jewishness as mutually constitutive templates for self-construction.

In chapter 7, Veta Greenstone and Shlomi Shmuel offer a sociolinguistic analysis of how Jewish speakers of Hebrew and English respectively understand the concept of animal suffering, as well as the role that language may play in shaping those ideas. They find that most respondents to their surveys share an aversion to causing animals unexpected harm or harm perceived to be unnatural. Surprisingly, Greenstone and Shmuel note that meat eaters, more than vegans and vegetarians, tend to associate such types of suffering with human actions. The linguistic divisions between the respondents do not seem to matter strongly.

New Directions

The second part of this book opens with three chapters that look to the Jewish religious tradition to inspire and also challenge the adoption of veganism and vegetarianism as a Jewish practice. David Seidenberg argues that the Torah asks ancient Israelites to think about their relationships with animals on covenantal terms, which reflect and inform how they understand their relationship with God. He traces this idea as a minority position through centuries of rabbinic thought. Although Seidenberg acknowledges that this covenantalist framework may prove inspiring for people invested in developing Jewish vegan cultures, he also warns that it may not be fully commensurable with the absolute withdrawal from animal use typical among vegans.

In chapter 9, Geoffrey D. Claussen shows, in a deeply personal essay, how wisdom gleaned from the Musar movement of nineteenth-century Poland and Lithuania can enrich Jewish vegan practices. Careful not to misrepresent the movement's luminaries as having adopted (much less advocated for) vegetarianism, Claussen nonetheless suggests that the methods they developed for cultivating "loving-kindness, compassion, empathy, and self-restraint" not only maintain their value today but may also inspire us to make contextually based lifestyle choices that they did not.

In chapter 10, Richard H. Schwartz and David Sears find in the rulings, writings, and life of Rabbi Abraham Isaac Kook, chief rabbi of Mandatory Palestine, *halakhic* (Jewish legal) and ethical imperatives for contemporary Jews to eschew animal products. Not the first to rely on Kook for such support, they distinguish their contribution by offering responses to eight common objections levied by people skeptical of such interpretations of Kook's teachings—not the least of which is that the rabbi himself ate limited quantities of meat.

The authors of the following two chapters wrestle with the commensurability of Jewishness and veganism, stemming from conflicts over speciesism. While many vegans fundamentally reject the notion that human lives are more valuable than animal lives, the Jewish tradition tends not only to have endorsed but even to have been based on such a hierarchy. In chapter 11, Alan D. Krinsky evaluates the classic argument against speciesism, as articulated by the influential philosopher Peter Singer, in light of rabbinic texts and rulings stretching from the medieval period to today.[22] With specific regard to the medieval commentary of Rabbi Joseph Albo (1380–1444) on the biblical story of Cain and Abel, Krinsky not only concludes that speciesism is anathema to the rabbinical tradition, but he also raises additional practical and philosophical objections to that position (without dismissing other possible Jewish arguments for avoiding animal use and consumption).

In chapter 12, Shmuly Yanklowitz argues that Jewish ethics encompass both the anthropocentric (or speciesist) framework discussed by Krinsky and a more egalitarian vision of the ideal relationship between humans and (other) animals, perspectives that often come into conflict. Yanklowitz explores how Jews have negotiated this tension in the past and reveals that competing moral imperatives have served a generative function in the development of Jewish ethics. This chapter situates contemporary Jewish thought and practice in wider intellectual currents and in the history of American legislation on animal welfare.

The final two chapters feature works that include elements of autoethnography and reflection. They offer perspective on the range of reasons that can motivate contemporary Jews, specifically nonobservant Jews, to adopt veganism as a Jewish practice. Sherry F. Colb divides chapter 13 into two sections. In the first, she reflects on the power of naming to mark groups of humans and animals alike as appropriate for slaughter. Colb thus calls attention to her own experience as the child of Holocaust survivors to account for the closeness she feels with "farmed animals" and her choice to adopt a vegan lifestyle. While Jacob and Shmuly tend to be skeptical about the invocation of the Holocaust to promote veganism, Colb's revelations show how such connections can arise organically and that they can have merit and personal relevance worthy of scholarly consideration.[23] In the second part of the chapter, Colb addresses, as a question of theodicy, the tensions between the vegan ideal found in the creation story and the permission that the Torah subsequently grants to eat meat.

In chapter 14, Jacob Ari Labendz presents his practice of Jewish veganism as cultural technology or a tool for self-construction that can help secular (nonreligious and nonnational) Jews like him experience Jewishness as a central aspect of their lives and one that has the potential to transcend the divisions of our modern, fragmented selves. His autobiographical study relies on insights from the fields of history, anthropology, social psychology, and religious studies. It concludes with suggestions for how to create Jewish vegan cultures effectively and sensitively and to advocate for veganism as a progressive within and beyond the Jewish community.

ACKNOWLEDGMENTS

We thank the contributors to this volume for their erudition, diligence, and partnership and for becoming our teachers. We also express our gratitude to SUNY Press for publishing this volume and to Rafael Chaiken, Aimee Harrison, and Laura Poole for their assistance throughout the editorial process. Two anonymous reviewers provided us and many of the contributors with challenging and useful criticism. They have helped make this a better book. We extend our appreciation to our friends at the Shamayim V'Aretz Institute, Jewish Veg, the Jewish Vegetarian Society, and the Jewish Initiative for Animals. Among them we would like to single out Sarah Chandler, Jeffrey Cohan, Aaron Gross, and Lara Smallman. We are grateful to Anna Elena Torres, Limor Chen, and Abraham J. Frost for their suggestions and counsel. This volume was made possible, in part, by financial support from Youngstown State University.

To the best of our knowledge, this book is only the second edited volume on Jewish veganism and vegetarianism. Its roots lie in the production of the first, *The Jewish Vegan*, a collection of articles, essays, and poetry, edited by Shmuly Yanklowitz, to which both he and Jacob contributed.[24] We express our gratitude to the authors and editors who published earlier works on these and related themes. Not only have they informed the contributions to this volume, they have inspired and enriched our lives.[25]

Jacob thanks Shmuly for his many years of friendship and for encouraging him to embrace a (nearly) animal-product-free lifestyle. He is grateful to Megan Kramer for joining him in that decision and for the many delicious meals they have shared. Jacob also acknowledges his parents, who taught him the values on which he bases his veganism and Jewishness. He further extends his gratitude to his colleagues and students at Charles University, Pennsylvania State University, and Youngstown State University, who have supported this project. Finally, Jacob dedicates his labors toward the publication of *Jewish Veganism and Vegetarianism* to the memory of his father, Ralph Labendz z"l, and of his grandparents, Marianne and Martin Labendz z"l and Pearl Shain z"l.

Shmuly thanks Jacob for his friendship and partnership over the years. Since their days together at the Wexner Graduate Fellowship, Jacob has challenged Shmuly to think more deeply and critically about historical and cultural issues. Shmuly also thanks his wife, Shoshana, for becoming a vegan with him on their wedding day and for raising their children together as vegans. He thanks the staff, board, and members of the Shamayim V'Aretz Institute for supporting his vision and partnering to grow the Jewish vegan and Jewish animal welfare movements. Last, Shmuly thanks the Creator for granting us life in an era when it is so easy to be a vegan in America.

NOTES

1. Major Jewish vegan and vegetarian organizations include the Shamayim V'Aretz Institute and Jewish Veg (formerly Jewish Vegetarians of North America) in North America, the Jewish Vegetarian Society in the United Kingdom, and Ginger—The Vegetarian Community Center in Jerusalem, Israel.

2. Jonathan Safran Foer, "Against Meat," *New York Times Magazine*, October 7, 2009, http://www.nytimes.com/2009/10/11/magazine/11foer-t.html; Shmuly Yanklowitz, "Why This Rabbi Is Swearing Off Kosher Meat," *Wall Street Journal*, May 29, 2014, https://www.wsj.com/articles/shmuly-yanklowitz-why-this-rabbi-is-swearing-off-kosher-meat-1401404939.

3. In North America, the Jewish Institute for Animals helps Jewish organizations to work through this process. However, the organization does not advocate for strict veganism and belongs more fully to other food and farming movements.

4. Tova Cohen, "In the Land of Milk and Honey, Israelis Turn Vegan," Reuters, July 21, 2015, http://www.reuters.com/article/us-israel-food-vegan-idUSKCN0PV1H020150721; and Daniella Cheslow, "As More Israelis Go Vegan, Their Military Adjusts its Menu," *Food for Thought*, NPR, December 10, 2015, http://www.npr.org/sections/thesalt/2015/12/10/459212839/why-so-many-israeli-soldiers-are-going-vegan.

5. Mary Douglas, *Purity and Danger: An Analysis of Concept of Pollution and Taboo* (London: Routledge Classics, 2002).

6. Gary A. Rendsburg, "The Vegetarian Ideal in the Bible," in *Food and Judaism*, ed. Leonard J. Greenspoon, Richard A. Simkins, and Gerald Shapiro; Studies in Jewish Civilization 15 (Omaha, NE: Creighton University Press, 2005), 319–34; see 320–21 and 329 for the quotes at the beginning of this section.

7. Ibid., 327.

8. This was part of Seidenberg's response to talks given by Jacob Ari Labendz and Adrienne Krone, which drew from their contributions to this volume.

9. David Biale, "Preface: Toward a Cultural History of the Jews," in *Cultures of the Jews: A New History*, ed. David Biale (New York: Schocken Books, 2002), xxi.

10. Ibid., xxiii.

11. Ibid., xxiv.

12. Roberta Rosenthal Kwall, *The Myth of the Cultural Jew: Culture and Law in Jewish Tradition* (Oxford: Oxford University Press, 2015).

13. For example, see Erica Weiss, "'There Are No Chickens in Suicide Vests': The Decoupling of Human Rights and Animal Rights in Israel," *Journal of the Royal Anthropological Institute* n.s. 22 (2016): 688–706; Nir Avieli and Franz Markowitz, "Slavery Food, Soul Food, Salvation Food: Veganism and Identity in the African Hebrew Israelite Community," *African and Black Diaspora: An International Journal* 11 (2017), 205–20. doi: 10.1080/17528631.2017.1394612. We thank Limor Chen for bringing these articles to our attention.

14. Limor Chen, "Between Preservation and Subversion: Meanings of Vegan Food among Religious Jews in Israel," M.A. thesis, Ben Gurion University of the Negev, 2016.

15. Aph Ko lists the following books as resources on social justice and critical studies: A. Breeze Harper (ed.), *Sistah Vegan: Black Female Vegans Speak on Food, Identity, Health, and Society* (New York: Lantern Books, 2010); Lisa A. Kemmerer (ed.), *Sister Species: Women, Animals, and Social Justice* (Urbana-Champaign: University of Illinois Press, 2011); Aph Ko and Syl Ko, *Aphro-ism: Essays on Pop Culture, Feminism, and Black Veganism from Two Sisters* (New York: Lantern Press, 2017); Sunaura Taylor, *Beasts of Burden: Animal and Disability Liberation* (New York: New Press, 2017); and Carol J. Adams, *The Sexual Politics of Meat: A Feminist-Vegetarian Critical Theory* (New York: Bloomsbury, 2015). See http://www.blackvegansrock.com/resources (accessed December 31, 2017).

16. Esther Alloun cites the following sources in an article in which she addresses, through a feminist and postcolonial framework, the differences she perceives among Jewish-Israeli and Palestinian vegan activists: Carol J. Adams and Lori Gruen (eds.), *Ecofeminism: Feminist Intersections with Other Animals and the Earth* (New York: Bloomsbury, 2014); Erika Cudworth, "Beyond Speciesism: Intersectionality, Critical Sociology and the Human Domination of Other Animals," in *The Rise of Critical Animal Studies: From the Margins to the Centre*, ed. Nik Taylor and Richard Twine (New York: Routledge, 2014), 19–35; Maneesha Deckha, "Intersectionality and Posthumanist Visions of Equality," *Wisconsin Journal of Law, Gender and Society* 23, no. 2 (2008): 249–67; and Kemmerer (ed.), *Sister Species*. See Esther Alloun, "'That's the Beauty of It, It's Very Simple!' Animal Rights and

Settler Colonialism in Palestine-Israel," *Settler Colonial Studies* (2017), doi: 10.1080/2201473X.2017.1414138.

17. Julia Feliz Bruek, introduction to *Veganism in an Oppressive World: A Vegans of Color Community Project*, ed. Julia Feliz Bruek (Sanctuary Publishers, 2017), 18.

18. Ibid., 28.

19. Saryta Rodríguez, "Move to Berkeley! and Other Follies," in *Veganism in an Oppressive World: A Vegans of Color Community Project*, ed. Julia Feliz Bruek (Sanctuary Publishers, 2017), 89–104.

20. Aaron S. Gross, *The Question of the Animal and Religion: Theoretical Stakes, Practical Implications* (New York: Columbia University Press, 2015).

21. Shaul Magid, *American Post-Judaism: Identity and Renewal in a Postethnic Society*, (Bloomington: Indiana University Press, 2013).

22. Peter Singer, *Animal Liberation: The Definitive Classic of the Animal Movement* (New York: Harper Perennial Modern Classics, 2009).

23. Jewish Veg, the Jewish vegan organization formerly known as Jewish Vegetarians of North America, features Alex Hershaft among its most prominent speakers. Hershaft is a survivor of the Warsaw Ghetto who invokes his wartime experiences and the lessons he has drawn from them to advocate for animals. See "Alex Hershaft: From the Warsaw Ghetto to a Life of Compassion," Jewish Veg, https://www.jewishveg.org/hershaft; and "Alex Hershaft: From the Warsaw Ghetto to a Life of Compassion," YouTube, July 24, 2015, https://www.youtube.com/watch?v=7-ohM0-6-C0.

24. Shmuly Yanklowitz (ed.), *The Jewish Vegan* (Shamayim V'Aretz Institute, 2015).

25. Monographs on this topic include Louis A. Berman, *Vegetarianism and the Jewish Tradition* (New York: Ktav, 1982); Roberta Kalechofsky, *Rabbis and Vegetarianism: An Evolving Tradition* (Marblehead: Micah Publications, 1995); Roberta Kalechofsky, *Vegetarian Judaism: A Guide for Everyone* (Marblehead: Micah Publications, 1998); Donald Bernard Roodyn, *Alternative Kashrut: Judaism, Vegetarianism and the Factory Farm* (London: Reform Synagogues of Great Britain, 1978); Richard Schwartz, *Judaism and Vegetarianism* (New York: Lantern Books, 2001); David Sears, *The Vision of Eden: Animal Welfare and Vegetarianism in Jewish Law and Mysticism* (Spring Valley: Orot, 2003); and Julian S. Shindler, *Animal Rights, Shechita and Vegetarianism: A Traditional Jewish Perspective* (London: Union of Jewish Students, 1987). More resources, including many articles, may be found on the websites of the Shamayim V'Aretz Institute, Jewish Veg, and the Jewish Vegetarian Society. See the following for discussions or chapters on themes related to Jewish veganism and vegetarianism: Rynn Berry, *Food for the Gods: Vegetarianism and the World's Religions: Essays, Conversations, Recipes* (New

York: Pythagorean, 1988); Alfred S. Cohen (ed.), *Halacha and Contemporary Society* (New York: Ktav Publishing House and Rabbi Jacob Joseph School Press, 1984); Mary Douglas, *Leviticus as Literature* (Oxford: Oxford University Press, 1999); Leonard J. Greenspoon, Richard A. Simkins, and Gerald Shapiro, *Food and Judaism*, Studies in Jewish Civilization 15 (Omaha, NE: Creighton University Press, 2005); Aaron S. Gross, *The Question of the Animal and Religion: Theoretical Stakes, Practical Implications* (New York: Columbia University Press, 2015); Roberta Kalechofsky (ed.), *Judaism and Animal Rights: Classical and Contemporary Responses* (Marblehead: Micah Publications, 1992); Jonathan Safran Foer, *Eating Animals* (New York: Bay Back Books, 2009); Richard Schwarz with Rabbi Yonassan Gershom, *Who Stole My Religion? Revitalizing Judaism and Applying Jewish Values to Help Heal the World* (Raleigh, NC: Lulu Press, 2011); David Mevorach Seidenberg, *Kabbalah and Ecology: God's Image in the More-Than-Human-World* (New York: Cambridge University Press, 2015); Kerry S. Walters and Lisa Portmess (eds.), *Religious Vegetarianism: From Hesiod to the Dalai Lama* (Albany: SUNY Press, 2001); Mary L. Zamore (ed.), *The Sacred Table: Creating a Jewish Food Ethic* (New York: Central Conference of American Rabbis, 2011); and Benjamin E. Zeller, Marie W. Dallam, Reid L. Neilson, and Nora L. Rubel, *Religion, Food, and Eating in North America* (New York: Columbia University Press, 2014).

Part One **Studies**

1 The Slipperiness of Animal Suffering
Revisiting the Talmud's Classic Treatment

BETH A. BERKOWITZ

THE RACCOON IN THE KITCHEN

The landlord of a Brooklyn apartment building dismissed their complaints when the tenant couple, Will and Malya, told him about the crying they could hear inside their walls. But Will and Malya could not tolerate the strange whimpers they heard at night, so they took matters into their own hands. One night when the crying was particularly bad, Will moved the stove, where the cries seemed loudest, and started to hack away at the wall with a hammer. Malya began to video-record Will as he knelt down behind the stove, wanting to capture whatever was going to happen. Will hammered and hammered until he had made a hole a little larger than the size of his hand. While Malya filmed, Will put on a rubber kitchen glove and plunged his hand into the dark space behind the wall. His gloved hand emerged out of the hole clasping a baby raccoon, like a rabbit being pulled out of a magician's hat. Will's first instinct was, for some reason, to bring the shocked raccoon to the bathroom mirror so that the two of them could look at their reflection. He moved on to the bathtub, apparently to wash off the raccoon from the drywall dust, but that is when Malya stops the video. The posted YouTube video went viral, bringing CBS News and local fame to the Brooklyn couple.[1] The odd juxtaposition of forest critter and urban kitchen, the couple's quirky Brooklyn vibe, and the adorable baby raccoon must have been what drew people to the story.

A reader of Peter Singer's *Animal Liberation* may find it strange when, a little ways into the book, the author gives extended treatment to the question of whether animals are capable of suffering.[2] Watching the video of Will and Malya, one wonders how anyone could doubt the capacity of animals to suffer. Yet even with this couple, who were so moved by an animal's suffering that they were compelled to break through their kitchen wall, one finds signs of doubt: the landlord who could not be bothered to answer their calls and the joking of the news anchors, who when they wrap up the story, laughingly remark that the outcome could have been different: "That sucker could have come out angry." One of the anchors pretends to be a scary raccoon baring his claws.

A fine line distinguishes responses to this story. If the cry of the raccoon had instead been the squeak of a rat, the couple might have called the exterminator instead of hacking through the wall. If the raccoon had died immediately when she fell from her family's den in the roof (which is what happened, it turns out), the couple would have been disgusted by the stench of her decaying corpse rather than moved by her crying.[3] But this baby raccoon, with her black bandit mask already visible and her tiny paws splayed out on the kitchen glove, got a new home in the woods of upstate New York, where the wildlife service relocated her. Her suffering touched the lives of Will, Malya, and the many viewers who gasped, along with Malya, when the raccoon emerged from behind the wall. In the end, if one follows the comments on YouTube, it was Will's bushy beard and shirtless chest that drew more attention than anything else.

As a major concern motivating veganism and vegetarianism, animal suffering is this chapter's interest, along with the complexity of human responses to it. In some cases, that suffering activates empathy, and in other cases, that suffering is ignored, denied, feared, or ridiculed. The same instance of suffering more often than not invokes conflicting responses, as was the case for the raccoon in Will and Malya's kitchen. To better understand why so many people are not vegan or vegetarian and do not consider becoming so, despite their sometimes love for animals, this chapter seeks a perspective on animal suffering that can make sense of those conflicting responses. It seeks a perspective that can help us understand why the same people who delight in the baby raccoon in the kitchen would be quick to exterminate a rat, or how the off-color remarks about Will's bare chest coexist with the compassion that the couple and their video viewers had for the critter stuck in the wall.

The argument of this chapter is that the Babylonian Talmud offers such a perspective. In the Talmudic passage I examine, the classic treatment of animal suffering in Bava Metzia 32a–33a, the Talmud's concern is to get at the complexity of human responses to animal suffering. The case addressed in this passage is the animal struggling beneath his burden found in Exodus 23:5 and Deuteronomy 22:4. Like the raccoon stuck in the wall—is it pet or pest? cute critter or nasty intruder?—the burdened pack animal is subject to double viewing. The pack animal on one hand evokes empathy, since we all know what it feels like to be too tired to continue with a difficult task. On the other hand, he or she may be viewed as little more than the Iron Age version of a pick-up truck broken down by the side of the road. The Talmud plays with the double character of the burdened animal to highlight the contradictions regarding animal suffering in the inherited sources. The suffering of the exhausted pack animal could not be more clearly in view, even more so than it was for Will and Malya, who could hear but not see the helpless raccoon. But is the suffering of the animal really the problem? To what extent does animal suffering—in a scenario where an animal is, to all eyes, doing just that—matter at all? Are the Bible and the Mishnah concerned with that suffering or not? These are the questions posed by the Talmud.

This chapter starts with Peter Singer and his critics to frame the problem of animal suffering. I first consider the insufficiencies in Singer's rationalist utilitarianism that have been pointed out, especially by his feminist readers, since that critique paves the way for understanding the Talmud's discourse. I proceed to the biblical and early rabbinic laws that treat a scenario where an ox or donkey has collapsed under his burden, considering whether animal suffering motivates these laws and, if so, in what way and to what extent. I cover some of the highlights of the Talmudic passage. I am particularly interested in how the Talmud offers several testing grounds for animal suffering: the financial interests of the Jewish animal owner, the relationship of the Jewish animal owner to non-Jews, and the relationship of the Jewish animal owner to fellow Jews. These testing grounds help the Talmud's editors highlight the complexities of animal suffering by showing all the forces that might compete with or eclipse it. My goal is to show how in the eyes of the Talmud framers, and still for us, animal suffering can seem so real, it can exert such a powerful demand on us, but at the same time, when looked at in the same events with the same eyes, can also seem trivial or invisible.

PETER SINGER AND HIS CRITICS

Animal suffering was at the heart of Peter Singer's *Animal Liberation*. For Singer, animal suffering was the factor that allowed one to speak of animals as having interests that could be recognized and was the phenomenon that animal liberation movements could dedicate themselves to eliminating. Animals might not be able to voice or reflect on their suffering in the same way humans do, but they could experience it in a way that, in Singer's example of a schoolboy kicking a rock, the rock cannot. Singer brought new prominence to a line from utilitarian philosopher Jeremy Bentham: "The question is not, Can they *reason*? nor, Can they *talk*? but, Can they *suffer*?"[4]

The problems in Singer's arguments are already evident in the line he pulls from Bentham, which implies that despite the fact that animals can neither reason nor talk, their suffering qualifies them for equal consideration (which he distinguishes from equal treatment—granting a pig's interest in not being caged makes sense in a way that granting a pig the right to vote does not). Ethologist pioneers like Jane Goodall, Marc Bekoff, and Frans de Waal, now joined by many a Nova special and Animal Planet, have shown that animals exercise a great deal of reason and speech, particularly if we broaden our conceptualizations of those things to include the kinds of which other species are capable. Research shows that other species are in fact much better than humans at certain kinds of communication or cognitive processing. For animal liberationist thinkers today, the question is neither can animals suffer, nor can they reason, nor can they talk, but how does the fact that animals can clearly do all these things change how we should conceptualize the moral demands they make on us and how we think about ourselves as one species among many.

Animal ethicists in the utilitarian tradition have tried to correct the problems in Singer's approach to animal suffering.[5] Other philosophers, questioning the utilitarian principle that advocates the most pleasure for the most sentient creatures, have offered alternative ways of thinking about animal liberation, such as Tom Regan with his rights-based approach or Martha Nussbaum in her orientation toward "capabilities."[6] Still other thinkers, inspired by the insights of Freud and feminism, advocate abandoning the rationalist framework altogether to pay closer attention to the affective and subconscious forces at work in human responses to animal suffering.[7] Instead of asking in Singer-like style—if we must choose to kill a "retarded" human baby or a highly intelligent border collie, whom are we justified in choosing?—let us ask what makes it hard or easy for us to kill either one, and why we are posing such an unsettling question to begin with. Cora Diamond asks why, if by all philosophical accounts a vegetarian or vegan is justified in eating a steak from a cow who was struck by lightning and whose suffering was not therefore engineered by human force, many vegetarians and vegans would still not eat that steak.[8] Drawing on children's ditties and poems rather than Bentham or other philosophical tracts, Diamond observes that a vegetarian or vegan probably thinks of that cow as a "fellow creature."[9] A vegetarian or vegan would no more think of eating that cow than they would think of eating their uncle. The feminist care tradition criticizes the classic analytic tradition for its demotion of affective forces, which are frequently associated pejoratively with the feminine.[10] With that challenge in mind, feminist animal ethicists tend to get personal and talk about their own experiences with individual animals and sometimes to thank those animals in their acknowledgments. At the same time, feminist thinkers are highly sensitive to the larger structures of domination that shape people's lives. They regularly and systematically challenge those structures.

Another critique of Singer's approach comes not from feminist philosophy but from theology and religious studies. Singer's book makes Western religion into the culprit responsible for much of the animal suffering wrought by humans.

One of its chapters is devoted to the dominion model of Genesis, in which the catastrophic consequences, according to Singer, were exacerbated by highly influential Christian thinkers like Augustine and Thomas Aquinas.[11] One need not be a defender of Western religion to point out—as Singer does in later discussion—that there are Abrahamic traditions sensitive to animal suffering, such as the Hebrew Bible's requirement for work animals to rest on the Sabbath, the Talmudic tale of Judah the Patriarch taking pity on a family of weasels, the hadith in which a sinner is pardoned by Allah after giving water to a thirsty dog, and the stories of Francis of Assisi preaching to animals.[12] Recent religious studies approaches point out that dividing religious traditions into good or bad for animals misses their complexity. It also misses the complexity of responses to animal suffering. Tracing the path of Singer and his critics tells us that analytical logic, affective bonds, structures of domination, and various religious traditions all play a role in producing human responses to animal suffering. Whether or not we see animal suffering at any one moment, and how we see it, is subject to a thousand forces. This is an insight the Babylonian Talmud furnishes as its editors discuss the biblical and early rabbinic traditions to which I now turn.

THE RESTING DONKEY AND THE EXHAUSTED OX

Exodus 23:5 appears to require a person to assist his enemy if he should come across him on the road in need of assistance: "When you see the ass of your enemy lying under its burden and would refrain from raising it, you must nevertheless raise it with him." We might picture a man who happens upon a neighbor with whom he has had some spat, and that neighbor's donkey has collapsed underneath his cargo. The issue facing the man is: Help out or ignore the neighbor's plight, given the bad blood between them. The verse says, "Do not ignore him. Help out, and put aside the grudge."

That understanding runs according to the Jewish Publication Society (JPS) translation, but the translation is forced to fudge a few things along the way.[13] The verb associated with the enemy's ass, *rovetz*, is understood by JPS to refer to the donkey "lying" or struggling under his burden, but the semantic range of the word suggests that the donkey is merely taking a rest.[14] JPS is also forced to rely on a rare etymology for the main verb when it translates *azov* as "raise" rather than the more usual "leave," and it has to supply the direct object "it" for that verb. With these problems in mind, Bible scholar Alan Cooper suggests that the verb *azov* be read in the more typical way, as meaning "leave," and that the addressee is being instructed not to help but to walk on:[15] "you must nevertheless leave [with] it/him." According to this reading, the verse features a sworn enemy against whom the passerby wishes harm and a donkey merely taking a break. When the addressee happens upon the donkey, he is tempted to take advantage of the donkey's resting state and grab either his enemy's donkey or the cargo atop the donkey or, worse, assault the man, assuming he is nearby. The verse is intervening to say: Leave him, his donkey, and his cargo well enough alone. This understanding solves the problem of the verb's usage and avoids reading Exodus through a Christianizing lens, according to which people are being instructed, in effect, to turn the other cheek. The lesson is not to go out of one's way to be nice to a person whom one despises, argues Cooper, but to hold oneself back from theft or assault and battery.

This reading raises other problems, however, such as what the verse means at the end when it instructs the person to "leave *with* it/him." Cooper suggests that the verse is instructing the man to leave the cargo with the donkey—"leave [it, the cargo] with him"—but this requires reading a direct object into the sentence. These various cruxes must have been the motivation for Deuteronomy to clarify the scenario.[16] According to Deuteronomy 22:4's restatement, the animal is clearly stuck rather than resting, and the addressee is instructed to help: "You shall not see your fellow's ass or ox fallen on the road and ignore them; you must surely raise up with him." In this reformulation, the verb associated with the animal is *noflim* ("fallen") rather than *rovetz* ("lying"), making clear that the animal is in distress. The final verb is "raise up," which indisputably refers to helping. Deuteronomy's instruction regarding what not to do ("You shall not... ignore them") is also clearer than the murky "and would refrain from raising it" of Exodus. Deuteronomy's shift from enemy to friend similarly helps clarify the intent of the verse, which is to require a person to go out of his way to assist his fellow in need. Deuteronomy's trend toward clarification of Exodus begins in the first words, which is the imperative "you shall not see" rather than the casuistic "when you see" that starts the Exodus verse. The prepositional phrase "with him," which is the last word in both verses, plays a clearer role in Deuteronomy, where one can easily visualize the addressee cooperating with his fellow.

Is there animal suffering at stake in these verses and, if so, in what way? Could one just as easily replace the donkey or ox with a tractor and would the verses essentially preserve the lesson for which they were intended? Because Exodus 23:5 is an ambiguous verse, it is difficult to determine the role of the animal in the scenario. If Cooper is correct that the command of the verse is essentially "do not steal from your enemy or commit assault and battery against him when given a good opportunity to do so," then the scenario involves no animal suffering whatsoever, and the addressee is assisting neither the person nor the animal. The animal is important not because he is suffering or because he requires assistance, but because he makes his owner vulnerable to attack by anchoring him to a particular location and tempting the enemy with a valuable cargo, ripe for theft. In updating the scenario, we might replace the animal with an expensive car loaded with purchases and maintain the spirit of the verse. This reading accords with the broader interest of Exodus 23 in preventing injustice, especially toward easy targets like the poor or in tempting situations like this one.

The animal plays a less replaceable role in Deuteronomy. The addition of the ox (a work animal) to the donkey (a pack animal) and the absence of any mention of cargo suggests that the animal is not being invoked strictly as a vehicle that an owner would not want to have stolen from him or to abandon. Other features of the Deuteronomy verse suggest that the creatureliness of the animal is integral to the scenario: the verb "fallen" to describe the condition of the animal; the instruction not to ignore "them," the person and the animal; the featuring of "your brother" rather than "your enemy," which might be making the point that one is obligated to help not only one's brother but even one's brother's animal. Even if the animal matters in Deuteronomy, as I am suggesting he does, one should not draw the conclusion that the animal's suffering is the verse's main concern, which is incontrovertibly the relationship between the two men. The final word of the verse speaks to the two men's cooperation: "raise up *with him*." The intraspecies relationship matters more than the interspecies relationships. Although the animal in the Deuteronomy verse is not as utterly fungible as he seems to be in the Exodus verse, neither is he irreplaceable.

LAZY, SICK, AND ELDERLY DONKEY DRIVERS

Mishnah Bava Metzia 2:10 does not follow Cooper's reading of the Exodus verse in which the donkey is a tempting target ("Walk on!") but instead presumes the JPS translation of a donkey in distress ("Stop and help!"):

> One unloaded [the animal] and reloaded, one unloaded and reloaded, even four or five times, one is [still] obligated [to help unload again], as it is said, "You must nevertheless raise [it]" (Exodus 23:5).
> He (the animal owner) went and sat himself down [and] said to him, "Since the commandment is upon you, if you want to unload, unload"— one is exempt, as it is said, "with him" (Exodus 23:5).
> [If] he (the animal owner) was old or sick, one is obligated.
> It is a commandment from the Torah to unload, but not to load.
> Rabbi Shimon says: Even to load.
> Rabbi Yose the Galilean says: [If] there was upon him (the animal) more than his [appropriate] burden, one is not bound with respect to

him—as it is said, "under his burden" (Exodus 23:5)—a burden that he is able to withstand.[17]

A number of rulings can be distilled from this mishnah:

1. One must repeatedly fulfill the obligation to unload the animal if need be.
2. One is exempt from the obligation if the owner of the animal does not himself make reasonable efforts.
3. All authorities agree on a fundamental scriptural obligation to unload, but they disagree over whether loading is also a scriptural obligation.
4. According to one authority (Yose the Galilean), one is exempt from the obligation (to unload, presumably) if the owner has placed on the animal an unreasonably heavy load.

Considering these rulings together, we might speculate that this mishnah's aim is a mutually satisfying and socially constructive cooperation between the two men who find themselves in this situation.[18] The man called on to assist must do so repeatedly. The man requiring assistance must make real efforts and not land himself in this situation through bad judgment or greed. By raising these possibilities, the Mishnah seems bent on assuring the person giving the assistance that his generosity will not be exploited, and the person receiving assistance that he will receive as much help as he needs.

We should notice—the Talmud will—that securing trust between the two men comes at the expense of the animal in a couple of cases. The repeated help required by ruling 1 would benefit the animal, but if the owner is lazy as he is in ruling 2, the animal pays for it, since the owner's cavalier attitude means that his animal is denied assistance. Ruling 4 operates similarly, since the owner who has loaded too much cargo onto the animal deprives the animal of aid, according to Yose the Galilean. Of all the circumstances imagined by the Mishnah, the animal in Yose the Galilean's ruling is the one who needs help the most. Yet the passerby is not obligated to help and is possibly discouraged from doing so, presumably because it would undermine the cooperative spirit this set of laws is meant to foster.

I have so far mentioned rulings 1, 2, and 4. The role of animal suffering is more difficult to sort out with respect to ruling 3: "It is a commandment from the Torah to unload, but not to load. Rabbi Shimon says: Even to load."[19] This ruling differentiating the status of loading or, in this case, reloading, from unloading will suggest to the commentary in the Talmud that the Mishnah possesses a concern for animal suffering. As the Talmud points out, the task of unloading presumes harm to the animal in a way that reloading the animal does not. If the animal is struggling under the weight of his cargo, he might sustain injury or die. Reloading, by contrast, is a pressing need of the animal owner but not of the animal himself, who if anything might prefer a little extra time unsaddled. All that being the case, might not the Sages' privileging of unloading over reloading suggest that they believe Scripture evinces a concern for animal suffering and, indeed, for that concern to be at the core of this entire set of laws?

I say with some assurance: no. First, the exclusion of loading from the Torah's sphere of command exists only in the Mishnah and its parallel, the Tosefta, and not in the contemporaneous midrash collection the Mekhilta, where reloading is considered to be at least derived through logic from Scripture and at most explicit in Scripture.[20] Second, while it is not impossible to see animal suffering at stake in these rulings, there is still no reason to think that animal suffering is operating as an independent concern that transcends the interpersonal stakes of the commandment. As the Talmud points out, animal suffering and human loss are coextensive in the case of a burdened pack animal. If the animal is injured under the burden of a load, the owner incurs damage to a valuable piece of his property (his animal). How can a concern for animal suffering be disentangled from a concern for the human's material loss if the two are so closely related? If we want to see which value is the driving force behind the commandment, we would need a test case in which the suffering of the animal is at odds with either the material flourishing of the owner or with the desired interpersonal relationship between owner and passerby. In fact, we already have that. As the Talmudic editorial voice observes, the other rulings in this mishnah make clear that animal suffering is not the driving concern, since those rulings seem all too tolerant of animal suffering when helping alleviate it would contravene the interpersonal aims of the commandment.

Finally, it is doubtful that even human suffering is at stake in ruling 3. The chief motivation for the Sages' preference for unloading over reloading may well be the maddening relationship between the two verses. When the Sages say, "It is a commandment from the Torah to unload, but not to load," why not take them at face value to be making primarily an interpretive claim? After all, the Sages do offer a better reading of Scripture than does Rabbi Shimon, who along with many other early rabbis seems to construe Deuteronomy 22:4 as issuing an obligation to help reload the animal. But as I noted, Deuteronomy 22:4 does not mention a load at all. The Sages' view, which seems to see both Exodus 23:5 and Deuteronomy 22:4 as referring to unloading, offers a fairly compelling reading of the verses, although it leaves them somewhat redundant, which is likely why Rabbi Shimon and some of the positions mentioned in the legal midrash take the alternative approach that sees the first verse as commanding unloading and the second verse commanding reloading.

To sum up before moving on to the Talmud's commentary, the Mishnah features a struggling animal, to be sure, but there is no moment when we can say that the animal's suffering makes any claims that go beyond the person whom that suffering would most affect. The larger set of interests in this section of the Mishnah, which deals with obligations generated by lost objects, reinforces the sense that here the animal is little more than an example of valuable property, along with the coins, food, clothing, utensils, and books that appear also in the chapter.

RAVA'S REVOLUTION

I am sometimes tempted to read the history of Jewish interpretation as a comedy of errors, and reading Rava's claim in the Talmud about animal suffering is one such time (if suffering can be comic). That "error" begins with Deuteronomy 22:4's revision of Exodus 23:5. Whereas Exodus 23:5 seems to feature neither a person in need of assistance nor an animal suffering under his load, Deuteronomy 22:4 introduces both, probably in the interests of greater clarity and out of a different ethical-legal orientation. The Mishnah produces a second "error": the suffering animal "travels" from the second verse (Deuteronomy 22:4) to the first (Exodus 23:5). Reading Exodus 23:5 now through the lens of Deuteronomy 22:4, the Mishnah sees in Exodus 23:5 an animal struggling under his burden and sees in Deuteronomy 22:4 an animal who is ready for reloading.

The next "error" is Rava's reading of the Mishnah, to which I now turn. The Babylonian rabbi Rava in the early fourth century CE is said to take the dispute about these verses as a sign that scripture is concerned with animal suffering: "Rava said: From the words of both of them it can be learned: The suffering of living creatures is from the Torah" (Babylonian Talmud Bava Metzi'a 32a–b). Rava's idea seems to be that the combination of the two positions in the Mishnah yields some information. I would venture to guess that Rava's logic hinges on an innocent, easily missed word in the Mishnah, "even": "It is a commandment from the Torah to unload, but not to load. Rabbi Shimon says: *Even* to load." Rava's thinking may be fueled by the fact that Rabbi Shimon, even while he holds reloading (where no animal suffering is at stake) to be just as much of a scriptural obligation as unloading (where animal suffering is at stake), still presents reloading as the less likely obligation to be included within the Torah ("*even* to load"). In short, *even* the disputant who holds that assistance where no animal suffering is entailed is just as scripturally mandated as assistance where animal suffering is entailed, concedes that it is a little bit surprising—a little less obvious—that assistance would be required where no animal suffering is involved. Thus does Rava infer that all early rabbinic parties take the Torah to evince a concern for animal suffering.

This reading strategy of Rava's is, in my view, radical because the Mishnah hardly seems preoccupied with animal suffering. The very language of Rava's claim reflects its innovative character. Neither the biblical verses nor the Mishnah ever speak explicitly of any kind of distress, except perhaps in the verb "fallen" in Deuteronomy, which is at any rate a more purely physiological description than is Rava's "suffering" (*tza'ar*). "Suffering," by contrast, is a highly emotion-laden and normally human term in the Babylonian Talmud.[21] Rava's term for animals, "possessors of life" (*ba'alei chayim*), is also distinctive, a largely Babylonian invention, used only once or twice in legal midrash and in the Palestinian Talmud but about twenty-five times in the Babylonian Talmud.[22] Rava's complete phrase—literally "the sorrow of possessors of life," normally and here translated as "animal suffering"—is used in a number of other Talmudic passages, always within the anonymous editorial literary strata of the Talmud, to alternatively query, legitimate, or elaborate on norms of behavior or a particular rabbi's practice with respect to animals.[23] Rava's declaration about animal suffering is, in sum, revolutionary, not only in his inferring it from a mishnah that is highly resistant to such a reading, but also in its very language and conceptualization, which marks a watershed in rabbinic thinking regarding animals, suffering, and the capacity of the one for the other.

THE TALMUD'S TESTING GROUNDS

In this closing section, I would like to suggest that the redactors' choices, if not motivated by the wish to illustrate the "error" of Rava's ways, at least had the impact of doing so. In other words, we are led by the Talmudic dialectic to see the ingenuity of Rava's claim and, along with that, the difficulties of reading animal suffering back into the sources as Rava wishes us to do. The authors of the passage accomplish this by setting up several testing grounds for animal suffering: (1) financial loss to the Jewish animal owner, (2) relationships between Jewish animal owners or users and non-Jewish animal owners or users, and (3) ethical self-cultivation. In these testing grounds, the composers of the passage weigh whether animal suffering is determinative of early rabbinic teachings or discarded by them or, in a third option, whether it is impossible to tell where the early rabbinic teaching stands on the question. That final possibility is ultimately, in my reading, the impression the Talmudic composers wish to convey, but I also consider other readings of the passage recently offered by Joshua Cahan, Dov Linzer, and Aaron Gross.

On the first testing ground, the composers of the passage try unsuccessfully to disentangle the animal owner's concern for the animal as his property, that is, for his economic interests, from his concern for his animal in and of itself, that is, for animal suffering:

> And if [for] loading, where there is no financial loss, one is obligated, then unloading, where there is financial loss, [should not one be obligated] all the more so? But is there no financial loss with loading? Are we not dealing with where he loses time from the marketplace in the meantime? Or, alternatively, thieves come and take everything he has with him?[24]

This section challenges Rava's inference from the Mishnah. Perhaps the Mishnah's preference for unloading over loading (in the sense that it considers unloading but not loading to be a scriptural obligation) stems from the financial loss that the owner incurs when his animal sustains injury in the course of bearing a burden. The editorial voice within the passage is pointing out that animal welfare and economic interests, when they converge, become indistinguishable. Who is to say whether the obligation to unload the animal stems from one or the other? Why not assume that human interests are paramount?

Why not, indeed, retort the redactors. The redactors retract in the next step not by asserting the moral significance of animal suffering but by admitting to the ubiquity of human economic interests. Unloading the animal simply entails a different kind of economic stress than loading does, which if delayed causes the owner to lose valuable transaction time in the marketplace or to become a target for thieves. The redactors suggest that human economic interests will always pervade human interactions with animals (as they pervade interactions with other humans). The pervasiveness of property interests ironically frees us, according to the Talmud's logic, to consider the moral significance of animal suffering. If financial concerns are a factor in every interaction, they cancel out and allow other kinds of concerns to become visible.

The second testing ground for animal suffering is the relationship between Jews and non-Jews:

> Say that [the following early rabbinic teaching] supports him (Rava): The animal of a gentile—one must care for her like the animal of an Israelite. If you say, this is well if animal suffering is a scriptural concern, that is why one must care for her like the animal of an Israelite. But if you say that animal suffering is not a scriptural concern, why must one care for her like the animal of an Israelite? There, [it is] because of enmity.[25]

This early rabbinic teaching obligates a Jew to attend to a non-Jew's animal in the same way he would attend to a fellow Jew's. Of all the early rabbinic teachings so far featured in the passage, this would seem to be the one that speaks most directly to a concern for the animal. Obligations to non-Jews are few and far between in rabbinic literature. If a rabbinic teaching requires a Jew to attend to a non-Jew's animal, then that obligation, so goes the Talmud's logic, must stem from an interest in the animal rather than in the non-Jewish owner. The redactor handily refutes the evidence, however, with the often cited principle "because of enmity."[26] One must help gentiles not because of any fundamental obligation toward them but because they might retaliate were they to get shabby treatment from Jews. The requirement to help the gentile is shown to rebound back to the Jewish and human self.

The third testing ground of animal suffering is the inner world of the self:

> Come and learn: [One's] friend (literally, "lover") is to be unloaded, and [one's] enemy to be loaded, it is a commandment with respect to the enemy, in order to compel his (i.e., the bystander's) *yetzer* (i.e., a putatively normal human tendency towards self-interest).[27] And if it arises to your mind that animal suffering is a scriptural concern, this (the obligation to unload the friend's animal) would be preferable for him! Even so, in order to compel his *yetzer* is preferable.

Faced with a choice between helping unload the animal of a friend or loading the animal of an enemy, which obligation should one fulfill first? Even though the friend is a worthier recipient of aid, and the friend's animal more in need of it, the early rabbinic teaching prioritizes the enemy, explaining that the value of overcoming one's tendency to help one's friend and dismiss one's enemy (that tendency is embodied by the *yetzer*) supersedes the needs of the friend. In its commentary on this teaching, the Talmud concedes the significance of animal suffering but claims that overcoming one's hostility toward other people has more.

Here at the end of the passage, Rava's claim about animal suffering is undone, yet again, as it meets other interests. The editor does not go so far as to deny Rava's claim and, with it, the significance of animal suffering. On the contrary, the passage closes with an affirmation of Rava and a marginalization of early rabbinic teachings that do not seem to support him. Those teachings are assigned to the dissenting opinion of Yose the Galilean: "It is Rabbi Yose the Galilean who says that animal suffering is [a concern] of [merely] rabbinic status."[28] Yet the passage raises serious questions regarding whether animal suffering can ever be isolated as the ground of obligation and, even when it can, whether it carries much weight when compared with other concerns within rabbinic culture. The testing grounds in the passage serve to stress the revolutionary character of Rava's claim along with the challenges of identifying animal suffering as a concern within authoritative rabbinic traditions.

CONCLUSIONS: COMPETING CONCERNS, LAW AND ETHICS, SLIPPERY SLOPES

This Talmudic passage in modern times has been buried under an apologetic reading that reduces it to Rava's statement—that animal suffering is a "Jewish value"—and loses sight of the literary complexities that I have tried to untangle here.[29] Recent readings of the passage have moved past the apologetics, however, and I wish to showcase their contributions before situating my own reading among them.

Talmud scholar, teacher, and Conservative Rabbi Joshua Cahan reads this passage and a short parallel passage on Shabbat 154b as an exercise in weighing competing goods.[30] What does one do when multiple goods (or evils) come into conflict? "How do we adjudicate the tension between this and other principles, both in explaining why we do things and in deciding what we should do?"[31] Cahan reads the Talmudic passage on animal suffering as a demonstration of the processes by which a person selects one value over another. He also considers the medieval legal traditions that accumulated around this passage, showing that over time the concern for animal suffering diminishes and almost entirely drops out, leading to a much less dynamic Jewish legal stance. Published in *Conservative Judaism*, Cahan's essay, "Tza'ar Ba'alei Ḥayim in the Marketplace of Values," seems aimed at restoring what he perceives to be the lost legal dynamism of Talmudic and early medieval traditions. Although animal suffering may seem like a modern concern, Cahan argues that it is in fact native to Jewish law and that the restoration of the concern would take Jewish law back to its roots. Cahan sees the narrative of Jewish law as one in which "the rabbis fit that value into the real-life challenges of Jews in different eras."[32]

Head of Yeshivat Chovevei Torah Rabbi Dov Linzer similarly sees in the talmudic and medieval traditions on animal suffering a juggling act of sorts.[33] Whereas for Cahan the balance is among competing values, each of which vies with the other for dominance and which together contribute to the dynamism of Jewish law, for Linzer the dialectic is between "Torah value" and *halakha* (Jewish law). Coming from an Open Orthodox perspective, Linzer explores whether and how a value considered to come from the Torah might inform the shaping of law. Linzer's question, he himself points out, is not the one often asked of whether there are values outside the Torah that might influence its interpretation. Rather, Linzer is interested in internal interpretive dynamics, in whether there are values inside the Torah that can be read back into the Torah to shape its interpretation. Animal suffering is a particularly fertile case for Linzer's inquiry because it is a value whose biblical status is explicitly addressed by the Talmud. Linzer is thus able to use the case of animal suffering to trace the extent to which Jewish legal decisors give weight to Torah values in the course of determining *halakha*. Linzer works his way through various medieval commentators on the passage, characterizing how each configures the relationship between the value of avoiding animal suffering and the commandment of unloading the pack animal. Linzer describes some commentators (Rashi and Tosafot) who see value and law as autonomous, nonintersecting spheres, and others (Ritvah, Rabbenu Peretz, and Ra'avad) who according to a variety of conceptualizations see the value shaping the scope of the law.

For Linzer and Cahan, the passage on animal suffering illustrates a larger dialectic within Jewish law. For religious studies scholar and animal activist Aaron Gross, the passage illustrates a larger dialectic within Jewish ethical culture, between what Gross calls "ascendancy" and "kindness" in the Jewish relationship to other species, which produce something he conceptualizes as the "humane subject."[34] Gross sees in the Talmud passage on animal suffering the jostling of ascendancy with kindness. The moments in the passage that resist the Torah status of animal suffering are on the side of ascendancy, a stance in which human beings take themselves to be ascendant over other creatures. The voices in the passage that defend Rava's claim embrace the opposite pole of kindness, when humans see themselves as kindred spirits with other species and as having obligations toward them that flow from that similarity. Gross sees this passage as expressing an anxiety about the broader implications of kindness.[35] Were animal suffering to be recognized as a concern of scriptural status, he argues, and kindness fully ensconced as a foundational legal principle, the entire scaffolding of Jewish practice could crumble. Animal husbandry, slaughter, and sacrifice would all come into question. The resistance in this passage to recognizing the scriptural status of animal suffering stems not just from the familiar ascendancy model, Gross speculates, but from an awareness that animal suffering lies deep within the heart of Judaism.

I find each of these readings compelling but part company with them when it comes to seeing the passage as an illustration of a broader dialectic within Jewish law or culture. For Cahan, Linzer, and Gross, the passage represents an irresolvable conflict between poles: between one value and another, between value and law, between ascendancy and kindness. The fundamental question, in my reading, is not what values does a concern for animal suffering compete with, what laws can a concern for animal suffering be read into, or what practices does the concern for animal suffering challenge. Rather, it is: *Is animal suffering there at all?* Rava stakes a claim for animal suffering that is undone by the passage, time after time, when tested against the sources in the different scenarios those sources imagine. In my reading this passage is less about the slippery slope of logic than about the slipperiness of animal suffering itself, which sometimes rises to the surface and at other times sinks into the ether. The talmudic passage features all the other interests—legal, ritual, economic, political—that can eclipse animal suffering, keeping us from noticing it or caring about it. We sometimes simply get distracted, as is the case in the blogosphere on the Brooklyn raccoon. The talmudic treatment of animal suffering wishes us to see that the threat of distraction is real. Just when we think we see animal suffering, the Talmud suggests, it always seems to disappear, displaced by other concerns and interests that somehow end up seeming more important. Like the Talmud, I offer no grand solutions for how we might transcend our tendency toward distraction and denial, but I follow the Talmud's lead in bringing attention to the unruliness of our hearts and minds so that we may better understand the obstacles we face in attending to animal suffering.

NOTES

1. William Levin, "Baby Raccoon Rescue in Brooklyn," YouTube, April 29, 2014, https://www.youtube.com/watch?v=C0dWq8lRBfU. CBS New York, "Brooklyn Man Pulls Raccoon out of Apartment Wall," CBS, May 2, 2014, https://www.youtube.com/watch?v=x-Abp9QZYOE.

2. Peter Singer, *Animal Liberation: The Definitive Classic of the Animal Movement* (New York: Ecco, 2009), 10.

3. The raccoon turned out to be female.

4. Singer, *Animal Liberation*, 7.

5. Raymond Gillespie Frey, "Utilitarianism and Animals," in *the Oxford Handbook of Animal Ethics*, ed. Tom L. Beauchamp and Raymond Gillespie Frey (New York: Oxford University Press, 2001), 172–97.

6. Tom Regan, *Defending Animal Rights* (Urbana: University of Illinois Press, 2001); Tom Regan, *The Case for Animal Rights* (Berkeley: University of California Press, 1983); Martha C. Nussbaum, "The Moral Status of Animals," in *Animal Rights: Current Debates and New Directions*, ed. Martha Craven Nussbaum and Cass R. Sunstein (New York: Oxford University Press, 2004), 30–36; Martha C. Nussbaum, *Frontiers of Justice: Disability, Nationality, Species Membership* (London: Belknap, 2007).

7. On the problem of logocentrism in these philosophical works and the feminist critique along these lines, see Matthew Calarco, *Thinking through Animals: Identity, Difference, Indistinction* (Palo Alto, CA: Stanford University Press, 2015), 22–24.

8. Cora Diamond, "Eating Meat and Eating People," in *Animal Rights: Current Debates and New Directions*, ed. Martha Craven Nussbaum and Cass R. Sunstein (New York: Oxford University Press, 2004), 96.

9. On the "literary turn" among Anglo American philosophers in the field of animal ethics, see Tzachi Zamir, "Literary Works and Animal Ethics," in *The Oxford Handbook of Animal Ethics*, ed. Tom L. Beauchamp and Raymond Gillespie Frey (New York: Oxford University Press, 2011), 932–56.

10. On the feminist ethic of care, see Carol J. Adams and Lori Gruen (eds.), *Ecofeminism: Feminist Intersections with Other Animals and the Earth* (New York: Bloomsbury, 2014); Josephine Donovan and Carol J. Adams (eds.), *The Feminist Care Tradition in Animal Ethics: A Reader* (New York: Columbia University Press, 2007). I am associating this approach with feminism, but one can see the emphasis on affect in many animal ethics works—for instance, Michael Allen Fox and Lesley McLean, "Animals in Moral Space," in *Animal Subjects: An Ethical Reader in a Posthuman World*, ed. Jodey Castricano (Waterloo, ON: Wilfrid Laurier University Press, 2008), 147–75; and Kathy Rudy, *Loving Animals: Towards a New Animal Advocacy* (Minneapolis: University of Minnesota Press, 2011).

11. His treatment of Hebrew Scriptures claims to represent its "basic position," but he dedicates no more than a paragraph to the matter. Singer, *Animal Liberation*, 188.

12. For subsequent discussion from Singer on religion and animal liberation, see Peter Singer, "Animal Protection and the Problem of Religion," in *A Communion of Subjects: Animals in Religion, Science, and Ethics*, ed. Paul Waldau and Kimberley Patton (New York: Columbia University Press, 2006), 616–28. For a collection of writings that attempt to deal comprehensively with the approach to animals taken by various religious traditions, see Paul Waldau and Kimberley Patton (eds.), *A Communion of Subjects: Animals in Religion, Science, and Ethics* (New York: Columbia University Press, 2006).

13. Marc Zvi Brettler and Adele Berlin (eds.), *The Jewish Study Bible: Featuring the Jewish Publication Society Tanakh Translation* (New York: Oxford University Press, 2004).

14. See the entry for r-v-tz in Francis Brown, *The Brown, Driver, Briggs Hebrew and English Lexicon: With an Appendix Containing the Biblical Aramaic: Coded with the Numbering System from Strong's Exhaustive Concordance of the Bible* (Peabody, MA: Hendrickson Publishers, 1996). The root is translated there as "stretch oneself out, lie down, lie stretched out."

15. Alan Cooper, "The Plain Sense of Exodus 23:5," *Hebrew Union College Annual* 59 (1988): 1–22.

16. On Deuteronomy's reworkings of Exodus, see Bernard M. Levinson, *Deuteronomy and the Hermeneutics of Legal Innovation* (New York: Oxford University Press, 1997).

17. This translation is based on the version of the Mishnah found in the Kaufmann manuscript.

18. Arguing that sometimes the early rabbis explicitly refer to ethical principles as the determining force behind their exegesis, and therefore it is warranted to imagine such principles operating elsewhere, is Moshe Halbertal, *Mahapekhot Parshaniyot Be-Hithayutan: 'arakhim Ke-Shikulim Parshaniyim Be-Midreshe Halakha* [Interpretive revolutions in the making] (Jerusalem: Magnes Press, 1999).

19. We can surmise from this ruling that it represents some disagreement about how to read Scripture ("it is a commandment from the Torah"), but it is hard to say anything definitive about the nature of the disagreement; the textual details and parallels are not sufficiently relevant to merit the extended discussion they require.

20. Tosefta Bava Metzia 2:28; Mekhilta de-Rabbi Yishma'el Mishpatim Masekhta de-Kaspa Parashah 20, s.v. *azov ta'azov imo*.

21. Shulamit Valler, *Sorrow and Distress in the Talmud*, trans. Sharon Blass (Boston: Academic Studies Press, 2011), 17–53, chap. 1.

22. Mishnah and Tosefta use the rich language of *davar she-yesh bo ruah chayim* ("a thing that has within it the spirit of life").

23. See Babylonian Talmud (henceforth, TB), Shabbat 117b, 154b; Betzah 26a; Bava Batra 20a; Avodah Zarah 13a; Hullin 7b. The contexts vary—transmission of impurity, Sabbath and festival observance, superstition of evil animals, counteracting idolatry—but "suffering" in all these cases refers to either the maiming or the starving of an animal, with the animals all belonging to the category of livestock.

24. TB, Bava Metzi'a 32b.

25. Ibid.

26. For a study of this and related terms, see Michael Pitkowsky, "Mipnei Darkhei Shalom ('Because of the Paths of Peace') and Related Terms: A Case Study of How Early Concepts and Terminology Developed from Tannaitic to Talmudic Literature," Ph.D. dissertation, Jewish Theological Seminary of America, 2011, esp. 198–204.

27. TB, Bava Metzi'a 32b. For discussion of the *yetzer* with this meaning, see Ishay Rosen-Zvi, *Demonic Desires: Yetzer Hara and the Problem of Evil in Late Antiquity* (Philadelphia: University of Pennsylvania Press, 2011), 16.

28. TB, Bava Metzi'a 33a.

29. A good example of this approach can be found in Noah J. Cohen, *Tsa'ar Ba'ale Hayim—The Prevention of Cruelty to Animals: Its Bases, Development and Legislation in Hebrew Literature* (Washington, DC: Catholic University of America Press, 1959). A quick Google search on animal suffering in Judaism will produce a plethora of websites that feature this type of approach.

30. Joshua Cahan, "Tza'ar Ba'alei Ḥayim in the Marketplace of Values," *Conservative Judaism* 65, no. 4 (2014): 30–48.

31. Ibid., 36.

32. Ibid., 31.

33. Dov Linzer, "Tza'ar Ba'alei Chaim (Animal Suffering): A Case Study in Halakha and Values," in *Mishpetei Shalom: A Jubilee Volume in Honor of Rabbi Saul Berman*, ed. Yamin Levy (Riverdale, NY: Ktav, 2010), 383–402.

34. Aaron S. Gross, *The Question of the Animal and Religion: Theoretical Stakes, Practical Implications* (New York: Columbia University Press, 2015).

35. Ibid., 165–67.

2 Vegetarianism as Jewish Culture and Politics in Interwar Europe

NICK UNDERWOOD

Some say vegetarianism began as a Jewish movement. It is in the Bible. Gary Rendsburg even argues that the vegetarian ideal is at the root of the two Genesis stories.[1] First, says Rendsburg, "God creates a world characterized by vegetarianism."[2] For him, Genesis implies a vegetarian world when it reads, "Both thorns and thistles it shall grow for you; And you will eat the plants of the field" (3:18). Then, after humans are seemingly unable to live up to God's ideals, God gives permission to eat animals, saying, "Every moving thing that is alive shall be food for you; I give all to you, as I gave the green plant" (Genesis 9:3). But most Jews are not vegetarians, so embracing vegetarianism cannot be framed only around biblical mandates. As we will see, the development of new Jewish vegetarian practices in interwar Europe eschewed biblical influence in favor of other social, cultural, and political forces.

In 1918, Europe struggled to collect itself from a catastrophe that had left European Jews searching for new ways to define and organize themselves. The Minorities Treaties laid the groundwork for a collective Jewish communal voice that had the potential to legitimate Jews' tenuous social, cultural, and political statuses across Eastern Europe.[3] The concurrent rise in nationalism and increasingly authoritarian governments in countries like Poland, however, stalled these movements; as a result, Eastern European Jewish communities had to search for new ways to legitimate their belonging in countries where they had lived, in some cases for centuries. With the rise of Nazism in Germany, Jews were faced with new social, cultural, and political restrictions. Antisemitic legislation compelled many to emigrate. The Jewish population of Germany was still significant in 1939, numbering approximately 241,000.[4]

In the early twentieth century, those Jews who embraced vegetarianism did not only or always do so in an attempt to virtuously fulfill biblical mandates. In particular, Europe's post-World War I years provided the stage from which vegetarianism could act as a Jewish practice that intertwined identity with politics. "Politics" here means an attempt to affect social change, which we can understand as change in community and national identity as much as change in governmental policy.[5] Pacifism, a major political and social movement of these postwar years, helped create the social climate necessary to make private choices, such as food practices, a public, cultural, and political venture.[6] The interwar years featured new kinds of politics where moral positions could find active expression in the public spheres.

This chapter focuses on the effects that meat-free gastronomic decisions had on Jewish identity and politics during the interwar years in Eastern and Central Europe, including a discussion on Vilna and the context within which Fania Lewando published her *Vegetarish-Dietisher Kokhbukh*. In the United States, Jewish vegetarianism was almost explicitly about "healthy living" during the early twentieth century.[7] By contrast, Jewish vegetarians in Europe explicitly folded the politics of the day into their advocacy for healthier and more "Jewish" lifestyles. The upheaval of early twentieth-century European life led to a variety of Jewish political movements, such as Yiddishism and Jewish diaspora nationalism, that envisioned and treated culture as an integral part of their community and national projects.[8] Yiddishists (proponents of Yiddishism, which included a pacifist streak) advocated for the Yiddish language as a legitimate (if not the only) Jewish national language. In Eastern Europe, proponents of Yiddishism felt that Yiddish would be the base for a Jewish national and cultural renaissance.[9] Diaspora nationalists, who were closely connected to Yiddishists, sought to achieve lasting Jewish cultural autonomy wherever they found themselves.[10] These movements catalyzed a particular Jewish national identity that insisted on establishing Jewish national rights within the diaspora, not Palestine. Food is not typically seen as a political marker of national identity in Eastern European Jewish history, but we will see how legal and social forces would make vegetarianism both a healthy and a Jewish choice.

Marginalized from the political sphere by their lack of franchise in interwar Poland and Nazi Germany, women were at the heart of the interwar Jewish vegetarian movement. Perhaps this should come as no surprise since women were, according to Paula Hyman, "the primary transmitters of Jewish culture."[11] On a more basic level, women were responsible for cooking. As a result, we will see that vegetarianism in 1930s Europe was a way for Jews, by way of women, to enact a new community ideal that was as much about promoting healthy living as it was about making clear claims in opposition to antisemitic legislation that at best restricted and at worst sought to end Jewish communities. If laws declared certain types of Jewish foods (i.e., kosher meats) illegal, then cooking vegetarian meals was a clear act to redefine what it meant to be Jewish.

Jewish food practices were politicized in April 1933 when Nazi Germany outlawed kosher butchering.[12] Poland did the same in 1936. In Nazi Germany, but not in Poland, the import of kosher meat was eventually banned in 1938. These laws carried with them communal cultural and political implications.[13] In Poland, for example, the antisemitism that catalyzed these laws was so widespread that, as Eva Plach has argued, "while contemporary animal protectionists were genuinely interested in animal suffering... they were also committed to raising Poland's reputation as a civilized and humanitarian nation."[14] Groups seemingly disconnected from nationalist politics were not immune to the implications of national and, by extension, biological "purification" of these laws.[15] In limiting access to a fundamental marker of traditional and secular Jewish cultural life, the basis of some Jews' culinary practice was made illegal in Poland and Nazi Germany. These constraints forced most Jews to rethink the place of meat in defining what could be considered "Jewish" food and practice.[16]

Anti-*kashrut* laws and vegetarian movements were related events that unfolded within a context of heightened interests in pacifism and Jewish diaspora nationalism. The social forces of vegetarianism and pacifism were so closely intertwined in these interwar years that historian Colin Spencer reminds us that World War I "provoked new peace groups to emerge... [and]... the public perception of the vegetarian diet [to grow] a little kinder."[17]

While Central and Eastern European Jews between the sixteenth and eighteenth centuries maintained a primarily meat-free diet, it was not until the early twentieth century that Jews began to tie vegetarianism to politics in earnest. This was largely dependent on Jews' socioeconomic status rather than deliberate choices.[18] In fact, any notion of identifying as "vegetarian" would not have found prudence among sixteenth-, seventeenth-, or eighteenth-century Jews because the term was not part of European nomenclature until after 1840.[19] In the immediate post-failed revolutionary world of Eastern Europe, the connection between vegetarianism and politics was most clearly made in Uri Nisan Gnessin's *Se'udah mafseket* (The Meal before the Fast [1906]), which describes the relationships between a traditional father and his vegetarian and revolutionary daughter. It ought to come as no surprise that linking Jews to the politics of vegetarianism was made after the failed revolution of 1905—an era that many believe awakened politically a new generation of Eastern European Jews.[20]

Jews and their foods are constantly changing. Accordingly, where people ate has also changed. Since the invention of the restaurant in eighteenth-century France, "restaurants have become a sort of laboratory for studying the relationship between social position and the foods that we eat," according to Sidney Mintz.[21] This was similarly the case in 1930s Poland.

Scholars have often taken interest in food as a way to home in on the question of cultural and social innovation among Jews and within Jewish tradition.[22] Recent work has also stressed developments within Jewish food practices and national identities, demonstrating that what Jews ate revealed as much about their Jewishness as the books they read, the songs they sang, and the languages they spoke.[23] Yael Raviv argues, "food is central to [one's] perception of 'home' and identity," even arguing for what might be called "culinary nationalism."[24]

For Jews, food has also possessed the ability to mitigate contested identities among Jewish migrants in their new homes.[25] Many studies tend to make the historic links between Jews and vegetarianism through the aforementioned biblical connection.[26] Eve Jochnowitz, however, broadens this perspective by urging us to consider "foodscapes," which tie together mouth, body, kitchen, table, and street to show how "the cuisines of uprooted and rearticulated Jewish communities selectively retain traditions and innovate at each point in the food system."[27] If we consider interwar Europe as a space of Jewish movement, migration, and experimentation, then we may see the potential for applications of Jochnowitz's notion of foodscapes and Raviv's notion of culinary nationalism. Where and how people ate their food were changing, and so were notions of Jewishness. When states imposed antisemitic laws denouncing ancient Jewish food practice as antimodern, Jews conceived of a Jewishness that did not rely on meat or deference to kosher slaughtering.

Another problem with existing scholarship on the topic is that general histories of vegetarianism have tended to focus heavily on elite intellectuals. When or if these studies engage Jewish food practices, the focus is generally on the connections between the Bible, Jews, and the development of *kashrut*.[28] When the politics of vegetarianism are addressed, the scholarship typically centers on idiosyncratic figures such as Mahatma Gandhi, Henry David Thoreau, and even Adolf Hitler, to demonstrate how issues of ecology stood at the center of these figures' vegetarian choices.[29] As a result, these histories paint vegetarianism as a marginal movement. The exception to this historiographical rule is James Gregory, who argues that within Victorian England, vegetarianism was important because many Victorians thought about vegetarianism, even if they did not actually become vegetarians.[30] Important for our conceptualization of Jewish vegetarianism in interwar Europe, Gregory shows how vegetarianism could be "counter-cultural and conventional."[31]

Cookbooks, and by extension recipes published in magazines and newspapers, are "artifacts of culture in its making," as Arjun Appadurai claims.[32] Cookbooks and recipes published in Jewish journals and newspapers illustrate how vegetarianism appeared and was used as a multifaceted political tool in 1930s Europe. Barbara Kirshenblatt-Gimblett argues that cookbooks "project an image of the ideal Jewish woman and the world she manages from her post in the home."[33] They also provide (women's) voices absent from many official accounts. Cookbooks can act as bottom-up accounts of "recipes" for an ideal national culture.[34] They can also represent the codification of the particularities and universal qualities of Jewish foods to the same end.[35]

Vegetarian cookbooks and recipes published in 1930s Poland and Nazi Germany illuminate the effect of context—in politics and culture—on Jewish life and identity. By focusing on publications from Poland and Nazi Germany in Yiddish and German, we can better understand the transnational implications of Jewish vegetarian foodways during the interwar period, a topic that has remained hitherto underexplored. Embedded within debates and practices about Jewish meat eating was a profound political and cultural statement about the place of Jews in modern European societies.[36] In the wake of the birth of modern Jewish politics during the fin-de-siècle, food—which was tied to issues of women's Jewish identity and questions of modernity—and vegetarianism moved away from their religious roots to stand against antisemitism and for a new meatless Jewishness.[37]

VEGETARIANISM AND JEWISHNESS IN VILNA

In the 1930s, in the heart of interwar Vilna's Jewish quarter, at 14 Niemiecka Street, one would have found Fania Lewando's popular vegetarian restaurant. A few blocks away was her cooking school. It was a bustling restaurant, even though being a vegetarian during the interwar years was uncommon.[38] In addition to serving up a wide variety of meatless dishes, her restaurant and related cookbook, *Vegetarish-dietisher kokhbukh: 400 speyser gemacht oysshlishlekh fun grinsen* (Vegetarian Dietetic Cookbook: 400 Recipes Made Exclusively from Vegetables), featured vegetarian versions of traditional Jewish dishes, even those that are traditionally carnivorous. Lewando's restaurant and cookbook stood as an important piece of a small-scale, yet still important interwar Jewish cultural and political movement: vegetarianism.[39] In addition, because the restaurant and cookbook centered on how women contributed to the health of the Jewish community and their families, Jewish vegetarianism in interwar Poland placed women on the front lines of this domestic brand of political action and Jewish identity.

Communal Health in Unsanitary Conditions

Alleviating Jews' poverty-stricken unsanitary living conditions became the focus of many Jewish public health advocates in early twentieth-century Poland. This became urgent as Jewish communities began to experience breakouts of typhus and favus, a chronic inflammatory skin infection.[40] Quoting Iris Borowy and Wolf D. Gruner's assertion that "the history of health in interwar Europe is in many ways the history of interwar Europe,"[41] Nadav Davidovitch and Rakefet Zalashik argue:

With the rise of the welfare state, governments became involved in social policy supporting the creation of hygiene, education, and consultation institutes. In addition, there was a shift from charity to broader strategies promoting welfare related to the developing scientific understanding of factors affecting health. In the post World War I era, health became a potential focus to rebuild communities and nations. The changing political context of the interwar era brought the issue of minority health rights to the fore as well as the important role of international relief organizations that were operating in various countries in Europe. One of these ethnic minorities was the Jewish communities in Eastern Europe.[42]

Vegetarianism played a vital role in these larger debates on health and wellness. These particular discussions had origins in the pre-World War I era.[43] In a 1912 issue of *Der idisher hoyz-doktor* (The Jewish House Doctor), a supplementary periodical published by the Warsaw-based daily newspaper *Haynt*, Dr. K. Norden discussed the types of foods that vegetarians avoided and concluded that if one had indigestion, which may have resulted from eating unsanitary or spoiled foods, they might consider eating a vegetarian diet.[44] At least one entry in the restaurant's guest book hints at the unsanitary conditions in Vilna: Nathan Buxbaum (leader of the left-wing Po'alei Zion in Poland) and Khayim Shloyme Kazdan, and Shloyme Mendelson (who were both involved with the Yiddish socialist secular school system TSYSHO) wrote, "Truly clean, nice, and delicious. If only we could say the same for Vilna."[45]

This emphasis on vegetarianism as a means to combat unsanitary living conditions and promote Jewish communal health continued well into the interwar years. From 1923 to 1933, Vilna was home to the biweekly Yiddish periodical *Folksgezund* (Popular Health), which became a major organ for the Jewish community's focus on improving their living conditions. One of Tsemah Szabad's many projects, *Folksgezund* was part of a larger social justice campaign that sought to elevate Jews' living conditions.[46] Szabad was a physician; founder of the organization OZE, YIVO (along with others), and the journal *Folkspartei* (along with Simon Dubnow);[47] and a member of the Polish Sejm (Senate). He positioned *Folksgezund* to promote preventive medicine through healthy daily practices. Within its articles, vegetarianism featured from time to time as a means through which to boost the cleanliness of one's food; one such article was written by Dr. B. Dembski, and Lewando later reproduced it in her cookbook.

To illustrate the broad coverage vegetarianism received within the interwar Yiddish press in Poland, *Haynt* published articles on the topic by two of its more well-known writers, Leo Kenig, a London-based Yiddish-language writer and art critic, and Menakhem Kipnis, a singer and humorist. For these writers, vegetarianism was not just about keeping clean and healthy; it was actually a Jewish act to not consume meat. For example, two April 1938 articles extolled the virtues of vegetarianism. In "Vegetarian," Kenig asks the reader, "Do you love vegetarians?" and then goes on to answer that he does. Kenig says that vegetarians and anti-vivisectionists, to him, are remarkable because they hold so strongly to their idealism during times of "persecution" (*negishes*).[48] Kenig writes that there is something "noble" in their actions. In "Why I Became a Vegetarian," Kipnis writes about eating meat as a "*goyish*" (not Jewish) act, tying together vegetarianism and Jewishness.[49] The articles highlight how in the late 1930s vegetarianism was seen as idealist, noble, and "Jewish" among Yiddish speakers.

Interwar Poland and Anti-Kosher Laws

Within this far-reaching Yiddish and Jewish context, Lewando published her cookbook in Vilna in 1938. It is chock full of recipes and full-color illustrations. The cover features beautiful images of red cabbage, beets, and peppers (naming them in both Yiddish and English), and the front pages contain illustrations of parsley root, melon, onion, celery root, spinach, fennel, leeks, lettuce, kohlrabi, cauliflower, peas, and turnips.[50] The images use both Yiddish and English because the cookbook was sold in Eastern Europe, England, and New York. However, the photo captions of the vegetables are the only place where English appears. Employing bilingualism solely in the images in the cookbook indicates that the book was created specifically for Yiddish speakers, although it was exported to US and British markets. It is therefore tempting to compare the import of Lewando's cookbook to Jewish and non-Jewish vegetarian movements in the United States and England, which focused almost primarily on the health benefits of a vegetarian diet. It is as important to remember the larger Polish national and political context within which this book was produced as much as its global vegetarian and particularly Jewish contexts.

When Poland gained its independence from Germany, Russia, and the Austro-Hungarian Empire in 1918 and reemerged as a sovereign state, it was a poor and ethnically diverse country. It was established as a democratic society, but political parties failed to develop any long-lasting parliamentary majority. The overall population breakdown was approximately 65 percent Polish, 16 percent Ukrainian, 10 percent Jewish, 6 percent Belorussian, and 3 percent German. Ten percent of the Polish population amounted to approximately three million Jews—the largest Jewish population in Europe. Many Polish Jews adhered to the authority of the *kehillot*, which were the self-governing institutions that regulated

Jewish religious and other community affairs. Important for our understanding of interwar Poland, the *kehillot* were typically religiously observant. Therefore, the Polish Jewish community relied on ritually slaughtered meat.

The situation for Jews in post-World War I Poland seemed promising, and there was hope that a "strong, stable Poland would act as the cornerstone of a stable East Central Europe."[51] Questions about territory and borders, however, dominated much of the newly (re)formed state's early years. In early 1922, for example, in its quest to reestablish the expanse of pre-partition Poland, the Polish military captured and annexed Vilna, which had until then been a part of the newly established Lithuanian Commonwealth.

In 1926, following the establishment of a far-right coalition government, renowned Polish political leader Józef Piłsudski carried out a successful leftwing military coup against the Polish state. This put an authoritarian regime in place in Poland, which was eventually succeeded in 1939 by Nazi and Soviet control. Piłsudski's Poland centered on the *sanacja* (cleansing) of the state. Eva Plach has shown that many of Piłsudski's followers imbued *sanacja*, which emphasized loyalty to the state, with "varied and creative meaning."[52] She has also shown that toward the late 1930s, animal rights activists took up cause in favor of the anti-kosher butchering laws and couched their advocacy in antisemitic terms,[53] therefore imbricating animal rights activism, which we can understand to some extent as advocacy for a meat-free diet, with Polish, anti-Jewish, nationalism.

At first, *Piłsudskiites* "shared an attachment to nineteenth-century Polish romanticism and to the idea of a brotherhood of nations and were steadfastly committed to maintain the multiethnic heritage of the old Polish-Lithuanian Commonwealth."[54] As the period of *sanacja* took hold during the Piłsudski years, however, *sanacja* began to gain a wider cultural meaning; one emphasizing "purification, health, and rebirth." "By popularizing a vocabulary of rebirth and change, of moral responsibility, civic duty, and citizen accountability, work and collective action, the *sanacja* sparked a widespread debate about the meaning of Poland and Polish national identity in the modern era."[55] Ezra Mendelsohn demonstrates that:

> Piłsudski's Poland, far from implementing new social programs or advancing new ways of solving the nationalities problem, proved itself to be no less conservative and nationalistic than the Poland dominated by the Endeks [the conservative right-wing party that, in coalition with other parties, dominated the Polish political scene until 1926].... One of [Piłsudski's] last acts [in 1935] was to replace the old constitution with a new, nondemocratic one which invested power in the president rather than the [parliament].[56]

These changes set the stage for an increasingly nationalist and fascist-influenced post-Piłsudski regime.[57] The debates over Polish national identity excluded Jews in favor of a chauvinistic vision of Polish national belonging. As a result, a series of laws centered on Jews, such as the adoption of anti-kosher butchering laws in 1936, which were at their heart exercises in state-sanctioned antisemitism.

The interwar Polish context was fixated on building Polish national identity and had ripple effects within the Polish Jewish communities. Seen as the cradle of Eastern European Jewish culture, Poland was also home to several Jewish community movements, most notably Yiddishism and diaspora nationalism. Within these Polish and Jewish political, social, and national contexts we can read Lewando's cookbook as a cultural production with inherently political and Jewish national implications.

Lewando's Cookbook and Ideals for a New Jewishness

Fania Lewando's cookbook opens with a series of short pieces that act as a serving platter, highlighting its meanings and implications for the interwar Jewish community. When read alongside the recipes, Lewando's "Tsu di balebostes: a por verter un aynike praktishe anvayzungen" (To the Housewife: A Few Words and Practical Advice); Dr. B. Dembski's "Far vos zaynen azoy vikhtik farn organizm frukhtn un grinsn?" (Why Are Fruits and Vegetables So Important for the Organism?); and Ben-Zion Kit's "Vegetarizm als idishe bavegung" (Vegetarianism as a Jewish Movement) highlight how Lewando imagined a new Jewishness by way of the virtues of meat-free cooking. Her amended Jewish dietary practice made way for a new way of eating Jewishly in a Polish and global context that was increasingly hostile to traditional, daily Jewish life.

In "To the Housewife," Lewando writes:

> It has long been established by the highest medical authorities that food made from fruits and vegetables is far healthier and more suitable for the human organism than food made from meat.... We know, furthermore, that in these unhealthy times there is almost no house in which you will not find one of more family member who cannot eat meat and must follow a special vegetarian diet.[58]

Lewando reminds the reader that the vegetarian movement was founded on the principle of not killing animals, but when she hears people say that there is "no meat to cook," she understands that "we Jews think of not eating meat as a hardship, a sign of mourning."[59] For these reasons, she writes, she published the cookbook: "to promote vegetarian cuisine in general, and to serve in particular housewives who must maintain a dietetic kitchen."⁶⁰ Lewando makes the case for vegetarianism as both a healthy and humane dietary lifestyle and one that, because of the "unhealthy" times, has direct effect on the Jewish household and therefore the Jewish community. The reproduction of a piece by Dembski gives further details about the health aspects of eating a vegetarian diet highlighted in Lewando's introduction.⁶¹

Following Lewando's call to housewives and Dembski's report on the nutritional science supporting vegetarianism, the cookbook features Ben-Zion Kit's piece, "Vegetarianism as a Jewish Movement," which is a brief history of the vegetarian movement. It begins by lauding the nourishing aspects of a vegetarian diet and claims, "as we can see, vegetarianism has solid scientific as well as social, cultural, and historic justification."⁶² After telling the reader that vegetarians think their dietary choices are suited to nature, he says, "killing living creatures is against human nature."⁶³ Before concluding by naming famous vegetarians such as Leo Tolstoy, Romain Rolland, Mahatma Gandhi, George Bernard Shaw, and Ilya Repin, Ben-Zion Kit writes,

> It is worth noting that, according to the Bible, the first permitted foods were plants. In Genesis 1:29 it is written: "And God said, 'I give you all seed bearing grasses that grow on the earth and all trees that bear fruit and this shall be for you to eat.'" Meat became permitted only after the flood, when there were not yet any new plants to eat.⁶⁴

In this final introductory piece, Kit marks Jews as the progenitors of vegetarianism. He shows that vegetarianism may have first developed as a modern secular idea in France and may have first been institutionalized in England, but its true origins are in the Bible and are therefore Jewish. Given the social and cultural context from which Kit wrote, we can read the implications of calling vegetarianism a "Jewish movement" as a polemic that had nationalist, internationalist, antiracist, and antifascist implications.

After these essays, Lewando's recipes shape the dietary aspect of her ideal for Jewish food and Jewish living. The recipes feature full descriptions of ingredients and directions on how to prepare them. There are recipes that some may consider traditionally meat-free Jewish standards, such as blintzes, for which there is a special section including five recipes, and borscht, which use cheese or fruit and beets, respectively, as their main ingredients. There are also sections for frittatas (*faynkukhns*) and salads and an eight-piece section for Passover recipes. The latke section lists ten recipes. Perhaps surprising to some, the cookbook also contains recipes that radically redefine dishes that seemingly demanded meat as part of their essential Jewish makeup, like cholent and schnitzel. In

Lewando's creation, cholent, a traditional slow-cooked stew prepared so that Jews could eat on the Sabbath without having to break the laws prohibiting work or the lighting of fires, does not have to include meat. Her versions are marked by their six-hour cooking time rather than the longer twelve hours usually associated with cholent. In traditional European cuisine, schnitzels are made from tenderizing meat by beating it with a mallet, then covering it with flour and beaten eggs and frying it. Lewando's schnitzel recipes feature carrots and peas as their primary ingredients. Her "Cauliflower Weiner Schnitzel" is a simple re-creation:

> Chop 1 small piece cooked cauliflower, mix with 1 large egg, 1 tablespoon bread crumbs, and some salt, and beat well. Melt 1/4 cup butter in a frying pan, add the batter and cook on both sides [until it starts to brown]. Serve topped with a fried egg, and garnish with fried new potatoes and a gratin of carrots.[65]

This recipe reimagines a staple of the European diet and, by inclusion in her cookbook, the Jewish diet as a meat-free dish. Here, schnitzel is no longer a tenderized, battered, and fried meat dish; it is a vegetable fritter, not unlike the latke really, but made of cauliflower, carrots, peas, and celery root or cabbage. In fact, one of the two carrot schnitzel recipes is titled "*Shnitzelkes fun mern*," which Eve Jochnowitz translates as "Carrot Fritters (Little Carrot Schnitzels)."[66]

4 Niemiecka Street

Lewando's restaurant was quite popular among vegetarians and nonvegetarians, attracting some interwar Jewish cultural royalty. Among many others, the guest book features entries from Marc Chagall, the famed Russian Jewish painter who was visiting from Paris, and Itzik Manger, the popular Yiddish poet, playwright, and Bundist. The few photos that remain of Fania Lewando's eatery show a bustling scene.

The photos reproduced in the English translation of the *Vilna Vegetarian Cookbook* give us a glimpse of what it may have been like to eat at Lewando's restaurant. In one photo of the restaurant kitchen, Lewando appears standing to the side of the frame to show how she oversees the culinary operations. Each person in the photo is looking at the camera, so it is not a candid or spontaneous shot, but the image captures the backbone of the operation. It was a large kitchen, big enough to comfortably fit four women cooks and Lewando. The walls are covered with shelves, supporting an array of cooking instruments and place settings: pots, pans, bowls, plates, and wine glasses. One of the cooks is working a shredder and holding a potato above it. As soon as the photographer's shutter finished clicking, that potato certainly found its way in. Perhaps someone in the dining room had ordered Lewando's potato latkes.

Another photograph captures the dining area. There are men and women wearing middle-class suits and dresses seated at the five tables visible in the photo. Two women are seen serving the tables, which are covered with tablecloths, adorned with flowers in vases, and set for a full-service meal, including pitchers of water. In this photo, too, Lewando stands toward the back of the room, but she is still the focal point. In an interesting twist on Jewish imagery, the cookbooks are set on a bookshelf to Lewando's right. The shelf is framed by a curtain, which gives the look of a Torah Ark in a synagogue, elevating the cookbook to canonical Jewish status. It is perhaps the housewives' cooking Torah.

There were several reasons it would make sense to refigure Jewish dietary practice and law through a vegetarian lens in interwar Poland. With the rise of antisemitism, resulting in the ban on kosher butchering, and the rise of Jewish diaspora nationalism, the time was ripe to refigure vegetarianism as a political (because of its antiracist and antifascist implications) and secular Jewish movement.[67] Fania Lewando was at the forefront of the rebirth of this Jewish movement, using her cookbook, restaurant, and cooking school, which was not strictly vegetarian at first, to catalyze a new Jewish dietary and national identity, one that did not rely on meat to provide the backbone of nutritional or cultural practices.[68]

VEGETARIANISM AS ANTIFASCISM IN NAZI GERMANY

Vegetarianism in early twentieth-century Germany was a varied cause. Both leftists and those on the right, including fascists, adhered to the tenets of the movement. Within a leftist context, vegetarianism became embedded into some of Weimar Germany's "back to nature" campaigns.[69] Broadly conceived, vegetarianism in Weimar Germany was associated with the *Lebensreform* movement, which also promoted nudism and attempted to realign Germans' relationships to their bodies and advocated for a return to the natural.[70] On the right in Germany, vegetarianism was seen as a tool for "purification."[71] According to Tristram Stuart, "the Nazis aspired to lead humanity back to 'nature,' and although their concept of 'nature' was abhorrent, it was one that was chillingly compatible with the language of vegetarianism."[72] Despite this and Hitler's purported vegetarian diet, the vegetarian movement in Nazi Germany was squashed shortly after Hitler became chancellor on January 30, 1933. Colin Spencer writes that "Vegetarian societies were declared illegal and their magazine ceased publication in Frankfurt in 1933."[73] This was most likely due to leftist affiliations.[74] When independent societies were made illegal under Nazi law in 1935 and mandated to either close or join the Deutsche Gesellschaft für Lebensreform (German Society for Life Reform), the Deutscher Vegetarierbund (German Vegetarian Society) voted to disband.[75] Therefore, promoting a vegetarian lifestyle, especially within Jewish communities and in print in Jewish periodicals such as the *Frankfurter Israelitisches Gemeindeblatt*, *Blätter des Jüdischer Frauenbundes*, and *Central-Verein-Zeitung*, could be considered an act of resistance and antifascism.

The ban on kosher butchering in April 1933 followed the Nazis' failed boycott of Jewish businesses.[76] Unlike the boycott, the ban had far-reaching effects into German Jewish communities. According to Marion Kaplan, "the early prohibition against kosher butchering caused great hardship for the Orthodox community but also affected other Jews who had continued to purchase kosher meats."[77] For example, the ban caused religious problems for some Jews, as well as malnutrition.[78] Some kosher slaughterers continued their work in secret, but it was not enough to meet the underground demand; illegal kosher butchering was the exception, not the rule.[79] As a result, many Jews in Nazi Germany began to live with meatless dishes because even though they could import kosher meats, those imported products proved too costly.

In May 1933, one month after the ban on kosher butchering, in the *Frankfurter Israelitisches Gemeindeblatt*, the official newspaper of Frankfurt's Jewish community, Ida Wolf made it clear that the ban would introduce a new role for the housewife, who "maintained household rituals."[80] Women, Wolf wrote, "must [now] provide for their family with meatless food that is as nutritious and not more costly than before."[81] She was quick to note, "this is not as difficult as it seems, it only requires relearning."[82] If one were to replace meats with dairy as the primary ingredients in dishes, "the required amount of protein, which cannot alone be achieved by eggs, vegetables, and fish, will be met."[83] This would not be considered a vegetarian diet by contemporary standards, nor even by Lewando's as her meat-free cooking did not include fish. These were, however, the means by which *Frankfurter Israelitisches Gemeindeblatt* defined "meat-free" in early 1933.

Whereas Lewando and vegetarians in Poland connected their particular Polish experiences to the global vegetarian movement, in Nazi Germany the focus was primarily on the German context. This affects how we are to understand the political and Jewish implications of advocating meat-free cooking to Jewish households in Nazi Germany.

Jüdischer Frauenbund's Vegetarian Recipes

In 1935, the Jüdischer Frauenbund (League of Jewish Women) published a cookbook that highlighted many vegetarian dishes. This was in contrast to their earlier cookbooks that featured meat in many recipes.[84] The 1935 cookbook went through four publications in that year alone.[85] The league's newsletter, *Blätter des Jüdischer Frauenbundes* (*BJFB*), also published vegetarian recipes. By 1937, the Jüdischer Frauenbund's emphasis on vegetarian cooking was a primary focus of their publications. "A typical day's menu included oatmeal, cabbage stuffed with rice, and steamed apples for the main meal, and salad, a hard-boiled egg, and cooked plums for the lighter one."[86]

Recipes published in the *BJFB* demonstrate the extent to which vegetarian cooking and recipes provided Jewish families in Nazi Germany the means to maintain some semblance of Jewish daily life. In November 1937, on the "Housewives' Page," *BJFB* published "Some Suggestions for the Winter Kitchen."[87] To set up the readers' understandings of the suggested recipes, Stephanie Forchheimer, a colleague of Bertha Pappenheim, the founder of the Jüdischer Frauenbundes, wrote:

> We are giving housewives a few suggestions for their recipe lists for the next few weeks. Given the conditions [the cost of buying meat] we want to limit ourselves to meatless, but nonetheless nutritious and delicious, food.... Of course, depending on preference or opportunity, the housewife may always add meat or fish dishes. However, the preparation of meat-free—not vegetarian—courses may not be as common.[88]

Curiously, Forchheimer differentiates between a meatless and vegetarian menu, perhaps to combat any conflicts with the typical German Jewish diet that was meat-based or perhaps because, as mentioned before, printing "vegetarian" recipes was banned. It is also possible that *vegetarian* means meat- and dairy-free, what we would call vegan now, as some recipes call for eggs or cheese.

Forchheimer's introduction is followed by seven recipes for "meatless" lunches and dinners. For lunch there is a series of soups, wraps, and salads. For dinner, she suggests a noodle dish, a cauliflower and cheese dish, an egg-dipped bread similar to French toast, and a potato dish along with a few salads. The recipes, like those in Lewando's cookbook, are straightforward and easy to follow. In fact, like Lewando, Forchheimer introduced meatless cooking to the Jewish household in a way that would allow their families to eat both nutritiously and "Jewishly." The food was nutritious because it was based a wide variety of vegetables and included healthy amounts of proteins, carbohydrates, fats, minerals, and vitamins. It was "Jewish" because of the context within which the recipes were published, in the

BJFB, a newsletter for an organization that actively sought to "alleviate the worsening conditions of all Jews."⁸⁹

CVZ's Vegetarian Recipes and Toni Benario's Nutrition Column

The *Central-Verein-Zeitung* (*CVZ*) functioned with a similar mandate to the *BJFB* and, after the Nuremberg Laws of 1935, took to publishing vegetarian recipes.⁹⁰ For example, in the articles "Everyone Learns to Cook" and "Even Peter Cooks," *CVZ* began to make cooking a household event. Marion Kaplan writes, "these articles emphasized how children, particularly daughters, could help their mothers. They suggested introducing work as fun, giving children, especially small ones, *permission* to help out and warned against demanding too much."⁹¹ The articles were community centered and pedagogical.

In 1938, *CVZ* began to demonstrate to its readers the healthy aspects of meat-free (*fleischlose*) cooking. In February 1938, Toni Benario wrote a "Meat-free Nutrition Guide," including a list of meat-free sources of protein, fat, carbohydrates, minerals, and vitamins, as well as an explanation for why one would want to choose a meat-free diet.⁹²

The tone used and reasons provided for cooking meat-free dishes in Nazi Germany reads in stark contrast to those printed in Poland. The focus is not on the unsanitary conditions, because even during the late prewar years in Nazi Germany, German Jews' living conditions were not (yet) as destitute as they were Poland, and they retained some of the middle-class habits they had developed during Germany's imperial years.⁹³ In fact, Kaplan says of *CVZ*'s efforts, "they urged a complete reevaluation of the class privilege formerly permitted the middle-class housewife and daughter but stopped short of assailing the gender hierarchy within the family."⁹⁴

Early on in Benario's nutrition column, she writes, "What is 'our' staple food [*Hauptnahrungsmittle*]? Meat!"⁹⁵ Considering that this declaration of "their" food was published as the Nazis were banning the import of kosher meats, we can understand "our" to mean "Jewish" as much as "German." The claim seems to be that "as German Jews, we eat meat." However, Benario suggests eating meat-free because of the "hot'climate," which could be taken literally and figuratively. Literally because, as she says, the summer is coming; it is hot during the summer. Benario claims that if you cut meat from your diet, you could live a "lighter" life. The figurative reading of this considers how the ban on kosher butchering and then on importing kosher meat created a climate hostile to the continuation of Jewish daily life.

In prewar Nazi Germany, the outlaw on kosher butchering and then importing kosher meats had both immediate familial and larger cultural and political ramifications for Jews. In his essay on what counted as "resistance" in Nazi Germany, Yehudah Bauer uses the Hebrew word *amidah* ("standing up against") to define a broad range of both armed and unarmed resistance:

> What does amidah include? It includes smuggling food into ghettos; mutual self-sacrifice within the family to avoid starvation or worse; cultural, educational, religious, and political activities taken to strengthen morale; the work of doctors, nurses, and educators to consciously maintain health and moral fiber to enable individual and group survival; and, of course, armed rebellion or the use of force (with bare hands or with "cold" weapons) against the Germans and their collaborators.[96]

In some respects, Bauer claims that resistance is any attempt made to maintain Jewish (daily) life. In Wolf's, Forchheimer's, and Benario's writings, we see an evolution of how and for what reasons Jewish women, as heads of the households and therefore progenitors of Jewish culture, seemingly embraced meat-free cooking. First, as Wolf wrote in early 1933, Jewish women needed to relearn some of their practices so they could continue to provide for their family without increasing their household budgets. In late 1937, Forchheimer, reflecting the deteriorating economic situation for Jews who remained in Germany, advocated meat-free cooking as a way to help alleviate the cost burdens of keeping meat in the family diet. Forchheimer's column indicates that although advocacy for meat-free cooking began in 1933, it was not widespread by 1937. A year later, Benario acknowledged that eating meat was considered "Jewish" and "German," but perhaps Jews' current situation called for a change in culinary practices.

Taken together, these articles demonstrate how Jewish activists in Nazi Germany tried to prolong a "normalized" daily life for as long as possible. This resistance took on both cultural and political importance. It was cultural resistance, because advocating for meat-free cooking was an attempt to maintain Jewishness within the household; it was political because the very act of advocating anything in print that might be considered vegetarian could be viewed as criminal. In Nazi Germany, preparing meat-free meals at home had the potential to support German Jewishness and oppose the Nazis' hypernationalist, antisemitic, and modernist brand of fascism.[97]

CONCLUSION: ROMANTICIZING JEWISH FOOD IN FRANCE

Western Europe, and France more specifically, was no stranger to vegetarianism, as Ben-Zion Kit has made clear. The modern movement was supposed to have begun in France, and advocates of vegetarianism counted among themselves many

French people, most famously Romain Rolland. In France, as in Weimar Germany, vegetarianism was tied to naturalist movements. As in Poland, in France it was tied to the purification of society, as well as the French Third Republic's attempt to provide "health for all," a public health campaign that sought to boost the number of hospitals.[98] Unlike in Piłsudski's Poland and Nazi Germany, there was no far-reaching advocacy for Jews to adapt to a vegetarian lifestyle. This was most likely because laws were not put in place before Vichy that dictated what Jews could and could not eat, even if there was certainly an increase in antisemitism in the 1930s.[99] Even during Vichy, kosher butchering was not banned.[100] Of the major Jewish newspapers in France, both French and Yiddish, none published columns on vegetarianism like those in Poland and Germany. One of the French Jewish newspapers, *Parizer haynt*, was even an outpost of the Warsaw-based *Haynt*, which was publishing on vegetarianism.

There were clearly Jews in France who followed a vegetarian lifestyle, however. For example, an ad in the weekly newspaper *Le Journal juif* for the restaurant Carmel in the old Jewish quarter of the Marais read that it served " 'lacto-vegetarian' meals at all hours" of operation.[101] It ought to be noted that *Le Journal juif*, other than publishing this advertisement, did not run any columns advocating vegetarian cooking for Jewish families.

Publications on Jewish cooking in France talked about it as both nostalgic and simple. Édouard de Pomaine published his memoir/cookbook, *Kasher: Cuisine juive ghettos modernes*, in 1929, which presented Jews in Eastern Europe as a group of people who "retained a special language, their own style of dress, ancient customs, and ritual cuisine."[102] Suzanne Roukhomovsky published *Gastronomie juive: Cuisine et patisserie de Russie, d'Alsace, de Roumanie et d'Orient* (1929), in which she advocated Jewish cooking as simple home cooking. Barbara Kirshenblatt-Gimblett quotes Roukhomovsky as saying "the reader does not have to search here for quasi-pharmaceutical complications of a cuisine that is too modern, nor the royal luxury of truffles, *foie gras* and champagne that one freely adds to all sauces, at least in the books."[103] Perhaps we can understand "quasi-pharmaceutical" as vegetarian, implying that in France, Jews had the luxury to cook whatever they wanted for whatever reasons.

In Poland and Germany during the 1930s, the particular political, social, and cultural climates in which Jews found themselves catalyzed new ways of conceiving Jewishness through foods, or lack thereof. In Poland, anti-kosher butchering laws seemingly compelled some Jews to tie their particular situation to the global vegetarian movement by advocating for the healthy aspects of vegetarian cooking, which could be interpreted as part of the new Yiddishism percolating in interwar Poland. In Nazi Germany, women activists advocated vegetarianism or, more precisely, meat-free cooking as a means to provide for the family on a budget and maintain the middle-class bourgeois German lifestyle to which they were accustomed. As result, both movements became political acts in their own ways. In Poland, Jews' actions can be understood as political because of how they advocated for a new Jewish identity through food practices that implicated Jews as part of, rather than in opposition to, "modern" society, ironically undermining the interpretation of Eastern European Jewish food culture put forth in France by Édouard de Pomaine. In Nazi Germany, Jews' promotion of meat-free cooking was a political act because of its inherent resistance to the Nazi system and how it was an attempt to maintain Jewish daily life. In both Poland and Nazi Germany, there seemed to be a sense of antifascism that underscored the proposals for meat-free menus.

Jewish ties to vegetarianism in 1930s Poland and Germany also make it clear how women were woven into conversations about community, modernity, and Jews' places within society. Jewish vegetarianism in interwar Poland and Germany further demonstrates how women were becoming integrated into political movements through the vanishing imaginary divide between public and private Jewish and familial spaces. Jewish women were recognized for their contributions to the homes, which in these particular political and social climates propelled them to the front line of a brand of Jewish politics that tied together the Jewish home, Jewish culture, and Jewish society. As Lewando, Wolf, Forchheimer, and Benario demonstrate, if Jews were to maintain their Jewishness in these times of cultural and political crises and catastrophe, women would maintain order within the family and introduce a new Jewish identity. Women would also bridge the public and private Jewish spheres to articulate a new kind of Jewish identity through a first radical, then necessary political strategy: not eating meat.

NOTES

I thank Rob Adler-Peckerar, Erin Corber, Eve Jochnowitz, Alexandra Loshe, Marion Kaplan, Frank Wolff, Clare Fester, and Jacob Ari Labendz for their help with and comments on earlier drafts of this article.

1. Gary Rendsburg, "The Vegetarian Ideal in the Bible," in *Food and Judaism*, ed. Leonard J. Greenspoon, Ronald A. Simkins, and Gerald Shapiro (Omaha, NE: Creighton University Press, 2005), 319–34.

2. Ibid., 320.

3. See Carole Fink, *Defending the Rights of Others: The Great Powers, the Jews, and International Minority Protection, 1878–1938* (Cambridge: Cambridge University Press, 2006). On how states managed to wrestle away from private institutions the right to monitor citizens' movements in the post-World War I era, see

John Torpey, *The Invention of the Passport: Surveillance, Citizenship and the State* (Cambridge: Cambridge University Press, 1999). On the parallel development of police surveillance of immigrant communities, see Clifford Rosenberg, *Policing Paris: The Origins of Modern Immigration Control between the Wars* (Ithaca, NY: Cornell University Press, 2006).

4. Germany's Jewish population in January 1933 was approximately 523,000.

5. Ezra Mendelsohn, *On Modern Jewish Politics* (New York: Oxford University Press, 1993), 5.

6. On the rise of the pacifist movement, specifically in France, see Norman Ingram, *The Politics of Dissent: Pacifism in France 1919–1939* (Oxford: Oxford University Press, 1991). On the rise of nationalisms and its effect on Jewish communities in Eastern Europe, see Ezra Mendelsohn, *The Jews of East Central Europe between the World Wars* (Bloomington: Indiana University Press, 1987).

7. For example, see Elisée Reclus, *Vegetarizm* (New York: Nyu Yorker vegetaryer fareyn, 1921); A. B. Mishulow, *Vegetarishe kokh bukh: 'ratsyonale nahrung'* (New York: Better Health and Correct Eating Institute, 1926); Lena Brown, *Kokh-bukh far gezuntheyt: geshribn vi tsu balansirn natirlekhe vegetarishe esns nokh der visnshaftlikher metode* (New York: Braun, 1931); B. Liber, *Darfn mir esn fleysh* (New York: Jacob Fine, 1956); and E. Dimshits, *Der vege taryaner gedank: a zamlung fun vegetaryaner ophandlungen* (Philadelphia: Filadelfyer vegetaryaner fereyn, n.d.).

8. See Stefani Hoffman and Ezra Mendelsohn (eds.), *The Revolution of 1905 and Russia's Jews* (Philadelphia: University of Pennsylvania Press, 2008).

9. For one, see Kenneth Moss, *Jewish Renaissance in the Russian Revolution* (Cambridge, MA: Harvard University Press, 2009).

10. For an overview of the development of Jewish diaspora nationalism and a related collection of documents, see Simon Rabinovitch (ed.), *Jews and Diaspora Nationalism: Writings on Jewish Peoplehood in Europe and the United States* (Waltham, MA: Brandeis University Press, 2012).

11. Paula Hyman argued, "the gendered differences in the experience of assimilation and the growing representation of women as the primary transmitters of Jewish culture shaped modern Jewish history on the battlegrounds of sexual politics." Paula Hyman, *Gender and Assimilation in Modern Jewish History: The Roles and Representations of Women* (Seattle: University of Washington Press, 1995), 9.

12. Robin Judd shows that in late nineteenth- and early twentieth-century German history, before the Nazi years, Jewish practices such as circumcision and kosher butchering were at the forefront of attention for "four generations of Jews and non-Jews and several different political regimes in the German lands." Although German Jews and non-Jews paid attention to these practices and debated

their merits, kosher butchering was not widely banned as it was in April 1933. See Robin Judd, *Contested Rituals: Circumcision, Kosher Butchering, and Jewish Political Life in Germany, 1843–1933* (Ithaca, NY: Cornell University Press, 2007), 3. On "new kosher" cooking in Nazi Germany, see Frank Wolff, "Der Traum vom deutsch-jüdischen Bauern: Das Auswandererlehrgut Groß-Breesen (1935–1938) und die verspätete Emigrationspolitik des CV," in *"Was soll aus uns werden?" Quellen und Forschungen zur Geschichte des Centralvereins deutscher Staatsbürger jüdischen Glaubens im nationalsozialistischen Deutschland*, ed. Regina Grundmann et al. (Berlin: Metropol, 2016).

13. Eva Plach, "Ritual Slaughter and Animal Welfare in Interwar Poland," *East European Jewish Affairs* 45, no. 1 (2015): 1–25.

14. Ibid., 19.

15. Plach argues that interwar Polish political culture of "cleansing" had clear implications for the development of Polish national identity during the Józef Piłsudski years (1926–1935). See Eva Plach, *The Clash of Moral Nations: Cultural Politics in Piłsudski's Poland, 1926–1935* (Athens: Ohio University Press, 2006).

16. Ezra Mendelsohn, in his typology for Jewish politics, argues that movements defining what is Jewish over who is Jewish is a fundamental component in recognizing and defining "Jewish politics." Mendelsohn, *On Modern Jewish Politics*, 5.

17. Colin Spencer, *The Heretic's Feast: A History of Vegetarianism* (Hanover, NH: University Press of New England, 1995), 310 and 312.

18. On Jewish diets during the sixteenth and eighteenth centuries, see John Cooper, *Eat and Be Satisfied: A Social History of Jewish Food* (Northvale: Jason Aronson, 1993), chap. 8.

19. Spencer, *The Heretic's Feast*, 252.

20. See Jonathan Frankel, *Prophecy and Politics: Socialism, Nationalism, and the Russian Jews, 1862–1917* (Cambridge: Cambridge University Press, 1984).

21. Sidney Mintz, "Introduction," in *Jews and Their Foodways*, ed. Anat Helman (Oxford: Oxford University Press, 2016), 5. On the history of restaurants in France, see Rebecca Spang, *The Invention of the Restaurant: Paris and Modern Gastronomic Culture* (Cambridge, MA: Harvard University Press, 2001).

22. Robert Liberles, *Jews Welcome Coffee: Tradition and Innovation in Early Modern Germany* (Waltham, MA: Brandeis University Press, 2012)

23. For recent studies on the relationships between Jews, food, and notions of national belonging, see Yael Raviv, *Falafel Nation: Cuisine and the Making of National Identity in Israel* (Lincoln: University of Nebraska Press, 2015), and Ted Merwin, *Pastrami on Rye: An Overstuffed History of the Jewish Deli* (New York: New York University Press, 2015)

24. Raviv, *Falafel Nation*, 2.

25. See Julia Bernstein, *Transnational Contested Identities and Food Practices of Russian-Speaking Jewish Migrants in Israel and Germany* (New York: Campus Verlag, 2010).

26. See Daniel Breslauer, "The Vegetarian Alternative: Biblical Adumbrations, Modern Reflections," in *Food and Judaism*, ed. Leonard J. Greenspoon, Ronald A. Simkins, and Gerald Shapiro (Omaha, NE: Creighton University Press, 2005).

27. Eve Jochnowitz, "The Culinary Landscapes of Russian-Jewish New York," in *Jewish Topographies: Visions of Space, Traditions of Place*, ed. Julia Brauch, Anna Lipphardt, and Alexandra Nocke (New York: Routledge, 2016), 295. See also Eve Jochnowitz, "A Younger World: Vegetarian Writings and Recipes in Yiddish as Political Strategies," in *Tastes of Faith: Jewish Eating in the United States*, ed. Leah Hochman (West Lafayette, IN: Purdue University Press, 2017).

28. The two most comprehensive histories of vegetarianism are Spencer, *The Heretic's Feast*, and Tristram Stuart, *The Bloodless Revolution: A Cultural History of Vegetarianism From 1600 to Modern Times* (New York: Norton, 2006).

29. Stuart most directly takes this approach. He is quick to point out that both the left and the right advocated for vegetarianism in early twentieth-century Europe. Stuart situates Hitler's vegetarianism within early twentieth-century German attempts to reinvigorate "health and beauty in the face of the pathological effects of urbanization," which was based on the concepts of *Lebensreform* (life reform) and *Körperkultur* (body culture). Stuart is also careful in his categorization of Hitler's vegetarianism in that although he categorizes Hitler as a vegetarian, he allows for what other historians believe was more propaganda than full adherence to the movement. Stuart, *The Bloodless Revolution*, 435–44. Spencer situates Hitler's vegetarianism in the context of his admiration for Wagner, who advocated vegetarianism based on his equation of animal and human life. Spencer, *The Heretic's Feast*, 282–83. For more on the cultivation through propaganda, specifically rooted in his domestic lifestyle that tried to depict Hitler as a congenial, orderly, and humane leader, see Despina Stratigakos, *Hitler at Home* (New Haven, CT: Yale University Press, 2015).

30. See James Gregory, *Of Victorians and Vegetarians: The Vegetarian Movement in Nineteenth-Century Britain* (New York: Tauris Academic Studies, 2007).

31. Ibid., 188.

32. Arjun Appadurai, "How to Make a National Cuisine: Cookbooks in Contemporary India," *Comparative Studies in Society and History* 30, no. 1 (1988): 3–24.

33. Barbara Kirshenblatt-Gimblett, "The Kosher Gourmet in the Nineteenth-Century Kitchen: Three Jewish Cookbooks in Historical Perspective," *Journal of Gastronomy* 2, no. 4 (1986/87): 53.

34. Raviv, *Falafel Nation*, 7.

35. Alice Nakhimovsky, "You Are What They Ate: Russian Jews Reclaim Their Foodways," *Shofar* 25, no. 1 (2006): 63–77.

36. Ben-Tsiyon Liber, *Darfn mir esn fleysh: gedanken vegn vegetarizm* (Brooklyn: Fine, 1956). For Yiddishists, highlighting the contributions of Yiddish culture to the development of modern society and modernity during the rise of fascism in Europe was part and parcel to many of their programmatic efforts, most notably the presentation of Yiddish and Jewish culture on display at the Modern Jewish Culture pavilion at the 1937 World's Fair in Paris. See Nick Underwood, "Exposing Yiddish Paris: The Modern Jewish Culture Pavilion at the 1937 World's Fair," *East European Jewish Affairs* 46, no. 2 (2016): 160–75. Also see David Shneer, "How Eastern European Jewish Immigrants, Modernist Yiddish Culture, and Anti-Fascist Politics Dragged the Netherlands into the Twentieth Century," *East European Jewish Affairs* 46, no. 2 (2016): 139–59.

37. On the birth of modern Jewish politics, see Zvi Gittelman (ed.), *The Emergence of Modern Jewish Politics: Bundism and Zionism in Eastern Europe* (Pittsburgh: University of Pittsburgh Press, 2003); Mendelsohn, *On Modern Jewish Politics*; and David Biale, *Power and Powerlessness in Jewish History* (New York: Schocken Press, 1986).

38. Jenna Weissman Joselit, "When Vegetarians Were Rare," *Jewish Daily Forward*, August 3, 2007, http://forward.com/culture/11273/when-vegetarians-were-rare-00217.

39. See recently published articles by Leah Koenig, "Vilna's Moosewood Cookbook," *Jewish Daily Forward*, October 5, 2011, http://forward.com/articles/143902/vilna-s-moosewood-cookbook; Melissa Clark, "Finding, then Publishing a Rare Yiddish Vegetarian Cookbook from the '30s," *The Splendid Table*, July 15, 2015, https://www.splendidtable.org/story/finding-then-publishing-a-rare-yiddish-vegetarian-cookbook-from-the-30s; Ofer Aderet, "Veggie Burgers in 1930s Vilna a Jewish Chef Ahead of Her Time," *Haaretz*, May 26, 2015, http://www.haaretz.com/life/books/.premium-1.657969; and Joselit, "When Vegetarians Were Rare."

40. Nadav Davidovitch and Rakefet Zalashik, " 'Air, Sun, Water': Ideology and Activities of OZE (Society for the Preservation of the Health of the Jewish Population) during the Interwar Period," *Dynamis* 28 (2008): 127–49.

41. Iris Borowy and Wolf D. Gruner, "Introduction," in *Facing Illness in Troubled Times: Health in Europe in the Interwar Years, 1918–1939*, ed. Iris Borowy and Wolf D. Gruner (Frankfurt: Peter Lang, 2005), 1.

42. Davidovitch and Zalashik, " 'Air, Sun, Water'," 129.

43. This connection between health and vegetarianism was part of the larger global vegetarian movement during these years. See Spencer, *Heretics Feast*, chap. 12, and Stuart, *Bloodless Revolution*, epilogue.

44. Dr. K. Norden, "Vegn vegetarianism," *Der idisher hoyz-doktor*, May 28, 1912, no. 11: 5–6.

45. Fania Lewando, *Vegetarish-Dietisher Kokhbukh: 400 speyser gemacht oysshlishlekh fun grinsen* (Vilna: G. Kleckina, 1938), 234.

46. For more on Szabad, see Yulian I. Rafes, *Doctor Tsemakh Shabad: A Great Citizen of the Jewish Diaspora* (Baltimore: VIA Press, 1999). See also Davidovitch and Zalashik, "'Air, Sun, Water'."

47. OZE stands for Obshchestvo okhraneniia zdorov'ia evreiskogo naseleniia (Society for the Protection of the Health of the Jews). It was later known as Obschestvo zdravookhraneniia evreev. It is now based in Paris and is known as OSE, Oeuvre de Secours aux Enfants. YIVO (Yidisher visnshaftlekher institut/Yiddish Scientific Institute), now known as the Institute for Jewish Research, was founded in 1925 and became the leading institution for scholarship in Yiddish and about the history and culture of Eastern European Jews and their emigrant communities. It is currently in New York City. The Folkspartey was a political party that formed in 1905 in St. Petersburg and advocated for Jewish national autonomy. Simon Dubnow (1860–1941) was a Russian Jewish historian and ideologue of Jewish diaspora nationalism.

48. Leo Kenig, "Vegetarier," *Haynt*, April 1, 1938, 7.

49. M. Kipnis, "Vi azoy ikh bin gevorn a vegetarianer...," *Haynt*, April 7, 1938, 8.

50. Lewando, *Vegetarish-Dietisher Kokhbukh*, n.p.

51. Mendelsohn, *The Jews of East Central Europe between the World Wars*, 11.

52. Plach, *The Clash of Moral Nations*, 8.

53. Plach, "Ritual Slaughter and Animal Welfare."

54. Plach, *The Clash of Moral Nations*, 2.

55. Ibid., 6.

56. Mendelsohn, *The Jews of East Central Europe between the World Wars*, 16

57. Ibid.

58. Fania Lewando, "To the Housewife: A Few Words and Practical Advice," in Fania Lewando, *The Vilna Vegetarian Cookbook: Garden-Fresh Recipes Rediscovered and Adapted for Today's Kitchen*, trans. Eve Jochnowitz (New York: Schocken, 2015), 3. I use Jochnowitz's translation of these introductory pieces. The original Yiddish is Fania Lewando, "Tsu di balebostes: a por verter un aynike praktishe anvayzungen," in Fania Lewando, *Vegetarish-Dietisher Kokhbukh*, iii.

59. Ibid.

60. Lewando, "To the Housewife," 4.

61. Dr. B. Dembski, "Why Are Fruits and Vegetables So Important for the Organism?," in Fania Lewando, *The Vilna Vegetarian Cookbook: Garden-Fresh Recipes Rediscovered and Adapted for Today's Kitchen*, trans. Eve Jochnowitz (New York: Schocken, 2015), 5–8.

62. Ben-Zion Kit, "Vegetarianism as a Jewish Movement," in *The Vilna Vegetarian Cookbook: Garden-Fresh Recipes Rediscovered and Adapted for Today's Kitchen*, trans. Eve Jochnowitz (New York: Schocken, 2015) 9.

63. Ibid., 10.

64. Ibid.

65. Lewando, *The Vilna Vegetarian Cookbook*, 68.

66. Ibid., 70.

67. Although historians do not tend to consider Piłsudski a fascist, some Jews in interwar Europe did, such as the writers and editors of the Parisian communist *Naye prese*. See *Naye prese*, June 29, 1935.

68. In a photo of the cooking school, one shelf of pots reads "*fleyshik*," meaning the kitchen was kosher, not vegetarian. It is unclear in what year this photo was taken, however. It is most likely that it predated the 1936 kosher laws in Poland. Lewando, *The Vilna Vegetarian Cookbook*, xxxiv.

69. For more on resurgence of "nature" in Weimar Germany, see John Alexander Williams, *Turning to Nature in Germany: Hiking, Nudism, and Conservation, 1900–1940* (Stanford, CA: Stanford University Press, 2007); and John Alexander Williams, "Friends of Nature: The Culture of Working-Class Hiking," in *Weimar Culture Revisited*, ed. John Alexander Williams (New York: Palgrave Macmillan, 2011). On vegetarianism as part of a larger post-World War I German national rehabilitation, see Erik Jensen, *Body by Weimar: Athletes, Gender, and German Modernity* (Oxford: Oxford University Press, 2010), 4.

70. On *Lebensreform* and vegetarianism, see Anton Kaes, Martin Jay, and Edward Dimendberg (eds.), *The Weimar Republic Sourcebook* (Berkeley: University of California Press, 1994), 673, and W. L. Guttsman, *Art for the Workers: Ideology and the Visual Arts in Weimar Germany* (Manchester: Manchester University Press, 1997), 145.

71. Stuart, *Bloodless Revolution*, 435.

72. Ibid.

73. Spencer, *The Heretic's Feast*, 308.

74. Spencer cites no sources for his claims about the closing of vegetarian societies in 1933, so the summary he presented is an attempt to frame this purported

ban around the political climate of Nazi Germany in 1933. It is unlikely that Nazi officials singled out vegetarian societies as vegetarian during this period, but it is possible that these groups, like many others, would have been shut down because of their leftist affiliations.

75. Ursula Heinzelmann, *Beyond Bratwurst: A History of Food in Germany* (London: Reaktion Books, 2014), chap. 10, n.p.

76. On the boycott as a "failure," see Richard Evans, *The Third Reich in Power* (New York: Penguin Books, 2005), 15. On the outlawing of kosher butchering, see Marion Kaplan, *Between Dignity and Despair: Jewish Life in Nazi Germany* (New York: Oxford University Press, 1998), 33.

77. Kaplan, *Between Dignity and Despair*, 33

78. Ibid.

79. Ibid., 34.

80. Ida Wolf, "Jüdische Küche," *Frankfurter Israelitisches Gemeindeblatt* 9 (May 1933): 215. For a study on Jewish women as the primary transmitters of Jewish culture, see Hyman, *Gender and Assimilation in Modern Jewish History*.

81. Wolf, "Jüdische Küche," 215.

82. Ibid.

83. Ibid.

84. *Kochbuch für die jüdische Küche* (Düsseldorf: Jüdischer Frauenband, 1926). MF 1286, Leo Baeck Institute, New York.

85. Ibid.

86. Ibid.

87. Stephanie Forchheimer, "Einige Vorschläge für die winterliche Küche," *Blätter des Jüdischer Frauenbundes* (November 1937): 13.

88. Ibid.

89. Kaplan, *Between Dignity and Despair*, 47.

90. Michael Burleigh and Wolfgang Wippermann argue that 1935 was a major turning point in Nazi Germany in terms of Jewish daily life and racial persecution. See Michael Burleigh and Wolfgang Wippermann, *The Racial State: Germany 1933–1945* (Cambridge: Cambridge University Press, 1993).

91. Kaplan, *Between Dignity and Despair*, 55.

92. Toni Benario, "Fleischlose Ernährung," *Central-Verein-Zeitung* 8 (February 24, 1938): 17.

93. Marion Kaplan, *The Making of the Jewish Middle Class* (Oxford: Oxford University Press, 1991).

94. Kaplan, *Between Dignity and Despair*, 55.

95. Benario, "Fleischlose Ernährung," 17.

96. Yehuda Bauer, *Rethinking the Holocaust* (New Haven, CT: Yale University Press, 2002), 120.

97. Hitler's fascism was just one of many forms of fascism in early twentieth-century Europe. For more on fascism as a disparate "movement" made up of several forms, see Eugen Weber, *The Varieties of Fascism: Doctrines of Revolution in the Twentieth Century* (Malabar, FL: Robert E. Krieger Publishing Company, 1982).

98. Arouna Ouédraogo, "Food and the Purification of Society: Dr Paul Carton and Vegetarianism in Interwar France," *Social History of Medicine* 14, no. 2 (2001): 225. For more on the relationship between food and identity in interwar France, see Lauren Janes, *Colonial Food in Interwar Paris: The Taste of Empire* (New York: Bloomsbury Academic, 2016).

99. On the rise in antisemitism in 1930s France, see Vicki Caron, *Uneasy Asylum: France and the Jewish Refugee Crisis, 1933–1942* (Stanford, CA: Stanford University Press, 2002).

100. Daniel Lee, *Pétain's Jewish Children: French Jewish Youth and the Vichy Regime, 1940–1942* (Oxford: Oxford University Press, 2014), 85–86.

101. *Le Journal juif*, November 15, 1935, 5.

102. Édouard de Pomaine, *Kasher: Cuisine juive ghettos modernes* (Paris: Albun Michel, 1929), 12.

103. Suzanne Roukhomovsky, *Gastronomie juive: Cuisine et patisserie de Russie, d'Alsace, de Roumanie et d'Orient* (Paris: Flammarion, 1929). Barbara Kirshenblatt-Gimblett, "Cookbooks," YIVO Encyclopedia, http://www.yivoencyclopedia.org/printarticle.aspx?id=2517.

3 "I Am a Vegetarian"
The Vegetarianism of Melech Ravitch

IRAD BEN ISAAK

This chapter discusses the development of the vegetarianism of Melech Ravitch (1893–1976), a prolific Yiddish poet, editor, autobiographer, and documenter of Yiddish culture in the twentieth century. Ravitch's vegetarianism and his critique of animal suffering found a unique and clear expression in his journalistic and creative oeuvre, including journal articles, autobiographical texts, and most prominently his poems. Ravitch became vegetarian at the age of nineteen in Vienna, and his vegetarianism become one of the fundamental pillars of his worldview. By setting an example and using his literary creativity, he managed to convert other people to vegetarianism, among them prolific Yiddish author and Nobel Prize winner Isaac Bashevis Singer, who became a vegetarian icon himself.[1]

Here I present the development of Ravitch's vegetarianism and discuss his "vegetarian poetry." I describe how he became a vegetarian and what it was like for him to "come out" as a vegetarian in front of his family—a family that happened to make a living by importing meat—in times when the concept of vegetarianism was hardly heard of. Then I analyze the key lines of Ravitch's vegetarian thought as it emerges from his articles and autobiographies, locating it within ethical and philosophical frameworks. At the end, I present a selection of what Ravitch described as his vegetarian poems, which formed the ultimate expression of his vegetarian sensitivity. I interpret these poems as an attempt to draw attention to animal suffering in a modernist poetic form and then analyze his means of humanizing the animal while dehumanizing its perpetrator.

BIOGRAPHY

Melech Ravitch—the pseudonym of Zekharye-Khone Bergner—was a prolific Yiddish poet and essayist and a very involved cultural activist. He was born in 1893 in the shtetl of Radymno in eastern Galicia, which was then part of the Habsburg Empire and became part of Poland in 1918. Ravitch's family was multilingual, speaking Polish, German, and Yiddish. His education included both secular and

Jewish traditional content; however, the secular component was more pronounced compared with the experiences of other Yiddish writers of his generation. Ravitch went to business school, which offered him opportunities for well-paid jobs in banks in Lemberg (Lwów) and Vienna in his early years. He was deeply inspired by the Czernowitz Language Conference, which discussed the idea of Yiddish as a national language of the Jewish people and took place in 1908 when he was fifteen. Under its influence, he dedicated his life to writing in Yiddish. When he settled in Vienna in 1912, he began to publish books of his Yiddish poetry.

In his poetry volume, *Naked Poems* (נאַקעטע לידער), which he published in 1921 at the end of his Viennese period, Ravitch turned toward modernism in its expressionist form.[2] In this volume, he dealt with a variety of diverse social themes, speaking against the norms and beliefs of bourgeois society in the name of his own ideological values.[3] This volume was the one where he devoted the largest space to vegetarian-themed poems. Its last chapter, "The Vegetarian Gospel" (וועגעטאַריש עוואַנגעליום), is discussed later in this essay.

By moving from Vienna to Warsaw in 1921, Ravitch started a new period in his life in which he was highly involved in the Yiddish literary scene of the Polish capital. At the beginning, his cultural activity was centered in the literary group known as Di Khalyastre (The Gang), which also included the iconic poets Perets Markish and Uri Tsevi Grinberg. The avant-garde trio together experienced their transformational processes from late neo-romanticism to modernism, each in his own way. In those times, Ravitch edited the journal *Di Vog* (The Scale), which inaugurated his long career as a journal editor. Beginning in 1924, Ravitch was the executive secretary of Association of Jewish Writers and Journalists in Warsaw, popularly known by its address in Warsaw, 13 Tłomackie. This association and its circle was the elite center of Yiddish secular literature and culture in interwar Poland. Ravitch was a co-founder and coeditor of *Literarishe Bleter* (Literary Pages), the association's influential literary and artistic Yiddish-language journal.

In the 1920s and 1930s, Ravitch continued publishing poetry books with a rich thematic, emotional, and linguistic range. In 1933 he left Poland and continued his life in constant movement, living in Australia, Argentina, Mexico, and eventually settling in Montreal in 1941 until his death in 1976. Next to his poems, Ravitch is best known for the rich documentation he produced of his life and his cultural scenes, through his personality lexicons, his three-part autobiography, and his archive.

I AM A VEGETARIAN: RAVITCH'S FIRST TWENTY-FOUR HOURS AS A VEGETARIAN

In his autobiography *The Story Book of My Life* (דאָס מעשה בוך פון מיין לעבן), Ravitch dedicated a chapter to a curious story about the night in Vienna when he became a vegetarian.⁴ The chapter's title, "I am a vegetarian…" (… איך בין אײן װעגעטאַריער) echoes his statement of "coming out" as a vegetarian at an extremely carnivorous family dinner at his uncle's, who happened to be one of the largest meat importers in Vienna. Ravitch opens the chapter with the statement that his turn to vegetarianism was related to Vienna.⁵ For young Ravitch, this city was a place of self-discovery, a space where he could develop his worldview. He arrived there as a young person, craving intellectual and emotional stimulation. In Vienna he found a freedom he had lacked in Galicia, as well as a more Western form of Jewish culture and life. He described his time in Austrian capital as a time of rebirth.⁶

This transformative night in Vienna occurred in 1912, two years before the outbreak of World War I, which shattered European political and social hierarchies. That night, Ravitch was barely nineteen, new in the Austrian metropolis, and deeply enchanted by its diversity and glory. He described his turn to vegetarianism that night as the effect of the influence of a friend, who literally "converted" him to vegetarianism. That friend was Jacob Funkelstein-Rosner, to whom Ravitch later dedicated his first vegetarian poem. Funkelstein-Rosner was portrayed as a particular archetype of an Eastern European Jew of that time: a Talmudic prodigy who left his shtetl in favor of Vienna, an urban homosexual assimilationist, a fan of the new Jewish writers in German, and a dreamer. Funkelstein-Rosner had been an *iluy*, a promising yeshiva student, back in his shtetl of Vishnitz in Bukovina, and at some point he was attracted to the Austrian metropolis by the fame of the Jewish poets and novelists of the German-language space: Stefan Zweig, Albert Ehrenstein, and Franz Kafka, who were also known as vegetarians, as well as Arthur Schnitzler, Franz Werfel, and others.⁷

Funkelstein-Rosner used to visit Ravitch every other night, each time coming up with new "strange ideas." He tried to talk Ravitch into writing his poems in German rather than Yiddish, while Ravitch attempted to convince Funkelstein-Rosner to do the opposite. Ravitch described Funkelstein-Rosner's German as "as rich as Franz Werfel's," but with a dominant Yiddish accent. His thick curly brown hair made him look like a sheep just before sheering. Ravitch implicitly mentioned Funkelstein-Rosner's homosexuality. Funkelstein-Rosner had a friend "of a similar type" named Isaac Schreier, a blond type with a *goyish* face and distinct European manners, who also wrote poems in German. The two presumably "loved each other like David loved Jonathan and Jonathan loved David."⁸

The night in which Funkelstein-Rosner turned Ravitch into a vegetarian began like many of their meetings. Funkelstein-Rosner visited Ravitch, sharing his new ideas with him late into the night. This time, he told Ravitch that earlier that day he had come to the conclusion that horses speak to each other at night in human language. Through all their years spent among humans, horses had presumably learned to speak, but they usually avoided showing off their human-language knowledge, fearing that the humans might think that a *dibbuk* had gotten into them and they were possessed. In Funkelstein-Rosner's vision, among the horses there were prince horses, poet horses, and philosopher horses, who possessed highly sophisticated intellectual qualities.[9]

Funkelstein-Rosner added, as if to emphasize the highly noble character of horses, that all of them were abstinent and they were all vegetarian. Saying the word *vegetarian*, Funkelstein-Rosner stopped talking as if something had hit him, said "good-night," and left Ravitch's place. At that point, late at night and before a long workday at a bank, Ravitch was left alone, confused, and haunted by these curious thoughts about "prince horses, poet horses, and philosopher horses" who speak human languages when people are not around.[10]

Right before dawn, Ravitch heard a quiet knock on his door and his name being called. He went down with his oil lamp to see who it was. Funkelstein-Rosner had come back. He nervously said to him: "It's been a whole night since I have become a vegetarian and you too must become a vegetarian, and I give you not more than fifteen minutes to think it over and decide—yes or no!?" Shivering and shocked from this strange happening, Ravitch did not let Funkelstein-Rosner back into his small flat, but simply told him through the door's eyehole that he should give him at least one day to think it over before he would make such a decision. But Funkelstein-Rosner answered him with the surprising "anger of an *iluy*," that he would not give him a whole day to decide and he was also taking time off the original fifteen minutes.[11]

Overwhelmed by the urgency in Funkelstein-Rosner's tone, Ravitch told him voluntarily that he would give him his answer within ten minutes. Then Ravitch laid down on his bed and started to get angry at his friend. After five minutes, he jumped up from his bed, intending to shout at Funkelstein-Rosner that he would not let him terrorize him like that, especially as someone who did not even work and sat around the whole day thinking weird thoughts, while he was working hard at the bank. On the way to the door, however, he stopped for a moment and his anger slightly faded. When he arrived at the door, Funkelstein-Rosner told him that five minutes of his time had already passed. Ravitch answered him calmly, with a smile on his face, "For me that's long enough. I am already a vegetarian. You have been a vegetarian already the whole night and I have been a vegetarian already for a whole minute."[12]

In the morning Ravitch went to his work at the bank "already having been a vegetarian." At this point, he mentions that it had already happened before that he did not eat meat for an entire day, and so his first day as a vegetarian passed without any difficulty. But a problem awaited him later that evening, as he was invited to a family dinner at his uncle's home. Surrounded by numerous family members, Ravitch could not stop thinking about what he was going do when they started serving the usual dishes, presumably liver, followed by chicken soup, followed by a thigh and a stew. Before he knew it, "a whole mountain of livers" had been placed on his plate. When everyone had been served and started eating, his aunt and his uncle asked him why he was not eating, noticing that he had not touched his plate. Ravitch answered them, somewhat embarrassed but very decisively, "I am a vegetarian."[13]

This one sentence, "I am a vegetarian," started an argument at the dinner table. The old generation made fun of Ravitch, the middle generation said they were sorry for him, and the young generation showed a lot of interest in what he had to say and even supported his stand, all while eating chicken thighs. His aunt, trying to maintain a polite atmosphere around the table, said that "the kid" would give up his youthful ideas at some point, portraying them as a natural and normal phase of being an adolescent.[14] Ravitch, however, kept to his decision "for the rest of his life."[15]

About a decade later, in 1922, Ravitch was living in Warsaw, and he made a short visit to Vienna. He was walking on the same street, Obere Donaustraße, where he used to live during in his Vienna times, when he suddenly saw Funkelstein-Rosner in a surprising location: a typical Vienna goulash restaurant. Sitting and eating a plate of goulash, Funkelstein-Rosner told Ravitch in his typical tone of "holy seriousness," "Come here, I have something very important to tell you." But Ravitch told him that this time he would not follow any of his fantastic orders even if he would give him a whole week to think them over. He assured Funkelstein-Rosner that he was still following his order regarding vegetarianism and that he would keep it for the rest of his life.[16]

RAVITCH AND HIS VEGETARIAN IDEOLOGY

Ravitch's vegetarianism was rooted in ethical and moral debates about killing animals, rather than in a religious approach. This reflected his primarily secular upbringing and was typical for modernist Yiddish authors' uneasy relationship with Judaism and Jewish Orthodoxy. In the Ravitch archive in Israel's National Library, I located an article he wrote celebrating thirty years of vegetarianism.[17] It is the only place where I found him mentioning the term *tza'ar ba'alei chayimnik*, a particularly Jewish phrase, and not the Latin Western term of *vegetarianism*. He writes, "You might have noticed that here and there that I have been writing something about myself being a vegetarian." He added that over the years, people became vegetarian just from looking at him. It seems that since the Sturm und

Drang days of *Naked Poems* in Vienna, Ravitch had become milder in his approach to spreading vegetarianism. In his autobiography, he wrote that in the beginning he had been very "missionary" regarding vegetarianism, which annoyed his boss at the bank.[18] It seems that later in life, his preferred means for disseminating his vegetarian message was simply setting a good example and gently throwing out refined hints here and there in his texts.

Ravitch referred later to one of the philosophical principles guiding him in his vegetarianism, a rather Jewish one, "aveire goreyres aveire" (עבירה גוררת עבירה), the idea that one crime leads to another. He stated that carelessly and unnecessarily shedding the blood of innocent animals was bound to lead to the careless bloodshed of humans. This argument is similar to the one at the heart of the 2002 book, *Eternal Treblinka*, which suggested that the practices of slaughterhouses and their wide acceptance led to and enabled the Holocaust.[19] This idea led Ravitch to a further conclusion: that the world would not be able to become a better place until the vegetarianism got its official and legal acknowledgment:

> וואס ווייטער איך לעב, אלץ מער גלויב איך, אז די וועלט וועט פריער נישט גוט ווערן איידער די אידעע פון וועגעטאריזם וועט באקומען מלוכה'שע אנערקענונג און וועט אריינגעשריבן ווערן אין געזעץ-ביכער.[20]

[The longer I live, the more I believe that the world will not become any better unless the concept of vegetarianism will receive a state recognition and would be introduced into the legal codes.]

Later in this article, Ravitch addressed the question of whether vegetarianism was healthy, if it was "good for the body." To that question, he answered clearly, "I don't know and it doesn't interest me." That is a strong statement, implying that the moral question was so significant and crucial for him that issues related to the human body were not even worth the smallest footnote in this debate. Ravitch's vegetarianism was clearly an ethical one. In his autobiography he mentioned a friend named Uriel Birenboym, who was also vegetarian but for totally different reasons. Birenboym was an "aesthetic vegetarian," who believed that it was not proper for a human to put substances made of lower-level creatures in his mouth. Ravitch distanced himself from that kind of thought, defining himself as an ethical vegetarian:

> ער איז געוורן (יעדנפאלס אין יענע יארן) א וועגעטאריער צוליב עסטעטישע טעמים. עס פאסט נישט, אז א מענטש זאל באהעפטן זיין מויל מיט דער סובסטאנץ פון נידעריקע באשעפענישן.... און איך—שוין דעמאלט עטלעכע יארן לאנג—אן עטישער וועגעטאריער.[21]

[He was (at least in those years) a vegetarian due to aesthetic reasons. It does not fit for a man to place in his mouth substances made out of lower-lever creatures.... And I am, already a number of years, an ethical vegetarian.]

Similarly, if today one of the main reasons motivating the spread vegetarianism relates to environmental concerns, it seems obvious that for Ravitch there was no such issue.

In his autobiography, Ravitch wrote that his mother, Hinde Bergner, was rather supportive concerning his vegetarianism.[22] When he visited his parents, she prepared for him a special dairy corner on their dining table on a separate piece of table cloth. His father found it hard to accept this change. His father was mourning the death of Ravitch's brother, and he cried when confronted with Ravitch's vegetarianism. He seemed like an outsider to him, a stranger, a foreign guest at the family's dinner table:

און דער טאַטע האט איצט נאָך אַ באַזונדערע סיבה צום וויינען. ער באַמערקט איצט, אַז אויך דער יונגערער זון זיינער, דער דערציילער פון דער דאָזיקער מעשה, זיצט עפעס אין גאַנצן אַ זייטיקער און אַ פרעמדער ביים טיש. ער זיצט גאָר אין אַ ווינקל, ווו די מאַמע האָט אויפגעהויבן אַן עק פון גרויסן, געפראַנזטן טישטעך און אויסשפרייט אַ קליין מילכדיק טישטעכל און דאָרט אין ווינקל, ווי עפעס אַ גאָר פרעמדן אורח, האָט זי דערלאַנגט דעם זון פון ווין זיין מילכדיקע מאָלצייט. דער זון איז שוין עטלעכע יאָר אַ וועגעטאַריער און מען קען נישט עסן מילכיקס און פליישיקס אויף איין טישטעך.[23]

[And the father had a special reason to cry. He noticed now that also his younger son, the narrator of this story, suddenly sits at the table as someone foreign, as an outsider. He sits in the corner, where the mother pushed a side of a big embroiled tablecloth, placed there a little tablecloth, and there, in the corner, as to some kind of a foreign guest, she passed to the son his dairy meal. From several years the son is a vegetarian, and one cannot eat the diary on the same table with the meats.]

Later in his life, Ravitch was involved with the Yiddish Vegetarian Union in the United States (דער אידישער וועגעטאַרישער פאַראיין). The organization had been established in 1907 and was reestablished in 1939 by Shmuel David Mat (1880–1949). Ravitch wrote the opening words for the organization's Yiddish volume *The Voice of the Vegetarian*, which appeared in the United States in 1952. Nathan Shmuel Davis, the journal's editor, stated that the purpose of the journal was to use the written word to reach the world, particularly the Jewish intelligentsia. Davis was an ethical vegetarian, and he was convinced that vegetarianism would bring world peace and more understanding between peoples:

אַ בלוטלאָזע דיעטע מוז ענדלעך פירן צו אַ וועלט אָן בלוט—פֿאַרגיסונג צווישן מענטשן. ס׳איז דאָ
אַ נאָענטע שייכות צווישן שלאַכט—הויז און שלאַכטפֿעלד.[24]

[The bloodless diet must finally lead to a bloodless world, a world without spilling human blood. There is a direct link between the slaughterhouse and the battlefield.]

This reasoning is similar to that of Ravitch, who had written "one crime leads to another." Ravitch opened his introduction to the journal with his personal story of becoming a vegetarian in Vienna.[25] He wrote the story of his friend challenging him to become vegetarian, to which he agreed with a smile. Funkelstein-Rosner had returned to eating meat after only two or three years, "but I held on," Ravitch wrote, "and will keep holding on in vegetarianism until the end of my life, with the same smile that I had in the moment when I became a vegetarian."[26] Ravitch then questioned the common use of the verb "to hold on" [אויסהאַלטן] in the context of vegetarianism, arguing that it was not the right word for it. A true vegetarian, as he believed, did not need to "hold on" to his vegetarianism. The vegetarian should not feel at all the fact that he is a vegetarian, rather "it should be like air, like water, like light." Ravitch wrote that "holding on" was something he needed to do during his long ship journeys around the world, in getting used to new countries, or during World War I, but vegetarianism was not something one needed to hold on to or bear. Vegetarianism was "like fresh air for both body and soul."[27]

Ravitch referred here to vegetarianism as something ancient and to vegetarians as a group of people that dated back to the twenty-first century before Jesus, but who also "might need to wait another twenty-one centuries until the vegetarian ideal will be fulfilled." For him, a true vegetarian not only avoids eating birds but also is not tempted to eat "the bird of false hope." He wrote that he was not tempted into false illusions and understood that vegetarianism was then an avant-garde idea, but, he added, humanity was already more than half the way to fulfilling this ideal. Even though many vegetarians were aware that their ideal still seemed *velt-fremd*, new and strange for everyday people, they knew that it was the best solution and its time would come. He declared that "we," the vegetarians, were not a political party: "We are not forcing anyone into our 'Garden of Eden.'" The vegetarians were only "knocking gently on hearts and souls, saying that the time has come to start a new, green life."[28]

Ravitch addressed and answered a well-known counterargument against vegetarianism. He wrote that the counter-vegetarians always had 101 arguments prepared against "people like us." One of the most popular was the "but everything lives" argument. It is a popular counterargument up to today. According to its reasoning, since everything we eat is a living thing that can feel pain, even fruits and vegetables, then we might as well eat cows, pigs, chickens, and so on, rather than granting them special mercy. Ravitch addressed this argument in an interesting way:

דערויף ענטפער איך: אמת. און אין וייס עס. אָבער אין דער יוריסטיק זענען פאַראַן גראַדן פון מאָרד. ערשטער גראַד, צווייטער. און הערגענען אַ ברודער-אָקס איז אַ מאָרד פון פערטן, צי פינפטן גראַד. נו, וויל איך בעסער באגיין דעם גראַד מאָרד ... לעבן מוז מען דאָך.²⁹

[My answer to that is: That's true. And I know it. But also in the field of law there are different levels of murder: first level, second level, and so on. So too the killing of a brother-Ox is a murder of the fourth, maybe fifth level, and the killing of a plant is also a murder, but a murder of twentieth level. Well, I'd better choose to commit this level of murder... I need to live, after all.]

RAVITCH'S VEGETARIAN POEMS

Ravitch's first published "vegetarian poem" appeared in Vienna in 1917, in his second book of poetry, *Ruin Grass* (רואינענגראָז) under the name "Butchers" (קצבים). This poem also appears in the collection *Di lider fun mayne lider*, with a dedication to Jacob Funkelstein-Rosner "with holy thankfulness for turning me to vegetarianism."³⁰ The poem begins with sharp butcher knives lying in their place, ready for another day of slaughter and with cutting boards still dripping with yesterday's blood, and graphically describes the way of a slaughtered animal from the slaughterhouse through the butcher shop to a family dinner table.

The greatest portion of Ravitch's vegetarian-themed poems appeared as a chapter titled "A Vegetarian Gospel," the last chapter of his 1921 volume, *Naked Poems*, published in Vienna. *Naked Poems* marked the conclusion of Ravitch's Austrian period (he soon left for Warsaw) and followed the suicide of his brother, Moshe Bergner. The "Vegetarian Gospel" chapter begins with a prologue poem (פּראָלאָג), followed by the poems "Horse" (פערד), "Meat-Glutton" (פליישפרעסער), "Emergency Slaughtering" (נויט-שחיטה), and "Cow Children" (קוה-קינדער). *Naked Poems* was described by Nakhmen Mayzel (1887–1966), a Yiddishist editor, critic, and cultural activist, as the most typical and representative example of the new modern Yiddish poetry.³¹ The previous Yiddish poetry, Mayzel wrote, was a poetry of soft-hearted harmony, sentimentalism, and tender feelings. The modern Yiddish poetry of the post-World War I era could no longer stay in its small, narrow world. It was, intentionally or not, influenced by global happenings and problems. Consequently, it had lost much of its inner harmony. Mayzel wrote that the voice of the new poetry was more like a scream breaking out of the heart into the world, rather than gentle rhymes cuddled in love and pleasant harmony. The *Naked Poems* were *kampflieder*, fighting songs, loaded with militant social criticism heading out in all directions. It was poetry of אויס־רוף, of exclamation and outcry. Ravitch indeed wrote *Naked Poems* during an extreme, Sturm und Drang time in his life, after World War I and shortly after his brother's suicide. In this short period, he wrote feverishly day and night and during his workday the bank.

The prologue poem (פּראָלאָג) is a monologue Ravitch where addresses the animal, "the creature" (קרעאטור). It opens with a call:

פֿון דער אומענדליכער ליבע צו פֿרייהייט,
קום איך באַפֿרייען דיך, קרעאטור!
דיינע אויסגעשרעקטע, אויסגעשטאָכענע העלזער וואָס העגגען פֿון אַ וואָגן,
ווען זיינע רעדער שלאָגען אָן,
טאַנצענדיג אויף שטעטישע שטיינער, און בלוט הענגט פֿון די ווייסע לאַנגע לעמער־האָר.[32]

[Out of my endless love of freedom,
I am coming to set you free, creature!
Your stretched, slaughtered neck hanging from a wagon,
while its wheels are banging,
dancing on city stones, and blood hangs from the white long sheep hair.]

This introductory poem is a manifesto describing a mission that Ravitch has taken on himself—whether as a poet or as a person—to set the animal free. The mission refers to a social issue, yet it is an "I poem." It is "I," not "we," who is supposed to come and set the "creature" free. It is not clear how he intends to do what he calls to be done, and in that sense, the poem is both a manifesto and a personal wish. However, since this poem is presented as a prologue to the rest of the vegetarian poems, we can assume that the calling "I am coming to set you free, creature" refers to the poems and indicates Ravitch's hope to free the animals through his words.

Ravitch uses the German and generally European word *creature*, קרעאטור, rather than, for instance, the Hebrew word בריאה, which also means "creation," or any other "Jewish" word. This suggests that he did not consider his moral motivation as emerging from Judaism but from a broader European, modern set of values, perhaps from the world of German thought and poetry. Similarly, Ravitch uses the word *frayhayt* to describe the value in whose name he will come to save the "creature." It is not, for instance, the Hebrew חירות (*herut*, freedom) but the German-origin term, *frayhayt*, that he selects in his discourses on modernization and human rights. The use of those German, Western, and European words in the prologue, implies that Ravitch did not see his mission as rooted in Jewish tradition but as a consequence of Western cultural trends.

The second poem in the "Vegetarian Gospel" is titled "Horses" (פערד).³³ It is dedicated to two old workhorses, exhausted from eighteen hard years of carrying wood. Now, in their old age, they were being led to the slaughterhouse. After four verses describing their suffering, the horses open their mouths and talk to each other in human language. As in the image described by Funkelstein-Rosner and in *Di Kliatshe* by the Yiddish classic novelist Mendele Moycher Sfoyrim, a horse opens his mouth to tells his "brother-horse" how tired and weary he has become after so many years of work. The horses talk about those years and the damage left on their bodies. Later, the poem describes the cold deal struck by their owner and a horse butcher, who sat at a bar, negotiating the sale of the old horses for the slaughter. The final part of the poem tells about the last day in the horses' lives, going to work while not being fed anymore, and their last moments, when they look back at their hard and lonely lives as workhorses.

Ravitch wrote this poem in a short period between the time his brother Moshe confessed to him that he had decided to commit a suicide and the day he actually did so. In his autobiography, Ravitch wrote that he showed this poem to his brother, and it was one of the few Moshe had liked. One can trace the connection between the horses who addressed each other as "my brother" and shared with each other their pain, shortly before their deaths, looking back on the hard lives they had spent side by side, and the actual situation of Bergner brothers.³⁴

The next poem, "Meat-Glutton" (פלייִשפרעסער), tells the story of a goose liver from the slaughter yard to the plate.³⁵ It begins with a peaceful atmosphere of waking up in the morning in a lovely countryside house in a friendly courtyard with a shining sun. It develops by showing the contrast with the other side of the courtyard, where geese are fed in the morning and slaughtered at noon, their livers to be served with the evening's dinner. The next poem in the "Vegetarian Gospel," "Emergency Slaughter" (נויט-שחיטה), tells the story of a cow called Gviazdula (a starlet), who has just given birth. Gviazdula wounded her leg with a stone when she made a wrong step along the way, which leads to her premature slaughter by the drunken village bully, Stach.³⁶

The last poem of the "Vegetarian Gospel" chapter and the closing poem of *Naked Poems*, is titled "Cow Children" (קוה-קינדער).³⁷ Ravitch's autobiography suggests that a night during the war, when he was a soldier in the countryside of Szombathely, Hungary, provided the inspiration for this poem. He wrote that one day his landlady brought four calves from the farm and tied them to a stick right outside the window where he was sleeping. The next day they were supposed to be sold for meat production. The calves were crying the whole night, the crying of creatures torn apart from their mothers. The poem describes them one by one, with their exact age in days, the specific cry that they let out through this long, sleepless night. This night "left a deep wound on Ravitch's soul" (די נאַכט האָט זיך אײַנגעקריצט אין מײַן נשמה) and shaped his poems and his beliefs for the rest of his life.[38]

The last vegetarian poem that I identified was published in Ravitch's volume קאָנטינענטען און אָקעאַנען (Continents the oceans), in a special chapter named "Vegetarian Poems" (וועגעטאַרישע לידער),[39] as well as in the vegetarian volume *The Voice of the Vegetarian*.[40] It is titled "A Ballade of Seven Cows."[41] It begins with a description of an agreement between a meat dealer and a farmer and goes on to describe the journey of the cows to slaughter led by a shepherd who constantly beats them with a stick.

In his vegetarian poems, Ravitch uses different means to humanize his animals. One of way is the focus on the animal's eyes. In "Prologue," Ravitch approaches the animal, the "creature," and asks it not to give him "this heart-breaking look" (און שטרעק מיר נישט אַנטקעגען דעם בערעכנדיגען בליק).[42] He portrays the gaze of the eye as a place of expression that evokes strong emotions in his heart and eventually in the heart of the reader. Also in "A Ballade of Seven Cows," Ravitch peers into the eyes of a cow and sees its expression and emotion. When describing the cow's way to slaughter, he calls attention how her big, brown cow eye sheds a tear. Later in the poem, he talks about animals who have "light in their eyes" (חיות מיט ליכט-אויגן) a description usually reserved for people.

Ravitch also gives animals a human status by placing them within time categories and family orders. In his vegetarian poems, the animal is often a mother, a son or daughter, a sister or brother, or a rooster who is a master of his "hen harem." In "Horses," the two horses are "a couple" (אַ פּאָר) who address one another as "brother" (ברודער).[43] The animals in his poems have specific ages, counted in years, weeks, or days, as if describing the age of a person. In "Emergency Slaughter," the protagonist is the cow Gviazdula. Ravitch not only gives her a name, he describes her as a "mother at the age of six" (זעקסיהעריגע מוטער) who has a four-week-old child (גוויאזדולאַס פֿירוואָכענדיק קינד).[44] The same device appears in "The Cow's Children." When Ravitch describes the young calves he heard crying through the night, right outside of his window, he proceeds one by one to note their ages, "One of them is three weeks old, two of them are four weeks old, and the youngest one is seven days old," (איינס דרייוואָכענ-אַלט, פֿירוועכענטליך צוויי, און דאָס יונגסטע איז זיבען טעג אַלט). Reading this, we feel how small, fragile, and lovable those baby cows were, and we think about them in human terms, in categories of time and age. The "proud rooster" in "Meat-Glutton" is a king, a polygamist patriarch, who has a "harem of his hens" over which he fights bravely:

> אוּן דער שטאָלצער האָן שרייט אין שאַרפֿן טאָן,
> חי-קרי-קאָ—זײַן האַלץ װערד פֿאַר מאַכטלאָזן שרייען אַזש בלאָ;
> דער שטאָלצער האָן, דאָס אָרימע עוף,
> קעמפֿט מוטיק פֿאַר זײַן האַרעם-הױף.⁴⁵

[And the proud rooster shouts in his sharp tone
Hi-kri-ko—and his neck turns blue from powerless shouting;
The proud rooster, the poor poultry,
fights bravely for his harem-yard.]

Ravitch further humanizes the animals in his poems by giving them a voice. His animals do not just yowl or crow, they cry (װײנען) and shout (שרײען), verbs that are usually reserved for human beings. The "proud rooster" from "Meat-Glutton" "shouts with a sharp voice" (אוּן דער שטאָלצער האָן שרייט אין שאַרפֿן טאָן) when protesting and fighting for his harem. In the same poem, the geese, whose livers will soon be served in their own fat, express themselves through "suffocated voices of fear" (דערשטיקטע אַנגסט קולות). In the coughing of a sick young calf in the cold night, Ravitch hears a "somewhat human voice" (און הוסט אַזוי שטאַרק/ מיט עפּעס אַ מענשליכן קול). Another unique way of humanizing animals is done by adapting their voice to sound like human words. The seven-day-old calf, separated from his mother, cries through the night: "Ma-ma-me!" which sounds like a cow's lowing and like calling to his mother in Yiddish, "Mame!"⁴⁶

Ravitch presents animal voices in human terms (crying and shouting) and creates vocal similarities between the animal voices and Yiddish, but he does not stop there. In some cases, he also gives them human language, for example, in his poem "Horses." He lets his horses open their mouths and have a dialogue, speaking out their pain in an eloquent human language. In "Cow's Children," he gives voice to the baby calf crying outside his window: "do not sleep while I, a child, suffer" (שלאָף נישט בשעת מײַן קינדער-פּײַן). In "Ballade of Seven Cows," the cow Gviazdula, in the latter stage of her journey to slaughter, turns her head back to the fields where she used to live, opens her mouth, and cries to all directions: "Let me go back!"

> אויף דער בריק האָט גוויאַזדולאַ דעם קאָפ אויסגעדרייט
> צו די דערפֿער, צו דער נאַכט, צום פֿאַרגאַנגענעם גליק,
> און האָט זיך צעוויינט: -לאָמיר גיין צוריק!⁴⁷

[On the brick, Gviazdula turned her head,
to the villages, to the night, to the forgone happiness.
And cried: Let me go back!]

In parallel to the humanization of animals, humans are made animalistic. For example, Ravitch's verb for eating meat is פרעסן, and his term for meat eaters is פלײשפרעסער—a word normally reserved for animals only (instead of the human עסן, "to eat"). The slaughterer in turn is described derogatorily, as a heavy smoker and drinker who cannot walk straight. His clothes shone with the black-red color of blood:

קומט אָן דער שוחט, און זיין געוואַנד
(דאָס ווייס איך נאָך פֿון מיין קינדערלאַנד)
גלאַנצט שוואַרץ-רויט פֿון בלוט,
און זיין אָטעם, ווייס איך, איז שנאַפּס און טאַבאַק,
און זיין וועג צום שעכטען געהט אין זיגזאַק.[48]

[The butcher comes, and his clothes
(I know this from my homeland)
glow from the blood with red and black.
He smells after vodka and tobacco,
and he zigzags to the slaughterhouse.]

This is similar to the case of the village bully Stach, who happens to be the one who drags Gviazdula to slaughter in the poem "Emergency Slaughter," and who shares character traits with the drunken and bloodied butcher:

און דער דאָרפֿשלעגער סטאַך שטינקט תמיד פֿון בלוט,
און שכור איז ער און באַוועגט זיך שווער.[49]

[And Stach, the village bully, always stinks of blood.
He is drunk and moves heavily.]

CONCLUSION

This chapter explored the meaning of the vegetarianism of Yiddishist poet and essayist Melech Ravitch, one of the key figures of modern, secular Yiddish culture. To address this subject, I presented and analyzed various texts in which Ravitch referred to vegetarianism and his story of becoming a vegetarian. This included his autobiographies, journal articles, and particularly his poetry, or as he labeled it, his "vegetarian poems."

We saw how Ravitch became vegetarian in his stormy Vienna decade (1912–1921), which began when he was barely nineteen. The Austrian metropolis was a place of freedom and exploration, where he developed his Weltanschauung and absorbed a hybrid Jewish and Western culture. Inspired by his free-minded friend,

Jacob Funkelstein-Rosner, Ravitch became a vegetarian overnight. From that point forward, the young poet experienced tension in his family; his uncle was a large-scale meat importer. His family members' reactions ranged from undermining his decision by describing it as a childish whim, to pitying him, to the expression of curiosity by his younger cousins. We saw that his mother attempted to accommodate his new diet by dedicating one corner of her dinner table to dairy products, otherwise meant for meat dishes alone. His father mourned this situation, feeling that his son had grown alienated from the family and had become as a stranger, an outsider, a guest.

Ravitch's vegetarianism was clearly a "moral vegetarianism," focused on animal suffering. He believed that hurting animals leads inexorably to hurting humans. He stated specifically that his vegetarianism had nothing to do with health concerns and that the health benefits of this diet held barely any meaning for him. He distanced himself from what he called "aesthetic vegetarianism," as embodied by his friend Uriel, who did not want to place in his mouth substances derived from "lower-level creatures." The "environmental" argument for vegetarianism, which has become common in our days of globalized, industrial meat production, is not mentioned at all in his writings.

Ravitch's concept of vegetarianism was a prevegan one. He did not mention at any point the notion of veganism, and not even the idea of a "pareve" diet for that matter, but wrote only about vegetarianism, a word that appears often in his different writings. The centrality of the notion of vegetarianism in his texts and the complete lack of the vegan concept may help us follow the development of vegetarian-vegan thought and practice in the twentieth century in Central and Eastern Europe, particularly among its Jewish proponents.

Ravitch's concept of vegetarianism had a strong relation to the Jewish idea of "milk" in the sense of *kashrut*, as opposed to "meat." As noted, his mother established for him a "milky" corner at the family's "meaty" table. This issue was particular to Jewish culture. Even though Ravitch's lifestyle was largely secular, he turned to a model from the Jewish repertoire to create a diet reflective of his moral values. This phenomenon implies the particularity of Jewish vegan-vegetarian choices and patterns, marking a difference when compared with other cultures and religions.

An additional element that may be considered a Jewish aspect of Ravitch's vegetarianism is the absolute absence of pigs from his "vegetarian poems." He addresses cows, horses, chickens, geese, and other animals with passion and mercy, but he does not even mention one pig, even though we may assume that he had encountered the slaughter and abuse of pigs more than once. Ravitch may have been one of the most secularized Yiddish poets of his time. Nonetheless, the fact that out of all the farm animals, the pig does not receive the same intensive and merciful poetic treatment from him as the rest can be seen as a trace of the Jewish religion.

In his vegetarian poetry, Ravitch used interesting measures to humanize or personify the animals he described, as well as dehumanize their persecutors. One of these strategies was to focus the big eyes of the animals, which have a color, defined expressions, and even tears. Ravitch described the animals in human categories of age and family order: the horses, geese, cows, and chickens were usually described as someone's mother, brother, child, and so on. They were also of a certain age, as he sometimes described them one by one with their age given in years, months, or days. The animals are humanized by being given a voice. They do not yowl or crow, but cry or shout. In some cases, the animals open their mouths to speak in human language. The human, usually a meat eater, a butcher, or anyone else in the chain of animal torture, is in turn dehumanized by the poet, who characterizes their status and actions with words usually reserved for animals, such as "carnivore" and "feeding." The butcher is portrayed as a drunken bully, stinking from tobacco and blood, who cannot even walk straight.

Ravitch's vegetarian poetry, chiefly the chapter "Vegetarian Gospel" in *Naked Poems*, was a pioneering work of Yiddish poetry in terms of its straightforward vegetarian message and as one of the most representative turning points from a harmonic romanticism to modernism. Struck by the horrors of World War I and his brother's suicide, Ravitch created a souring, straightforward, bleeding poetry, breaking the forms of earlier Yiddish poetry that usually had a rather harmonic and silent spirit and melody. The Sturm und Drang atmosphere of the times when he wrote his vegetarian poems created an explicit, graphic, and blooded poetry. This kind of poetry well suited the cruel happenings in the slaughterhouses he described, much better than the aestheticized harmonic form of the "premodern," or rather "pre-Ravitch," Yiddish poetry. If we understand Theodor Adorno's statement that "writing poetry after Auschwitz is barbaric," to refer to the unsuitability of an overaestheticized poetry for describing the ultimate horrors, we might say that Ravitch's poetry found a suitable way to address the subject of mass killing.

NOTES

1. Armin Eidherr, *Sonnenuntergang auf eisig-blauen Wegen* (Göttingen: V&R Unipress, 2012), 137.

2. Melech Ravitch, נאַקעטע לידער [Naked Poems] (Vienna: Farlag Der Kvel, 1921).

3. Nakhmen Mayzel, "Melech Ravitch, Naked Poems, Vienna 1912," in נאענטע און ווייטע [Close and remote], vol. 2 (Vilna: Vilner Farlag fun B. Kleskin, 1929), 223–32. In Yiddish.

4. Melech Ravitch, דאָס מעשה-בוך פון מיין לעבן [The storybook of my life] (Tel Aviv: Y.L. Peretz Publishers, 1976).
5. Ibid., 193–200.
6. Eidherr, *Sonnenuntergang,* 136.
7. Ravitch, דאָס מעשה-בוך פון מיין לעבן [The storybook of my life], 193–95.
8. Ibid., 194–95.
9. Ibid.
10. Ibid., 195.
11. Ibid., 197.
12. Ibid.
13. Ibid., 198.
14. Ibid., 199.
15. Ibid., 200.
16. Ibid., 200.
17. Melech Ravitch, "... אַ וועגעטאַריער פראוועט אן איינזאמען יובל און רעדט זיך דורך מיט זיינע לעזער" [The vegetarian celebrates a lonely jubilee and talks with his readers...], אויסטראלישע יידישע נייעס *Oystralish Yidishe Nayes* [Australian Jewish news], September 17, 1943.
18. Ravitch, דאָס מעשה-בוך פון מיין לעבן, [The storybook of my life], 168.
19. Charles Patterson, *Eternal Treblinka* (New York: Lantern Books, 2002).
20. Ravitch, "... אַ וועגעטאַריער פראוועט אן איינזאמען יובל און רעדט זיך דורך מיט זיינע לעזער" [The vegetarian celebrates a lonely jubilee and talks with his readers...].
21. Ravitch, דאָס מעשה-בוך פון מיין לעבן [The storybook of my life], 387.
22. Ibid., 226.
23. Ibid.
24. Nathan Shmuel Davis (ed.), א זאמלשריפט געווידמעט דעם עטיש-וועגעטארישן געדאנק. דאָס קול פון דעם וועגעטאַריער [The voice of the vegetarian. A volume devoted to ethical-vegetarian thought] (New York: Yidisher Vegetarisher Farayn, 1962), 8.
25. Ibid., 12–14.
26. Ibid., 12.
27. Ibid.
28. Ibid., 14.
29. Ibid., 13.
30. Melech Ravitch, די לידער פון מיינע לידער [The poems of my poems] (Montreal: Melech Ravitch Book Committee at the Jewish Public Library Montreal, 1954), 42.
31. Mayzel, "מלך ראוויטש, נאַקעטע לידער, דער קוואל, וויו, 1921" [Melech Ravitch, Naked Poems, Vienna 1921], 225.
32. Ravitch, נאַקעטע לידער [Naked poems], 167.
33. Ibid., 168–70.

34. Ravitch, דאָס מעשה-בוך פון מיין לעבן [The storybook of my life], 451–58.
35. Ravitch, נאַקעטע לידער [Naked poems], 171–72.
36. Ibid., 173–74.
37. Ibid., 175–76.
38. Ravitch, דאָס מעשה-בוך פון מיין לעבן [The storybook of my life], 332.
39. Published by ליטעראַרישע בלעטער [Literary pages] (Warsaw, 1937).
40. Davis, דאָס קול פון דעם וועגעטאַריער [The voice of the vegetarian].
41. Ibid., 25–27.
42. Ravitch, נאַקעטע לידער [Naked poems], 167.
43. Ibid., 168–70.
44. Ibid., 173–74.
45. Ibid., 172.
46. Ibid., 175–76.
47. Ravitch, די לידער פון מיינע לידער [The poems of my poems], 265–68.
48. Ibid.
49. Ravitch, נאַקעטע לידער [Naked poems], 173–74.

4 Farm Animal Welfare in Jewish Art and Literature

HADAS MARCUS

In the midst of our high-tech, ostentatious, hedonistic lifestyle... there are the "black boxes"... factory farms, and slaughterhouses—faceless compounds where society conducts its dirty business of abusing and killing innocent, feeling beings.... We rationalize that the killing has to be done and that it's done humanely. We fear that the truth would offend our sensibilities and perhaps force us to do something. It may even change our life.
—Dr. Alex Hershaft, president of Farm Animal Rights Movement (FARM) and survivor of the Warsaw Ghetto

Respect for animals is really the issue of respect for life as such. Great seers such as Gandhi and Schweitzer also suggest that life is a continuum, and that one cannot make arbitrary cuts anywhere in the chain without doing injury at all levels... if ever again on this anguished planet we are to realize that His tender mercies do indeed extend over all His works... then somehow all of us must ourselves regain, and help our society itself regain, some considerable regard for the lives of our beasts.
—Rabbi Everett Gendler, "The Life of His Beast" (1967) in *Religious Vegetarianism: From Hesiod to the Dalai Lama*

Several times a week, I find myself in a car or a bus behind an enormous truck crammed with cattle, sheep, or poultry being transported to slaughter. As I sit witnessing this horrific scene, I cannot avert my attention from the undeniable suffering in front of me. I can distinguish the bulging, glazed eyes of exhausted cattle through the metal slats, parched with thirst and paralyzed with fear in the scorching heat, nearly toppling over one another as they struggle to remain standing while the truck moves jerkily along. Other times, I see a chaotic mass of chickens shoved into such tiny spaces that their bodies are literally mutilated and contorted, with feet and broken wings sticking out of the wire containers, as a rain of feathers hits the windshields of cars. This experience is so upsetting that I am shaken for many hours afterward, overwhelmed by a sense of helplessness to do anything to stop this outrage. As the years go by, I notice these livestock trucks with increasing frequency, and each time, I am grieved by the sight of their sad load of frightened animals doomed to endure a tortuous journey and an unspeakably cruel death.

When I first moved from an urban neighborhood into an agricultural area in the Jezre'el Valley, I was swept away by a romantic illusion of reverence for nature, and I admired the people who worked the land and were deeply rooted to it. Unconsciously, I glossed over any evidence of mistreatment and neglect on the huge farms nearby. I remained oblivious until my vegan daughter Galit opened my eyes to the harsh realities of the livestock industry, particularly regarding dairy cows. She made me aware of the numbered plastic tags dangling from their ears, the rotted hooves from standing in puddles of muck, the painfully swollen udders, the bawling calves torn from their mothers only hours after birth, and other signs of abuse. Gradually, I began to realize that many city dwellers never bear testimony to the ubiquitous, appalling conditions of livestock, and I began to understand that if they could, it might persuade some of them to reconsider their consumer habits. Yet how does one broach the barbed subject of animal welfare without proselytizing?

The interdisciplinary field of ecocriticism—the study of literature and other cultural media dealing with environmental themes—focuses on writing, art, cinema, and other forms of creative expression dealing with issues related to ecojustice, environmental problems, veneration of nature, the animal-human bond, and other relevant topics. With ecocriticism now a burgeoning scholarly domain, what once was a rather narrow and esoteric field of inquiry has widened its scope to encompass broader aspects of the nonhuman material world, and the "question of the animal" as put forth by Jacques Derrida has become embedded into the realm of posthumanist thought and ethics. The theoretical framework of critical animal studies seeks to promote a paradigm shift from anthropocentrism, which embraces the superiority of human beings, toward biocentrism. The latter, more egalitarian approach dethrones humans from our self-appointed position of unquestioned sovereignty over all creatures and empowers other species and whole ecosystems by imparting them with greater value.

In the Old Testament and ancient Jewish texts, ample evidence can be found of the paradoxical and contradictory attitudes expressed in Judaism toward nonhuman species, which are sometimes treated with compassion and reverence, and at other times with a pitiless, purely utilitarian perspective. This chapter suggests that an ecocritical approach can be a useful tool in dealing with the manifold aspects of the human-animal divide, especially regarding livestock, and how these are represented in Jewish works of art and literature.

VEGANISM: A NEW TREND?

To quote songwriter Bob Dylan, a recipient of the Nobel Prize in Literature, "the times they are a-changin'." Yes, times most certainly are changing; this is especially true when it comes to veganism, in Israel and globally. Over the past several years, ethical veganism as a social and ideological movement in Israel has skyrocketed, partly due to the immensely popular lecture (available online) of an outspoken, rabble-rousing Jewish American, Gary Yourofsky. His inflammatory "Best Speech You Will Ever Hear," with highly contentious allusions to the Holocaust, has been viewed by millions and converted many sworn meat eaters to ardent vegans. Much more radical and shocking than Yourofsky's lecture are the public rituals carried out by 269Life (the number of a rescued calf), an organization that enables individuals to be voluntarily tattooed, or even branded with a hot iron, in solidarity with factory farmed animals, thus leaving a permanent mark on their bodies.

Such rather fanatic behavior is certainly not typical, but nevertheless veganism has become a mainstream dietary choice and unswerving ideological stance for many Israeli citizens from all walks of life. This surprisingly rampant cultural trend has drawn international attention, and many people boast that Israel, especially Tel Aviv, has become the vegan capital of the world. Indeed, there is a plethora of fairly new upscale restaurants and fast-food places in the country that offer sumptuous vegan delights. Despite all the hype and glamour of the elegant vegan cuisine now readily available, we must not forget that the most popular national food for many decades—falafel, hummus, French fries, and salad in a pita, often messily scarfed down as a quick meal—has also been vegan. To illustrate how much easier things have become, in the old days, compulsory Israeli military service usually felt like becoming a faceless cog in a wheel with ironclad rules, and few concessions were made for an individual's tastes. But today, vegan soldiers are entitled to special military boots made of faux leather, a food stipend in addition to vegan meals, and the right to refuse vaccinations if they are opposed to animal testing.[1]

How did this "vegan revolution" happen? What elements of Judaism and Israeli life, secular or observant, might have led to this surprising culinary and ethical movement? Is it something recent that has been the result of a powerful surge of ubiquitous social media and widespread dissemination of videos, lectures, online and face-to-face groups and the like? Or is it a wave that has been slowly gaining momentum, bit by bit, permeating our collective historical, cultural, and religious conscience in a slow but steady trickle, thanks to many voices from the past? Could it be the aftermath of centuries of adversity, persecution, vulnerability, and alienation that has enabled the Jewish people to experience deep empathy for animal Others? In an attempt to clarify these issues, I examine a broad sample of literary and artistic works and investigate what lasting contributions they have made to Jewish consciousness regarding animal welfare. I contend that today's fashionable trend of veganism and vegetarianism in modern Jewish thought was significantly influenced by artists and writers, from centuries ago up to modern times, who grappled with the problem of cruelty toward humans and animals alike.

For the past four years, I have traveled from Israel to Oxford University to deliver papers on ecocriticism that reflect our complex relationships with animals—showing how various works of art, literature, and film throughout history have influenced our perceptions of nonhuman Others. In 2014, the first time I participated in a roundtable, organized by an Israeli woman, titled "Making Sense of the Animal," I spoke about the early origins of the animal rights movement. In 2015, 2016, and 2017, I attended the annual Summer School at the Oxford Centre for Animal Ethics, held at St. Stephens House, a theological college, under the direction of Rev. Professor Andrew Linzey. In 2015, we dealt with the ethics of live animal experiments (vivisection) and in 2017, the theme of the summer session was the fur industry. In 2016, "Eating Animals" was the topic of discussion, and it was an unforgettable experience. After countless hours of discourse and lectures, I came away with much food for thought, if you will pardon the pun. Secular scholars, courageous activists, and devout people from a wide spectrum of faiths congregated to explore and debate the worldwide mass suffering of livestock, primarily in factory farms, and discuss how best to persuade others that veganism or vegetarianism is the most sustainable and humane dietary choice.

At each session of the Oxford Summer School, I shared delicious vegan meals over intriguing conversations about animal welfare among eloquent nuns, Buddhists, reverends, professors, activists, and so forth, and this propelled me to contemplate the Jewish position on this topic. In 2016, I delivered a paper about contemporary works of art and cinema that promote veganism or vegetarianism, exploring visual culture from a wide range of historical periods, places, and media. I challenged the efficacy of showing viewers overtly graphic or violent documentary footage from slaughterhouses shot by underground activists and filmmakers (such as Shaun Monson's *Earthlings* or Frederick Wiseman's *Meat*). Two of my vegan female colleagues from Israel presented papers about diametrically opposed situations: one of them was writing her doctoral dissertation at Bar-Ilan University based on interviews with Jewish ritual slaughterers (*shochtim*) about their feelings toward the animals they kill, and the other, a graduate student at

Tel Aviv University, spoke about the phenomenal success of a burgeoning online movement in Israel known as Etgar 22, designed to create a critical mass of vegans.

Starting in eighteenth-century England and then fast-forwarding to recent times, this essay examines works created by mostly secular Jewish individuals—with varying degrees of observance and culturally religious identification—who promoted empathy toward animals raised for consumption or questioned humankind's relationship with meat itself. Yet an obstacle arises in doing so because critics have a strong penchant to interpret works of art and literature about animals on a purely metaphorical level and ignore other possible layers of meaning (for instance, the barnyard animals in Chagall's paintings). When dealing with literary analysis, critics and readers often contend that many fictional works focusing on animal protagonists are meant to formulaically reduce these nonhuman characters to a merely anthropomorphized, cute, or trivial rank, in which case they are treated as superficial stories for children (as in Bashevis Singer's "Zlateh the Goat") or are automatically assigned symbolic or allegorical status representative of antisemitic persecution (for example, Mendele Mocher Sforim's "The Calf"). Yet such an approach limits and denudes the text of its potential richness. Contemporary scholars in ecocritical animal studies, such as Erica Fudge, who has conducted commendable research on attitudes toward cows and other domesticated species in early modern literature, refute this one-dimensional, simplistic methodology that belittles and excludes the animal as a way of elevating the human. These scholars beckon us to reconsider, in historical and fictional accounts, the centrality of the real animal as a flesh-and-blood being who actively participates in the narrative. As Fudge states:

> We must write a history which refuses the absolute separation of the species; refuses that which is the silent assumption of humanist history. By rethinking our past—reading it for the animals as well as the humans—we can begin a process that will only come to fruition when the meaning of "human" is no longer understood in opposition to "animal."[2]

The aim of this chapter is not to reiterate what others have said by showering lavish praise on the Jewish "celebrities" of the animal welfare movement, particularly when it comes to veganism or vegetarianism. Most readers of this book are probably well acquainted with many of the seminal writings and teachings spanning Orthodox Judaism to ecofeminist treaties on animal ethics. There are many examples of these, and they include such diverse works as Rav Kook's *A Vision of Vegetarianism and Peace* (*Chazon ha-Tzimchonut ve-ha-Shalom*), Peter Singer's classic *Animal Liberation*, Richard Schwartz's *Judaism and Vegetarianism*, Roberta Kalechofsky's *Vegetarian Judaism: A Guide for Everyone*, Jonathan Safran Foer's

Eating Animals, and so on. Thus, I do not dwell on these "classics," but will focus on less familiar, underappreciated, or long-forgotten works in terms of how they address and promote vegetarianism. I explore the common threads of empathy for nonhuman Others that bond the creative production of Jewish icons who also have significance for animal welfare—whether or not they ate meat. This includes artists such as Chaim Soutine and Marc Chagall, and writers such as Isaac Bashevis Singer and Franz Kafka, as well as a few other Jewish figures whose works promote ethical veganism or vegetarianism.

EUROPEAN VOICES FROM THE PAST

In *The Cry of Nature: Art and the Making of Animal Rights*, Stephen Eisenman chronicles the development of the animal welfare movement, largely due to the indefatigable efforts of audacious philosophers, artists, and writers. The most well-known of these is the oft-quoted utilitarian philosopher Jeremy Bentham, who in 1789 proclaimed in *An Introduction to the Principles of Morals and Legislation*, "The question is not, Can they *reason*? nor, Can they *talk*? but, Can they *suffer*?" In his book, Eisenman delves into the cultural role of animals in eighteenth- and nineteenth-century England and expounds on those free thinkers, artists, and writers, from William Hogarth to Alexander Pope, who made great strides in improving conditions for animals—especially beasts of burden and animals abused in blood sports such as bear baiting. As an art historian, vegan, and activist, Eisenman emphasizes the influential role of fine art in the recognition of animals as sentient beings from the eighteenth century to today. He states that "the longstanding hierarchy that placed humans at the pinnacle of creation must be overturned in the name of a new, posthumanist logic that understands people as one among many animal species and due no more deference than any other."[3]

As Kathryn Shevelow, author of *For the Love of Animals: The Rise of the Animal Protection Movement*, points out, discord within the animal welfare movement traces as far back as the 1830s. This was exemplified by the newly formed Society for the Prevention of Cruelty to Animals (the SPCA, later the RSPCA) in Britain, which splintered under the stewardship of Jewish animal advocate, inventor, and entrepreneur Lewis Gompertz (1784–1861). In an era when fox hunting, cockfighting, and feasting on meat were popular and pleasurable activities, Gompertz's strict vegan dietary regime was met with derision and considered overly zealous, and his aggressive prosecution of animal abusers was deemed to be too severe. A precursor of Peter Singer, this misunderstood man was ostracized partly because of his radical ideas about animal welfare but also because of the

SPCA's adopted antisemitic attitudes based on "Christian faith, and on Christian principles." Forced to resign from his position as secretary of the SPCA because he was a Jew who promoted "Pythagorean doctrines" (i.e., that animal feelings were of equal value to those of humans), Gompertz subsequently established the Animal Friends Society. His book, *Moral Inquiries on the Situation of Man and of Brutes* (1824), was a remarkable achievement far ahead of its time in terms of awareness of animal sentience.[4] Astounded to discover how similar Gompertz's progressive concepts were to his own, Peter Singer wrote in the preface to *Moral Inquiries* that "Gompertz may well have been the first modern Western thinker to take so strong a stand in favour of equal consideration for animals, to argue for this position in a logical and philosophical way, and to act accordingly."[5]

In his exhaustive book, which methodologically resembles yeshiva learning based on debate over philosophical issues, Gompertz presents a hypothetical conversation between two men about slaughtering animals

> First, how do you prove that mankind is invested with the right of killing them, and that brutes have been created for the purpose you assert them to be? Secondly, it is to be observed that the flesh of man himself possesses the same nourishing and palatable qualities? Are we then to become cannibals for that reason?[6]

The author extrapolated his understanding of Jewish teachings on kind-hearted treatment of animals into a rudimentary form of veganism. He obdurately shunned eggs, meat, and leather and traveled everywhere on foot rather than riding in carriages out of pity for horses. Yet Gompertz was not opposed to consumption of animals that had died of natural or accidental causes (definitely not kosher!), because their bodies would otherwise decay and they had not been killed intentionally. Likewise, he believed that it was permissible to use a cow's milk only if her calf died, as otherwise it would go to waste. But Gompertz did not agree with eating meat or dairy products under any other circumstances.

Moving on through history, several famous authors of Yiddish, Hebrew, or world literature who felt a deep affiliation with their Jewish roots were vegetarians, condemned cruelty to animals in their fictional writings, or both. The best known of these authors is Isaac Bashevis Singer (1902–1991), born Icek-Hersz Zynger, the indisputable champion of Yiddish literature and animal rights. He is unceasingly cited for his motivation to become a vegetarian "for the health of the chickens," and he openly proclaimed that vegetarianism was "his religion." Although he had attended a rabbinical seminary in Warsaw for a brief time, he turned his back on Orthodox Judaism. In the introduction to his book on Singer, Seth L. Wolitz states:

Bashevis writes not as an ideologue of some political persuasion, nor as a prophet with a didactic moral stance, but as an author functioning within, and drawing inspiration from, the linguistic and cultural parameters of his own Eastern European Ashkenazic Jewry—a people basically disenfranchised, but possessing an ancient heritage, a distinctive religious perspective, and a unique lifestyle. . . . Bashevis's personal existential condition mirrors the conflict within modern European Jewish culture, which fractured itself between traditional religious observance decreed by its Halakhic world view and secular accommodation to Westernization. Many Jews sought to unburden themselves of intense if unsatisfactory religious practice in order to participate in the modern secularism of the surrounding majority. . . in the newly emerged Yiddish-speaking secular culture of 1900, art as an esthetic undertaking was problematic for a significant sector of this linguistic community.[7]

Animal rights activists today frequently repeat the controversial quote from Singer's "The Letter Writer" where the main character, Herman, eulogizes his tiny mouse companion by saying "for the animals, it is an eternal Treblinka."[8] This problematic concept, which has shocked and offended many Jews, was later expanded into a book of the same title and theme by Holocaust expert Charles Patterson. Explaining why he made the decision to become a vegetarian in 1962, Singer lamented: "For years I had wanted to become a vegetarian. I didn't see how we could speak about mercy and ask for mercy and talk about humanism and against bloodshed when we shed blood ourselves—the blood of animals and innocent creatures."[9]

Soon after being awarded the Nobel Prize in Literature in 1978, Bashevis Singer stated in an interview:

Why is one born? Why does one suffer? In my case, the suffering of animals also makes me very sad. I'm a vegetarian, you know. When I see how little attention people pay to animals, and how easily they make peace with man being allowed to do with animals whatever he wants because he keeps a knife or a gun, it gives me a feeling of misery and sometimes anger with the Almighty.[10]

In one of Singer's masterful stories, "The Slaughterer," we sympathize with the tragic protagonist Yoineh Meir, whose unfortunate circumstances thrust him into a downward spiral of insanity and eventual suicide. Guilt-ridden, the unwilling *shochet* (ritual slaughterer), whose profession has been forced on him by the community, is tormented by unrelenting anguish over the injustice of killing innocent animals. "He felt as though he were immersed in blood and lymph.... The bodies refused to know any justification or excuse—every body resisted in its own fashion, tried to escape, and seemed to argue with the Creator to its last breath."[11] At the end of the story, Yoineh is constantly haunted by thoughts of self-retribution and has hallucinations of "shouts, screams, the stamping of running feet" and a bloody swamp in which intestines, livers, and kidneys hang from the trees. These nightmarish thoughts ultimately drive him to throw himself into the river:

> The forequarters of beasts rose to their feet and sprayed him with gall and slime ... Myriads of cows and fowls encircled him, ready to take revenge for every cut, every wound, every slit gullet, every plucked feather. With bleeding throats, they all chanted, "Everyone may kill, and every killing is permitted."[12]

Bashevis Singer also wrote a children's story, "Zlateh the Goat" (included in the anthology by the same title, 1966), a touching, meaningful piece for readers of all ages, particularly those who deal with the animal-human divide in which the distinguishing lines between species becomes blurred. It is a tender story of the close relationship between a boy named Aaron and his cherished old she-goat, Zlateh. He had been commanded by his father, a furrier with a cold, utilitarian approach to animals, to escort Zlateh to the local butcher as a means of supplementing the family's dwindling income. Aaron's forlorn journey leading the unwary goat to slaughter is interrupted by a sudden blizzard. The blinding snowstorm threatens to kill them both, but they are saved by hiding in a haystack, and the goat's life is ultimately spared. In many parts of the story, the boy and the goat share feelings and "conversations" as he confides in her as he would a human being ("he had always loved Zlateh, but now she was like a sister"); she also appears to demonstrate deep insight and sympathy, as she gladly nourishes the ravenous boy with her milk and keeps him warm with her body heat.

> For three days Aaron and Zlateh stayed in the haystack. Aaron had always loved Zlateh, but in these three days he loved her more and more. She fed him with her milk and helped him keep warm. She comforted him with her patience. He told her many stories, and she always cocked her ears and listened. When he patted her, she licked his hand and his face. Then she said, "Maaaa," and he knew it meant, "I love you too."[13]

Unlike "The Slaughterer," the story ends on a joyful note when the boy and his goat are reunited with their grieving family, who believed they had perished in the storm. From that day forward, they all regarded Zlateh as a beloved pet:

> Aaron's sisters kissed and hugged Zlateh and gave her a special treat of chopped carrots and potato peels, which Zlateh gobbled up hungrily.... Nobody ever again thought of selling Zlateh.... When Hanukkah came, Aaron's mother was able to fry pancakes every evening, and Zlateh got her portion too. Even though Zlateh had her own pen, she often came to the kitchen, knocking on the door with her horns to indicate that she was ready to visit; and she was always admitted... Zlateh sat near the stove watching the children and the flickering of the Hanukkah candles.[14]

Another Yiddish author is Mendele Mocher Sforim (1836–1917), born Sholem Yankev Abramovich, who wrote a story titled "The Calf," which is categorically interpreted as an allegory for the persecution of the Jewish people. The tale can also be approached from the angle suggested by Erica Fudge: placing the animal in the center of the narrative, thus enabling us to read it on a more literal level—one that expresses profound sensitivity for the animal-human bond. In "The Calf," the devout narrator, a gaunt Yeshiva boy, is driven to madness over the inconsolable grief he feels for his beloved cow and the slaughter of her newborn calf (reminiscent of Yoneh Meir in Singer's story).

> I had visions of milk, sour cream, cheese, a whole loaf of bread spread with butter. Then I conjured up a roast, with chunks of meat sautéed in fat and onion. I grew faint with hunger. I could no longer bear it. I tossed about on the floor, turning from side to side. A bell rang in my ears: the second act. A young calf, about eight days old, struggles out of the slaughterer's hands and runs off, crying bitterly, the slaughterer in hot pursuit. The calf cries desperately for her mother, but she is in the pasture and cannot help.... The slaughterer casts her to the ground, presses her down with his knees, pulls her neck taut, raises the knife, begins the benediction, "Blessed art thou, Master of the Universe," and strikes.... I could no longer distinguish between dream and reality. Sweetmeats hung over my nose, made up of the calf's roasted liver and lungs. I was being slapped, pricked with needles. Burning coals scorched my pocket. Two gold coins sprang out. I looked at them—and a pair of blood-swollen calf's eyes stared back at me. The same day they carried me off to the hospital, babbling incoherently.[15]

We must also not forget the words of S. Y. Agnon, a pescatarian, who featured several vegetarian characters in his stories as well as animals with human traits and capabilities (e.g., the dog Balak in *Tmol Shilshom*). In his acceptance speech for the Nobel Prize in Literature in 1966, Agnon stated these moving words:

Lest I slight any creature, I must also mention the domestic animals, the beasts and birds from whom I have learned. Job said long ago (135:11): "Who teacheth us more than the beasts of the earth, And maketh us wiser than the fowls of heaven?" Some of what I have learned from them I have written in my books, but I fear that I have not learned as much as I should have, for when I hear a dog bark, or a bird twitter, or a cock crow, I do not know whether they are thanking me for all I have told of them, or calling me to account.[16]

Another distressed, assimilated Jewish icon of world literature, Franz Kafka was adept at empathetically portraying the nonhuman protagonist's experiential reality (*umwelt*) and point of view in his fiction, as can be seen by the unforgettable characters he created in some of his short stories. Examples of these protagonists are Gregor Samsa, the man-turned-roach, in "The Metamorphosis" (1915) and Red Peter, the anthropomorphized ape in "A Report to the Academy" (1917), first published in the monthly periodical *Der Jude*. In "A Hunger Artist," Kafka addresses the topic of eating meat and the disgust it provokes. In the story, the emaciated protagonist, who sits in a cage fasting for prolonged periods of time to entertain the crowds, feels "very upset and constantly depressed by the stink from the stalls, the animals' commotion at night, the pieces of raw meat dragged past him for the carnivorous beasts, and the roars at feeding time."[17] Eventually the hungry artist starves to death, admitting to his keepers with his final weak breath that he "couldn't find a food that tasted good." Max Brod, Kafka's biographer and closest friend—a Czech Jew who later immigrated to Israel—relates how he was once told by a lady who accompanied Kafka to the Berlin aquarium how he suddenly "began to speak to the fish in their illuminated tanks, 'Now at last I can look at you in peace, I don't eat you anymore.' It was the time that he turned strict vegetarian."[18]

CONTEMPORARY AUTHORS AND ANIMAL WELFARE

A number of contemporary Jewish authors from Israel and the United States have also touched on the subject of vegetarianism in writing that is either semi-autobiographical or vicariously reflected through their characters. Although apparently the much-loved novelist Amos Oz is not a vegetarian, in his poetic writing he seems to admire or sometimes poke harmless fun at the carefully honed ideals and sensitivity of those who refrain from eating meat.[19] Oz, who was the son of Holocaust survivors and whose mother committed suicide when he was twelve, wrote *A Tale of Love and Darkness* (*Sipour al Ahava ve-Hoshekh*, 2002) as an autobiographical account of growing up in Jerusalem when Israel was on the threshold of achieving statehood. In the novel, Oz describes his Russian neighbors as Tolstoyans who were incapable of properly tending to their own potted plants, yet they were nevertheless

> without exception devout vegetarians, world reformers with strong feelings for nature, seekers after the moral life, lovers of humankind, lovers of every single living creature, with a perpetual yearning for the rural life, for simple agricultural labor among fields and orchards.[20]

The novel was adapted into a Hebrew screenplay for a movie directed by and starring Israeli American Natalie Portman, one of the most celebrated advocates for veganism and animal rights. In his book *Between Friends* (*Bein Haverim*, 2012), Oz beautifully portrays the inner struggle of a new immigrant, Moshe, who tries to integrate himself into a fictional kibbutz society in the 1950s. Moshe willingly rejects his religious upbringing in an effort to be accepted within the insular and conventional organization of the kibbutz, even though this wedges an uncomfortable distance between him and his mentally ill Orthodox father. At the same time, he is profoundly remorseful and morally torn by his assignment to work in the chicken coop and cannot bear the sight of the birds' cramped, filthy conditions. In a poignantly written description of this inner conflict and his revulsion at animal suffering, Oz depicts Moshe's dreadful task and his silent, painful thoughts:

> Even from a distance, the smell of the coop enveloped him: the stench of chicken excrement, of the dust that rises from the feed, of torn-out feathers that stuck to the wire netting, along with another vague smell of overcrowding and suffocation.... When here and there he found a dead chicken in a cage, he opened the cage, took out the carcass and placed it gently on the concrete walk behind him. When he finished distributing the feed into all the troughs, he went back to collect the carcasses. Low moaning filled the air as if the hens, squeezed together by two-by-two in the cages, were keening a low, persistent, lost lament. Only now and then did a sharp screech of fear burst from one of the cages, as if a chicken had suddenly guessed how all of this would end. After all, no two chickens are or ever have been exactly alike.... Moshe had already decided to become a vegetarian one day, maybe even a vegan, but he had postponed implementing the decision because being a vegan among the kibbutz boys would not be easy. Even without being a vegetarian, he had to work hard day and night to seem like everyone else here.... He thought of the cruelty of eating meat and of the fate of those hens, doomed to spend

their entire lives packed tightly in wire cages, unable to move even one step. Someday, Moshe thought, a future generation will call us murderers, unable to comprehend how we could eat the flesh of creatures like ourselves, rob them of the feel of the earth and the smell of the grass, hatch them in automatic incubators, raise them in crowded cages, force-feed them, steal all their eggs before they hatch, and finally, slit their throats, pluck their feathers, tear them limb from limb, gorge ourselves on them and drool and lick the fate from our lips.[21]

Oz's *Suddenly in the Depths of the Forest* (*Pitom b-Omek ha-ya'ar*, 2011) has been described by the author as "a fable for all ages," and reviewers label it as a children's fairy tale or an allegory. The book also relays an underlying message of how humans flagrantly inflict needless cruelty on animals. In the story, two children from a gray, dreary village search for an answer to the frightening mystery of why all the animals—from dogs to cows to snails to fish—have completely vanished. It is a reprehensible, taboo topic, one that none of the inhabitants wants to discuss with the children. The shame over what happened to the animals and the reason for their disappearance leads them to remain silent.

Popular author Etgar Keret reminisces about a childhood outing gone awry when his well-meaning father, a Holocaust survivor, took him to see *Bambi* in the theater when he was five years old. Traumatized by the scene in which Bambi's mother is shot down by a hunter, Keret announced he would become a vegetarian, a vow he never broke, much to his parents' chagrin. No matter how hard she tried, Keret's mother was unable to tempt her son to eat meat with the inviting odor of her homemade schnitzels. Today as an adult who does not like to cook, Keret claims he is addicted to hummus, which he eats at every opportunity, even if it is not very good. He fondly recounts memories of his early days as his mother tried to accommodate his "bizarre" dietary choices:

> In those years, the concept "vegetarianism" didn't exist in Israel, but the first natural-food store had opened a bus ride away from our house, and one day my mom came home with a large bag of dry, lumpy, yellow-brown stuff that had the texture of Styrofoam and was labeled "meat substitute"... Soon, bags of the stuff were piled up in our house. My mom cooked it in huge pots and froze it in small portions, and I ate it every day.... No one else in my family dared to taste it, but a friend who came over one day, tried it and loved it. Soon, a rumor spread through the neighborhood that Etgar's mom served a special dish you couldn't get anywhere else in the world. Some said it was camel meat, others claimed it had been created

in a Weapons Development Authority lab, but all the neighborhood kids agreed that it was the food of the gods, and they lied and schemed their way to our kitchen table to partake of it.... I kept eating the stuff on a daily basis until I was thirteen.[22]

Presumably, most readers are familiar with the groundbreaking bestseller *Eating Animals*, by Jonathan Safran Foer, and are aware of its immense contribution to veganism by transforming a fringe movement into a mainstream trend. Natalie Portman, the aforementioned actress and animal rights activist, co-produced and narrated a feature-length documentary about factory farming (2017), inspired by Foer's *Eating Animals*. Among some of his most persuasive excerpts is the following:

> Just how destructive does a culinary preference have to be before we decide to eat something else? If contributing to the suffering of billions of animals that live miserable lives and ... die in horrific ways isn't motivating, what would be? ... And if you are tempted to put off these questions of conscience, to say not now, then when?[23]

Some of you may have also read *Everything Is Illuminated* by the same author or seen the cinematic adaptation of the novel. The protagonist is Jonathan Safran Foer himself (played by Elijah Wood), an eccentric, stern Jewish American whose facial features are swallowed up behind thick spectacles. He carefully hoards remnants and artifacts of his own life and his genealogical Jewish heritage in zip-top bags. Accompanied by two local tour guides, Jonathan goes on a sort of spiritual pilgrimage to the rural landscapes of the Ukraine, obsessed with the detective work of locating the elderly woman who rescued his grandfather from death. He goes to a hotel restaurant where he learns that there is not one thing on the menu without meat. A humorous dialogue transpires as he attempts to explain his dietary preferences to his bewildered tour guides and the waitress:

> "I'm a vegetarian." "I do not understand." "I don't eat meat." "Why not?"... "I just don't." "How can you *not* eat meat?" "I just don't." ..."Why not?" "I just don't."... "No meat." "Pork?" "No." "Meat?" "No meat." "Steak?" "Nope." "Chickens?" "No." "Do you eat veal?" "Oh, God. Absolutely no veal." "What about sausage?" "No sausage either."[24]

PAINTINGS OF SLAUGHTERED OXEN

As the twentieth century unfolded, a number of poor Jewish emigré artists flocked to Paris. Among them, Chaim Soutine and Marc Chagall were two of the most notable. Not only did they originate from a similar *shtetl* background of austerity and religious ritual, they lived and worked in the same beehive of studios known as La Ruche, a residence for struggling artists in Montparnasse. Both became swept up in avant-garde movements, as they infused their own brand of originality onto the art scene. Although they are recognized as universal (rather than as Russian Jewish) artists, their childhood memories and Orthodox upbringing (which they both cast aside) definitely influenced their paintings. This is especially obvious in the vivid, surrealistic works by Chagall and alluded to in the tormented, sometimes repugnant paintings by Soutine. Both artists featured farm animals, alive and dead, in their works.

These Parisian artists created works that are somewhat similar to the famed *Slaughtered Ox* (1655) by Rembrandt (see figure 4.1). In the Dutch master's painting, a huge bovine carcass hangs from a crossbeam by its truncated hind legs, spread apart so that the bone and muscle of the inner body are fully visible. The headless body, hung in a manner reminiscent of a crucifixion, expresses a mood of sober tranquility rendered with broad brushstrokes and subdued colors. The earlier rendition of the Rembrandt painting was done by Chaim Soutine (1893–1943), of Belarusian origin, whose deep admiration for Rembrandt's piece in the Louvre led him to paint two versions of the shocking and vivid *Carcass of Beef* (1924 and 1925). The latter piece is so famous that it was featured in the film *Mona Lisa Smile* (2003) and recently sold for an enormous sum of money. I viewed the earlier version at the Minneapolis Institute of Art (the MIA) on a trip to the United States last summer.

Some years before those nightmarish paintings were created in the mid-1920s, the artist had already begun to produce a series of somewhat less shocking, more abstract pieces with unappealing titles such as *The Beef* (1920; see Figure 4.2), *Butcher's Meat Rack* (1919; see figure 4.3), and *Mutton* (1920). Obsessed with morbidity, especially between 1920 and 1925, Soutine repeatedly created unsettling works of small, dismembered, and dead creatures—a significant number of paintings show fish with gaping mouths, flayed and skinned hares, and twisted, plucked fowl cadavers nailed to walls (see figures 4.4 and 4.5)—as subjects for his still-life compositions. Avigdor Poseq describes these eerie paintings as erotic metaphors, stating that "the allusive character of these images, especially their oblique reference to sexual experiences, reflects deeply ingrained taboos, which seem to have conditioned Soutine's emotional attitudes."[25]

Although both versions of *Carcass of Beef* (1924 and 1925) are less realistic than Rembrandt's finely detailed ox, Soutine's animal subjects are much more expressionistic, central to the canvas, and visceral, mirroring the anguish of his own tormented soul. Plagued by phobias, refusing to maintain any personal hygiene, and living in abject poverty, the Lithuanian Jew led a miserable existence in Paris, which culminated in his death at the age of forty-nine, following years of hiding during the Nazi occupation.[26]

The process of painting *Carcass of Beef* led to some odd circumstances. Soutine hung a side of beef purchased at a Parisian slaughterhouse in his studio and ordered his obedient female model/assistant to pour a bucket of fresh cow's blood on it every few days to maintain its bright color. As his brush flew at a frenetic pace, he also told her to shoo away the swarms of flies that were drawn to

Figure 4.1. Rembrandt, *Slaughtered Ox*, 1655, oil on board. (Image from Wiki art, https://www.wikiart.org/en/rembrandt/the-carcass-of-an-ox-slaughtered-ox-1655.)

Figure 4.2. Chaim Soutine, *The Beef*, c. 1920, oil on canvas. (Image from

Figure 4.3. Chaim Soutine, *Butcher's Meat Rack*, c. 1919, oil on canvas. (Image from The Athenaeum, https://the-athenaeum.org/art/detail.php?ID=85959.)

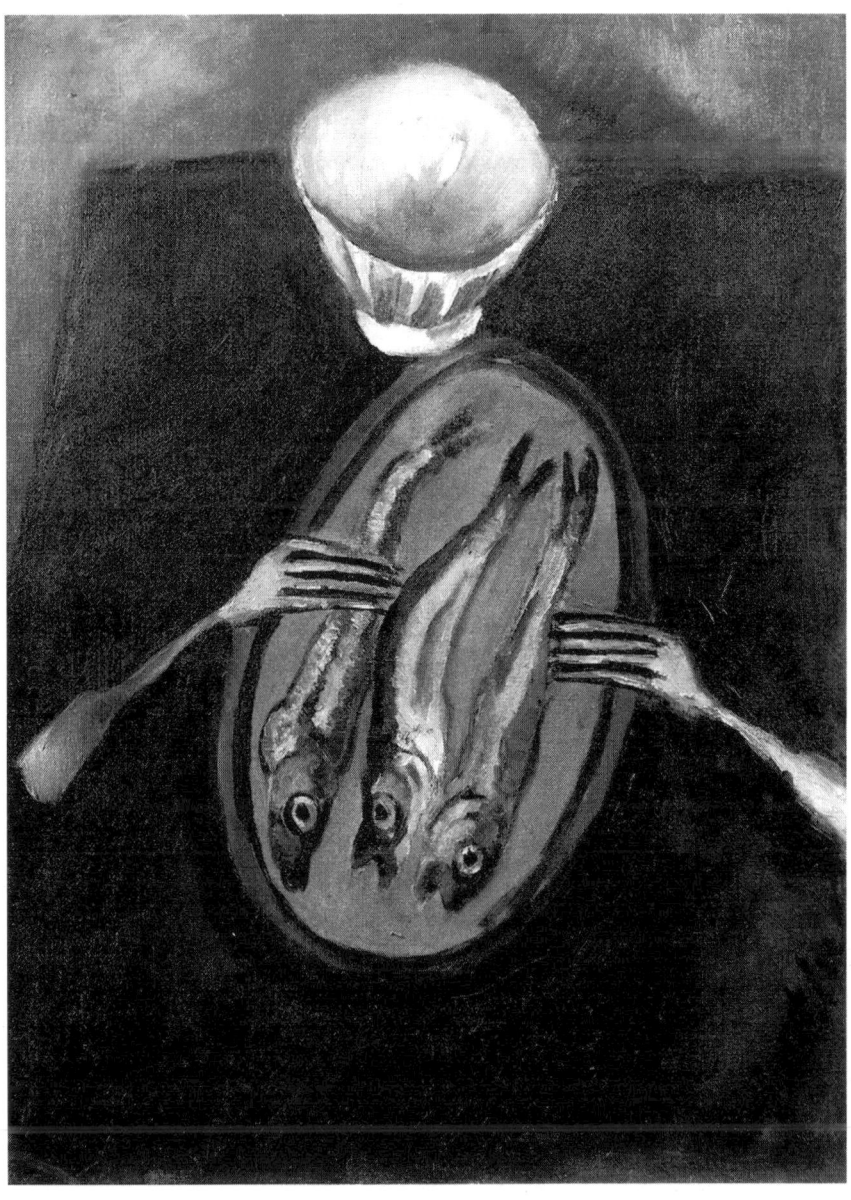

Figure 4.4. Chaim Soutine, *Still Life with Herrings*, c. 1916, oil on canvas. (Image from The Athenaeum, https://the-athenaeum.org/art/detail.php?ID=56399.)

Figure 4.5. Chaim Soutine, *Still Life with Chicken*, c. 1918, oil on canvas. (Image from The Athenaeum, https://the-athenaeum.org/art/detail.php?ID=56410.)

the rotting flesh. Not surprisingly, his neighbors on the Rue du Mont St. Gothard complained about the stench, almost causing health inspectors to confiscate the subject of his painting before he could finish. The authorities agreed to let him keep the putrid cow cadaver on condition that he treat it with ammonia and fumigate the apartment.[27] It is said that Chagall became alarmed and began to scream when he saw cow's blood leaking from Soutine's studio, thinking that the artist had been murdered.[28] Fortunately for Soutine, he was allowed to complete what is today considered his greatest masterpiece, which sold in 2015 at Christie's for nearly $30 million. Due to his chronic stomach problems (he died following complications from surgery to repair a perforated ulcer) and destitution, he ate a very sparse diet for much of his life, usually eschewing meat. But besides his failing health, Soutine admitted that he could not bear to see animals suffer and that he was continually haunted by memories of slaughter.

> I once saw how a village butcher cut the throat of a goose and let the blood pool out. I wanted to scream, but his cheerful look constricted my throat. I still feel this cry here. When I drew a self-portrait as a child, I tried to free myself of this cry; I wanted to get rid of it. Up until now, I have not succeeded.[29]

Born in Vitebsk in 1887, the beloved Marc Chagall (Moishe Shagal), whose famous windows embellish Hadassah Hospital in Jerusalem, was another Russian French Jewish artist inspired by Rembrandt and who created a painting titled *The Flayed Ox* (1947). This work has been widely interpreted as an allegory for the irretrievable loss of innocent Jewish lives during the Holocaust. In the painting, a brightly colored red ox, its abdomen split vertically by the butcher's knife, hangs upside down. Its limp tongue tumbles out of its mouth, almost touching the blood that fills the wooden bucket beneath its head. While most critics agree that Chagall's vivid, surrealistic paintings are symbolic (although he claimed this was not intentional), there are elements in his work that show close identification with farm animals in the *shtetl*. His paintings are often populated with anthropomorphized cows, horses, chickens, and goats engaged in activities such as floating freely and blissfully in the sky, playing violins, or embracing villagers and brides, or depicted as hybridized with humans. It is unclear if Chagall had sympathy for barnyard animals in terms of his everyday dietary choices. It is noteworthy that he was the most prominent guest to dine at Fania Lewando's successful vegetarian restaurant in the 1930s, whose delightfully illustrated Yiddish *Vilna Vegetarian Cookbook* was rediscovered, translated into English, and published in 2015.[30]

Almost none of Chagall's depictions of animals are as grim as *The Flayed Ox*. As a child, Chagall, the eldest of nine children in a Hasidic household, was enrolled in traditional Jewish primary education. He and some of his siblings spent their childhood summers with their grandfather, a *shochet*, who appears in at least one of the artist's paintings. Yet typically, even these works are less harsh; the earthy-toned *Butcher* (1910; figure 4.6) is a rather subdued innocent-looking portrait of his grandfather at work while holding a hatchet. The colorful *The Cattle Dealer* (two versions, 1912, shown in figure 4.7, and 1923) emanates a sense of renewal, as embodied by the image of the foal in the womb of the mare pulling the carriage to market. The latter painting recalls fond memories of his uncle's farm, where all the animals had names and were treated as members of the family, even when they had to be transported to market for slaughter. We can sense Chagall's wistful yearning for the lost simplicity of his youth in the cubist painting *I and the Village* (1911), in which a green-faced human and an anthropomorphized cow are mesmerized in an interlocking gaze, as if man and animal had finally reached the acme of mutual understanding, egalitarianism, and harmony.

Perhaps it would be best to conclude this essay on a more optimistic note, with one more uplifting example of the human-animal bond in artistic expression. It is both inspiring and comforting to view the bucolic canvases of a distinguished painter whom many people do not even realize was Jewish, even though he was the target of overt antisemitism. He is none other than the renowned

Figure 4.6. Marc Chagall, *Butcher*, 1910, gouache on paper. (Image from Wiki art, provided by Tretyakov Gallery [Moscow, Russia], https://www.wikiart.org/en/marc-chagall/butcher-1910.)

Danish French Impressionist artist Camille Pissarro (1830–1903), a completely assimilated Jew, whose nostalgic landscapes capture a vanished era of agrarian simplicity. If anyone's work exemplifies the way domesticated livestock should be allowed to live—treated with love, empathy, and respect, while roaming free in an open and natural setting—it is Pissarro's paintings. Many of his pieces depict peasant women in the fields as they harvest crops, or serenely watch over their placid animals, mainly cows but also sheep and chickens. The amicable relationship that is suggested in many of his paintings is one of great tenderness and patience toward one individual animal, as if she were a pet, or perhaps a few of them, as they languish in the sun, imbibe fresh water from a pond, or graze in the meadows. If only today's cows could enjoy the idyllic scenes which Pissarro created in his stunning series entitled *The Cowherd* (various works from 1874–1892, see figures 4.8 and 4.9) and *Autumn, Montfoucault Pond* (1875, see figure 4.10), their existence would be vastly superior to the appalling conditions they endure today.

FINAL REMARKS AND ACKNOWLEDGMENTS

Among the dust-covered family albums of my ancestors that I keep as souvenirs of my legacy, there are two slim booklets in Yiddish with crumbling yellow pages that were written by my maternal great-grandfather, who had been a scholarly *shochet* in Romania. Although I cannot read the Yiddish, I was told by my aunt that these booklets deal with the stringent rules regarding the knife's sharpness.

Figure 4.7. Marc Chagall, *The Cattle Dealer*, 1912, oil on canvas. (Image from The Athenaeum. (Image from Wiki art, https://www.wikiart.org/en/marc-chagall/the-cattle-dealer-1912.)

Figure 4.8. Camille Pissarro, *The Cowherd*, 1875, oil on canvas. (Image from The Athenaeum, https://the-athenaeum.org/art/detail.php?ID=12381.)

Figure 4.9. Camille Pissarro, *Cowherd, Pointoise*, 1882, gouache on paper. (Image from The Athenaeum, https://the-athenaeum.org/art/detail.php?ID=11870.)

I sometimes wonder what it would be like if my great-grandfather and I could have somehow met in the distant past and shared a conversation in a language we both understood. What would we have said to one another?

After so many hours of research and writing, I have worked up quite an appetite, and could easily devour a heaping plate of locally grown vegetables and tahini. But I am even hungrier for more knowledge from books about the fascinating and intricate relationship between humanitarian values and the ethical treatment of animals that are so deeply entrenched in Judaism. I wish to thank those empathetic Jewish artists and writers who conveyed their heartfelt pity for innocent chickens, sheep, goats, and cows with their paintbrushes and pens. I am also deeply indebted to my youngest daughter, Galit Govezensky—a photographer and a vegan —whose sensitivity and intimate portraits that foster identification with farm animals have taught me so much. I am grateful to all of them for serving as my muse through their touching works, and I am also inspired by their efforts to create a gentler and more compassionate world that disdains cruelty to animals.

Figure 4.10. Camille Pissarro, *Autumn, Montfoucault Pond*, 1875, oil on canvas. (Image from The Athenaeum, https://the-athenaeum.org/art/detail.php?ID=12376.)

NOTES

1. Veganism as a growing movement in Israel has been widely publicized, see for example, Tova Cohen, "In the Land of Milk and Honey, Israelis Turn Vegan," *Reuters*, July 21, 2015.
2. Erica Fudge, "A Left-Handed Blow: Writing the History of Animals," in *Representing Animals Theories of Contemporary Culture*, ed. Nigel Rothfels (Bloomington: Indiana University Press, 2002), 3–18, p. 16 for quote.
3. Stephen F. Eisenman, *The Cry of Nature* (London: Reaktion Books, 2013), 18.
4. Kathryn Shevelow, *For the Love of Animals: The Rise of the Animal Protection Movement* (New York: Henry Holt, 2008), 276–78.
5. Peter Singer, preface, in Lewis Gompertz, *Moral Inquiries on the Situation of Man and of Brutes* (Lewiston: Edwin Mellen Press, [1824] 1997), 12.
6. Ibid., 84.
7. Seth L. Wolitz, introduction, in *The Hidden Isaac Bashevis Singer*, ed. Seth L. Wolitz (Austin: University of Texas Press, 2001), xiv–xv.
8. Isaac Bashevis Singer, "The Letter Writer," *New Yorker*, January 13, 1968, 26.
9. Quoted in Peter S. Prescott, "Singer the Magician," *Newsweek* 92 (October 16, 1978): 97–98.
10. Quoted in Peter S. Prescott, *Encounters with American Culture: Volume 2 (1973–1985)* (New Jersey: Transaction Publishers, 2006), 12.
11. Isaac Bashevis Singer, "The Slaughterer," in *The Seance, and Other Stories* (New York: Farrar, Straus & Giroux, 1968), 20.
12. Ibid., 30.
13. Isaac Bashevis Singer, "Zlateh the Goat," in *The Oxford Book of Animal Stories*, ed. Dennis Pepper (Oxford: Oxford University Press, 2002), 246.
14. Ibid., 247.
15. Mendele Mocher Sforim, "The Calf," trans. Jacob Sloan, in *A Treasury of Yiddish Stories*, 2nd ed., ed. Irving Howe and Eliezer Greenberg (New York: Penguin Books, 1953/1990), 97–111.
16. Quoted in Richard H. Schwartz, *Judaism and Vegetarianism* (New York: Lantern Books, 2001), 172.
17. Franz Kafka, "The Hunger Artist" in *One Hundred Great Stories*, ed. James Daley (New York: Dover Publications, 2015), 720.
18. Quoted in Jonathan Safran Foer, *Eating Animals* (New York: Little, Brown, 2009), 36.
19. In the second chapter, "How to Cure a Fanatic," included in his book bearing the same title, Oz criticizes the "uncompromising self-righteousness" of a number

of movements. In that essay, he mentions the "vegetarians who will eat you alive for eating meat!" along with other ideological and religious groups.

20. Amos Oz, *A Tale of Love and Darkness* (London: Vintage, 2005), 4.

21. Amos Oz, *Between Friends*, trans. Sondra Silverston (UK: Chatto and Windus, 2013), 66–69.

22. Etgar Keret, "Going Vegetarian in Israel," *New York Times Magazine* (October 29, 2015).

23. Foer, *Eating Animals*, 243.

24. Jonathan Safran Foer, *Everything Is Illuminated: A Novel* (New York: Perennial, 2003), 65.

25. Avigdor W. G. Poseq, "Soutine's Dead Fowl as Metaphors of Sexuality," *Konsthistorisk Tidskrift* 66, no. 4 (1997): 251–260, 258.

26. Esti Dunow and Maurice Tuchman, *Life in Death: Still Lifes and Select Masterworks of Chaim Soutine* (New York: Paul Kasmin Gallery Publications, 2014).

27. Stanley Meisler, "Soutine: The Power and the Fury of an Eccentric Genius," *Smithsonian Magazine* (November 1988).

28. Jackie Wullshlager, *Chagall* (New York: Knopf, Borzoi Books—Random House Books, 2008), 154.

29. Carl H. Klaus, *Chaim Soutine* (United Kingdom: Parkstone Press, 2015), 79.

30. See chapter 2 in this volume by Nick Underwood for more information on Fania Lewando.

5 Vegetarianism and Veganism among Jewish Punks

MICHAEL CROLAND

Jews disproportionately played leading roles as the pioneers of punk, and many Jews have remained actively involved in punk. This includes Jewish musicians in prominent punk rock bands as well as those who overtly put their Jewishness front and center by playing Jewish punk. Among both categories, vegetarianism and veganism are seen frequently.

Punk has attracted against-the-grain, free-thinking individuals since its inception. Punk rock began in the mid-1970s with bands like the Ramones and the Dictators in New York and the Sex Pistols and The Clash in England. Punk rock is characterized by loud, abrasive, dissonant, fast-paced songs. *Punk* refers not just to the music but also to the subculture, which includes musicians, show organizers, show attendees, creators of zines (self-published magazines), and other people involved with the scene and community surrounding the music.

Veganism has become widespread among punks and in punk culture.[1] Some key, well-known Jewish punks were vegetarian or vegan, and overtly Jewish punks have discussed vegetarianism, veganism, and animal protection in their songs and other communications. The prevalence of veganism among Jewish punks can also be seen in key cookbook projects. The examples in this chapter, drawing from both music and cookbooks, show that vegetarianism and veganism are common among Jewish punks and, in some instances, even expected.

The prevalence of vegetarianism and veganism among Jewish punks is partly explained by their interests in social justice, radicalism, individualism, and questioning. These factors provide common ground between Jewishness and punk and help shape Jewish punks' identities, making it more likely for them to adopt a vegetarian or vegan diet. These factors have led most Jewish punks who go vegetarian or vegan to do so out of concern for animal issues, rather than health considerations. A blanket statement about why so many Jewish punks are vegetarian and vegan would be unwarranted. Jewish punks embrace vegetarianism or veganism on their own for varied reasons.

This chapter gives an overview of veganism among punks followed by connections between Jewishness and punk. It will then offer examples of intersections between Jewishness, vegetarianism and veganism, and punk in the realms of music and cooking.

VEGANISM AMONG PUNKS

Numerous punk rock bands and individuals have made a connection between veganism and punk rock. Some vegan cookbooks have been guided by a punk aesthetic or the punk ethos, including *Please Feed Me: A Punk Vegan Cookbook*, *This Ain't No Picnic: Your Punk Rock Vegan Cookbook*, *Please Don't Feed the Bears!: A Vegan Cookbook*, and two volumes of *Soy, Not Oi!* The editors of the original *Soy, Not Oi!* noted that encouraging people to go vegan was "not a unique message: anyone faintly in touch with punk rock... has certainly heard it before."[2]

In *Soy, Not Oi! Volume 2*, an essay titled "Punks and Veganism" explained that compassion is a "key element of punk."[3] "Behind all of the political idealism is a desire for those that don't have it so great to do a little better," the author wrote. "It may seem odd to match a fundamentally caring message with screaming and distorted guitars, but it's caring nonetheless. To reject the eating of meat and the exploitation of animals is also compassionate and caring." *Tikkun olam* (healing the world) will be discussed in the next section, but it should be noted that the social justice-oriented mind-set of punk is conducive to veganism.

This chapter examines subjects who relate to punk rock and the punk ethos, including many who are not part of the underground punk subculture. It looks at vegetarianism and veganism among those subjects and does not specifically deal with the so-called vegan punk subculture, identified by some scholars as a subculture that, in addition to following a vegan diet, champions anarchism and dumpster-diving and eschews overly processed and commodified foods.[4] Although this view of vegan punks is too narrowly defined for the scope of this chapter, scholarship on the subject provides beneficial insight into people who embrace both veganism and punk.

Cultural anthropologist Dylan Clark noted that veganism gained traction in the punk world by the 1990s.[5] Clark largely attributed this to the popularity of the straight-edge movement—which shunned alcohol, drugs, and promiscuous sex—within punk. Although veganism was not a tenet of straight edge per se, it appealed to many straight-edge punks interested in a pure, clean, and ethical lifestyle. Clark explained, "To be vegan in America is to perpetually find oneself in the minority, chastised, excluded, challenged, and reminded of one's difference. In this sense, veganism also served as an incessant critique of the mainstream, a maker of Otherness, and an enactment of punk."[6] In Clark's view, veganism was an expression of punk values and identity.

Religious studies scholar Julie Sylvestre addressed the vegan punk subculture in her master's thesis. She wrote, "Although veganism is not the ubiquitous dietary practice of punks, it is a popular expression of resistance within the movement, and serves as a tool of critique. In the context of punk, veganism becomes a powerful force dedicated to upholding a way of life that promotes awareness and responsibility."[7] She added, "By adopting a vegan diet punks literally embody their resistance.... For certain punks, veganism is a recipe of opposition and their bodies are vehicles of resistance through the ingestion of symbols."[8] While Clark's and Sylvestre's observations about the vegan punk subculture do not apply to all vegans who embrace punk, they shine light on the consistency and cohesion of veganism and punk.

SHARED VALUES AND BACKGROUNDS BETWEEN JEWS AND PUNKS

In the first chapter of my book, *Oy Oy Oy Gevalt! Jews and Punk*, I identified the predominant qualities among Jewish punks: "On the whole, they are humorous, tough, Holocaust-preoccupied, social justice-minded, radical, individualist, questioning outsiders, with the plurality of them coming from New York."[9] Each factor bridges Jewish and punk identities by drawing on both backgrounds, even if none is a hallmark of Jewishness or punk per se. Four of these commonalities—social justice, radicalism, individualism, and questioning—help explain the prevalence of vegetarianism and veganism among Jewish punks.

Tikkun Olam

Tikkun olam, the Jewish imperative to heal the world, has become intertwined—and at times synonymous—with social justice advocacy. Social justice is a focal point of punk as well. Punks often stand up for the disadvantaged and the marginalized, in the face of the unjust or corrupt powers that be. According to Lars J. Kristiansen and colleagues in *Screaming for Change*, the "overall mission" of punk is "the enablement of social change through reasoned action and persuasion."[10] Punk rock bands frequently discuss social injustice in song lyrics, in album liner notes, and in speeches during concerts. Punk rock bands sometimes participate in benefit shows for various causes, including animal rights. Frequently at punk shows, leaflets and pamphlets about social justice issues, including veganism, are readily available.

In the early 2010s, Matthew Honig worked on an unfinished documentary called *Tikkun Olam* about the connections between Judaism, *tikkun olam*, radical politics, and punk. Honig viewed *tikkun olam* as a punk—and do-it-yourself (DIY)—rationale for activism. He saw *tikkun olam* as an acknowledgment that healing the world was "not up to G-d" because "G-d's not going to do it."[11]

He said that "it's up to us [people] to fix the world"—to do it yourself. Honig explained that among the Jewish punks he interviewed for his film, many "saw a connection between the ethics of doing something in Judaism—and the idea that you're supposed to do something and not just pray and wait for G-d to do something—and punk." As he showed, some Jewish punks connected the Jewish concept of *tikkun olam* with their drive for social justice.

Tikkun olam can inspire individuals to work in behalf of many issues, including those related to vegetarianism and veganism. Concerns for core Jewish values—such as *tza'ar ba'alei chayim* (preventing unnecessary animal suffering), *pikuach nefesh* (prioritizing health and life), and *ba'al tashchit* (environmental stewardship)—can lead Jews to work on animal welfare and animal rights, public health, and environmental issues, respectively. These three concepts and their corresponding pragmatic applications are well-established reasons for embracing vegetarianism and veganism.

Moshiach Oi! has released three albums, been featured in the documentary *Punk Jews*, and been profiled in the *New York Times*. In 2008, Menashe Yaakov Wagner—who soon became the group's guitarist—described Moshiach Oi! as a "hardcore vegan straight-edge Orthodox Jewish punk band."[12] After Moshiach Oi! evolved from a one-man band—originally just singer Yishai Romanoff—into a quartet featuring Wagner, "vegan" was dropped from the band description. Moshiach Oi! switched to the more succinct label "Torah hardcore" instead.

Romanoff placed animal rights in a larger context of *tikkun olam*. In an interview for the documentary *Tikkun Olam*, he explained:

> I feel like the Jewish people have a deep-rooted longing and desire to bring healing to the world. They want to heal the world through being an anarchist . . . or animal rights, where you want to stop suffering to animals and stuff like that. It's all in this same desire to bring healing to the world, which I think is rooted in this desire to get close to G-d.[13]

Not only was animal rights part of an effort to heal the world for Romanoff, he saw it as interrelated to striving for a close relationship with G-d.

The Shondes has released five albums, toured internationally, and been profiled in the *Wall Street Journal*. Many songs by the Shondes focused on the theme of "valuing life and aliveness," according to singer Louisa Solomon.[14] For Solomon, a former rabbinical school applicant, the concept is rooted in *pikuach nefesh*, prioritizing the preservation of life. She linked *pikuach nefesh* to being a good person and fighting for social justice. "To the extent that I subscribe to a religious Judaism," she said, "that idea [of *pikuach nefesh*] is probably the guiding idea, and it's totally represented in our music."

In a 2008 interview, Solomon said that all four members of the Shondes were vegetarian. Although animal issues have not come up in the band's songs, Solomon did include them as part of her understanding of *pikuach nefesh*:

> For me personally the connections between Judaism and animal protection issues are really important.... I take the whole notion of *pikuach nefesh* to refer to our obligation to protect life in general, not just human life, so compassion for animals is an obvious piece of my worldview, along with social justice/human rights activism.... I love the opportunity to have intelligent discussion about how vegetarianism and animal rights connect to a broader anti-oppression politic.[15]

Pikuach nefesh conventionally refers to saving human life, but at least two other prominent Jewish vegetarians, Rabbi Fred Scherlinder Dobb and actress Natalie Portman, have questioned whether it should extend to animal lives.[16] Shondes members were active with social justice issues, and Solomon saw animal protection as interrelated—out of concern for *pikuach nefesh*.

As shown by Romanoff and Solomon, some Jewish punks grounded their attraction to veganism, vegetarianism, and animal rights in their embrace of *tikkun olam* and social justice.

Radicalism

Many Jewish vegans point to how vegetarianism and veganism are consistent with long-standing Jewish values and have become mainstream in recent years. They would not willingly portray veganism or animal rights advocacy as radical. At the same time, there is a tendency among punks to engage in radical activism and politics, including for animal rights. Among Jews, there is a long history of radicalism of which Jewish punks are proudly a part. Jewish punks are radical at least at a cultural level, and their radicalism may extend to social, political, and religious pursuits.

There have been a disproportionately high number of Jews involved in socialism, communism, anarchism, and other radical movements. Myriad Jews have expressed themselves as cultural radicals, including through punk rock. To some extent, this proclivity for radical politics and culture relates to an outsider identity and *tikkun olam*. As sociologist Jack Nusan Porter wrote, a Jew's impetus to embrace secular radicalism was rooted in the very religion and traditions that he or she usually rejected. Porter explained, "These rebels go beyond Judaism in their search for a more humane and just world . . . yet the origins are still Jewish—the prophetic vision of an ideal world."[17] For Jews who embrace radicalism, including punks, radicalism can be an expression of their Jewishness, even if their association with Judaism is not primarily religious in nature.

Individualism

Individualism is a key part of the punk ethos, which leads punks to think for themselves and determine what is right, regardless of social norms. *Individualism* describes a person's discretion to choose what is right him- or herself. In this context, it does not mean that the individual's interests are paramount and that the greater good should be ignored, which would be inconsistent with *tikkun olam* and social justice. In line with this DIY, individualist spirit, punks often look to create music, organize shows, and release zines on their own.

In contemporary US Jewish life, many Jews choose the elements of Judaism that they find the most personally resonant and relate to their Jewishness, culturally and religiously, in an individualist manner. This emphasis on individualism allows Jewish punks to embrace their Jewish identity, culture, and religious practices in a manner they deem appropriate, without sacrificing their punk outlook.

Several key studies by sociologist Steven M. Cohen show the DIY and individualist nature of US Jews' approaches to identity and culture. This is particularly evident among Jews who are young, single, and not formally affiliated with Jewish communal organizations—the demographic that most Jewish punks were a part of at the time they made their art. In a study of Jews under age thirty-five, Cohen and Ari Y. Kelman explain that subjects were concerned with "personal meaning" in their Jewish interactions and that their attraction to "community engagement" was through "individualist impulses."[18]

In their book, *The Jew Within*, Cohen and Arnold M. Eisen said that Jews had "turned inward in the search for meaning."[19] They noted, "Our subjects emphasize personal meaning as the arbiter of their Jewish involvement. Their Judaism ... assum[es] the rightful freedom of each individual to make his or her own Jewish decisions.[20] They wrote, "Today's Jews reject the notion that Judaism places demands upon them. Some even told us that Judaism requires them to choose those options that they find most personally meaningful."[21]

A DIY, individualist approach is prevalent in the Jewish community, and it is not a new fad. When Jewish punks do things their own way, it is consistent with this paradigm, not some rare example of breaking apart from the norm. Veganism is not proscribed by the Jewish "establishment." That is not an obstacle to Jews coming to veganism on their own, and this is particularly true of Jewish punks.

Questioning

One particular aspect of thinking for oneself as an individual is questioning the way things are and asking why. This is common to Jews and punks.

There is a cliché that religious observance depends on dogma, hierarchy, and conformity. That characterization is true for some religious practices, but there is a long-standing tradition in Judaism of asking "Why?" When G-d threatened to annihilate Sodom and Gomorrah, Abraham questioned His decision. The Talmud is full of lively debate, often with questions from multiple viewpoints that do not get resolved with unanimous acceptance. A segment of the Passover Seder addresses four sons—the wise son, the wicked son, the simple son, and the son who cannot formulate a question—and the latter seems the most facile and pitiable.

Punks, too, have sought to ask "why?" In *We Owe You Nothing*, *Punk Planet* editor-in-chief Daniel Sinker wrote, "Punk has always been about asking 'why' and then doing something about it."[22] He explained that DIY was "the answer to" the "why" question. Punks asked why something that seemed off was the way it was, and then they took action accordingly.

Much of the general public might sit back and accept the horrors of factory farming and slaughterhouse conditions, for example, without considering them to any significant degree. Jewish punks, on the other hand, are already accustomed to asking "why?" As questioning, individualist, social justice-oriented radicals, the table is set for Jewish punks to consider and embrace vegetarianism or veganism.

EXAMPLES FROM PUNK ROCK MUSICIANS

I now turn my attention to examples of vegetarianism and veganism among punk rock musicians. I look at prominent Jews involved in punk rock and Jewish punk bands (i.e., punk rock artists that put their Jewishness front and center). The musicians discussed their vegetarianism and veganism in song lyrics, interviews, and other communications. Some explicitly advocated for vegetarianism and veganism, and many proudly made their fans and listeners aware that they were vegetarian or vegan.

Prominent Punks

While prominent punks who were Jewish typically did not put their Jewishness on display overtly and frequently, it played a role in shaping who they were. Some were vegetarian or vegan or were otherwise animal advocates.

The Ramones is credited as being the first punk rock band. Iconic singer Joey Ramone (Jeffry Hyman) was Jewish, as was the quartet's original drummer, Tommy Ramone (Tamas Erdelyi). Whereas it was not widely known who else was Jewish in punk's 1970s heyday, it was common knowledge that Joey was a member of the tribe. In the early 1990s, Joey went vegetarian.[23] He had an accident that made him take stock of his life, and he became sober and health-conscious as a result. In addition to embracing a vegetarian diet around this time, Joey stopped consuming dairy products, which gave him a mucus problem that adversely affected his singing. Whereas most vegetarians and vegans in this chapter referred to ethical considerations, one of the best-known Jewish punks cut out meat and dairy for health reasons.

Michael "Mick" Jones was the guitarist of The Clash, one of the biggest punk bands to come out of England. Jones was Jewish on his mother's side, and he was primarily raised by his maternal grandmother, whom he described as religious, from the time he was eight years old.[24] In 2007, Jones told the *New York Times* that he had stopped eating meat and dairy products.[25] "I read about how animals experience fear on the way to slaughter," Jones said. "I didn't want to eat that. I figured it would make me a stronger person." Like Joey Ramone, Mick Jones gave up both meat and dairy products.

Some other well-known Jewish musicians, from proto-punk to present-day punk, were vegetarian, vegan, or animal advocates. Proto-punk singer/guitarist Jonathan Richman was vegan. MDC singer Dave Dictor was vegetarian for over four decades and was outspoken for animals in his music and beyond.[26] Former Gogol Bordello guitarist Oren Kaplan was vegetarian. New Found Glory bassist Ian Grushka was vegetarian and designed a graphic provegetarian shirt for People for the Ethical Treatment of Animals (PETA). NOFX singer Michael "Fat Mike" Burkett released a benefit CD for PETA through his record label, Fat Wreck Chords. Bad Religion guitarist Brett Gurewitz opined, "It's my view that if a being is capable of suffering, then the suffering should be minimized—period.... I feel that every sentient creature has a right to not suffer unnecessarily."[27] Gurewitz did not use the Hebrew term *tza'ar ba'alei chayim*, but his point about minimizing unnecessary animal suffering was consistent with this Jewish imperative.

Most of these musicians were not publicly outspoken about their Jewishness, let alone making a connection between their Jewishness and their vegetarianism, veganism, or animal advocacy. Nevertheless, the fact that some of the most prominent Jewish punks embraced these ideas and practices helps illustrate how popular they were among Jewish punks.

Outspoken Vegetarian Jewish Punks

Overtly Jewish punk bands are typically less popular and prominent than the artists in the previous section. Among this group, some artists have been outspoken about vegetarianism in connection with Jewish themes. These artists frequently noted their vegetarianism and incorporated their love for vegetarian foods into their public image.

Beyond just vegetarians, Jewish punk bands often referred to Jewish foods. For Jewish punk bands that overtly proclaim their Jewish identity without espousing religious messages, their overall approach depended on appealing to familiar, resonant cultural referents. It should not be surprising that food is a primary example. At concerts, Gefilte F*ck threw gefilte fish into the mosh pit, Jewdriver distributed bagels to concertgoers for food fights, and Yidcore got playful on stage with hummus, falafel, latkes, and Manischewitz wine.[28] Numerous bands discussed Jewish foods in their lyrics. The prevalence of food in Jewish punk facilitates assessment of dietary preferences.

Steve "Gangsta Rabbi" Lieberman is the self-professed "King of Jewish Punk" and has released more than seventy albums. Lieberman said that he went vegetarian to "glorify the commandments to be kind to animals."[29] In a 2010 interview, he explained:

> Originally, although G-d gave man dominion over the animals, both were given only plants for food. It wasn't until Genesis 9, after the fall of mankind, that He gave Noah and his sons the right to eat their fellow creatures. Although throughout the Scriptures there are commandments dealing with the kindness to animals (epitomized in Numbers 22, when G-d gives Bala'am's donkey the power of speech after his cruelty to her) . . . vegetarianism is not in itself required to serve G-d.
>
> I went to the Long Island Game Farm and was petting a cow, and she licked me, just like my puppy Buttons would do. . . . If this cow had a related soul to Buttons, I should no longer have her kind killed for my benefit. So on . . . 3/20/1995, in this spirit, I became vegetarian, never to stray for 15 years this month.[30]

Lieberman connected his vegetarianism to his understanding of Torah teachings about kindness to animals—essentially, *tza'ar ba'alei chayim*—and his firsthand experience with animals.

Lieberman boasted about being vegetarian in the song "Glad I Am a Vegetarian." The lyrics frequently repeated the title:

Glad I am a vegetarian
The animal kingdom and the kingdom of man
Ban the slaughterhouses then we'll pray for the land
Glad I am a vegetarian

Glad I don't eat no beef
The cows on the farm they are so sweet
They got big hooves instead of their feet
Glad I don't eat no beef

Glad I don't eat no pork
The Pig in the City, they taught him to talk
I'm the happiest guy in the state of New York
Glad I don't eat no pork

Glad I don't eat no fish
When they kill them they smell just like pish
Don't want anything like that on my dish
Glad I don't eat no fish

Glad I don't eat no deer
Bambi don't have to live in fear
I'll come back to feed him this time next year
Glad I don't eat no deer

Glad I don't eat no rabbit
Killing Thumper: That's a really bad habit
Glad I'm not John Wayne Bobbit
Glad I don't eat no rabbit

Glad I don't eat no chicken
The smell of Colonel Sanders it just makes me sicken
You won't get me there either screaming or kickin'
Glad I don't eat no chicken.[31]

Lieberman sang about how he would not eat a half-dozen different types of animals, and in three examples, he named anthropomorphized animals from popular movies to make his case. On his website, Lieberman explained the song by saying,

> I did it for the right reasons, as a protest [against] the slaughter of the L-rd's creatures for human consumption. Although permitted in the Torah

(certain animals anyway), many references are there to show kindness and compassion to animals, thus my way of doing that: not eating them."[32]

"Glad I Am a Vegetarian" was a vehicle for Lieberman to talk about his vegetarianism with pride.

In "The Meat I Eat," Lieberman sang about how it was not exactly meat that he ate. In the lyrics, he clarified that the "meat I eat" was derived from wheat and that the "meat I enjoy" was from soy.[33] He showed the viability of a plant-based diet by discussing mock meats made from seitan and soy. In his public persona, interviews, website, and song lyrics, Lieberman has been outwardly and proudly vegetarian.

Yidcore was as overtly Jewish as a punk rock band could be. The Australian band might have incorporated animal products into its shtick at times, but singer Bram Presser was vegetarian. When Yidcore members took "chicken soup shots" (along the lines of taking shots of alcohol) on stage, Presser's were vegetarian. Yidcore included a shofar (ram's horn) among its instruments, and Presser ethically grappled with using an animal's body part. He affixed PETA stickers to the shofar, but he said they were not an effort "to make up in some sad way for what [he] was doing with a bit of a murdered animal."[34] Rather, just as punks often adorn their guitars with stickers, he put stickers for "things [he] believed in" on his instrument. Despite its animal origin, the shofar became a platform for "I Am Not a Nugget" and other animal rights messages.

In the song "They Tried to Kill Us. They Failed. Let's Eat!" Yidcore posited that despite facing hard times, the Jewish people persevere—and celebrate their thwarted annihilation with food. Presser sang, "We struggle just so we can eat."[35] An animated video for the song depicted Nazis as pigs and Jews as chickens.[36] The video drew on a controversial comparison between the Holocaust and factory farming, which has been made by Isaac Bashevis Singer, PETA, and Charles Patterson's book *Eternal Treblinka: Our Treatment of Animals and the Holocaust*, among others. In the video, the chickens defeated the pigs.

At least as part of his public persona, Presser was obsessed with hummus. As contemporary Jewish studies scholar Sarah Bunin Benor noted in her essay about hummus and Israel, among diaspora Jews, hummus is widely perceived as an Israeli food and a way of connecting to Israel.[37] She explained that hummus is one of many Israeli examples of what can be "important in the construction of Diaspora Jewish identities."[38] On Presser's MySpace profile, he described himself as "more hummus than hummus."[39] In the Yidcore song "(I Wanna Be A) Hummusexual," he sang about having sexual fantasies for chickpeas.[40] He sometimes smeared hummus over his body and clothing during concerts, and he boasted that there were "endless possibilities for hummus as a spreading-on-self condiment."⁴¹ At the band's final concert in 2009, Presser drenched himself in hummus, covering his face, hair, beard, fingers, and shirt. He utterly embraced a popular vegetarian food that suggests connections to Israel as part of diasporic Jewish identity.

Another Presser obsession was Natalie Portman, probably the world's most famous Jewish vegan. In "Natalie Portman, This Is Your Last Chance," Presser addressed the extent of his crush as well as his compatibility with Portman, saying that the two were "meant to be."⁴² He noted that both were "vego yiddin," a creative way of saying vegetarian Jews. It was not an afterthought to Presser that he and Portman were both vegetarian and Jewish. He rattled off both factors at the top of his list of reasons why they should be together.

Yidcore's comic shtick could be downright zany. But as Yidcore pointed out in the liner notes to one album, the band "supported a cruelty-free, egalitarian lifestyle. Despite the dumb stuff they do."⁴³

Useless ID was the most famous punk rock band to come out of Israel and released multiple albums on the American label Fat Wreck Chords. All four band members were vegetarian. Useless ID spoke out in its music and otherwise about vegetarianism and the band members' love for falafel.

Guitarist Ishay Berger talked openly about being vegetarian and thought that doing so fell in line with the tradition established by other punk rock bands. He said:

> We feel that it's legitimate to let people know that we don't eat meat and [that we're] going against the cruel [meat] industry that we always hated. If people don't want to hear about it, it's a good enough reason to inform them about what's the alternative to a cruel, mindless lifestyle. We don't push anything down anyone's throat, though; we just feel it's important to be somewhat vocal about it, 'cuz after all, I think bands . . . had a lot to [do] with why I've been a vegetarian for most of my life, so it's a good tradition, I think.⁴⁴

Opposing cruelty to animals was the basis for the band members' vegetarianism and support for animal rights.

In the 2016 song "Without a Choice," Useless ID discussed how "innocent creatures" have their young taken away from them and are slaughtered for food.⁴⁵ "Stop animal abuse," the lyrics declared. The song noted that while animals might not have a say in whether they are killed for food, people do have a say.

In the animated video for "Without a Choice," the members of Useless ID were trucked to a slaughterhouse.⁴⁶ They were stunned by a rooster, injected by a cow, decapitated by a chicken, and had their limbs cut off by a bull. After a cow made ground meat from one musician's leg, a "Kosher" sign was visible. Berger explained:

> Animal rights and punk rock go hand in hand. If you care about making a change in this crazy world, you should try and start the revolution within yourself. Useless ID is not a preachy band, but we always felt that Animal Liberation is essential to self-freedom and that it is hypocritical to strive for freedom, while giving a hand to death machines. This animated video . . . the point of it is pretty simple, don't do to others what you don't want them doing to you.[47]

The video was covered by punk news sites, getting the message out to a wider audience.

Useless ID promoted animal rights in other ways, too. The band's website referred fans to several animal protection organizations. Multiple albums' liner notes directed fans to PETA's website and boasted, "Useless ID still support the animal rights movement and believe in a cruelty-free lifestyle."[48]

Whereas Presser's chickpea preference was hummus, Useless ID sided with falafel. This is not surprising considering how common—and representative—falafel is in Israeli cuisine.[49] In his essay about falafel and Jewish identity, historian Shaul Stampfer described falafel as an iconic Israeli food.[50] He explained that consumption of and references to falafel suggest connections to Israel and Israelis, at least in Israeli or Jewish contexts.[51] For Useless ID, the role of falafel as an iconic Israeli food and a staple vegetarian food combined to make it so significant to the band members that it was intertwined with the group's public identity. Useless ID noted on its website, "well, falafel is the fuel and the main force behind useless id. see, even if we weren't all broke, lazy, vegeretian [sic] punx, we'd like to think that falafel was [the bomb]. we eat falafel all the time, and we talk about it even more."[52] Useless ID started a record label named Falafel Records. Even Presser came around to understanding Useless ID members' falafel focus after they introduced him to what he called "the best falafel ever in the world" in Haifa.[53]

Lieberman, Presser, and Useless ID were outspoken about their vegetarianism. All three were vegetarian for ethical reasons, and they connected their vegetarianism to different facets of their Jewish or Israeli identities, including Torah teachings, a crush on a famous Jewish actress, and chickpea dishes associated with Israeli cuisine. They addressed their vegetarianism in a variety of formats, including song lyrics, videos, interviews, liner notes, online content, a record label name, stickers on a shofar, and direct interactions with food during performances.

References by Nonvegetarians

Several Jewish punk bands had songs referring to vegetarians or vegans despite not having such members. Befitting the nature of Jewish punk, they typically did so in a humorous way. As these examples demonstrate, vegetarians and vegans are not alone in recognizing that vegetarianism and veganism are common among Jewish punks. Other Jewish punks see it that way, too.

In the Schmekel song "Dumpster Dive," the narrator was romantically interested in "a vegan with a heart of kale."[54] Schmekel's singer said that the song was in part about dumpster-diving, vegans, and anarchists.[55]

In the Jew Cocks' "Semen Vegan," the lyrics discussed a vegan woman who would not "eat meat" but would consume human semen.[56] The band's keyboard player typically sought to engage vegans in attendance at live shows, introducing the song by saying, "Do we have any vegans out there? Show of hands."[57]

In Jewdriver's "Pastrami on Rye," the meat-glorifying narrator took issue with someone who thought that everybody should "be a veggie Jew."[58] The narrator boldly voiced his objection by cursing against the supposed vegetarian Jewish listener and declaring, "I pissed in your tofu!"

Not all of these references portrayed vegetarianism and veganism in a glowing light. Recurring discussion of the topic by artists who were not vegetarian helps show how prevalent vegetarianism and veganism are among Jewish punks, in terms of adherence to the diet, expectations thereof, and discussion about the topic.

EXAMPLES FROM THE FOOD WORLD

Moving beyond music, I discuss the Jewish, punk, and vegan intersection in vegan food and cookbook projects. I focus on Isa Chandra Moskowitz and the NewKosher cookbook.

Other Jewish punks have been active in the vegan food world. Popular vegan cookbook author Sarah Kramer acknowledged that she "came from an '80s punk DIY" background, and her debut cookbook featured a variety of Jewish dishes, including Oi-Vey! Mock Chopped Liver, matzo ball soup, matzo pizza, and various kugels.[59] Kerry "The Hardcore Chef" Weber discussed keeping kosher in his youth and made F*ck Nazi Sympathy BBQ Tofu on his *Vegan Cooking for Animal Lovers* DVD, and he blogged about matzo ball soup.[60] Kramer and Weber, however, did not directly integrate their Jewishness, veganism, and punk to the same extent as the following examples did.

Isa Chandra Moskowitz

Isa Chandra Moskowitz is a revered vegan food personality and a bestselling vegan cookbook author. She has written nine vegan cookbooks and opened vegan restaurants in Omaha, Nebraska, and Brooklyn, New York. While her Jewish and punk identities did not come across in everything that she did, both were parts of her public persona. In Moskowitz's cookbooks and beyond, she sometimes integrated her Jewishness, veganism, and punk.

Moskowitz burst onto the vegan food radar in 2003 with the *Post Punk Kitchen*, a public access television show. In accordance with the DIY spirit of punk, she took it upon herself to create the media and entertainment she thought should exist rather than hoping that someone else would. She put "Punk" in the name because she thought it should sound "vaguely punk because punk was the culture I grew up in and the culture that made me the woman I am."[61] She maintained a *Post Punk Kitchen* website and blog for more than a decade after launching the show.

At times, Moskowitz's punk approach involved putting her own spin on something instead of falling in line with the way things had always been done. She explained,

> I think it's important to know what "authentic" food is, but I definitely don't let the idea box me in. Especially as a vegan chef, I'm constantly playing with traditions and concepts, creating vegan translations of classics and breathing new life into old favorites.[62]

Other times, Moskowitz's punk culinary tactics meant being shambolic. She advised that one "super punk-rock" way to frost cupcakes would be "messy and unpredictable, but that's anarchy for you."[63] She called her Mashed Potatoes with Punk Rock Chickpea Gravy "punk rock" because it "depends on almost every spice in your spice rack; it would make any 'real' chef gasp."[64]

Making use of punk rock bands also helped add a punk element. In the Passover episode of the *Post Punk Kitchen*, Moskowitz explained that she and her cohost were going to make their own matzo meal and that one could do so by placing matzo in a food processor. Alternatively, she advised, "If you have a punk rock band in your living room, just give it to them and they'll crush it up for you."[65] As a punk rock band performed, the singer crushed the matzo. The band members played around with kitchen utensils, such as using a soup ladle as a drumstick. The episode included songs by the punk rock bands NOFX, Minutemen, and the Dead Kennedys. The *Post Punk Kitchen*'s Passover episode was Moskowitz's most overt integration of Jewishness, veganism, and punk.

Both hummus-happy Presser and falafel-fueled Useless ID would approve of Moskowitz's recurring spotlight on chickpea dishes. Moskowitz said that hummus was "quintessentially vegan" and that there is no food "more comforting and cozily vegan."[66] She quipped that "hummus is to vegans what air is to the rest of humanity: we need it to live."[67] She used a falafel recipe as an opportunity to reflect on "humiliating acts" from her Jewish day camp experiences.[68] She claimed that "every punk... knows that chickpeas are the punkest legume there is."[69] She tied in her Jewish, vegan, and punk identities as part of her discussion of chickpea dishes.

Even before her 2016 holiday cookbook, Moskowitz featured traditional Jewish foods in her books, including matzo brei, latkes, kugel, and cholent. She did so despite acknowledging that she often reads online comments saying that "some of my recipes are 'weird' and 'ethnic.'"[70] She did not back down from the naysayers, explaining that "no matter what culinary roads I travel, my food will always be a reflection of the world as seen by a Jewish-American woman from Brooklyn."[71] She humorously incorporated her Jewishness into descriptions for some recipes. For example, for a cholent featuring textured vegetable protein, she wrote, "Warning: You might start inexplicably calling people *meshugahs* and *putzes* after you've eaten this."[72] Moskowitz put her Jewish pride on display for readers—including a largely non-Jewish audience—to see.

Moskowitz's most recent work, *The Superfun Times Vegan Holiday Cookbook*, featured more overtly Jewish recipes and references than any of her previous works. The book's holiday focus resulted in three chapters on Jewish holidays: Passover, Rosh Hashanah and Yom Kippur, and Hanukkah. There were vegan versions of traditional Jewish dishes (some of which are vegan to begin with), including bagels and "nox," blintzes, challah, charoset, hamantaschen, kasha varnishkes, kugel, latkes, mandelbrot, matzo ball soup, rugelach, sufganiyot, and tzimmes. There was even a recipe for "Gefilte Chickpeas"!

From the *Post Punk Kitchen*'s Passover episode to her beloved cookbooks, Moskowitz integrated her Jewish, vegan, and punk identities.

NewKosher

PunkTorah is a nonprofit organization that encourages people to relate to Judaism on their own terms, through several websites, books, and an online educational program. The "punk" part of PunkTorah pertains to a rebellious, against-the-grain spirit as well as the DIY ethos at the heart of punk. PunkTorah largely appeals to outsiders who do not feel satisfied by the mainstream Jewish community, including LGBT Jews and converts.

In 2011, PunkTorah published a Jewish vegan cookbook, which fit its larger approach of presenting an unconventional side of Judaism and appealing to Jews who may feel that they are outside the mainstream. *NewKosher Cookbook: Your Favorite Jewish Vegan Recipes!* offered recipes for vegan versions of traditional Jewish dishes, including blintzes, challah, egg cream, kishke, kreplach, kugel, matzo ball soup, rugelach, sufganiyot, and tzimmes. A section titled "The Jewiest, Vegan Essays Ever" featured several pieces by *Judaism and Vegetarianism* author Richard Schwartz and one by Matthue Roth, author of the Jewish punk novel *Never Mind the Goldbergs*.

The cookbook's opening chapter discussed veganism vis-à-vis *kashrut* and acknowledged that Jewish vegans have varied motivations, including ethical, health, and environmental reasons as well as adhering to what could be seen as "G-d's initial intention for humanity."[73] The book's editors noted that "a vegan diet and traditional Jewish law go hand-in-hand" and that "traditional Jewish recipes can be (or already are) compl[e]mentary to a vegan diet."[74]

The editors explained that their approach to the cookbook relied on a spirit of inclusion, as was consistent with the punk ethos and common for PunkTorah. They welcomed recipes from a varied field of professional and amateur chefs, as long as they were original recipes (i.e., DIY).[75] They featured contributors who self-identified as Jewish "by whatever definition you wish to use."[76] They saw this open-door policy as enabling inclusion to "remove the barriers which prevent people from participating in a religious community."[77] In conclusion, in line with a DIY approach, they encouraged readers to consider veganism, noting that "whatever choice you make is entirely yours."[78]

Moskowitz's work and the NewKosher cookbook showed how well Jewishness, veganism, and punk gelled in the realm of cookbooks and food.

CODA

This chapter began by outlining established connections between vegetarianism or veganism and punk as well as Jewishness and punk. It showed that vegetarianism or veganism, Jewishness, and punk could all be integrated. The subjects featured in this chapter represented the bigger picture of how popular vegetarianism and veganism are among Jewish punks, mostly because of animal reasons. The concepts of *tikkun olam*, radicalism, individualism, and questioning help illuminate why so many Jewish punks adopt a vegetarian or vegan diet. Some of the most prominent punk rock musicians were Jewish and vegetarian or vegan, as were lesser known, more overtly Jewish artists. These musicians expressed their

Jewish identity and their vegetarianism or veganism through their music and other ways. The intersection between Jewishness, punk, and veganism played out in cookbooks, as best evidenced by the country's bestselling vegan cookbook author and the NewKosher cookbook.

Punk encourages self-expression in a DIY manner. Considering the prevalence of veganism among punks and the roles of *tikkun olam*, radicalism, individualism, and questioning, it makes sense that so many Jewish punks are proud "vego yiddin."

NOTES

1. Will Boisseau and Jim Donaghey, " 'Nailing Descartes to the Wall': Animal Rights, Veganism, and Punk Culture," in *Anarchism and Animal Liberation: Essays on Complementary Elements of Total Liberation*, ed. Anthony J. Nocella II, Richard J. White, and Erika Cudworth (Jefferson: McFarland, 2015), 80.

2. Jack and Joel, introduction to *Soy, Not Oi!*, comp. The Hippycore Krew (1989; repr., Oakland, CA: AK Press, 2005), 2.

3. Todd Wolenski, "Punks and Veganism," *Soy, Not Oi! Volume 2*, comp. The Hippycore Krew (San Diego, CA: Culture at All Costs Publishing, 2014), 16.

4. Julie Sylvestre, "Fringe Food and Renegade Words: Symbol and Meaning in the Vegan Punk and Zine Subcultures," M.A. thesis, University of Ottawa, 2009, 27–29.

5. Dylan Clark, "The Raw and the Rotten: Punk Cuisine," *Ethnology* 43, no. 1 (Winter 2004): 24.

6. Ibid., 24–25.

7. Sylvestre, "Fringe Food and Renegade Words," 16.

8. Ibid., 37.

9. Michael Croland, *Oy Oy Oy Gevalt! Jews and Punk* (Santa Barbara, CA: Praeger, 2016), 21.

10. Lars J. Kristiansen, Joseph R. Blaney, Philip J. Chidester, and Brent K. Simonds, *Screaming for Change: Articulating a Unifying Philosophy of Punk Rock* (Lanham, MD: Lexington Books, 2010), 136.

11. Quoted in Croland, *Oy Oy Oy Gevalt!*, 14–15.

12. Michael Croland, "Moshiach Oi: Punk with an Authentic Jewish Focus," *heebnvegan* (blog), November 30, 2008, http://heebnvegan.blogspot.com/2008/11/moshiach-oi-punk-with-authentic-jewish.html.

13. "Tikkun Olam Documentary–Trailer," YouTube, posted by punkCDsampler, November 29, 2012, https://www.youtube.com/watch?v=a7rvjwWm47M.

14. Croland, *Oy Oy Oy Gevalt!*, 74.

15. Temim Fruchter and Louisa Solomon, email to the author, December 30, 2008.

16. David A. Teutsch, *Community, Gemilut Ḥesed, and Tikun Olam* (Wyncote, PA: Reconstructionist Rabbinical College Press, 2009), 37; and Michael Croland, "Natalie Portman: 'The Center of Judaism for Me Is Not Taking Life,'" *heebnvegan* (blog), January 12, 2010, http://heebnvegan.blogspot.com/2010/01/natalie-portman-center-of-judaism-for.html.

17. Jack Nusan Porter, *The Jew as Outsider: Historical and Contemporary Perspectives, Collected Essays, 1974–1980* (Washington, DC: University Press of America, 1981), 5.

18. Steven M. Cohen and Ari Y. Kelman, "The Continuity of Discontinuity: How Young Jews Are Connecting, Creating, and Organizing Their Own Jewish Lives," Berman Jewish Policy Archive, 2007, 45, https://www.bjpa.org/search-results/publication/327.

19. Steven M. Cohen and Arnold M. Eisen, *The Jew Within: Self, Family, and Continuity in America* (Bloomington: Indiana University Press, 2000), 2.

20. Ibid., 36.

21. Ibid., 192–93.

22. Daniel Sinker, *We Owe You Nothing: "Punk Planet": The Collected Interviews* (New York: Akashic Books, 2001), 10–11.

23. Donna Gaines, "My Life with the Ramones," *Village Voice* 41, no. 3 (January 16, 1996): 26.

24. Joe Strummer, Mick Jones, Paul Simonon, and Topper Headon, *The Clash* (New York: Grand Central Publishing, 2008), 28 and 31.

25. Zoe Wolff, "Two Punks Go into a Bar," *New York Times*, December 23, 2007, http://www.nytimes.com/2007/12/23/fashion/23nite.html.

26. Dave Dictor, *MDC: Memoir from a Damaged Civilization* (San Francisco: Manic D Press, 2016), 27.

27. "peta2 Exclusive Interview: Brett Gurewitz," YouTube, posted by peta2TV, June 10, 2014, https://www.youtube.com/watch?v=wbpQu-BdYgE.

28. Michael Croland, "Meet the Jewish Punk Bands That Throw Gefilte Fish, Bagels, and Hummus," *Forward*, February 5, 2017, http://forward.com/food/361056/nosh-or-mosh-meet-the-jewish-punk-bands-that-throw-gefilte-fish-bagels-and.

29. Steve Lieberman, email to the author, October 13, 2005.

30. Michael Croland, "The Four Questions: Gangsta Rabbi," *heebnvegan* (blog), April 2, 2010, http://heebnvegan.blogspot.com/2010/04/four-questions-gangsta-rabbi.html.

31. Steve Lieberman, "Glad I Am a Vegetarian," *Bad'lania Rising*, 2002, Gangsta Rabbi Bad'lan USA Records, CD.

32. GangstaRabbi.com, accessed January 18, 2016, http://gangstarabbi.com/buycds.html.

33. Steve Lieberman, "The Meat I Eat," *My Magic Last Days*, 2012, self-published, CD.

34. Bram Presser, email to the author, May 25, 2017.

35. Yidcore, "They Tried to Kill Us. They Failed. Let's Eat!," *They Tried to Kill Us. They Failed. Let's Eat!*, 2006, Rubber Records, CD.

36. "They Tried to Kill Us. They Failed. Let's Eat!," YouTube, posted by yidcore, May 1, 2007, https://www.youtube.com/watch?v=M5D5Ww7PKN4.

37. Sarah Bunin Benor, "Hummus, Challah, and Gefilte Fish: Israel in Diaspora Jewish Culture," in *Dynamic Belonging: Contemporary Jewish Collective Identities*, ed. Harvey E. Goldberg, Steven M. Cohen, and Ezra Kopelowitz (New York: Berghahn Books, 2012), 219–22.

38. Ibid., 222.

39. Michael Croland, "Vegetarian Jewish Punk Rockers," *heebnvegan* (blog), September 17, 2006, http://heebnvegan.blogspot.com/2006/09/vegetarian-jewish-punk-rockers.html.

40. "YIDcore (2008)—The Hummusexual-EP-PUNK 100%," YouTube, posted by Music Explorer, April 4, 2016, https://youtu.be/VkCczXicD-Q.

41. Bram Presser, email to the author, October 13, 2005.

42. Yidcore, "Natalie Portman, This Is Your Last Chance," *They Tried to Kill Us. They Failed. Let's Eat!*

43. Yidcore, liner notes, *Eighth Day Slice/Fiddlin on Ya Roof*, 2005, Rubber Records, CD.

44. Michael Croland, "Useless ID: That Hard-Working, Real-Deal Band from Israel," *heebnvegan* (blog), October 23, 2008, http://heebnvegan.blogspot.com/2008/10/useless-id-that-hard-working-real-deal.html.

45. Useless ID, "Without a Choice," *State Is Burning*, 2016, Fat Wreck Chords, CD.

46. "Useless ID—Without a Choice (Official Video)," YouTube, posted by Fat Wreck Chords, November 21, 2016, https://www.youtube.com/watch?v=52E46mox7wE.

47. Andrew Sacher, "Watch Animals Slaughter Useless ID in Anti-Cruelty Video 'Without a Choice,'" *Brooklyn Vegan*, November 18, 2016, http://www.brooklynvegan.com/watch-animals-slaughter-useless-id-in-anti-cruelty-video-without-a-choice/.

48. Useless ID, liner notes, *The Lost Broken Bones*, 2008, Suburban Home, CD; and Useless ID, liner notes, *State Is Burning*.

49. Shaul Stampfer, "Bagel and Falafel: Two Iconic Jewish Foods and One Modern Jewish Identity," in *Jews and Their Foodways*, ed. Anat Helman (Oxford: Oxford University Press, 2015), 177.

50. Ibid., 181.

51. Ibid., 187–88.

52. Croland, "Vegetarian Jewish Punk Rockers."

53. Presser, October 13, 2005.

54. Schmekel, "Dumpster Dive," *The Whale That Ate Jonah*, 2013, self-published, digital album.

55. "Schmekel: 100% TransJews 'Dumpster Dive,'" YouTube, posted by Riley Kilo, July 18, 2011, https://www.youtube.com/watch?v=E7v9ADy8cRw.

56. Jew Cocks, "Semen Vegan," *Extended Play*, 2014, self-published, digital album, https://jewcocks.bandcamp.com/album/extended-play.

57. Todd, email to the author, January 27, 2016.

58. Jewdriver, "Pastrami on Rye," *Hail the Jew Dawn*, 2004, Impact Records, CD.

59. Sarah Kramer, introduction to *How It All Vegan! Irresistible Recipes for an Animal-Free Diet*, by Tanya Barnard and Sarah Kramer (1999; rpt., Vancouver: Arsenal Pulp Press, 2009), 9.

60. Kerry Weber and Elizabeth Dechant, *Vegan Cooking for Animal Lovers* (Halo 8, 2007), DVD; and Kerry Weber, "WTF Is a Kneydl Soup?," *Hardcore Chef* (blog), April 8, 2008, https://hardcorechef.wordpress.com/2008/04/09/wft-is-a-kneydl-soup.

61. Isa Chandra Moskowitz, *Vegan with a Vengeance: Over 150 Delicious, Cheap, Animal-Free Recipes That Rock* (New York: Marlowe, 2005), 3.

62. Isa Chandra Moskowitz, *Isa Does It: Amazing, Easy, Wildly Delicious Vegan Recipes for Every Day of the Week* (New York: Little, Brown, 2013), 171.

63. Isa Chandra Moskowitz and Terry Hope Romero, *Vegan Cupcakes Take Over the World: 75 Dairy-Free Recipes for Cupcakes That Rule* (New York: Marlowe, 2006), 18.

64. Moskowitz, *Vegan with a Vengeance*, 111.

65. "Post Punk Kitchen Episode 3: The Passover Episode," YouTube, posted by Isa Chandra, July 27, 2013, http://www.youtube.com/watch?v=i5ahFA1k_fU.

66. Moskowitz, *Isa Does It*, 201.

67. Isa Chandra Moskowitz and Terry Hope Romero, *Veganomicon: The Ultimate Vegan Cookbook*, 10th anniversary ed. (Cambridge, MA: Da Capo Press, 2017), 74.

68. Moskowitz, *Vegan with a Vengeance*, 98.

69. Ibid., 111.

70. Isa Chandra Moskowitz, *Vegan Brunch: Homestyle Recipes Worth Waking Up For—From Asparagus Omelets to Pumpkin Pancakes* (Cambridge, MA: Da Capo Press, 2009), 53.

71. Moskowitz, *Isa Does It*, 171.

72. Isa Chandra Moskowitz and Terry Hope Romero, *Veganomicon: The Ultimate Vegan Cookbook* (Cambridge: Da Capo Press, 2007), 182.

73. Jeremiah Satterfield, Patrick Aleph, and Michael Sabani (eds.), *NewKosher Cookbook: Your Favorite Jewish Vegan Recipes!* (Atlanta: NewKosher/PunkTorah, 2011), 19.

74. Ibid., 16.

75. Ibid.

76. Ibid., 17.

77. Ibid.

78. Ibid., 19–20.

6 Opening the Tent

Jewish Veganism as an Expression of an Ecological Form of Judaism

ADRIENNE KRONE

In April 2016, I discovered that hosting a vegan Passover Seder was difficult in ways that hosting vegetarian Passover Seders for the previous six years had not been. There were new hurdles to leap, and while I successfully managed to find adequate replacements for the animal products on the Seder plate, I fell flat in attempting to make a vegan version of the Passover classic matzo ball soup. My cohost was pessimistic about my attempt. She decided to bring her own vegetarian matzo ball soup long before my first batch of vegan matzo balls hit the boiling water (whereupon they almost immediately lost their shape and dispersed into a thin matzo film floating on top of the bubbles). After the similarly terrible second and third attempts, each with a different binder mixed in to replace the eggs, I stared in complete frustration at the three bowls full of cooked matzo mush I had produced and sent my cohost a text message to let her know she was right, I could not make vegan matzo balls. In the end, I drew on the knowledge I had gained through many years of watching cooking competition shows and baked the vegan matzo mush in a mini muffin tin. The end products, which I decided to call matzo muffins, were an odd but adequate complement to the vegan broth. The fifteen guests who attended the Seder were a mix of Jewish and not Jewish and represented a wide dietary spectrum, from vegan to omnivorous. They all dutifully tried the vegan and vegetarian versions of matzo ball soup. The empty pot of vegetarian soup and the pile of vegan matzo muffins that remained after the meal offered a clear verdict.

Preparing for Passover was the first true difficulty I had experienced after transitioning from vegetarian to vegan. The two chapters dedicated to Passover in the 2015 volume *The Jewish Vegan* suggest that I was not alone in this particular struggle.[1] Passover is a holiday that comes with stringent food restrictions: a prohibition on leavened bread and all foods that resemble it, including *kitniyot* for some Ashkenazim. *Kitniyot* is a category that includes the vegan staples beans and rice. This presents a rather steep challenge when it is combined with the similarly rigid restrictions of veganism: abstaining from all animal products and by-products.² Observing Passover as a Jewish vegan requires considering these two aspects of their identity in relation to each other. The fact that many Jewish vegans are practicing and writing about Passover proves that these two identities are not competing but are becoming syncretic.

In this chapter, I discuss the relationship between "Jewish" and "vegan" identities and the ecological worldview that I argue ties them together. Jewish vegans tend to see humans as one animal among many. Their sense of responsibility toward their fellow creatures allows them to combine two identities that each offer a dietary system undergirded by a set of values that influence many aspects of their lives. Jewish vegans live out their identities in many ways beyond consumption. I conclude this essay with a discussion of how these values are shaped and lived in the context of the Jewish community farming movement. The Jewish vegans I encountered on one Jewish farm offer an example of how these identities influence one another in spaces designed to encourage ecological thinking and living. For Jewish vegans, the set of values that enables their syncretic identity is based on an ecological outlook that requires humans to consider their relationship with other organisms and the Earth and informs what they eat and how they live.

JEWISH IDENTITIES

Shaul Magid, scholar of modern Judaism, describes the search for new Jewish identities in the postethnic United States in his book *American Post-Judaism*. He uses the terms *postethnic* and *post-Judaism* to describe what he sees as a problem: the strategies Jews usually deploy for survival assume "an 'ethnic' root of Jewish identity."³ This is the idea that Judaism has been passed from generation to generation and must continue to be passed on in that way if the religion is to survive. Magid argues that Judaism is postethnic because "Jewishness" is no longer the sole ethnic identity of US Jews, so "Jewishness" must be balanced alongside other identities. Jews no longer identify solely as Jews, or even American Jews. Instead, they may identify as a Chinese American Jewish bisexual. Magid suggests that in the postethnic world, "identities are mixed" and "allegiances are more voluntary than inherited, more the result of consent rather than descent."⁴ Dietary identities may be viewed as an allegiance that is voluntary, though they may also be inherited. Magid's argument is compelling and provides a useful framework for a conversation about forms of Judaism that prioritize identities that are not ethnically based.

Magid offers his discussion of postethnic Judaism as a starting point for a conversation about contemporary US Judaisms. He raises two points that are particularly useful for a study of one such Judaism: Jewish veganism. First, he notes that the dissolution of the connection between Judaism and "peoplehood" allows for "new rubrics" for constructing Judaism.[5] This move away from peoplehood allows for a new vision of the Jewish community that allows room for humans and nonhuman animals to be considered. Postethnic Judaism allows Jews to reconsider their place in the world. No longer tethered to notions of peoplehood and the survival of Judaism, Jews are free to focus their attention on the future of all people or all of creation. The second aspect of postethnic Judaism that Magid illuminates is that in this era "the past requires a combination of translation and abandonment, or translation *as* abandonment."[6] Magid contends that this approach, which he identifies in the Jewish Renewal movement, "reimagines Judaism from its very roots without the obligatory tie to *halakha* or its past authority."[7] So postethnic Jews do not have to take on the traditions of their grandparents. Instead, they feel free to seek answers and inspiration directly from texts and traditions from other communities of Jews and non-Jews.

Magid pinpoints a tendency among contemporary Jews to invent and reinvent new Judaisms that reconsider the past and allow for religious syncretism. He even mentions that they are "using Judaism as a template for world ecological concerns."[8] One might phrase that another way: some Jews are using world ecological concerns as a template for creating new Jewish spaces and practices. This flexible approach to tradition is crucial for a study of Jewish vegans. Using Magid's language, Jewish veganism can be seen as a contemporary translation of the dietary laws of the Bible by a community of people who are concerned with the realities of industrial agriculture and who abandoned the old system of *kashrut* in favor of a new set of dietary laws. Jews are not the only adherents to this set of plant-based dietary laws, so I now turn my attention to veganism and the construction of vegan identities.

VEGAN IDENTITIES

In an essay titled "Quasi-Religious American Foodways: The Cases of Vegetarianism and Locavorism," Benjamin Zeller scholar of religion in the United States, proposes that applying a religious studies lens allows for a better understanding of how some foodways go from food choices to what he describes as "ways of life, systems of values, and symbols of meaning."[9] Zeller describes the conversion process of vegans and vegetarians as well as locavores (who consume only food grown and produced where they live). He uses data from oral histories he gathered. He identifies religious language in the stories people told about how they became vegetarians. The stories he includes describe people who experienced a "crisis of faith" on discovering that chicken is chicken and then converted to vegetarianism.[10] Zeller argues:

> Something analogous happens among foodway converts who recognize some sense of discomfort present in their lives, understand this discomfort as rooted in their food and eating patterns, and finally encounter people, texts, or movements that inspire them to reject their current foodways and follow new ones.[11]

The new foodways that the converts find and adopt are enacted in religious ways as well. Zeller explains: "Like religious beliefs, practices, and membership in religious communities, beliefs practices, and communities based on food help assuage such anxiety and root people in space and society."[12] When people experience a crisis, usually through exposure to realities of animal agriculture, they adopt a vegetarian diet, begin reading texts about vegetarianism, and connect with other vegetarians to move through the crisis and settle into a lifestyle that avoids further anxieties over the treatment of animals and their role in that system. Zeller describes conversions to vegetarianism and locavorism, but similar patterns emerge in other vegan narratives, as identified by two scholars of veganism, Barbara McDonald and Laura Wright.

McDonald's article, " 'Once You Know Something, You Can't Not Know It': An Empirical Look at Becoming Vegan," considers transitions to veganism in relation to Jack Mezirow's transformation theory.[13] McDonald interviewed twelve vegans and determined that their process required slightly different steps than the ten included in Mezirow's theory. She describes these steps as the "elements of the vegan learning process."[14] The process includes a consideration of who the person was before the learning experience, a catalytic experience that introduced the person to an aspect of animal cruelty, a period of repressing that knowledge, a period where they learned more about animal abuse or how to live as a vegan, a decision moment when the person makes the choice to become vegan, and finally the adoption of a worldview that "guides the vegan's new lifestyle."[15] This process incorporates more aspects of the process than the crisis moment-conversion-lifestyle model Zeller laid out. McDonald accounts for worldviews the person held previously and for the learning process that happens in between the crisis moment/catalytic experience and the conversion/transition to veganism. She also offers a description of a vegan worldview (similar to Zeller's "lifestyle"): "The vegans' transformed worldviews were shaped by a felt connection with nonhuman animals and with nature, the moral rightness of veganism, and by experiencing the world as a vegetarian and vegan."[16] McDonald describes some of the difficulties the vegan participants experienced when they shared their worldview with their families and friends and the effects their transitions had on those relationships. Her approach offers a more holistic description of the process vegans go through than Zeller. These participants did not convert and adopt a new lifestyle on their own. They were people with pasts whose transitions were often made more complicated by social relationships. She describes vegans who struggled with their identities as marginalized individuals.[17]

The vegan learning process McDonald describes bears a strong resemblance to the one laid out by Zeller, except that it opens up the possibility that a vegan worldview can and often does exist alongside other perspectives the person had prior to their vegan learning process. Zeller's use of the terms *quasi-religion* and *convert* imply that the person transitions completely. He describes a person who converted to both locavorism and a new religion who told him, "I am a pathfinder in both."[18] This dual conversion leaves the reader with the impression that these identities are functioning separately. McDonald allows for a consideration of syncretic identities through her attention to the person who existed before they entered the vegan learning process. She explains:

> Each individual came to the learning event with a unique personal and cultural history, identified in this study as who I was. These histories shaped their original worldviews and, for most participants, influenced their learning to become vegan.[19]

Including the participants' past experiences and worldviews in their transition to veganism enabled McDonald to recognize how these vegans maintain multiple identities. They did not "convert" to veganism and adopt it as a quasi-religious practice; instead they went through a learning process wherein veganism was influenced by and subsequently influenced their worldview. From this, we could imagine a Jewish person who is motivated by Jewish tradition to learn more about veganism, adopt veganism, and incorporate a worldview that includes a connection to nonhuman animals into their preexisting Jewish identity.

In her book *The Vegan Studies Project: Food, Animals, and Gender in the Age of Terror*, Laura Wright adds even more complexity to this discussion of vegan identities. First, Wright describes veganism as an identity category that functions like race, sexual orientation, and religion and also as a practice.[20] In addition, Wright notes a tension that arises from the fact that "vegan identity is both created by vegans and interpreted, and therefore, reconstituted by and within contemporary (non-vegan) media."[21] This reality is related to the social difficulties that McDonald's interviewed vegans encountered at the end of their processes. Vegans are not the sole authors of the worldview they adhere to. As they avoid animal products for ethical reasons or for their health and develop a worldview that incorporates their new values, the people around them are similarly interpreting their actions. Wright offers this grim perspective: "Being vegan, no matter where and when, has always constituted a nonnormative position, one that has often inspired persecution."[22] It is worth mentioning that this description would work almost as well if the word *vegan* were replaced with *Jewish*. Wright's book offers an intersectional approach to veganism, where it is considered alongside gender, racial, and national identities, among others. This approach opens up a method for studying people with a multiplicity of identities that include veganism and Judaism.

Zeller, McDonald, and Wright all offer useful models for considering vegan identities. Zeller proposed that foodway conversions follow patterns similar to religious conversions. McDonald detailed the transition to veganism and allowed for the possibility of the development of syncretic identities through the vegan learning process. Finally, Wright offers an approach to the study of veganism that is similar to Magid's treatment of Judaism and allows for an attention to multiple aspects of a person's identity. Judaism and veganism are currently created and lived out in an era when multiple identities are the norm, and untangling those identities from one another and treating them as separate is a lost cause. Moving forward, "Jewish vegan" will be discussed as a syncretic identity in which each of the two pieces informs and enables the other, and both are informed by the adoption of an ecological worldview.

JEWISH VEGAN IDENTITIES

From this study of Jewish identities and vegan identities, it is clear that identities are worked out in relationship with others. The new forms of Judaism that have developed in Magid's postethnic age were forged in community spaces. Zeller, McDonald, and Wright all noted the importance of the community in the late stages of adopting veganism. Veganism is made possible by sharing resources, recipes, and stories. It is not surprising, then, that Jewish vegans are coming together to form communities. The interesting aspect of those communities is their inclusion of human and nonhuman members. The resources that are informing, sustaining, and growing the Jewish vegan community all use an ecological framework that considers humans as we exist in relation to each other and the nonhuman organisms with which we share the planet. The framework differs slightly across the small body of Jewish vegetarian and vegan literature, but this attention to humans as one organism among many pervades the genre.

There are two major texts on Jewish vegetarianism: Richard Schwartz's *Judaism and Vegetarianism* and Roberta Kalechofsky's *Vegetarian Judaism: A Guide for Everyone*. Both books take a similar approach and cover common topics. Schwartz and Kalechofsky both turn their attention to readings of biblical and rabbinic texts in the context of industrial agriculture. A shared set of values appears in both books. Schwartz's book includes chapters on *tza'ar ba'alei chayim*, which he translates as "compassion for animals," health, feeding the hungry, ecology, and peace.[23] Kalechofsky also divides her book into chapters focused on Jewish values: *pikuach nefesh* (guard your health), *tza'ar ba'alei chayim* (the pain of animals), *ba'al tashchit* (use nature prudently), *tzedakah* (charity), and *klal Israel* (community responsibility).[24] Although the connections between these tables of contents are clear in some cases, others require further explanation. Kalechofsky's chapter on *ba'al tashchit* (use nature prudently) and Schwartz's chapter on ecology both detail the environmental effects of animal agriculture and point to biblical precepts related to the protection of the Earth. Similarly, Schwartz's chapter on feeding the hungry includes a discussion of *tzedakah* and the Jewish responsibility to care for the Jewish community. These topics persist in the materials of Jewish Veg, a Jewish vegan organization in the United States. Their mission statement is "We encourage and help Jews to embrace plant-based diets as an expression of the Jewish values of compassion for animals, concern for health, and care for the environment."[25] The headings listed under a tab labeled "What's Jewish About Being Veg?" mirror the themes of the mission and include the following: "Enhancing Our Health," "Compassion for Animals," "What We Eat and the Environment," and "Feeding the World's Hungry." These four thematic areas—health, animal welfare, feeding the hungry, and the environment—exemplify the ecological-ethical framework that helped create and now supports Jewish vegetarianism and veganism. Even the recently published book *The Jewish Vegan* (edited by Rabbi Dr. Shmuly Yanklowitz), which appears on the surface (from section and chapter titles) to deal mainly with animal welfare, delves into the environmental effects of animal agriculture, the health benefits of veganism, and the need to feed humans directly instead of feeding animals to feed humans.[26]

It is interesting to note that Schwartz actually uses the term *ecology* and argues that vegetarianism and ecology are related in his chapter on this topic. He writes, "The aims of vegetarians and ecologists are similar: simplify our life styles, have regard for the earth and all forms of life, and thereby apply the knowledge that 'the earth is the Lord's.' "[27] Schwartz offers an explanation for why Jews tend to approach veganism ecologically. He explains, "Everything belongs to God. We are to be stewards of the earth, to see that its produce is available for all God's children."[28] Schwartz points to an imperative that shows up frequently in Jewish vegetarian and vegan resources. The Earth and all of its inhabitants are sacred, and humans, in these interpretations often Jews in particular, have a responsibility to protect creation. This idea of stewardship is not unique to Jewish texts about vegetarianism and veganism. Ellen Bernstein, editor of *Ecology and the Jewish Spirit*, writes in the introduction "The Creation story, Jewish law, the cycle of holidays, prayers, *mitzvot* (good deeds), and neighborly relations all reflect a reverence for the land and a viable practice of stewardship."[29] Bernstein had been studying the environment and experimented with different religious paths before finding the answers she was looking for in Judaism. She explains: "Judaism supported the values I was teaching: that Creation is sacred and humanity has the awesome and wonderful responsibility to guard and preserve it."[30] The Jewish environmentalism movement has grown since Bernstein published this in 1998, so it appears there is a community of Jewish people who agree with her. Approaching Judaism with stewardship in mind has led to the formation of education programs, camps, farms, bike rides, food conferences, and numerous other organizations and activities that allow Jews to explore and embrace an ecological outlook.

For many Jews, the abuses of industrial meat production conflict with how they understand their role as humans and as Jews in the world. The crisis moment that influences many Jews to become vegans is an inability to reconcile the worldview that encourages Jews to see themselves as stewards of their fellow creatures with the modern abuses that fly in the face of that vision. Stewards of the Earth and consumers of factory-farmed meat and animal by-products are not identities that work well together. There are a number of solutions to this irreconcilable reality, one of which is Jewish veganism. Embracing Jewish veganism allows people to live the values that encourage them to consider the lives and well-being of human and nonhuman animals and the Earth at every meal.

JEWISH VEGAN IDENTITY IN PRACTICE

Ellen Bernstein suggested that being in community with other Jews can help people "walk the stewardship path."[31] She founded Shomrei Adamah, "Keepers of the Earth," which she describes as "the first organization dedicated to cultivating the ecological thinking and practices that are integral to Jewish life."[32] This group inspired the founding of many others that proliferate today. The Jewish communal farming movement, currently comprising about twenty organizations, represents a practical ecological strategy enacted by Jews in North America. Hundreds of Jewish Americans are engaged in growing food, raising animals, preserving and creating habitats for pollinators, and planting indigenous species to restore native ecologies. These farms offer a valuable lens into how Jewish vegan identities are shaped, how they inform Jewish practice, and how they change.

A number of these farms offer fellowship programs for young adults that allow them to learn about sustainable agriculture and its connection to Jewish tradition. Through ethnographic fieldwork on sixteen of these farms, I have noticed that while some participants in these fellowship programs do experience a learning process that results in them adopting veganism, others arrive at the fellowship because they are already vegans. These sustainable farms offer an enticing opportunity for Jewish vegans looking for a community where they can live out their ecological values and continue their learning process. To provide a clear example of the different ways veganism can be explored on Jewish farms, I discuss two participants in the same program. Amelia and Rose (both pseudonyms) participated in the Adamah fellowship at the Isabella Freedman Jewish Retreat Center in summer 2015. They were both vegans when I met them, but their stories were remarkably different. The fact that there were two vegans in a group of ten fellows suggests that Adamah is either attracting or creating vegans because that percentage is much higher than one would expect. My conversations with them make it clear that Adamah is, in fact, doing both.

When I sat down with Amelia, I asked if the fact that Adamah was a Jewish program had appealed to her. She told me that she was "not into Judaism."[33] Her sister had found the program and thought Amelia would be interested. She reflected, "She knows I'm interested in farming and she knows that I'm a vegan, so I'm interested in organic stuff and health and being active."[34] She found the program was intriguing for these reasons and because she was a college student majoring in environmental policy. Amelia noticed that other participants had moved toward vegetarianism and veganism after arriving at Adamah, especially after they witnessed a kosher slaughter demonstration. Amelia experienced the reverse, remarking, "I think in some ways my diet brought me here, so that's kind of an interesting twist."[35] I asked her why she became a vegan, and she explained that it was not just one thing. She was initially drawn to the health aspects, but as she began reading about veganism, she "developed a really strong ethical connection to it."[36] This connection included a sense that "it's really wrong to kill other living things" and that "it's just so much better for the environment."[37] She continued, "When you're vegan, you use so much less resources, it's crazy."[38] Amelia summed up her veganism definitively: "If I can nourish myself very well without consuming animal products and save the environment and my health and animals at the same time, then I don't know why everyone isn't doing it."[39]

For Amelia, veganism is the obvious option, and the three reasons she listed are reminiscent of those described in the Jewish vegetarianism and veganism resources: health, animal welfare, and the environment.

Amelia's interest in living in a Jewish community dedicated to sustainable agriculture was motivated by her veganism, and her participation in the program helped her develop a Jewish identity as well. Amelia had attended a Jewish day school as a child and she didn't connect with the Judaism she experienced there in the morning prayer sessions. However, she enjoyed Avodat Lev, the morning prayer sessions at Adamah. She explained why she thought this was the case: "I think it's [Avodat Lev] more spiritual. We meditate, we sing beautiful songs. Even though they are prayers, they're just beautiful."[40] Amelia thought that the difference may have been in the approach to the morning prayers at Adamah, noting that "it's more just a holistic idea that the morning prayers are meant to start you."[41] Amelia entered Adamah with an interest in sustainable agriculture because of her veganism; participating in the Jewish aspects of the program was allowing her to explore aspects of her Jewish identity that she had not previously embraced.

Rose's experience at Adamah offers the opposite perspective. Rose was drawn to Adamah because of her strong Jewish identity. She had moved through a few different Jewish communities prior to her arrival including a Zionist summer camp and an Orthodox community. She was still seeking: "What I needed in my life was a space to explore my Jewish identity."[42] She had not found the Jewish practice she was seeking at Adamah. The Shabbat services and Avodat Lev sessions were too unstructured for her taste. She told me that was a big part of her religious practice and that she liked "doing tradition for tradition's sake."[43]

Rose was particularly interested in a program that would allow her to farm because she connects with land-based Jewish traditions. However, she found that aside from weeding, which she loved, she was not enjoying farming as much as she thought she would. She reflected, "I think I philosophize farming a lot more than actually being here."[44] However, since being at Adamah, she had found a way to live out her ecological Judaism in a way that did not involve farming. The kosher chicken slaughter that all the fellows watch as part of their program proved to be a crisis moment for Rose. She remembered her thoughts as she watched, "It was a kosher chicken slaughter, and they tried to make it seem like it was holy, but it still seemed very much like it wasn't."[45] She became a vegan that day. She explained her choice as one motivated by an interest in being a peaceful presence in the world: "I just realized that there's so much violence in the world, and there's only so much I could do about it. But I just felt like I didn't want to contribute to putting violence in the world. Eating animal products is a violent act."[46] Rose was reading Matthew Scully's book *Dominion* around that time, and his description of factory farming added to her conviction that becoming a vegan would help her avoid putting violence into the world. Although Rose did not list the common aspects of veganism that I discussed already, her interest in not being a violent presence in the world may be considered a type of ecological ethics. Her decision is premised on the idea that humans are currently a violent presence in the world and that stepping back from the violent systems involved in animal agriculture was a good solution to avoiding that violence. Rose was also reconsidering other areas where her actions might be perceived as violent. Although she found weeding "cathartic," she did worry about whether her love for killing weeds meant she was "a psychopath."[47] Rose came into Adamah with an interest in exploring her Jewish identity and found herself reevaluating her relationships with both animals and plants along the way.

Both Amelia and Rose explored veganism and Judaism while they were at Adamah and their journeys were quite different. Amelia was drawn to Adamah because of her veganism and was using her time there to rethink aspects of her plant-based diet. She was becoming conscious of the effects of her habit of buying fruits like mangoes and bananas that had to travel long distances to reach the shelves at her grocery store in Ohio. Meanwhile, Rose had experienced a crisis moment and was moving through the early stages of learning about and practicing veganism. She arrived with a lot of good Jewish experiences in mind and was looking forward to exploring another, whereas Amelia was initially less interested in the Jewish aspects of the program. In the end, Amelia found the prayer experiences at Adamah meaningful, and Rose found them to be a bit too detached from traditional Jewish liturgy for her taste. However, some aspects of the program appealed to both women. Amelia loved the physical labor she experienced on the farm, and Rose had found a meditative practice in weeding. They enjoyed learning about the connections between Judaism and agriculture and found those parts of Judaism meaningful. At Jewish community farms like Adamah, young adults are able to explore and experiment with Jewish vegan identities in ways that are meaningful to them. They do so in a supportive community of people whose ecological ethic binds them together.

CONCLUSION

Jewish vegan identities are emblematic of the postethnic Judaism Magid describes because they are always in flux. As I write this, Jewish vegans all over the world are studying Jewish tradition, experimenting with new Jewish practices, and finding new ways to live out their ecological values. Almost immediately after I experienced the great matzo ball disaster, I began doing the same to prepare for future Passover Seders. In the two chapters of *The Jewish Vegan* about Passover, the authors offer different visions of how vegans can approach the holiday in new ways.

In "New Traditions for a Vegan Passover," Jacob Ari Labendz offers thoughtful ideas for replacing the animal products that traditionally grace the Seder plate. Instead of using items that resemble their animal counterparts, as I did with a roasted pepper standing in for a shank bone and a small round white turnip acting as an egg, he suggests looking back to tradition to create new traditions. His ideas include colorful edible flowers to evoke spring and renewal and a new tradition of writing goals for a personal sacrifice to commemorate the sacrifice of the paschal lamb.[48]

In "My Plans for a Meaningful Vegan Passover," Mayim Bialik—actress, neuroscientist, and vegan—offers ideas for vegans who avoid *kitniyot* during Passover. Instead of returning to the texts to revisit the prohibition of *kitniyot*, as some Jewish vegans do, Bialik suggests that there are plenty of *kitniyot* and animal product free foods that can sustain vegans throughout the holiday. Quinoa, avocados, and nuts are described as staple foods for vegans on Passover.[49]

The approaches these authors and I adopted as we prepare for Passover exemplify Magid's suggestion that postethnic Judaism allows people to use or not use Jewish traditions of the past as they embrace new Judaisms. Jewish veganism motivated all three of us to make conscious decisions about what we would serve at our Seders and during the week. I tried to replicate the Seder plates and meals I was raised with using plant-based alternatives, which in the case of *kitniyot* meant revisiting the prohibition and determining that I would consume beans and rice during Passover, despite my Ashkenazi background. Bialik found protein sources that would allow her to avoid *kitniyot* and feed her family during Passover. Labendz offered new interpretations based on the symbolic meanings of the foods that traditionally adorn Seder plates. All three approaches were useful and meaningful for us, and all three represent our blended identities as Jewish vegans. Passover predicaments like these arise because Jewish vegans are dedicated to an ecological ethic that finds people prioritizing their relationship with all creation and reimagining the role and shape of Judaism in their lives along the way. Serving meat, roasting a shank bone, or cracking an egg to create successful matzo balls is simply not an option. The Haggadah, the text used for the Passover Seder, keeps us looking toward the future every Passover with hope. The spaces that have been and are being created for Jewish vegans to share resources, explore their identities, and repair human relationships with animals, plants, and land allow for a similarly optimistic outlook. Next year in Jewish veganism!

NOTES

1. Shmuly Yanklowitz (ed.), *The Jewish Vegan* (Shamayim V'Aretz Institute, 2015).

2. People approach both Passover and veganism in different ways. For the purposes of this chapter, veganism is defined as a plant-based diet where all animal foods, including meat, dairy, eggs, and honey, are not consumed. I return to a discussion of the Passover restrictions, and *kitniyot* in particular, in the conclusion.

3. Shaul Magid, *American Post-Judaism: Identity and Renewal in a Postethnic Society* (Bloomington: Indiana University Press, 2013), 1.

4. Ibid., 5.

5. Ibid., 4.

6. Ibid., 3; emphasis in original.

7. Ibid., 8.

8. Ibid., 34.

9. Benjamin E. Zeller, "Quasi-Religious American Foodways: The Cases of Vegetarianism and Locavorism," in *Religion, Food, and Eating in North America*, ed. Benjamin E. Zeller et al. (New York: Columbia University Press, 2014), 295.

10. Ibid., 297.

11. Ibid., 307.

12. Ibid., 309.

13. Barbara McDonald, "'Once You Know Something, You Can't Not Know It': An Empirical Look at Becoming Vegan," *Society and Animals* 8, no. 1 (2000): 1.

14. Ibid., 2.

15. Ibid., 6.

16. Ibid., 15.

17. Ibid., 17.

18. Zeller, "Quasi-Religious American Foodways," 308.

19. McDonald, "'Once You Know Something,'" 6.

20. Laura Wright, *The Vegan Studies Project: Food, Animals, and Gender in the Age of Terror* (Athens: University of George Press, 2015), 6.

21. Ibid., 2.

22. Ibid., 6.

23. Richard H. Schwartz, *Judaism and Vegetarianism* (New York: Lantern Books, 2001).

24. Roberta Kalechofsky, *Vegetarian Judaism: A Guide for Everyone* (Marblehead, MA: Micah Publications, 1998). The transliterations and translations here are Kalechofsky's.

25. "Mission Statement," Jewish Veg, https://www.jewishveg.org/about (accessed August 31, 2016).

26. Yanklowitz (ed.), *The Jewish Vegan*.

27. Schwartz, *Judaism and Vegetarianism*, 94.

28. Ibid., 80.

29. Ellen Bernstein, *Ecology and the Jewish Spirit: Where Nature and the Sacred Meet* (Woodstock, NY: Jewish Lights Publishing, 1998), 11.

30. Ibid., 11–12.

31. Ibid., 250.

32. Ibid., 12.

33. Amelia, interview with author, Isabella Freedman Jewish Retreat Center, July 8, 2015.

34. Ibid.

35. Ibid.

36. Ibid.

37. Ibid.

38. Ibid.

39. Ibid.

40. Ibid.

41. Ibid.

42. Rose, interview with author, Isabella Freedman Jewish Retreat Center, June 29, 2015.

43. Ibid.

44. Ibid.

45. Ibid.

46. Ibid.

47. Ibid.

48. Jacob Labendz, "New Traditions for a Vegan Passover," in *The Jewish Vegan*, ed. Shmuly Yanklowitz (Shamayim V'Aretz Institute, 2015), 115–16.

49. Mayim Bialik, "My Plans for a Meaningful, Vegan Passover," in *The Jewish Vegan*, ed. Shmuly Yanklowitz (Shamayim V'Aretz Institute, 2015), 164.

7 A Linguistic Appraisal
Jewish Perceptions of Animal Suffering

VICTORIA GREENSTONE AND SHLOMI SHMUEL

> Think occasionally of the suffering of which you spare yourself the sight.
> —Albert Schweitzer

Albert Schweitzer was a prominent Alsatian theologian and philosopher in the early twentieth century, as well as a renowned musician and doctor. In 1952, he was awarded the Nobel Peace Prize for what he considered to be his life's most important legacy, the "Reverence for Life" philosophy. Influenced by Jainism and the value of nonviolence, his ideology stressed that "I am life that wills to live in the midst of life that wills to live"[1] and that "we are brothers and sisters to all living things, and owe to all of them the same care and respect, that we wish for ourselves."[2] In keeping with his philosophy, Schweitzer was a vehement opponent of colonialism and European treatment of indigenous populations. He also considered vegetarianism to be an important application of his philosophy and became increasingly committed to the lifestyle toward the end of his life. His main ethical concern was the acceptance, validation, and preservation of all life.

Similarly, Judaism values life above anything else. Virtually any commandment can and must be overridden if that action can save a life. Unlike Schweitzer, however, Jewish sources make a distinction between human and animal life. In Genesis, it is clearly written that man has "dominion over the fish of the sea, and over the fowl of the air, and over every living thing that creeps upon the earth" (Genesis 1:28). Humanity is called on to be stewards of the Earth and treat animals with compassion. There are dozens of directives in the Tanakh that specifically deal with the proper treatment of animals and ban any unnecessary cruelty.[3] These are collectively referred to as the biblical mandate of *tza'ar ba'alei chayim*. Although these instructions are specific, most of them refer to agricultural practices that many modern Jews do not encounter or take part in through the course of their daily lives. Instead, scholars and rabbis have extrapolated the essence behind the instructions and, combined with *kashrut* laws, informed the modern understanding of the relationship between humans and animals.

Could this understanding of Jewish law also be compatible with a more egalitarian view like Schweitzer's or the one promoted by vegan culture? A topical glance at consumption habits in Israel,[4] recently named one of the most vegan countries, suggests that more and more Jews believe so.[5] As of 2015, 8 percent of Israelis were vegetarian,[6] and another 5 percent eschewed animal products altogether (a total of 13 percent).[7] This shows an astounding 400 percent growth over only five years; in 2010, only 2.6 percent of the population was vegetarian or vegan. Food consumption habits are not simply palatal preferences. They represent an active espousal of identity and the acceptance or rejection of cultural values and norms. The numbers seem to indicate an interesting shift in Jewish thought and culinary culture regarding the value of animal lives.

While roughly 80 percent of the Israeli Jewish populace self-identify as secular or traditional,[8] cultural practices are often rooted in a religious past. There is not, however, a unanimous consensus among scholars as to what Judaism's stance on abstaining from animal products means. British anthropologist Mary Douglas, an advocate of literary analysis of biblical myth, explores the concept of purity and taboo and finds that "the valorization of a purely herbivore existence is consistently considered suspect and problematic."[9] She points to the story of Cain and Abel:

> Now Abel kept flocks, and Cain worked the soil. In the course of time Cain brought some of the fruits of the soil as an offering to the Lord. And Abel also brought an offering—fat portions from some of the firstborn of his flock. The Lord looked with favor on Abel and his offering, but on Cain and his offering he did not look with favor. (Genesis 4:2–5)

Following the Lord's disappointment with his meatless offering, Cain becomes enraged and kills his brother. Réné Girard buttresses Douglas's claim with God's proclamation in the story of Noah that "every inclination of the human heart is evil from childhood" (Genesis 8:21). He argues that man is naturally violent and that the plant-based lifestyle does not provide a sufficient outlet for natural aggression, leading Cain to take out his fury on his brother.[10] Girard positions vegetarianism as "a symbol of some lost ideal, of a paradisiacal alternative."[11]

Other rabbinical scholars agree on this last point and instead use it as the foundation for their argument that vegetarianism is ideal and the lifestyle God originally intended. In the creation story, God bequeaths unto humans and animals "every seed-bearing plant on the face of the whole earth and every tree that has fruit with seed in it" for nourishment (Genesis 1:29). The Garden of Eden is therefore under a divine vegan mandate. Only after Genesis 9:3, during the flood of Noah, does God allow the consumption of animals. According to Gary Rendsburg, "the consumption of meat is a compromise, a divine acceptance of human inability to adhere to the utopia established at creation."[12] Rav Kook champions this concept of meat as a concession, but only as a temporary measure. While the move to carnivorous diets "testifies to the problems inherent in human nature," he suggests that such practices will become obsolete in the messianic age.[13] The messianic age will signify a return to the paradise of creation where "the wolf will live with the lamb and the leopard will lie down with the goat" (Isaiah 11:6). All animals, including humans, will live in harmony and purity and will not cause death and destruction by upholding a vegan existence.

Regardless of whether or not people are influenced directly by the biblical stories and rabbinical scholars, ethical considerations are a strong motivator for abstaining from animal-based diets. A survey of twenty-first-century vegans (of all religions) in the United States and the United Kingdom found that 87 percent of respondents stated they were vegan for ethical/moral reasons,[14] trumping other reasons such as health or environmental consciousness.[15] One of the major factors in the ethical argument for meat abstinence centers on the morality of compassion and suffering.[16] However, these are semantically vague terms that can mean vastly different things to different audiences. Our research aims to clarify the meaning of suffering, specifically animal suffering, in a Jewish context to better understand the growth of Jewish veganism.

DATA COLLECTION AND METHODOLOGY

To collect data, we created a semi-structured survey in both English and Hebrew that was then advertised through social and personal networks (see the Appendix to this chapter). The sample is undoubtedly opportunistic and not representative of all Jewish communities around the world, but it was meant to be an exploratory study since there is relatively little literature on the topic. The survey was closed once we reached 100 respondents from the United States (English version) and 100 from Israel (Hebrew version). The surveys were anonymous, and only adults above the age of eighteen were allowed to participate.

Due to the probative nature of the study, an abbreviated version of grounded theory was deemed the most appropriate methodology precisely because of its focus on open-mindedness. Grounded theory was born from the collaboration of US sociologists Barney Glaser and Anselm Strauss in the mid-1960s after their study on the interactions between terminally ill patients and medical personnel, documented in their book *Awareness of Dying* (1965).[17] They were disillusioned with the domination of quantitative positivist ideologies in the social sciences and "criticized the 'overemphasis' of verifying theories to the detriment of actually generating the theory itself."[18] Many of the existing theories were also based on a priori assumptions and deductive logic. Glaser and Strauss advocated for theory creation with an inductive approach based on empirical data to create more robust hypotheses, which could then bridge the "embarrassing gap between theory and empirical research."[19]

The methodology is "comparative, iterative, and interactive," relying on the use of multistage coding and category identification to create a theoretical framework.[20] This is accomplished by constant comparative analysis in which the researcher collects data and performs the analysis simultaneously. Initial analysis can include grouping similar data under descriptive labels, but as more data are introduced, the analysis should tend toward increasing abstraction and the use of analytic rather than descriptive labels.[21] By using labels that speak to the rationale of a phenomenon instead of simply describing it, the researcher can develop a more nuanced framework and more easily identify covert relationships between categories. It is important to distinguish between grounded theory coding and content analysis. In the former, the codes emerge from the data itself, while the latter relies on a predefined coding scheme. Because of this, content analysis codes are designed to be mutually exclusive, whereas grounded theory coding is not so rigidly limited and can evolve and overlap throughout the analytical process.[22]

There are three levels of coding: open, axial, and selective.[23] Open coding is the initial phase, which consists of comparing and contrasting raw data to group concepts together into categories and subcategories. By means of constant comparison, originally broad categories are broken down into dimensions and properties based on the patterns in the data. This prevents research bias from creeping into the developing theory because "fracturing the data forces examination of preconceived notions and ideas" and constant comparison negates the tendency to sort data into a category where it does not empirically belong.[24] The next step is typically axial coding, where categories are related to one another through a "'coding paradigm' of conditions, context strategies (action/interaction), and consequences."[25] This type of coding draws heavily from the two main sociological underpinnings of grounded theory: pragmatism and symbolic interactionism.[26] Together, these concepts assert that phenomena are dynamic rather than static and that actors and investigators actively respond to conditions and consequences, constructing a unique interactional dynamic. While we espouse these beliefs wholeheartedly, we were limited to a noninteractive data-gathering technique (online surveys) and thus had to perform an abbreviated analysis. As such, it was impossible to use the strict coding paradigm espoused by Strauss and Corbin, which focuses on the "manifestation of 'process' and 'change' "; instead we used a more fluid paradigm which arranged the categories into hierarchies of subordinate, superordinate, and lateral concepts.[27] Following this step, the last stage in coding is selective coding. This requires the researcher to organize all the categories into a unified model, with one core phenomenon at the center and the rest of the categories arranged in some kind of cohesive structure, typically represented visually in a diagram or flow chart.

Aside from coding, grounded theory has several other central tenets that help guide robust theory formation. The first one is openness to the fullest degree possible. To this end, researchers are encouraged not to complete a literature review until partway through or after the completion of data collection so as not to taint the coding process with preconceived notions and expectations. To counteract this lack of prior foundation, grounded theorists engage in a practice of theoretical sampling to the point of saturation. Theoretical sampling consists of collecting additional data based on the categories that arise from the current sample. As new categories and relationships emerge, investigators can perform negative case analysis to see which instances do not fit the current theory and revise it accordingly. They can also include data from a wider population pool if the categories suggest that a certain type of respondent might provide new or beneficial information. This process allows for clarification and refinement of the preliminary open coding. Ideally, this theoretical sampling should be executed to the point of saturation, when new patterns or variations cease to materialize. Another crucial component to grounded theory methodology is continuous memo-writing. Through the data-collection, sampling, and coding processes, the researcher should record trends, possible categories, preliminary hypotheses, and any other miscellaneous introspective insights about the process itself.[28] This helps systematize the researcher's progression and organize the developing theory.

Our research project about Jewish attitudes toward animal suffering was originally conceptualized with a different methodology in mind, and therefore some of the initial experimental design is inconsistent with grounded theory recommendations. The survey as a medium was chosen due to its accessibility; it was deemed preferable to have a large sample size and geographic and demographic diversity instead of conducting more interactive interviews with a small group of people from the researchers' circles. While decreasing control of the interview and eliminating the possibility for directed theoretical sampling, the online survey avoids issues of data skewing that could arise from only speaking to people within one geographical community, denomination, or other community of practice. For the sake of equity across the surveys and in the hopes of getting a large enough sample, the surveys were closed after reaching 100 respondents instead of being guided by analytic saturation, although this was also achieved.

One last important difference to point out lies within the surveys themselves. The English survey meant for US Jews and the Hebrew survey for Israeli

Jews approach the question of religiosity and religious denomination differently. This was done to reflect the cultural differences in how religion is understood in the two countries. In the United States, almost 50 percent of Jews identify with the Reform and Conservative movements, while only 5 percent of Israeli Jews do.[29] These movements have gained prominence in Europe and North America as an alternative to Orthodoxy, but they have been bitterly battled in Israel by an Orthodox rabbinate. The Chief Rabbinate has issued multiple statements accusing these movements of encouraging intermarriage and assimilation and "engrav[ing] on their shield the uprooting of the Torah of the Jewish people from its essence and from its uniqueness."[30] As such, these labels have not gained popularity, and Israeli Jews instead prefer a system of four basic labels: *haredi* (ultra-Orthodox), *dati* (religious), *masorti*[31] (traditional), and *hiloni* (secular).[32] These labels also carry an assumed statement of religiosity. While someone in the United States might identify with the Conservative movement but be nonpracticing, Israeli Jews would label them as secular despite the denomination in which the person was raised. In our survey, we fleshed out these labels to include the option for people who might consider themselves ethnically Jews but religiously atheist or agnostic. We also separated the *masorti* label into two categories—religious and not religious—to clarify the respondent's level of religiosity within the denominational marker. No other questions were modified between the two surveys.

RESULTS

Due to the evolving nature of the analytic process under grounded theory, the results are most comprehensible when presented in a chronological fashion, mirroring the original process. A review of the literature relevant to certain categories or patterns is interwoven to provide a point of comparison between our findings and those of researchers studying similar concepts in other disciplines. It is not within the scope of this work, nor would it be particularly insightful, to go through every survey response and detail the codes that were assigned. Instead, selected responses are included as exemplars of the patterns being described. We also focus on the first open response question ("How do you define animal suffering?") as the context for our final model describing the Jewish understanding of animal suffering. The second question ("What are the acceptable boundaries of animal suffering for food consumption (if any)?") is the topic of future studies to assess the precision of the model built to answer the first question.

The initial survey results returned some anticipated trends and circular definitions and quite a few more unexpected and intriguing patterns. Out of the first twenty responses, half of the respondents cited pain, discomfort, or torture as necessary conditions for animal suffering. These were all grouped together under the label "pain." Five out of the ten who mentioned pain qualified their answers, adding specific conditions, causes, or purposes of pain that made it unacceptable. These responses included concepts of unnatural causes of pain, unnecessary or unprovoked pain, extensive pain, and pain that does not benefit humans or the animal. These were united under a label of "necessity/propriety." The first respondent's answer is reproduced here unaltered because it is indicative of both labels shown above as well as another two that are discussed below: "Animals living in cruel conditions or caused pain by [sic] unnaturally (i.e., by human causes)." The answer specifies that suffering includes pain that is made inappropriate by its unnatural causes. However, it also brings two new and important themes forward: the role of humans and unnaturalness. We discuss the role-of-humans theme because it was paramount to the creation of our first working hypothesis. (We revisit the idea of unnaturalness later because it becomes increasingly important in subsequent stages of analysis.) Upon observing the trends above, we reexamined the other respondents' answers for similar proclamations of humanity's guilt in the propagation of animal suffering. Out of the first twenty responses, three specifically named humans as the cause of suffering. We filed these away under the category of "agency." Five other responses did not specifically name humans but implicated them through their syntactic structuring; for example, "Killing the animal and putting it through pain." The use of the present progressive for the verbs *killing* and *putting* implies an actor. The respondent could have said "when an animal is killed and put through pain," which would have described suffering passively in a stative construction, forgoing the need to implicate an active agent. These kinds of responses were also deemed to be assigning agency, so we moved "agency" to a superordinate category; those who lexically asserted the role of humans were given the label "named (agency)" and those who syntactically presumed it were given the label "grammatically implied (agency)."

We explored this phenomenon in the Hebrew survey responses as well. Of the first twenty responses, three explicitly cited humans as responsible for animal suffering. One such example is:

צער בעלי חיים הוא הסבל הנגרם לבעלי חיים כתוצאה מפעולות אותן עושה (או לא עושה) האדם.
המטרה היא מניעה של צער בע"ח באמצעות ניהול אורח חיים טבעוני

(Animal suffering is suffering as a result of activities done to them [or not done to them] by man. The goal is the prevention of animal suffering by means of a vegan lifestyle.)

Just as in the English survey, another five responses implicated humans. Unlike English, Hebrew does not have a present progressive or equivalent syntactic tense. It does, however, have an imperative mood. In English, an imperative command such as "open the door" has the implied grammatical subject "you," which plays the semantic role of the agent. The imperative mood in English implies a second-person subject, but other languages have a form of imperative mood that marks first and third person as well. These are known as the cohortative and jussive moods, respectively. Modern English is considered a weakly inflected language relative to many others, meaning that it has lost or collapsed many of its morphological markers that could signify differences in tense, mood, aspect, number, gender, case, voice, or person. Of particular importance here, English does not call for marking verbs in the jussive mood; Hebrew does employ the jussive in written contexts for both third-person commands and negative commands in which the subject is not physically present or is not a specified addressee.[33] The English equivalent for this would be a general "you" instead of a statement aimed at a specific person. The following example shows one respondent's answer that employs the jussive (in bold) as a negative directive toward a general human audience, which serves to grammatically imply agency:

לא לפגוע בחיות בלי סיבה מוצדקת.

(**Do not harm** animals without a justified reason.)

While delving into the grammatical differences between Hebrew and English constructions of agency, we realized another difference that could have bearing on the way speakers view animals as compared with humans. In prescriptive English, animals are referred to with the genderless *it* that is also often used to describe objects; in Hebrew, animals are described with "חוא/היא" (he/she) exactly as humans are, and not with the genderless "זה" (it) reserved for things. Under the tenets of a weak Sapir-Whorf hypothesis,[34] we thought that the deictic usages in each language might influence how speakers of each dialect view and categorize animals: as closer to objects or to humans.[35] Of the English survey responses, all respondents used standard conventions or no deictic usage at all, except for four who made of use of *he*, *she*, or singular *they*. All Hebrew survey respondents used standard gendered deictic conventions or avoided deictics entirely in their answers.

To gauge whether respondents equated animals more with humans or objects, we created a category called "comparisons to humans" and counted the number of responses flagged with this code. Responses were subdivided into two categories: people who compared animal and human suffering and people who equated the two.[36] We hypothesized that Hebrew speakers would show higher incidences of both codes than would English speakers because of the grammatical rules governing deictic usage in their language. Table 7.1 shows the numbers of each code present in the data.

Table 7.1 "Comparisons to humans" code results by language

	English	Hebrew
Compared to human suffering	3	4
Equated to human suffering	8	2
Total "comparisons to humans"	11	6

Some examples of responses belonging to each category are shown in Table 7.2. The empiasrical evidence proved contrary to our expectations. We thought this could have been the result of opportunistic sampling and theorized that perhaps there were simply more vegetarians and vegans in the English sample. Quite surprisingly, the opposite was true. There were only nineteen respondents who identified as pescatarian, vegetarian, or vegan in the English sample, compared with forty-three in the Hebrew sample.

Table 7.2 Sample responses of "comparisons to humans" code

	English	Hebrew
Compared to human suffering	Putting animals through processes humans would not want to go through and that are unnecessary to the goal outcome.	לראות את כל החיות כיצורים עם רגש הראויים ליחס של כבוד. To see all the animals as beings with emotions that deserve to be respected.
Equated to human suffering	Emotional or physical. Animals suffer the same as human animals.	כל מעשה הפוגע ברווחת בעל חיים שלא לשם הגנה עצמית, דהיינו שווה ערך לחיי אדם. Any act that harms the welfare of an animal not in self-defense, meaning its life is equivalent to human life.

These findings forced us to examine our own biases and realize that ascribing to a particular diet did not equate with a particular worldview. We thought it would be useful to continue to look at other demographic information to see what correlated most with different views on animals. This line of induction led us to our first hypothesis regarding the core issue underlying how Jews understand animal suffering.[37] We hypothesized that the root phenomenon driving respondents' answers and conceptualizations was their position on speciesism, or the belief that humans are inherently of a different moral status than animals. It seemed logical to us that those who held animals in the same moral regard as humans were more likely to be meat restricting (vegans, vegetarians, and pescatarians) and would have lower thresholds for their definitions of animal suffering.

Y. Michael Barilan, a practicing physician and bioethicist, argues that speciesism is a precondition to justice. From the philosophical perspective, he contends that "justice itself presupposes the possibility of social life without one society member's life plan or well-being *inexorably* dependent on frustrating others."[38] He argues that animals cannot be considered members in a society of justice because moral sociability consists of the "unconditional disavowal of exploitations of other members."[39] As such, any predator's lifestyle is simply incompatible with the precepts of moral sociability. He also argues that an ethics of rights does not apply because it is impossible to acknowledge rights that necessarily always violate other rights.[40] For example, granting a lamb the right to life would directly violate a lion's right to sustenance. Instead, Barilan presents two ways of approaching the moral status of animals: recipient-dependent (E1) and agent-driven (E2).[41] The ethics of rights and justice described above fall squarely under E1 because they are decided based on the characteristics and lifestyles of the recipient. E2 ethics place the onus on the agent; Immanuel Kant in particular endorses this view, saying, "we must treat animals mercifully for the sake of cultivating our own virtues."[42]

Taking these dichotomous approaches into account, Barilan offers two possible solutions to the question of the moral status of animals. The first model is a weak contractarian-like justice founded on the concept of E1 ethics. It has an unspoken contract between humans and animals in which we "decree that we shall never exceed nature's ambit of pain and suffering; we shall not visit [animals] with levels of destructions and suffering that reach beyond the fate of [animals] in a human-free nature."[43] Following this implicit contract, consumption, minimal experimentation, infliction of pain, and slow alteration of habitat are all acceptable because they are imitations of natural processes. However, many of the current industry practices would be deemed intolerable under this contract because of their departure from natural practices. These include

> factory farming [which] systematically and irremediably frustrate[s] natural animal behavior[,] genetic manipulations much more radical than

naturally occurring mutations[,] disfiguring and unusually painful experiments[,] and grandiose projects [which alter] whole ecosystems, along with the lives of creatures therein contained.[44]

An E2-based model would be based on upholding humanity's higher values of stewardship, love, mercy, and kindness. The limits placed on animal suffering would go far beyond those listed above because philosophical concerns, rather than natural practices, would be taken as the measure of acceptability.

Barilan's E1/E2 model is particularly relevant and illuminating to our study because it accounts for the two most prominent trends found in the data: naturalness (E1) and the role of the person (E2). Our hypothesis then represents an extreme version of E2 ethics where the definition of animal suffering is dependent on not only applying human values to the treatment of animals regardless of recipient characteristics but also equating human and animal moral worth.

To test our theory, we returned to the categories of "agency" and "comparisons to humans." According to an E2 model, unacceptable animal suffering would be a direct result of a failure on humans' part to live up to the values of kindness, stewardship, and cruelty avoidance. To test this, we looked at the number of respondents whose answers were coded either "named agency" or "grammatically implied agency." In the English survey, only 11 percent of respondents directly named humans as the cause of animal suffering and 17 percent implied it, making a total of 28 percent. In the Hebrew survey, 16 percent named humans explicitly and 26 percent implied it for a total of 42 percent. In the broader context of all the codes amassed, the agency tags composed only 9.9 percent (28 out of 284 codes) and 18.6 percent (42 out of 226 codes) of the total codes in the English and Hebrew samples, respectively. These numbers do not support an E2 model as the core concept in Jews' understanding of animal suffering. In the demographic characteristics of the respondents, the most common type of respondent in this category was a nonreligious, female omnivore in both the Hebrew and English surveys. Tables 7.3 and 7.4 illustrate the exact breakdowns.

In addition, our hypothesis went a step further and assumed that those who held animals and humans in morally equivalent positions would be most likely to avoid causing animal suffering, particularly in the form of consumption. Although our theory was discredited, we looked at the "comparison to humans" code to see if this second assertion was correct. The results diverge in the English and Hebrew responses. In the English survey, three respondents compared human and animal suffering and eight more fully equated them. As seen in Table 7.5, omnivores presented the majority. Of the six, five equated human and animal suffering.

In the Hebrew survey, four respondents compared animal and human suffering in some way, and two equated the two. In this sample, however, the majority of respondents with this code were vegans (see Table 7.6). The data regarding diet preferences and attitudes of moral equivalence thus proved inconclusive. To fully explore this, further study needs to be conducted on a larger and more representative sample.

Table 7.3 Demographics of respondents with "agency" codes in English survey

	Male		Female		Other	
Gender	11	39.3%	16	57.1%	1	3.6%
	Yes		Middle		No	
Religious	4	14.3%	4	14.3%	20	71.4%
	Meat eating		Vegetarian/pescetarian		Vegan	
Diet	23	82.1%	5 (4P/1V)	17.9%	0	0.0%

Table 7.4 Demographics of respondents with "agency" codes in Hebrew survey

אחר (Other)		נקבה (Female)		זכר (Male)		
0%	0	58.5%	42	54.1%	71	מין (Gender)
לא (No)		בינונית (Middle)		כן (Yes)		
61.0%	52	20.12%	5	26.8%	11	דת (Religious)
טבעוני (Vegan)		צמחוני (Vegetarian/pescetarian)		אוכל כל (Meat eating)		

A Linguistic Appraisal 143

The demographic patterns we found echo findings reported in Deemer and Labao's study on the public concern with farm animal welfare. In their literature review, they found that women and other marginalized groups were more likely to be supportive of protecting animals under Kendall's "underdog hypothesis."[45] An abundance of literature supports the trend that women tend to care more about animal welfare in general, although some attribute this to other causes,

Table 7.5 Demographics of respondents with "comparisons to humans" codes in English survey

	Male		Female		Other	
Gender	2	18.2%	9	81.8%	0	0.0%
	Yes		Middle		No	
Religious	3	27.3%	3	27.3%	5	45.4%
	Meat eating		Vegetarian/pescetarian		Vegan	
Diet	6	54.5%	3	27.3%	2	18.2%

Table 7.6 Demographics of respondents with "comparisons to humans" codes in Hebrew survey

אחר (Other)		נקבה (Female)		זכר (Male)		
0%	0	7.66%	4	33.3%	2	מין (Gender)
לא (No)		בינונית (Middle)		כן (Yes)		
6.66%	4	7.16%	1	7.16%	1	דת (Religious)
טבעוני (Vegan)		צמחוני (Vegetarian/pescetarian)		אוכל כל (Meat eating)		
66.6%	4	7.16%	1	7.16%	1	תזונה (Diet)

such as women's gender roles and their frequent socialization into caretaker positions.[46] They also reported that in the literature as well as in their results, there is an inverse relationship between theological conservatism and religiosity (as measured by frequency of attendance) and concern for animal welfare.[47] This trend was attributed to the idea that those who are more theologically conservative tend to interpret biblical texts more literally and are more likely to "subscribe to the 'dominion' injunction in Genesis (1:24–26) [which proclaims] the ascendancy of human beings over all creation."[48] Although their research was performed within a Christian context, we find no reason that the findings would not also apply to Jewish beliefs, as the dominion view expressed in Genesis is a foundation of both religions. On the scale of religious conservatism, other studies grouped Jews and nonreligious people together in terms of tolerance, so there may be a skewing of the effects of religiosity in our sample.[49] After performing their survey, Deemer and Labao found that "women, younger people . . . and vegetarians hold less dominionistic views."[50] Similarly, an analysis of our survey under E2 ethics found nonreligious women were more likely to condemn humans for the mistreatment of animals in contemporary food industry practices. The results on the relationship between diet preferences and concerns with animal suffering were inconclusive in our sample.

After discovering that our first hypothesis was not grounded in the data we collected, we turned instead to the second model mentioned by Barilan—the E1 weak, contractarian-like justice based on naturalness. According to this understanding, animal distress is allowed to a degree because it mimics nature. This approach focuses less on philosophically situating animals in a moral hierarchy and more on maintaining the status quo. Our updated hypothesis asserts that the Jewish understanding of animal suffering centers on the idea of abuse and transgression of "reasonable" boundaries, namely, the natural circumstances present in the animal's habitat had it been born in the wild and never interacted with humans. Since this view is rooted in dominionistic principles with a few added restrictions, Deemer and Labao's work suggests that there may be a positive correlation between the diet, gender, and religion (religiosity and level of conservatism) of participants and codes expressing the theme of unnaturalness.

In the early stages of coding, it became apparent that many of the respondents were focused on logistical and physical aspects of the animals' lives and deaths. Originally unaware of our biased E2 mindset, we dismissed these as secondary concerns and were disgruntled by the lack of more philosophically driven answers that were in line with what we had anticipated. We coded them regardless but because we were looking elsewhere. We failed to notice just how prevalent these codes were proportional to the entire data set. Upon completion of secondary coding, we had compiled a total of 284 codes in thirteen categories and five metacategories. We reviewed the codes through the unnaturalness lens and found 102 flagged codes across nine categories. Simply from a statistical standpoint, these codes account for 35.9 percent of the data. After subtracting out the codes from categories that were unrelated to the circumstances of the animals' lives or deaths (such as deictics, agency, and comparisons to humans as discussed previously), unnaturalness accounts for 43 percent of the codes. It is also important to note that the coding paradigm was very conservative and excluded ambiguous codes that were not explicitly compared to natural circumstances. Three such examples were the codes "malnourished," "pain," and "discomfort" because conceivably these same circumstances could be envisioned in nature and no explicit reference point was given. There were sixty-five such codes; had they been included, codes associated with the unnaturalness phenomenon would have accounted for 70.5 percent of the data regarding the animals' circumstances.[51] These numbers suggest that the second hypothesis is much more representative of the data and that unnaturalness is indeed the core issue in Jews' endeavor to define the term *animal suffering*.

Although the numerical representation does help illuminate the overarching trends in the data, it does not supersede the words themselves. To provide a framework for the upcoming selected examples, Figure 7.1 shows a graphic representation of the categories and metacategories that were defined in our secondary coding. Our first hypothesis was based on codes in the categories of agency, deictics, and comparisons to humans. These all fell into the metacategory concerned with blame and acceptability because our guiding theoretical construct was an

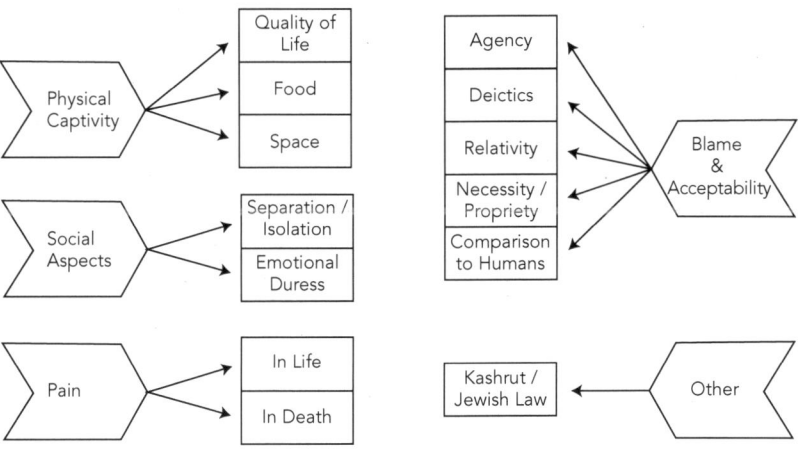

Figure 7.1. Secondary coding categories and metacategories.

E2 model that directly connected suffering on the part of animals with blame and criticism of human behaviors and, by extension, moral shortcomings.

The updated hypothesis includes codes in all subcategories included under physical captivity, social aspects, and pain, and those in the relativity and necessity/propriety subcategories under the blame/acceptability metacategory. Table 7.7 showcases selected examples of the data to buttress and clarify the argument we made statistically above. We have listed the categories and codes that were tagged for the response and indicated the relevant words that semantically convey the core issue: unnaturalness.

Table 7.7 Selected examples of secondary coding with response excerpts, codes, and metacategories

Category	Code	Data excerpts
Quality of life Space	"unnatural behavior" "unnatural habitat"	"Anything that forced the animal to do something **it wouldn't naturally do,** or be held in a location that **does not mimic its natural habitat**"
Necessity/propriety Quality of life Emotional duress Pain in life	"prolonged pain" "low quality of life" "emotional pain" "[physical] pain"	"Prolonged physical or emotional suffering of an animal, lowering its quality of life standard **compared to what otherwise be possible without the cause for pain and suffering**"
Space Pain in life Pain in life Pain in death	"captivity" "torture" "rape" "slaughter"	"Everything being done to an animal **that is not in nature** . . . captivity, rape, slaughter, torture"
Quality of life Emotional duress Emotional duress Emotional duress Pain in life Agency	"poor sanitation" "fear" "stress" "struggle to enjoy survival" "physical damage" "named"	"Acts such as housing animals in space with odors of other animals with tissue damage or who are in fear, psychological stress caused by **obstructing animal's instinct for self-protection, defense and survival**. Acts that cause damage to animal's bodies, organs and tissues by humans or other animals"

In accordance with grounded theory conventions, we have created a visual model to represent our hypothesis, shown in Figure 7.2.

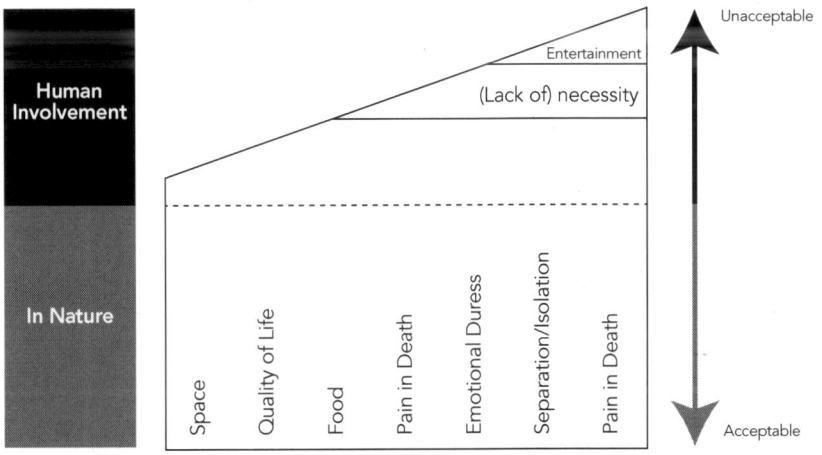

Figure 7.2. Visual representation of hypothesis regarding Jewish understanding of

In essence, we found that the Jewish understanding of animal suffering was not a categorical refusal of certain experiences (such as emotional duress or pain), but a call for moderation. The point of reference on the spectrum of acceptability is what happens in nature; animals in the wild still experience unpleasantries, so humans are not expected to create an idyllic life free of all suffering. Of course there are certain human practices that exceed the compass of "reasonable" discomfort that animals might encounter in the categories listed above. For example, an animal might be temporarily ensnared in the wild, but it will never be forced to spend its entire life in a small cage where it cannot turn around. Similarly, food may be scarce at times or animals might accidentally ingest something harmful; that, however, is a far cry from purposeful malnourishment or force-feeding with modified food that stimulates rapid growth. These types of activity would be above the dotted line that marks the threshold of acceptability.

The seven categories on the horizontal axis are listed from left to right in order of increasing code frequency in the survey results. Two codes were found exclusively in the human involvement domain and were found to always be in excess of acceptable boundaries: (lack of) necessity and entertainment. These were taken from the necessity/propriety and relativity categories, respectively, and were renamed for clarity. Essentially, an overwhelming majority of the survey respondents subscribe to a schema of nature as a temperate state where animals prey and are preyed on only as much as is necessary and for purely survival-driven purposes. As such, human practices such as factory farming are seen as transgressions of this implicit natural balance that bring unnecessary and disproportionate pain to the animals involved. This excess is only superseded by suffering inflicted on animals in the name of entertainment, according to the survey results. Several respondents pointed to hunting for pleasure and circuses as prime examples of a gross overstepping of natural boundaries.

CONCLUDING REMARKS

This research project led to many surprising discoveries, not the least of which was the unearthing of the mindset identified here. A brief survey of certain animals' behavioral patterns call this utopian view of nature into question; however, only 1 person out of the 200 surveyed mentioned that nature itself can be cruel. In his own words:

> הרג או התעללות שהיא לא לצורך מזון או הגנה. למרות זאת ניתן לראות כי הטבע בעצמו נוטה להיות אכזר ולהתעלל באוכל - חתולים מכל הגדלים לעיתים מתעללים באוכל שלהם לצורכי שעשוע

> (Killing or abuse that is not for food or defense purposes. However, we can see that nature itself has an inclination to be cruel and abuse food—cats of all sizes sometimes abuse their food for entertainment.)

Further research is needed to delve into the origins of this belief in natural balance. It is unclear if this schema is correlated with Jews in particular or whether it has a wider appeal to multiple ethnic and religious groups. The dominionistic attitude, which is founded on the concept of natural hierarchies and a divinely inspired balance, has been studied in the context of Christianity in US society; however, it would be beneficial to examine the beliefs of other religions in other parts of the world outside of the Judeo-Christian tradition to see how widespread this belief is.

Another unexpected pattern was the notable absence of respondents who referenced *kashrut* or Jewish law. Before the coding, we anticipated this to be one of the most common motifs in a question about the Jewish understanding of animal suffering. Because this was not a representative sample, we wish to refrain from making an overgeneralization about the possible implications of this finding. It seems, however, to suggest that in our sample religious dogma was not the primary factor in informing respondents' moral compasses, at least in relation to animal rights and consumption habits. Future analyses of these data should explore the extent to which certain elements of Jewish culture or community ethos in Israel and the United States contribute to or influence Jewish attitudes toward the relationship between themselves and animals.

Last, the most counterintuitive trend we encountered was that meat-eating respondents were more likely to blame humans for animal suffering. It seemed logical to us that those who consciously choose to avoid meat and animal products, such as vegetarians and particularly vegans, would be the most vocal group in promoting an ideology of personal accountability for dietary choices. This may well be influenced by negative stereotypes in popular culture which portray vegans as overly aggressive activists. The fact that many meat eaters are cognizant of their impact on animals can lead to dichotomous conclusions. On the one hand, the acknowledgment of guilt may actually "[keep] the focus on oneself [and] contribute to the reification of [one's] negative qualities (e.g. I *am* selfish), and become an obstacle for imagining oneself differently, and for changing one's behavior."[52] In other words, some might admit wrongdoing with no intention of actually changing their behavior. On the other hand, admitting to oneself that some behavior is problematic and focusing on change rather than guilt could be the impetus for a sustained lifestyle change. Awareness is essential because it bridges the disconnect that so many people have between the food on their plate and the animal that that food used to be. Anecdotally, this was the first step for many in their journey to becoming vegetarians and/or vegans.

This study was a small-scale pilot attempt to conceptualize the Jewish understanding of animals suffering in the hopes that this would provide some insight into the growing movement of Jewish vegans around the world. In the future, further studies should be conducted to evaluate the accuracy of the model developed herein. These studies should include larger and more representative samples of Jews around the world. It would also preferable to conduct interviews in person rather than through an online study to ensure more thoughtful and complete answers. The effects of these studies would be twofold: not only would they help tackle some very important questions about how humans relate to the world around them, but they would also be vehicles for opening up a crucial dialogue that is too often disregarded. Whether or not the studies would create a more effective model, they would be a catalyst for the participants to actively engage with, examine, and possibly challenge their own beliefs about animal rights and the ethical component of dietary choices. As Schweitzer would point out, the first step toward creating a more compassionate world is acknowledging the damage that is done by our hand. Once we are awakened to the impact of our choices, we become empowered to make informed decisions on how we choose to live. Why not start with our plates?

APPENDIX

English Survey

1. What is your age?
    - ☐ 18 to 24
    - ☐ 25 to 34
    - ☐ 35 to 44
    - ☐ 45 to 54
    - ☐ 55 to 64
    - ☐ 65 to 74
    - ☐ 75 and older

2. How do you identify?
    - ☐ Female
    - ☐ Male
    - ☐ Other/non-binary

3. What is your religious affiliation?
    - ☐ Reform
    - ☐ Reconstructionist
    - ☐ Conservative
    - ☐ Orthodox
    - ☐ Modern Orthodox
    - ☐ Ultra-Orthodox (*haredi*)
    - ☐ None
    - ☐ Other (please specify; textbox provided)

4. How would you describe your level of religiosity?
    - ☐ Not observant at all (atheist/agnostic/uninterested)
    - ☐ Secular but follow some cultural traditions
    - ☐ Somewhat observant
    - ☐ More observant (follow most halakhic rules but not all)
    - ☐ Very observant

5. How would you describe your current diet? (select all that apply)
    - ☐ Dairy-free
    - ☐ Kosher
    - ☐ Paleo

- ☐ Vegan
- ☐ Raw
- ☐ Omnivore
- ☐ Gluten-free
- ☐ Pescatarian
- ☐ Vegetarian
- ☐ Other [please specify; text box provided]

6. In what state or US territory do you live? [drop-down menu provided]

7. How would you define "animal suffering"? [text box provided]

8. What are the acceptable boundaries of animal suffering for food consumption purposes (if any)? [text box provided]

Hebrew Survey

1. ?מהו גילך
   - ☐ 18–24
   - ☐ 25–34
   - ☐ 35–44
   - ☐ 45–54
   - ☐ 55–64
   - ☐ 65 או מבוגר יותר

2. ?כיצד אתה מזדהה
   - ☐ נקבה
   - ☐ זכר
   - ☐ אחר

3. כיצד אתה מגדיר את עצמך מבחינה דתית?
   - ☐ אתאיסט
   - ☐ חילוני
   - ☐ מסורתי לא דתי
   - ☐ מסורתי דתי
   - ☐ דתי
   - ☐ חרדי
   - ☐ אף אחד מהנ"ל
   - ☐ אחר (נא לציין)

4. כיצד אתה מגדיר את אופי התזונה שלך?

☐ כשר
☐ נטול לקטוז
☐ פליאו
☐ טבעונאי
☐ צמחוני
☐ אוכל כל
☐ נטול גלוטן
☐ טבעוני
☐ פסקטריאן
☐ אחר (נא לציין)

5. היכן אתה מתגורר בישראל?

6. איך אתה מגדיר צער בעלי חיים?

7. מהם הגבולות המקובלים לצער בעלי חיים למטרות אכילה (באם קיימים)?

NOTES

1. Albert Schweitzer, *The Philosophy of Civilization*, trans. C. T. Campion (Buffalo, NY: Prometheus Books, 1987)

2. James Brabazon, *Albert Schweitzer: A Biography*, 2nd ed. (Syracuse: Syracuse University Press, 1975)

3. Some examples include Exodus 23:5, 23:12; Deuteronomy 11:15, 22:6, 22:10, 25:4.

4. Israel's population is roughly 75 percent Jewish, 21 percent Arab, and 4 percent other. Of the world's 14.3 million Jews, approximately 43 percent reside in Israel. It is not the author's intention to ignore other populations residing in Israel; however, for the purposes of this research, Israel and its consumption patterns are considered demonstrative of more general trends in the Jewish world. See "Vital Statistics: Latest Population Statistics for Israel," Jewish Virtual Library, http://www.jewishvirtuallibrary.org/latest-population-statistics-for-israel (accessed May 2017).

5. "Israel Is the 'Most Vegan Country in the World,'" *Israel National News*, October 22, 14, http://www.israelnationalnews.com/News/News.aspx/186427.

6. The survey did not distinguish between Jewish Israelis and Israelis of other religious denominations. For the purposes of this work, it is assumed that the rise

in the percentage of vegetarians and vegans nationally is also indicative of a rise in the number of Jewish vegetarians and vegans.

7. Tova Cohen, "In the Land of Milk and Honey, Israelis Turn Vegan," Reuters, July 21, 2015, http://www.reuters.com/article/us-israel-food-vegan-idUSKCN0P V1H020150721.

8. Central Bureau of Statistics of the State of Israel, "Persons Aged 20 and Over, by Religiosity and by Selected Characteristics," in *Statistical Abstract of Israel 2011*, 338, http://www.cbs.gov.il/shnaton62/st07_04x.pdf (accessed June 20, 2017).

9. Quoted in S. Daniel Breslauer, "The Vegetarian Alternative: Biblical Adumbrations, Modern Reverberations," in *Food and Judaism*, ed. Leonard J. Greenspoon, Gerald Shapiro, and Ronald Simkins (Lincoln: University of Nebraska Press, 2005), 83.

10. Ibid., 83.

11. Ibid.

12. Gary A. Rendsburg, "The Vegetarian Ideal in the Bible," in *Food and Judaism*, ed. Leonard J. Greenspoon, Gerald Shapiro, and Ronald Simkins. (Lincoln: University of Nebraska Press, 2005), 322.

13. Breslauer, "The Vegetarian Alternative," 92–93.

14. The labels "ethical/moral," "health," and "environment" were those chosen by the creators of the survey referenced and are not representative of the authors' beliefs regarding what constitutes an ethical or moral concern.

15. "Vegan Profile," Vegan Research Panel, 2003, http://www.imaner.net/panel/profile.htm.

16. Kerry S. Walters and Lisa Portmess (eds.), *Ethical Vegetarianism: From Pythagoras to Peter Singer* (Albany: SUNY Press, 1999)

17. Meabh Kenny and Robert Fourie, "Tracing the History of Grounded Theory Methodology: From Formation to Fragmentation," *Qualitative Report* 19, no. 52 (December 29, 2014): 1, http://nsuworks.nova.edu/cgi/viewcontent.cgi?article=1416&context=tqr.

18. Ibid.

19. Ibid., 2.

20. Kathy Charmaz, "Grounded Theory," in *Qualitative Psychology: A Practical Guide to Research Methods*, 3rd ed., ed. Jonathan A. Smith (Los Angeles: Sage Publications, 2015), 54.

21. Carla Willig, *Introducing Qualitative Research in Psychology*, 3rd ed. (New York: Open University, 2013), 70.

22. Ibid.

23. Juliet Corbin and Anselm Strauss, "Grounded Theory Research: Procedures,

Canons and Evaluative Criteria," *Zeitschrift für Soziologie* 19, no. 6 (December 1990): 423.

24. Ibid.
25. Ibid.
26. Ibid.
27. Willig, *Introducing Qualitative Research* 73.
28. Corbin and Strauss, "Grounded Theory Research," 422.
29. Michael Lipka, "Unlike U.S., Few Jews in Israel Identify as Reform or Conservative," FactTank: News in the Numbers, Pew Research Center, March 15, 2016, http://www.pewresearch.org/fact-tank/2016/03/15/unlike-u-s-few-jews-in-israel-identify-as-reform-or-conservative.
30. Jeremy Sharon and Sam Sokol, "Chief Rabbinate in Fierce Attack on Reform, Conservative Movements," *Jerusalem Post*, February 25, 2016, http://www.jpost.com/Israel-News/Politics-And-Diplomacy/Chief-Rabbinate-in-fierce-attack-on-Reform-Conservative-movements-446143.
31. *Masorti* in this context refers to the term commonly used by Israelis to describe Jews who pick and choose which elements of observance, *halakha*, or tradition they would like to follow or emphasize. While they do share many common beliefs, *masorti* in the way in which the authors are using it here must be differentiated from the Masorti Olami movement, which is the international Conservative movement based in Israel that stresses the intersection of tradition and modernity. For more information about the Masorti Olami movement, please refer to www.masortiolami.org.
32. Lipka, "Unlike U.S."
33. Edna Amir Coffin and Shmuel Bolozky, *A Reference Grammar of Modern Hebrew* (Cambridge: Cambridge University Press, 2005), 40.
34. The Sapir-Whorf hypothesis currently exists in two forms: strong and weak, which correspond to the concepts of linguistic determinism and linguistic relativism, respectively. Linguistic determinism dictates that language and its underlying structures dictate and organize human thought. Edward Sapir wrote that "human beings... are very much at the mercy of the particular language which has become the medium of expression for their society.... The fact of the matter is that the 'real world' is to a large extent unconsciously built up on the language habits of the group." Edward Sapir, "The Status of Linguistics as a Science," in *The Selected Writings of Edward Sapir in Language, Culture, and Personality*, ed. D. G. Mandelbaum (Berkeley: University of California Press, 1958), 162. As an example, Turkish encodes information about the source of an utterance, using one form for eyewitness testimony and another for reported speech. Meanwhile, certain grammatical tenses in English, such as the present perfect, are also encoded with

information about the current status of the individual, namely if they are alive or dead. If one subscribes to linguistic determinism, then these language differences would mean that Turkish speakers are more aware of different evidence types than are English speakers, while English speakers are more mindful of death than are Turkish speakers. Such generalizations about an entire population are very difficult to evaluate empirically and have largely been categorized as overreaching. However, there are some studies that have demonstrated a limited degree of determinism when comparing speakers whose languages describe spatial relationship based on the body (front/back or right/left) versus those that used fixed points (such as the cardinal directions). Those speakers whose language encodes space based on fixed external points have been proven to be more aware of their position relative to compass points than those whose language does not. Although there is still some disagreement as to the validity of linguistic determinism, most linguists agree that there is merit in a weaker version of this idea, which states that the language a person speaks may well influence their perception of the world. Language and cognition are very closely interrelated, but language is only one part of how humans experience and interact with the world. Therefore, many linguists consider it problematic to draw assumptions of causation and prefer instead to examine correlation. In this chapter, we based our assumptions on the more well-accepted weak form of the Sapir-Whorf hypothesis and looked only into correlation, making no assumptions of cause and effect. For more information and the quotes above, see "Language and Thought," Linguistic Society of America: Advancing the Scientific Study of Language, https://www.linguisticsociety.org/resource/language-and-thought.

35. Deixis refers to words whose semantic meanings are fixed, but they cannot be fully understood without additional information. In English, pronouns are deictic; for example, the meaning of "he" is set, but it is unclear who the referent of "he" is without further contextualization from the utterance.

36. Due to the methodology of grounded theory, codes are not preexisting and are created as they appear in the data set. In this case, the first statements that were encountered directly equated human and animal suffering. After that, we encountered other responses that did not explicitly say humans and animals suffer in the same way, but seemed to provide a weaker comparison. Many of these responses alluded to sentience, feelings, or other anthropomorphic qualities, which we then coded as "compared to humans" because they assumed shared aspects between animals and humans. It is important to remember that these codes do not exist in a vacuum and should be understood as relative to one another.

37. Though undoubtedly a nuanced and often debated subject, in this work we assumed that Jewish people from various geographical locations, levels of

religiosity, and political beliefs could all be classified into the single category of "Jews." This is not to say that this is homogeneous group by any means, but they share some commonality as a group, which makes the analysis of their differences even more relevant and interesting. It is difficult to define Jewish peoplehood; indeed, there is currently no single agreed-on definition, and many Jewish journals have dedicated entire issues to addressing this question. Because the authors of this study are not experts in this field, we chose to avoid operationalizing the concept of peoplehood and instead adopted a purposefully vague understanding of it as "being united by Jewish*ness* in some hard-to-articulate way rather than by *being Jewish* in an active way through portals such as religion, language, and culture." From the personal experiences of the authors (who met while working together on a Taglit-Birthright trip), every person understands and connects to Jewishness in their own way. For some, it is a matter of shared history, ethnicity, and tradition; for others religion; and for others it is simply an indescribable sense of belonging to a tribe. To us, it did not seem germane to the study to see why people identified as Jews. Participation was completely voluntary and marketed to Jews above the age of eighteen, so whoever completed the survey had self-selected themselves into the category of "Jew." For the purposes of this study, Jews are an intensely multifaceted group with diverse perspectives and experiences who all (for their own reasons) acknowledge membership in the same ethnoreligious group. See Erica Brown and Misha Galperin, *The Case for Jewish Peoplehood: Can We Be One?* (Woodstock, NY: Jewish Lights Publishing, 2009), 2.

38. Y. Michael Barilan, "Speciesism as a Precondition to Justice," *Politics and the Life Sciences* 23, no. 1 (March 2004): 24, emphasis added.

39. Ibid.

40. Ibid., 26.

41. Ibid., 23.

42. Quoted in ibid.

43. Ibid., 30. On covenantal relations between humans and animals in the Jewish tradition, see David Seidenberg's contribution to this volume in chapter 8.

44. Ibid.

45. Danielle R. Deemer and Linda M. Lobao, "Public Concern with Farm-Animal Welfare: Religion, Politics, and Human Disadvantage in the Food Sector," *Rural Sociology* 76, no. 2 (June 27, 2011): 172.

46. Ibid., 181.

47. Ibid., 173.

48. Ibid., 174.

49. Ibid., 173.

50. Ibid., 184.

51. We focused our statistical findings on the results of the English survey. The Hebrew survey had an unexpectedly high amount of circular definitions that did not give rise to any new insights. In addition, there was a slight misunderstanding with a few participants who mistook our prompt "צער בעלי חיים" [*tza'ar ba'alei chayim*] for a prominent animal welfare organization in Israel with the same name.

52. Carissa Veliz, "7 Reasons Not to Feel Bad about Yourself When You Have Acted Immorally," *Practical Ethics: Ethics in the News*, University of Oxford, December 4, 2014, http://blog.practicalethics.ox.ac.uk/2014/12/7-reasons-not-to-feel-bad-about-yourself-when-you-have-acted-immorally.

Part Two **New Directions**

8 Veganism and Covenantalism
Contrasting and Overlapping Moralities

DAVID MEVORACH SEIDENBERG

Veganism is often presented as the highest ideal for anyone who is concerned about animal rights or opposed to what deep ecology calls "speciesism." In this essay, I explore whether veganism is an ideal moral practice and whether veganism can be affirmed as an authentic or ideal Jewish practice.

If veganism represents the ideal, then people's choices from best to worst would fall on a spectrum from veganism to vegetarianism to eating a modicum of meat to eating meat frequently. This spectrum can fit within a wider spectrum, whose extremes run from not using animals at all to using them however one wishes. The fundamental question behind that wider spectrum is what kind of dominion or dominance, if any, humanity may exert over other animals.[1] If dominion is the principle underlying our current food system, the opposite ethic would be to reject any use of animals, not just as a source of food but for any other purpose, including entertainment or labor. This ethic, often called "abolitionist veganism," can be summed up in the words of one of its leading proponents, Gary L. Francione: "There is veganism and there is animal exploitation. There is no third choice."[2]

In Judaism, though, there is a clear third choice. The ideal of covenant that is so fundamental to the Torah's understanding of the human-divine relationship also shapes a mutualistic understanding of people's interactions with other animals.

Of course, dominion also plays a large role in Jewish thinking about animals. It is true that the concept of dominion has strong roots in God's declaration in Genesis 1:28 that humanity will "exercise dominion [*ur'du*] over the fish of the sea and the bird of the skies and over every animal treading upon the land." It is also true that in normative Judaism, dominion—or even more hierarchically, domination (either word could translate the rabbinic concept of *r'diyah* derived from this verse)—is seen as the foundation of humanity's relationship to animals. Looked at from the perspective of dominion, the many rules in the Torah protecting animals appear to be stopgap measures to prevent dominion from becoming full-blown exploitation, promoting what we would call animal welfare.

However, I hope to show that even though dominion is highlighted in Genesis 1, it cannot provide a sufficient explanation for the many laws about animals in the Torah. In fact, covenant provides a deeper explanation for those laws, as well as for the narrative evidence that describes ancient Israelites' relationships with their animals. Because covenant is based on mutuality, it provides a stronger foundation for ecological ethics. I call this approach "covenantalism" (without intending the Christian meanings of that term).

If covenant is the ideal, however, the question of veganism looks substantially different. The only way to create a covenantal relationship is for humans to be directly involved with animals. The normative vegan understanding would see rights as intrinsic to animals, giving them standing and moral worth independent of human choices and ideas. But the covenantal equivalent of rights—whether possessed by a human or animal subject—would instead be that there is a human or society-wide obligation to that subject.[3] Because a covenantal perspective recognizes that humanity, like all other species, must use its fellow species, it is concerned with how to use them well and how to be used well by them. Covenantalism necessarily affirms some of the ways animals may be used for human ends, as long as those ends are achieved in a way that is mutually beneficial on a species level. A vegan perspective might instead focus on minimizing or eliminating many human-animal interactions and dependencies out of a desire for purity or because it believes that the capacious power human beings have to control other creatures will distort every interaction toward exploitation.

Although elements of both perspectives can be found in Jewish texts, along with teachings that outright reject any concept of animal rights or subjecthood, in different historical contexts one or another of these perspectives dominates. The Torah's understanding of covenant can be used to establish a baseline to measure human-animal relationships in subsequent stages of Jewish literature and thought. Those eras and genres characterized by a covenantal perspective are less favorable to a purist vegan ideology, whereas those that base morality on the individual and extrapolate that morality to our relations with animals are more favorable to veganism.

DEFINING COVENANT

We can better explore this question by first defining covenant in contrast with symbiosis on one hand and contract on the other. In addition to being beneficial to both sides, like symbiosis, a covenant entails rights and responsibilities, like a contract.

Like a symbiotic relationship but unlike a contract, a covenant exerts its force across generations. However, symbiosis is determined by ecological necessity, whereas a covenant is rooted in more than biology and its power is more than unconscious or instinctual. Conversely, covenant is not confined to the realm of societal norms and human intention, the way a contract would be. Rather, a relationship that is covenantal can embrace what is human and what is more-than-human and can include the natural world or nonhuman creatures, as well as the divine. Unlike symbiosis or contract, a covenant may posit or define the nature of what is right and good, in a way that portrays its terms as "eternal" or divinely given.[4] Finally, covenant always has a sacred dimension.

DOMESTICATION

The centrality of covenant in all stages of Israelite religion is indisputable. What is less obvious is that the very idea of covenant is modeled on the Israelites' understanding of their relationships with their domesticated animals, as we shall see. The relationships humanity establishes with other animal species through domestication are world-changing and culturally determinative.[5] Although domestication can be understood as a process of domination, it can equally be understood as forging both a symbiosis and a covenant between a human community and another species. Plants and animals tamed by humans also in a real sense tame the human community, teaching humans to tend them and take responsibility for their well-being.[6] Neither exploitation nor dominion (as it is commonly understood) are the best lens for understanding such relationships.

Domestication creates a covenant-like relationship where the individual animals we use have the right to have their intrinsic needs met. These include being well nourished, being allowed to reproduce, and working only in ways that fit their capacities. On the human side, domestication imposes the obligation to allow animals to fulfill their needs, but it also includes the right to take an animal's life for food and sacrifice. Ethically speaking, the Torah's laws about animals focus on the covenantal aspect of our relationships with domesticated species. The Torah virtually bans hunting because the laws about taking the life of a wild animal are so restrictive. Theologically speaking, these covenantal relationships shaped the Israelite understanding of the divine.

COVENANT IN THE TORAH

The simplest definition of *b'rit* (covenant) in the Torah is that it is a kind of contract that is binding on future generations. Its ability to bind future generations is tightly bound to its sacred character. Explicit covenants that use the term *b'rit* are made between God and a human progenitor like Abraham. The Torah is often understood as the substance of the covenant between God and the Jewish people. Covenants are also made between individuals, like Jacob and Laban, and between peoples, like Isaac's household and the Gerari Philistines.

The very first covenant God makes is not with humans but with all animals. After the flood, God/*Elohim* informs Noah,

> And I, here I am erecting my covenant [*b'riti*] with you all and with your seed after you, and with the soul/life of every animal [*kol nefesh ha-chayah*] that is with you.... And I will establish my covenant with you all, and all flesh will not again be cut off by the flood's waters and there will never again be a flood to destroy (all) the land/Earth.... This is the sign of the covenant that I am giving between Me and between you all and between every living animal/creature [*nefesh chayah*] that is with you, for generations forever. My bow I put in the clouds, and it will become a covenant sign [*ot b'rit*] between Me and the land. And it will (happen) when I cloud over the land, and the bow appears in the cloud, and I will remember my covenant, and no more will waters become a flood to destroy all flesh.... an eternal covenant between God and between every living creature.... This is the covenant sign that I am erecting between Me and all flesh that is on the land. (Genesis 9:9–17)[7]

All other biblical covenants are preceded by and derive from this first covenant with all life, which is also a covenant with the land or Earth itself. Its importance is underscored by the sevenfold use of the term *b'rit* in this passage. Like every divine *b'rit*, this covenant, sometimes called the "rainbow covenant," protects all generations forever. Nevertheless, while the *b'rit mei Noach* is predicated on a divine obligation to all creatures, it is unlike most other covenants because it does not impose obligations on the animals or on humanity as covenantal partners.[8]

God's covenant with all animals ascribes a higher moral standing to animals than has been the norm in modern society. Animals are subjects and merit covenantal care, and here humanity is not granted a relationship with divinity separate from them. This point cannot be overemphasized. That animals have standing is reflected at a more fundamental level in the Torah's use of the same vocabulary for human and animal bodies: both are called a *nefesh*, soul or self.[9]

The part of the flood story immediately preceding the rainbow covenant, however, creates a radical distinction between humans and animals. In Genesis 1, even though humans are granted dominion, they are also told they will share the *yerek eisev*, the green plants, with the animals (1:29–30).[10] After the flood, human beings are invited to eat the other animals: "like the green grass I give you it all" (Genesis 9:3). At the same time, taking a human life, by animal or human, is condemned:

> Only your blood for your lives I will seek, from/by[11] the hand of every animal [*miyad kol chayah*] I will seek it, and from/by the hand of the human. One who spills the blood of the human, by the human, his blood will be spilled, for in *Elohim*'s image He made the human. (Genesis 9:5–6)

These verses imply that even though a covenant was established between God and all the animals after the flood, no such covenant was established between humans and other animals. On the contrary, the dominion described in Genesis 1:28, which may hint at domestication and *convivencia*, is replaced by "a terror of you and a dread of you [that] will be over every animal of the earth [*chayat ha-aretz*]" (Genesis 9:2).[12]

What substitutes for any covenantal relationship between humans and other animals is a check on humans: "Every crawling thing which lives will be for you for eating.... But the flesh with its *nefesh* [soul/life], its blood, you will not eat" (Genesis 9:4). The blood of every animal, declared to be off-limits, is not yet declared sacred, though it is sacrosanct. This rule is not made part of the rainbow covenant; it focuses not on establishing relationships but on limiting human power and abuse.

THE COVENANT OF ISRAEL AND THE COVENANT OF BLOOD

We need to examine the ritual life of biblical Israel to show that even though humanity was not called to have a covenantal relationship with animals, the Israelites were. A strong intimation of that relationship is that domestic animals were required to rest from work on the Sabbath, the same way that people were (Exodus 20:10, 23:12; Deuteronomy 5:14).[13] The Sabbath itself is described as "an eternal covenant" between God and Israel, not just in Torah but throughout scripture.[14]

Were the animals seen as partners in this covenant, or were they merely subsumed under the aegis of their owners? The language of Exodus 23:12 suggests the former: "You will stop *in order* that your ox and your donkey will rest, and the child of your maidservant and the stranger will be re-souled" (emphasis added).[15] Owners must keep the Sabbath so that they will let their animals and servants' children (not just their servants) rest—not vice versa.[16] The covenant of the Sabbatical year, "the Sabbath of Sabbaths" (Leviticus 25:4), includes even the wild animals as participants (Leviticus 25:7).

The prohibition against eating blood played a covenantal role in Israel's life. The blood, rather than simply being off-limits as it was described in the Noah story, is reserved for sacred use:

> Any man from the children of Israel who would slaughter an ox or sheep or goat ... and did not bring it to the entry of the meeting tent ... blood/bloodguilt is accounted to that man, he has spilled blood, and that man will be cut off from among his people.... In order that when the children of Israel will bring their sacrifices ... to *YHVH*, to the entry of the meeting tent ... And the priest will cast the blood upon *YHVH*'s altar ... an eternal statute this will be for them for their generations.... And every man that would eat any blood, I will set my face against the person/soul [*nefesh*] that eats the blood, and she will be cut off from among her people. For the *nefesh* of the flesh is in the blood, and I gave it to you all for the altar, to atone for your lives/souls [*nafshoteichem*], for the blood will atone through the *nefesh*. (Leviticus 17:3–11)

This passage from Leviticus assumes that everyone would be able to bring their animal to the meeting tent or *Ohel Mo'ed*, also called the *Mishkan*, for slaughter. Deuteronomy, imagining that the final resting place of the ark, the Temple, will be too far for some, allows slaughter away from the altar, so that "you may eat in your gates with all the desire of your *nefesh*" (12:21). Nevertheless, the sacredness of the blood is declared with equal force:

> Only be strong against eating the blood, for the blood is the *nefesh*, and you will not eat the *nefesh* with the flesh. You all will not eat it, onto the ground you must spill/pour it like water. You will not eat it, so that it will go well for you and for your children after you, when you do what is upright in *YHVH*'s eyes.... And the blood of your sacrifices you will pour out on *YHVH*'s altar ... and the flesh you may eat. (Deuteronomy 12:23–25, 27)

Because blood is reserved for the altar, it must be poured out "like water" whenever one is away from the altar to prevent it from being used for any other purpose. This imperative is enjoined in a way that is characteristically covenantal, "so that it will go well for you and for your children after you," defined by its impact on future generations.

The life or *nefesh* of the animal, localized in blood, had two sacred roles. One, reflected more strongly in Leviticus, was that the animal's blood/*nefesh* could be offered to facilitate atonement for a human supplicant's *nefesh*. In this manner, the blood served as an adjuvant in Israel's covenantal relationship with God. The other, reflected more strongly in Deuteronomy, was that offering the blood/*nefesh* on the altar is what enabled the flesh of the animal itself to be eaten.[17]

Sacrificial animals could only come from domesticated species, such as cows, sheep, or goats, which meant that people lived in close relation to animals that were sacrificed. Domestic animals played a role in society that was essential not only for material and economic reasons but also for spiritual ones. However, as we are seeing, animals were more than just providers of food, labor, and sacrificial blood. According to Mary Douglas, the consecration of the firstborn of the Israelites' flocks and herds, like the consecration of their own firstborn children, is strong evidence that "the herds and flocks which share the lives of their owners, travel with them, and provide their sustenance . . . come under the terms of the covenant of their masters."[18] Just as the people of Israel are "singled out for the honour of being consecrated to God," so are "the cloven-footed ruminants singled out."[19]

These passages about blood suggest that animals not only played a significant role in the human-divine covenant but were also part of a human-animal covenant. However, if animals are partners in the covenant, this creates a conundrum: how can it be permissible to slaughter and eat them?[20] A crucial piece of evidence that the Torah is aware of this problem is found in Leviticus 17:4, which teaches that one who does not offer the blood of a slaughtered animal on the altar has "spilled blood" and incurred "bloodguilt"—committed a kind of murder—with the consequence that "that man will by cut off from among his people."[21]

The altar rites solved this conundrum.[22] One part of the animal, its blood, was identified with its *nefesh*. Just as *nefesh* and *n'shamah* are related to breath, the blood is the internal breath flowing through the body, carrying the divine life force. By reifying the animal's *nefesh* as the blood, the "personhood" of the animal could be given to God, rendering the remaining body into usable parts.[23] In contrast, the human body in its entirety was called a *nefesh* and acquired holiness through its wholeness. People became *tamei*, cultically impure, when that wholeness was disrupted, and were made *tahor*, cultically pure, by rituals like the *mikveh* or ritual pool that restored wholeness.[24] The Temple was the shared center of these distinct ritual regimes: *korbanot* applied to other animals, and *taharah* applied to humans.

In structuralist terms, the Torah used rituals to inscribe difference onto animal bodies and human bodies. Instead of justifying slaughter by denying the subjecthood and subjectivity of animals, as later Western thought did, ancient Hebrew culture designed slaughter to symbolically or animistically protect that subjecthood.[25]

Were the animals offered up on the altar giving their lives for a holy purpose that served both human and animal? Could one imagine, or did the Israelites imagine, that the dominion asserted by humans over other species also served those species? The arguments I have given so far depend on an expansive interpretation of the sacrificial system. A more direct answer to these questions can be arrived at through the biblical metaphor of sheep and shepherd.

THE COVENANTAL ROLE OF THE SHEPHERD

Perhaps the most important evidence for covenantalism can be found in the fact that the human-animal relationship, in the figure of shepherd and flock, became a prophetic metaphor for God's relationship to Israel.

Shepherding is portrayed in the Torah as the originary human-animal relationship, both on the mythical level (in the person of Abel) and historically (the occupation of the patriarchs). One of the matriarchs is even named "ewe" or *rachel*. In the Joseph story, his brothers take pains to insist they are shepherds and not cow herders when they come before Pharaoh, contrary to Joseph's wishes (Genesis 46:31–47:4).

In the Torah, only Jacob, the master of animal husbandry and shepherd par excellence (Genesis 30:32–43), refers to God as shepherd, once when he blesses Joseph's sons in the name of "the God who shepherds me [*haro'eh oti*]" (Genesis 48:15), and once when he blesses Joseph (Genesis 49:24). Since the number of examples in the rest of scripture is overwhelming, I review just a handful. Psalm 23 contains one of the most well-known images of God as the good shepherd:

> *YHVH* is my shepherd, I will lack nothing. The One makes me crouch alongside rich fields of grass, leads me beside calm/restful waters.... Your staff and Your signet—these will comfort me. (23:1–2, 4)

Similarly, Jeremiah (31:9) says, "The One who scattered Israel will gather him and guard him, like a shepherd [would] his flock." As Israel's shepherd, God cares so tenderly for the lambs that He carries them like a nursing mother: "Here, *Adonay YHVH* will come with strength ... like a shepherd, the One will pasture His flock, in His arm the One will gather lambs, and carry them in His bosom" (Isaiah 40:11).

The shepherd is also the model for righteous human leadership. Ezekiel 34, an extended meditation on shepherding, offers a particularly rich example, comparing good leadership with the virtues of a good shepherd, condemning bad shepherds who feed themselves and not the sheep. Zechariah denounces the elite by comparing them to a shepherd who does not care about what happens to his sheep after they are sold (11:3–4) and describes the sinful shepherd as one who does not heal the broken or care for the young and who eats (!) the healthy (11:16).

More pointedly, in these chapters, God's covenant is explicitly compared to the shepherd's. Zechariah (11:10) cuts up his shepherd's staff to symbolize that God has annulled a divine covenant. In Ezekiel (34:25), God promises to establish a *b'rit shalom* or covenant of peace in which the sheep (Israel) will no longer be preyed on.[26]

Why is the primary human-animal metaphor not herder and cattle but shepherd and sheep? It may be because one can fulfill essential needs for food and clothing from sheep by harvesting milk and wool without killing the animal. Also, even though cows like sheep were herded and sacrificed, they were also used for agricultural labor, which was sometimes seen as a kind of enslavement (e.g., Ezekiel 34:27), whereas sheep were not. (This may explain why many sacrifices using cows required a heifer or calf that had never been worked.) There may be an allegorical dimension to sheep and shepherd: a shepherd will generally lead his or her sheep by walking in front of them or alongside them, whereas cows are driven from behind.[27] This detail suggests a more mutualistic relationship wherein both parties respond freely to each other.

THE ECOLOGICAL DIMENSION

The importance of shepherding also reflects the ecological constraints of the land of Canaan. Only a portion of the rocky, hilly land settled by the ancient Israelites could be farmed. Much of the land was better suited to herding sheep or goats. Some aspect of these differences allowed the ancient Israelites to see sheep as the species participating most completely in a covenant with their shepherd.

The constraints of the land are reflected in the rules for kosher animals. Mammals that chew their cud and have split hooves are the only land animals considered *tahor* (cultically pure) and permissible for food (Leviticus 13:3–8; Deuteronomy 1:4–8). I propose that it was not ritualism or symbolism but ecology that first determined the rules about which species of mammals were permitted to be eaten.[28] Ruminant animals can make use of marginal land growing grasses inedible to humans, and animals with split hooves can graze on rocky land that would make for poor farming. From a purely ecological perspective, these rules permit only species that do not compete with humans for land or food.[29]

These species allowed humans to sustainably derive the most sustenance from agriculturally marginal land by herding animals that can graze there, especially sheep and goats, and eating them. Conversely, these constraints of hoof and stomach would compel some people to live as shepherds and goatherds, leading their animals from one wild area to the next, maximizing the flock's growth while limiting its impact on the land. Moreover, the land would be used best for this purpose if it were not fenced off. This also meant it would remain part of the commons and continue to function as habitat for wild animals.

Land that could be cleared of rocks and was flat or could be made flat through terracing, and therefore farmed relatively easily, would have formed a separate realm that was more intensely managed by humans and would be subject to ownership. Each realm could maintain a variety of species in a self-contained way, with cows, for example, fitting more into the human agricultural realm and sheep more into the realm of unowned mountain wilds. This categorization fits an idealized model of Creation, where the proper species in their proper domains represent the divine order, each set of species having its own set of sacred relationships. Sheep would then represent the greater natural realm, and the possibility of harmony in that realm between humans, animals, and the land.

Of course, the ancient Israelites knew full well that a shepherd lived off his or her flocks not only by shearing and milking them but also by slaughtering them.[30] Nevertheless, this relationship, envisioned as a covenant, provided a model or image for them of how God would take care of them.[31]

From the metaphor of the shepherd, we can draw several conclusions about the concepts underlying the ideal relationship between humans and domesticated animals. Eating animals and using animals for sacrifice were not seen as events in which animals functioned as objects, even sacred ones. Instead, the relationship between human and animal was characterized by mutual support. This relationship in its totality was aimed at achieving a covenantal level of care and responsibility, which included both nurturing life and giving death. Most important, this relationship served as a model for the human relationship and covenant with the Divine.

DOMESTICATED ANIMALS VERSUS WILD ANIMALS

A shepherd and his or her flock wandering through wild pasture are also wandering in the space between domesticated and wild realms. Genesis already assumes a world where some animals are tame or domesticated, since the Creation story specifies that both the wild animal, the *chayah*, and the domesticated animal, the *b'heimah*, are created from the earth (Genesis 1:24–25, 2:20).[32] When the animals are brought to the first human to be named in Genesis 2:19, the act of naming has a quality of domestication.

Most laws about animals in the Torah enjoin people to protect what may be called the rights of domesticated animals: not muzzling an ox to prevent it from eating the grain it threshes (Deuteronomy 25:4), not yoking together two different species (Deuteronomy 22:10), lifting up a fallen animal and relieving it of its burden (Exodus 23:5, Deuteronomy 22:4), allowing a mother to nurse her young for seven days (Leviticus 22:27). All appear to have consideration for the subjectivity and intrinsic needs of the creatures we care for and can fit under the rubric of animal welfare.[33] Not taking the life of a parent and its offspring in the same day (Leviticus 22:28, called *oto v-et b'no*) can also be perceived in that light, even though it applies whether or not the parent and child are aware of each other. It is one of several laws that valorize the relationship between parent and child (see below). The same values may be at the root of the prohibition against "cooking a kid in its mother's milk" (Exodus 23:19, 34:26 Deuteronomy 14:21).[34] If that interpretation is correct, then the prohibition would primarily be about honoring the milk that gives life along with the blood that is life—a rule that has little or no direct impact on animal welfare but is redolent with covenantal significance.

If domestication in human-animal relationships has the nature of covenant, then one would expect the laws of the Torah to make ritual and ethical distinctions between domesticated and wild animals. In fact, there are three laws that focus explicitly on wild animals. In the case of the *Shmitah*, the Sabbatical year, agricultural lands rest from being worked by people and domesticated animals just as on the Sabbath. In addition, wild animals, along with people and domestic animals, have the right to enter any field and eat whatever grows by itself (Leviticus 25:7; Exodus 23:11). The inclusion of wild animals here widens the sphere of moral concern (and is reminiscent of Eden—see below).

The commandment to chase away a mother bird if one wishes to take her eggs or nestlings, called *shiluach ha-kein* (Deuteronomy 22:6–7), also concerns wild animals because the law applies "when a bird's nest happens to be before you on the way in any tree or on the ground."[35] Like the law of *oto v-et b'no*, this law commands respect for parent-child relationships, but wild creatures have rights not extended to domestic creatures. The end of Deuteronomy 22:7 further explains that the reward for sending away the mother is "in order that it will go well for you and you will lengthen days"—a covenantal phrase that echoes the commandment to honor one's parents "in order that your days will be lengthened and in order that it will go well for you" (Deuteronomy 5:16).[36]

The same covenantal reward of long life is promised for not eating blood (Deuteronomy 12:25). Since blood is the element of the body most connected to breath and soul, to flow, and hence most connected to life, all blood was out of bounds for human use, whether the blood came from a wild or domesticated animal, and the covenantal punishment for eating it was "being cut off" (Leviticus 17:10, 17:14). But the third law in question specifically differentiates the ritual treatment of a wild animal's blood. In Leviticus 17:13, we are instructed that if a person takes the life of any kosher wild animal (*chayah*) or bird captured in hunting, they must "spill/pour out its blood and cover it with dirt." This commandment, called *kisui ha-dam*, underscores the fact that one may not make use of a wild animal's *nefesh* even for the sacred altar. It is as if one were giving the essence of the animal a proper burial.[38]

Kisui ha-dam did not apply to domesticated species.[39] Their blood could be offered on the altar, but if that were not possible, their blood had to be poured out "like water" (Deuteronomy 12:16, 12:24, 15:23)—meaning the blood of domestic animals did not require special treatment beyond being spilled on the ground to make it unusable for any secular purpose. It seems paradoxical that a domestic animal's blood was treated with greater sanctity in the Temple but lesser sanctity outside it. One way to conceptualize these rules is to imagine that the blood poured out on the altar was offered not only on behalf of human petitioners but also on behalf of all the animals of that species that were slaughtered anywhere.

Why was a domestic animal treated differently? Its life was in the hands of its caretakers, herders, midwives, and farmers. Hands that nurtured the animal's life were permitted to give it death as well. Because all creatures must die, this was not considered a violation of life but an act of respect for the life that one had cared for, as one may infer from the metaphor of God as shepherd. Having such power over the life of an animal would make sense to most pet owners, who would choose to give their animal a "good death" at the end of its life, rather than wait until whatever natural cause of death overcomes it.

In contrast, human beings have done nothing to give wild animals life, so there is neither responsibility nor right to give them death.[40] This is reflected in the measures applied to their slaughter.

THE PROPHETS

Scripture returns to the theme of covenant repeatedly. But before covenant, there was the flood and the fall, and before those, Eden. Covenant happens when the Edenic state is already shattered, when God has to promise not to destroy the world because humanity will tempt God to destroy it again in the future (Genesis 8:21). When people think about veganism in the Torah, they tend to think first about the conditions of the Garden of Eden, before the first covenant, where human and animal ate a perfectly vegan diet and shared the same food:

> I have given to you all every plant/grass seeding seed which is on the face of all the land and every tree which has in it tree-fruit seeding seed, for you it will be for eating, and for every animal ... and for every bird ... and for every crawler ... in which there is a living soul [*nefesh chayah*]. (Genesis 1:29–30)

The laws of the Torah that delineate the ideal of Eden also delineate a world where Eden can be partly re-created every seven years for the whole Sabbatical year, when people stop farming and share whatever grows naturally with each other and with wild animals.[41] This echo of Eden, unlike Eden itself, is very distinctly bounded by covenant, as is clear from the blessings and curses of Leviticus 26 that come if the land is not allowed to rest.

But the prophets envision an end of time that will be a fully realized return to Eden, when predation will end; when lion and calf, leopard and kid, wolf and lamb will lie down together; and the lion will eat straw "like cattle" (Isaiah 11:6–7). It is hard to imagine that these images were meant as prescriptions for the redemption of nature, rather than as metaphors.[42] But if vegans are looking for a biblical model, they have both the original Eden and the future Eden. However, these worlds would seem to be ecologically impossible and contrary to Nature as we know it.

The model of the shepherd is not entirely absent from that future Eden. After enumerating its unlikely pairings of prey and predator, Isaiah 11:6 declares that "a child will lead them." Nor is the theme of covenant absent. Hosea (2:20) says in God's name, "I will cut a covenant for them on that day, with the wild animal of the field and the bird of the sky and crawler on the ground, that I will break bow and sword and battle from the land and they will all lay down in safety." In this verse Hosea returns us to a world that is fully like Eden, where all will be unafraid of each other and fully like the rainbow covenant, where all the animals are gathered under one dispensation with the people and the land.[43]

RABBINIC TEACHINGS ON ANIMALS

Classical rabbinic texts expand the covenantal dimensions of human-animal relationships in some ways and diminish them in other ways. The image of the good shepherd as a model for godliness lives on in the Midrash (collections of rabbinic interpretation) in stories about the prowess and compassion of shepherds Moses and David that illustrate their virtue.[44] The laws that the rabbis derive from the Torah entail even more obligations on the part of human beings toward their animals than can be found in the Torah. Among these was the principle that one must feed one's animals before feeding oneself (derived from Deuteronomy 11:15) and the prohibition against neutering animals (derived from Leviticus 22:24), both of which resonate with the idea of covenant.[45]

The rabbis also derived extensive laws from the requirement that wild animals have access to Sabbatical produce. Fences were to be left open or taken down during the Sabbatical year so that wild animals could reach the fields, and people were only allowed to eat a species of produce in their house if it was still growing in fields where wild animals could eat it.[46] The rabbis articulated the complex rules of slaughter as well, which maximized the fulfillment of two principles important in the Torah: that as much of the blood should leave the body as possible and that the animal should feel the least pain possible. Perhaps most important, the rabbis articulated an overarching rule against causing animals suffering, *tza'ar ba'alei chayim*, as a general framework to explain the detailed laws and attitude of the Torah.[47]

These rules, of course, applied to the Jewish people rather than to all humanity. In rabbinic literature, as in Torah, there seems to be no conception of covenant between animals and humans in general. It is true that the rabbis thought that taking any part of a living animal for food was forbidden to all humanity.[48] However, this principle, derived from the prohibition against eating blood enjoined on Noah in Genesis 9:4, is better characterized as harm reduction, without any hint of caretaking or mutuality. On the contrary, the response of animals to the advent of human predation after the flood—that they will have "a terror of you and dread of you" (Genesis 9:2)—was interpreted by *Genesis Rabbah* to mean that after the flood, humanity lost its dominion over the animals.[49] A commentary on this teaching attributed to Rashi even states that the meaning of dominion before the flood was exactly the opposite of "terror and dread": when Adam called, the animals would come to him.[50]

Even though the rabbis established an ethic of responsibility toward animals, the Midrash reports a question from Rav that undermines that ethic. Rav asks, "What does it matter to the Holy One whether one slaughters [by beginning to cut] from the throat or slaughters from the back of the neck?" He answers that God's only intention was "to refine the [human] creatures" by challenging them to uphold an arbitrary commandment.[51] According to Rav's opinion, the needs of the animal and even the importance of separating the sacral blood from the flesh are not the main points of the law. In a similar vein, rabbinic law expansively elaborated the rule against cooking a kid in its mother's milk to include cooking, eating, and benefiting from all mixtures of meat and milk, called *basar v-chalav* or *basar b-chalav*, while forswearing the quest for the rule's meaning.[52]

On the level of lore and legend, however, the rabbis explicitly extended the idea of covenant to other animals, even inventing what sound like new covenants that were hardly hinted at in the Torah. For example, the Midrash, discussing the instruction to throw nonkosher meat "to the dog" (Exodus 22:30),[53] explains that dogs deserve this gift as a reward for keeping silent when the Israelites were leaving Egypt.[54] God, as it were, establishes through this verse a covenant with dogs to be carried out by humans.[55] Similarly, the commandment to bury a wild animal's blood is interpreted as a reward for the wild animals and birds who, according to Midrash, buried Abel's body after he had been slain by Cain.[56] This explicitly elevates *kisui ha-dam* to the level of a covenant.

Furthermore, *Kisui ha-dam* became the rabbinic archetype for the requirement to carry out each commandment in a way that showed respect. The rabbis derived this principle, called *kavod la-dam* or *k'vod ha-dam*, "respect for the blood" or "respecting the blood," from the rabbinic understanding that a person is required to use their hands to spread earth over the blood of a slaughtered wild animal. The law could not be fulfilled by using one's foot to push earth over the blood.[57] Although Jewish law applied this principle to the way one carries out any *mitzvah*, the fact that it was applied first to the blood—the *nefesh*—has special meaning. At its root, *kavod la-dam* can be understood in our time as expressing an attitude of deep respect for everything associated with life, an attitude that may also explain the vast elaboration of rabbinic laws about *basar v-chalav*.

Rabbinic texts also denigrated the practice of hunting, turning hunters that appear in scripture, like Nimrod and Esau, into villains,[58] and rejecting the slaughter of wild animals (especially sport hunting) as a type of depravity.[59] Practically speaking, it was very difficult to kill a wild animal in a kosher manner that would allow its flesh to be eaten.[60] Of course, there are hunting cultures, as found among the Native Americans, that consciously see themselves as being in a covenantal relationship of giving and thanksgiving between prey species and humans. However, rabbinic Judaism inherited a shepherding tradition that never developed such an understanding.

It was also a given for the rabbis that animals have souls.[61] The relevant question was not whether they have souls but what kind of souls they have. Are their souls of such a different nature from a human soul that this belief has no bearing on our ethical stance, or is it consequential? Here the rabbis made a firmer distinction between other animals and humans than the Torah did.[62] At the same time, rabbinic lore imagined animals as moral actors in their own right. For example, the animals join Adam in worshiping God,[63] and they can be piously strict about what they eat or when they work.[64]

One important story is the tale of the calf being led to slaughter that runs and hides itself in the folds of Rabbi Yehudah Hanasi's robe. When Rebbe, as he is known, says, "Go, for this [purpose] you were made," the angels afflict him with suffering, saying that since he did not show compassion, he will not receive compassion. His ailment continues until the angels see Rebbe sparing the lives of wild animals living in his house.[65] If Rebbe was punished for sending a calf to do its covenantal mission, does this not mean that this mission was in some sense wrong?

Despite the fabulistic quality of such stories, their moral content was treated as real. The conflicted message of the story of Rebbe and the calf is that the use of an animal's life cannot be fully justified. Although the covenantal use of animals in the cult was never explicitly rejected, we find frequent expression of the idea that there is a higher moral calling that does not condone sacrifice.[66] A different kind of ambivalence about eating meat is evinced by the rabbinic statement that even though meat was permitted, it should not be eaten by anyone unlearned.[67]

These supererogatory calls to compassion and restraint did not impinge on the fact that rabbinic law requires several *mitzvot* to be performed with products made from parts of animals. Torah parchment, *mezuzah* scrolls, *tefillin* boxes and straps must be made from animal hide; shofars must be made from a ram's horn or the horn of a similar animal.[68] Although the commandments requiring animal products are few, they are central to Judaism.

The overall trend in both Midrash and *halakha* (Jewish law) was to expand on and add to the covenantal elements of the Torah's ethical rules governing human-animal relationships. At the same time, the covenantal framework that encompassed the sacrificial system was overwritten by interpretations that were more moralizing, whereas laws about animals concerning slaughter, milk and meat, and such were reinterpreted by many as *chukim* (statutes without ethical content or reason).

MEDIEVAL PHILOSOPHICAL PERSPECTIVES

Jewish thought from the tenth century onward imbibed the rationalism of Greek (especially Aristotelian) philosophy. Jewish philosophers tended to magnify and emphasize the difference between humans and all the other animals. Many philosophers completely instrumentalize animal lives, leaving no possibility that our relationship with them could have a covenantal element. Saadyah Gaon, the earliest and most extreme example, explains God's directive that humanity "will dominate over the fish of the sea and over the bird of the sky and over every animal and over the land" (Genesis 1:26) in this way:

> The word *v-yirdu* [they will dominate/rule] includes the entire range of devices with which man rules over the animals ... with fetters and bridles ... with ropes ... with weapons of the hunt ... [and] with cages....
> The word *vi-d'gat* [over the fish] includes the stratagems for catching fish ... their consumption, the extraction of pearls ... the use of ... skin and bones ... and He added the word *ha-yam* [of the sea] to include man's subjugation of water; for he finds it within the ground and raises it out....
> And thus he dams rivers ... and he uses it to power mills ... and [He hints at] the construction of ships and boats.... And His word *uv-oaf* [and

over the birds] corresponds to . . . snares . . . the process of taming . . . the preparation of them for foods . . . and potions.[69]

More broadly, Saadyah promulgated the radically anthropocentric position that everything exists to serve us: "When we see the many created beings, we should not be perplexed about what among them is the goal . . . for the goal is humanity."[70]

Maimonides was an exception to the general philosophical attitude toward animals. In *The Guide for the Perplexed*, he emphatically rejects Saadyah's anthropocentrism:

> All the existent individuals of the human species, and all the more, those of the other species of the animals, are things of no value at all in comparison with the whole [of Creation] that exists and endures.[71]

The title of his magnum opus is directed against Saadyah's claim, as Maimonides makes clear when he writes:

> [Many minds] are perplexed . . . over the question of the final end of existence. . . . It should not be believed that all the beings exist for the sake of the existence of humanity. On the contrary, all the other beings too have been intended for their own sakes and not for the sake of something else. Thus, the quest for the final end of all the species of beings collapses.[72]

Elsewhere, Maimonides ridicules the idea that everything is created for humanity's pleasure.[73] It is not surprising that the way he interprets laws concerning animals shows an understanding of their intrinsic needs and a willingness to see those needs on par with human needs. Most famously, he wrote concerning *oto v-et b'no*:

> It is forbidden to slaughter [an animal] and its young on the same day, this being a precautionary measure to avoid slaughtering the young animal in front of its mother. For in these cases animals feel very great pain, there being no difference regarding this pain between humankind and the other animals. For the love and the tenderness of a mother for her child is not consequent upon reason, but upon the activity of the imaginative faculty, which is found in most animals just as it is found in humankind.[74]

He applied similar reasoning to *shiluach ha-kein*: "If . . . the mother is let go and escapes . . . she will not be pained by seeing that the young are taken."[75] Here, however, Maimonides adds a crucial element: "In most cases, this [commandment] will lead to people leaving everything alone." *Shiluach ha-kein*, he claims, not only protects the mother from suffering but also discourages people from interfering in any way with the nest. This interpretation reflects a different attitude toward wild birds and animals than toward domestic animals, which humans have a right to use.

Not only did Maimonides insist that all creatures exist for their own purposes, he also asserted that the very goodness of Creation is built on this fact:

> If you consider [the] Torah, the notion that we have in view will become manifest.... For with reference to none of the things created is the statement made in any way that it exists for the sake of some other things. It only says that God brought every part of the world into existence and that it conformed to its purpose. This is the meaning of the saying: "And God saw that it [is] good." About the whole, it says: "And God saw everything that He had made, and, behold, it [is] very good."[76]

The inherent goodness of the whole of Creation is not grounded in any individual species, but in "the way they are mutually connected."[77] What is of ultimate value is not a single species but the whole woven from them all.

In these passages, Maimonides provides a foundation for animal rights within Judaism, rooted in radical empathy. Though he nowhere suggests that a vegan or vegetarian diet is an ideal to strive for, his positions correlate with aspects of a traditionally vegan perspective, while his radical assertion of empathy would fit with a more covenantal perspective.

While most Jewish philosophers before and after Maimonides were closer to Saadyah, at least two adopted a perspective resonant with animal rights: Yosef Albo and Isaac Arama (both fifteenth century).[78] According to Albo, while the state humanity was born into was vegetarian, something went gravely wrong in the second generation. Cain inferred from the "prohibition" against killing animals that human and animal life were equal. Because of this, says Albo, when Abel sacrificed animals from his flock as an offering, Cain understood Abel's action as murder and murdered him in response.[79]

After the flood, God permitted—or even, as Albo suggests, required—Noah to kill animals to guarantee that humanity would never make the mistake of equating human life with the life of animals from any other species.[80] Thus the precondition under which humans may aspire to return to the ideal state of veganism or vegetarianism is that they recognize humanity's spiritual and moral superiority over other species.

Arama explained that there were three levels of humanity: those without spiritual advancement who should not eat meat at all, per the teaching from the Talmud quoted already; those in the process of becoming learned, who could eat meat; and those who had achieved a level of completion and spiritual perfection. About the last group, Arama says that people who are "whole" in wisdom have always removed themselves from society and materiality, sought out the wilderness, and distanced themselves from eating anything "from animals."[81] Arama then describes a vegan diet: one should eat "grasses (herbage), seeds, and tree fruit, and other vegetables," based on "the correct advice that the Creator gave to the human species in the time of Creation." For both teachers, veganism was motivated by an aspiration to reach a higher level of spiritual purity, rather than be in a more perfect relationship with animals.

In sum, Jewish philosophy did not adopt the Torah-based rabbinic concept that humans should or could treat their animals with covenantal kindness. On the contrary, Jewish philosophers mostly espoused the idea that everything in Creation, including the animals, was created for the sake of humanity. Even those few like Albo and Arama, who saw veganism as an ideal and criticized humanity's use of animals, still strongly affirmed anthropocentrism. Maimonides uniquely taught that the world and its creatures do not exist for our sakes and that anthropocentrism is fundamentally a mistake. An outlier in most ways, Maimonides's teachings could be used to develop a robust vegan ethos.

KABBALAH AND THE SOULS OF ANIMALS

Kabbalah as it developed after the promulgation of *Sefer Bahir* in thirteenth-century Christian Spain was a reaction against philosophical rationalism, and it has the strongest bearing on our questions. *Sefer Bahir* was the first work to include the themes discussed below that characterize what most people think of as Kabbalah. But there is at least one earlier stratum of Jewish mysticism that is also important: *Sefer Chasidim*, authored by Yehudah Hechasid, one of the Chasidei Ashkenaz or "German pietists" of the twelfth century.

In *Sefer Chasidim*, Yehudah Hechasid insisted that a pious person should be thorough in covering the blood of a slaughtered animal.[82] In a passage that demonstrates the extreme sensitivity to animals shown throughout *Sefer Chasidim*, he wrote:

> When a person slaughters a wild animal [*chayah*] or bird, he should think in his heart, this one that did not sin was slaughtered.... How then can a person who is full of sin overcome spilling blood [*sh'fikhut damim*, a term usually meaning murder of a human being] and Hell [*Gehinom*]? And he should consider how the Holy One commanded him to cover an animal's or bird's blood (Lev. 17:13), lest the angel [having] authority over them should say, "How can the blood of this one that did not sin be spilled by the hand of a sinner whose sins are like scarlet and worm?" and they seal with the blood [the decree of] one who is decreed to die.[83]

This powerful perspective could justify vegetarianism at the very least, since it equates slaughter with murder. By enjoining a person to meditate "in his heart" on the animal's innocence, Yehudah Hechasid inculcates a strong moral identification with animals. However, the second half of his comment disassociates this *mitzvah* from respecting the animal itself and from any covenantal relationship between generations of animals and humans. Instead, covering the blood becomes a kind of magic trick to fool the angel who watches over that animal.

Jewish mysticism in Spain incorporated some aspects of Jewish philosophy but rejected many others. Most important, whereas Jewish philosophy on some level rejected the body, insisting that only the soul, mind, or reason was "in God's image," the Kabbalah, starting with *Sefer Bahir*, asserted emphatically that the body was also created fully in the image of God.[84] *Sefer Bahir* taught that only rituals carried out physically could effect cosmic healing and that the purpose of the commandments was to bring blessing to all Creation, not just to Israel or to humanity.[85] Last, *Sefer Bahir* introduced the idea of reincarnation, which evolved in later Kabbalah to include the idea that human souls could reincarnate into nonhuman animals.[86] In these ways, the sphere of moral concern was expanded greatly to include the more-than-human world, and notably all animals.

Moshe ben Nachman, also called Nachmanides or Ramban, was one of the first Torah commentators to thoroughly incorporate Kabbalistic ideas. He explained that humanity was not allowed to eat animals in Eden because their souls are similar in some ways to human souls, since

> they have choice/freedom [*b'chirah*] concerning their good and their sustenance, and they flee from pain and death, and [so] scripture says: Who knows if the spirit [*ruach*] of the children of Adam rises upward, and if the *ruach* of the beast descends below, to the earth? (Ecclesiastes 3:21)[87]

At the same time, Noah gained the right to slaughter and eat animals because he had saved them: "Because Noah rescued [the animals] to keep the species in existence, [God] gave him permission to slaughter and to eat, because their existence was because of him [*ba-avuro*]."[88] This is a step toward the idea of covenant.

There is also an echo of covenant in Ramban's understanding of Adam naming the animals. According to Ramban, Adam was searching for an animal that could name him, just as he could give it a name.

> Any species that would call to him "*Ha-adam*," like his name, and say about him that he [i.e., Adam] is a *nefesh chayah* like him [the animal] ... he would be a help corresponding to him. [But Adam] called to all of them and did not find for himself a helper that would call [back] to him.[89]

Though Adam's search holds out hope for a covenantal relationship, it is a covenant that is uncompleted or unfulfilled.

One more element of Ramban's thought is important here: his interpretation of *shiluach ha-kein*, sending away the mother bird. He rejects Maimonides's explanation that the reason for the commandment is to avoid causing suffering, instead offering three others: (1) to teach people to be compassionate (i.e., to each other); (2) to avoid any action that would destroy a species; and (3) to honor the "mother of the world," which in Kabbalah means the quality of *Binah* or Understanding that is the womb in which the world is created.

Ramban sees no element of compassion for individual animals in this *mitzvah*. Rather, the divine concern is to protect humans from becoming cruel. Significantly, in distancing himself from Maimonides, Ramban opens his readers' eyes to the idea of taking responsibility for species rather than individuals:

> Scripture will not permit doing [any manner of] destruction that would uproot a species, even though it permits slaughter of a particular species; and behold, one who kills [*ha-horeg*] the mother and the children in one day or takes them . . . it is as if he would cut off that species.[90]

Taking parent and child would not normally threaten a species, and the medievals did not even believe that species could go extinct. But for Ramban, the simple fact that taking mother and child would lead to extinction if extrapolated many times makes it prohibited.[91] There is an implicit covenant here, not limited to domesticated species, that has at its root honoring the source of all life by honoring the life of all the species.

Later Kabbalistic literature included many expressions of the idea that we have a covenantal responsibility to our animals and to all the living beings that we interact with. Moshe Cordovero, in sixteenth-century *Safed*, gave us one of our most explicit and powerful examples:

> [A person should] not uproot a growing thing except for need, nor kill any animal [*ba'al chayyim*] except for need. And he should choose a good/easy death [*mitah yafah*] for them, with a carefully examined knife, to show mercy however is possible. This is the principle: compassion [*chemlah*] [should be] over all existences, to not hurt them . . . unless [it is] to raise them from level to level, from growing to living, from living to speaking, for then it is permitted to uproot the growing thing and to kill the animal, the debt/harm [being outweighed] by the merit.[92]

According to Cordovero, kosher slaughter or *shechitah* has the goal of "a good death." Cordovero coined this application of the term *mitah yafah*, but it comes from the *Tosefta*, where it has a very different meaning. In the *Tosefta* and Talmud, *mitah yafah* only applies to human beings; specifically, when capital punishment was due to be meted out, the manner of execution had to be a *mitah yafah*, a good or easy death, as defined by the rabbis.[93] Practically speaking, this meant minimizing the victim's pain and not disfiguring their body.

The requirement of *mitah yafah* was derived by the ancient rabbis from the verse, "Love your neighbor/friend as yourself" (Leviticus 19:18), one of the most important ethical principles in the Torah. Classically, this principle applies only to human beings. Cordovero made a radical leap by calling *shechitah* a "good death," implicitly teaching that the command "Love your neighbor" includes animals, who may be seen as neighbors and friends—in other words, as persons.

What defines a good death for Cordovero is not just that an animal should not suffer pain or disfigurement. The animal's soul should also be elevated by the manner and intention through which it was killed and eaten. If one's treatment of any living thing one uses is less than that, "the debt [of killing or taking] outweighs the merit."

Cordovero set an extraordinarily high ethical standard for every act that involves taking from the natural world. Contemporary ecology adds much more depth to this quest for merit. Having responsibility to benefit the souls of the animals we use is the highest order of covenantal relationship one can imagine.

Cordovero can provide inspiration for Jewish animal rights activists, but many Kabbalists, including Isaac Luria and most Hasidic thinkers, tend to understand the elevation of an animal differently: we are not acting on behalf of the animal as a subject or soul but on behalf of the sparks of divinity it contains.[94] The animal is, as it were, a vessel without personhood—and in some teachings, the animal or other vessel we make use of, whether plant or tool or rock, is seen as a prison from which the spark must be liberated.[95] Although this would seem to conflict with the idea that human souls can reincarnate in animals, these perspectives were often integrated.[96] In neither case is the animal a subject in itself, and neither includes the element of covenant between humanity and other animal species.[97]

Nevertheless, according to every Kabbalist, how one treats animals profoundly affects one's ability to elevate the sparks or souls found in them. Kabbalah can therefore undergird a strong vision of animal welfare, but only the Cordoveran lineage leads toward a deeper convenantal vision of our relationships with animals.

ABRAHAM ISAAC KOOK

One of the most important voices in Jewish tradition that can be used to support veganism and animal rights is Abraham Isaac Kook, chief rabbi of Palestine before the state of Israel was established. Kook's explanations for the laws concerning animals focus on moral lessons. For example, he says that the purpose of *kisui ha-dam*, covering the blood, is to "hide your shame [about eating meat] and your moral weakness."[98] Though this sentiment is powerful, the framework of covenant is absent.

While *kisui ha-dam* applies to wild animals with which people do not have regular relationships, Kook offered similar interpretations of the commandments regarding domestic animals. For example, the laws of slaughter and the prohibition of taking parent and child are meant to implant in a person's heart that

> this must not be an encounter with some ownerless thing, in which there are nothing but automatic reflexes, but rather with a creature which lives and feels, and one must consider its senses and even the emotions of its heart, including sentiments for the life of its family and compassion for its offspring.[99]

The permission to eat meat, for Kook as for Albo, was necessary to teach people to respect human life, but he believed that in messianic times all people would understand that whenever humans take from animals, it is a kind of theft or murder. He even regarded taking wool and milk as an act of oppression:

> The human being in the weakness of self-love ... approaches the poor cow and the mute sheep, taking from this one its milk and that one its wool.... It is not a moral wrong to take wool from the sheep when the wool's owner, the sheep itself, would be relieved by its removal, or in any case, when to do so would neither distress it nor harm it. It is indecent, however, to take it for one's own benefit when the true, natural owners, the sheep themselves, need it. So it is fitting to see this ... as a wresting of justice that comes only by means of an attack upon a weaker being. And the case is the same with the milk.... According to the holistic view ... the mother does not live so that one might presumptuously exploit (the milk) for oneself, but rather so that she can suckle her tender young beloved to her with the milk of her teats.[100]

These extended passages show the depth of feeling Kook had for animals as autonomous subjects. There is very little room here for a covenantal interpretation of human-animal relationships because using animals is cast as contrary to justice. Nevertheless, Kook also understood that humanity's role was to lead all Creation and all creatures toward God and toward the good.[101] This role suggests a covenantal relationship to all creatures on a more abstract level.

Kook's strict moral code aligns with the prophetic vision of redemption as a peaceable kingdom where all species live in Edenic harmony. However, even

Kook did not advocate total vegetarianism for his own time, let alone veganism. His reasoning closely followed Albo. According to Kook, humanity had not yet evolved to the level where society could fully respect animal life and still understand how important it is to value human life.[102]

The widespread interpretation that the flood story teaches that divine permission to eat meat was granted as a concession to human violence only becomes normative in more recent times through the influence of teachers like Kook. In this view *kashrut* has the combined purpose of making it difficult to eat meat and spiritually elevating the desire for meat. Though some scholars believe this interpretation to be the intended message of the flood story itself, there are only hints of it found in earlier rabbinic texts. Kook, closest in time to modern veganism, is also its closest ally.[103]

BIFURCATING MORALITIES

The centrality of human-animal relationships in the Torah is not surprising, given that ancient Israelites depended on their draft animals to plow and haul and on their herds to harvest the nourishment of pasture lands. Like every ancient society, whether hunting or herding or farming, to survive they needed to be in close relationship not just to the land but to the animals and plants they shared it with. Covenant was the ancient Israelite concept that guided those relationships.

As we saw, when Jewish thought becomes distant from the world described by the Torah, there is a shift away from a covenantal approach to animals. Instead of seeing ethical rules about animals as the framework for a living, mutual relationship, people tend to interpret those rules through two disparate lenses: either animals are here to serve humanity and the rules about animals reflect human needs, or animals have rights that exist independent of any relationship to humanity, and the rules reflect those rights.

The first lens sees the dominion of Genesis 1 as the foundation of our relationships to other animals. The second is more apt to see the model of Eden in Genesis 2 as the foundation for those relationships.[104] Neither perspective fits the integral meaning of covenant. Whereas dominion is declared an essential characteristic of humanity in Genesis 1, in the context of covenant, dominion means nothing more than the ability to domesticate, to choose which species to ally with in close relationship. The rest of the Torah provides the rules and the spiritual framework for such relationships. The converse idea that the Torah is an extended polemic against meat eating can empower an animal rights or vegan perspective, but it also derails such mutualistic interpretations. Without a covenantal framework, our humanity becomes founded on what we refrain from doing to other animals, on leaving animals alone rather than being engaged with them. Even in Eden, it is a given that the first human must encounter all the animals before the need for human companionship between an Adam and an Eve can be known.

Paul Shepard said, "The human species emerged enacting, dreaming, and thinking animals and cannot be fully itself without them."[105] We could say the same about the ancient Israelites. The issues raised by the Torah's strictures are broad and significant. But they only make sense in the context of a lasting covenant with other animal species.

VEGANISM AND COVENANTALISM: TRANSCENDING DICHOTOMY

What should we make of the tension between veganism and covenantalism, or between veganism and any ethical system that insists on the importance of animals in society?

Only in a technologically advanced society, disconnected from the land, could one conceive of abolitionist veganism.[106] The ideal of not using animals at all is only imaginable because we have tractors with internal combustion engines that can plow without oxen or horses. But the extraction-based industrial economy that makes this possible is necessarily plagued by oil spills and contamination; by the degradation of soil health because of monocropping, pesticides, and artificial fertilizers; and by loss of habitat caused by development and extraction itself—not to mention global climate disruption. That economy causes far more harm to animals than any shift to veganism would mitigate.

Industrial agriculture could not be much further from a system that respects animals, whether from the perspective of animal welfare or human compassion, whether in terms of rights, covenant, or sustainability. More strongly, our human ancestors made a sacred covenant with the species they adopted, a covenant that is violated every minute that concentrated animal feeding operations exist. There are strong grounds to say that all meat produced through such a system should be forbidden to Jews, according to biblical and rabbinic Judaism.[107]

Other technologies and other methods (like no-till farming), hold the promise of a different kind of agriculture. Even though we cannot arrive at a perfect system without working many years to change our society, a humane system that respects animals is already practiced on a small scale, including in parts of the Jewish community influenced by environmentalism.[108] Even if one embraces veganism as a messianic ideal for the end of history, in the manner of Kook and the prophets, there are so many steps we can take in the interim that accord with both veganism and covenantalism: eliminating factory farming, decreasing every community's meat consumption, using permaculture methods that allow land to serve as both agriculture and habitat. There is one step that would fit covenantalism but not abolitionist veganism: where possible, returning to an agriculture powered by draft animals instead of petroleum.[109] Even so, changing the role of farm animals in society from consumer products to partners should be a worthy goal for most vegans.

We can measure every institution affecting animal rights and welfare against the sacred covenant that our ancestors believed was the heart of society's relationships with its domesticated fellow travelers. Most changes that help people relate to animals in a covenantal manner will move us in a direction that accords with veganism. Like the prophets, our model of reality can include a recall of Eden, the fantasy ecosystem, along with a covenantal understanding of the real ecosystem, which calls on us to engage with the other creatures and bring healing and blessing to them, rather than destruction.

NOTES

1. Although it is not traditional to refer to humans and "other animals," that is the language Maimonides uses throughout the *Guide for the Perplexed*. I use it here when appropriate.

2. Gary L. Francione, landing page of the Abolitionist Approach, http://www.abolitionistapproach.com (accessed June 7, 2017).

3. The meaning of animal rights in the context of Jewish law and practice is discussed in David Mevorach Seidenberg, "Animal Rights in the Jewish Tradition," in *Encyclopedia of Religion and Nature* (New York: Continuum, 2004), 64–66.

4. This correlates with David Novak's definition of covenant in *The Jewish Social Contract: An Essay in Political Theology* (Princeton, NJ: Princeton University Press, 2005), 33. Novak, like many interpreters, is not cognizant of the fact that the first covenant is with all creatures, not just with humanity (34).

5. Anthropologist Pat Shipman has even proposed that the reason humans supplanted Neanderthal hominids is because of the advantages provided by their alliance with dog-wolves. See Pat Shipman, *The Invaders: How Humans and Their Dogs Drove Neanderthals to Extinction* (Cambridge, MA: Harvard University Press, 2015).

6. David Rindos, *The Origins of Agriculture: An Evolutionary Perspective* (San Diego: Academic Press, 1984); and T. O'Connor, "Working at Relationships: Another Look at Animal Domestication," *Antiquity* 71, no. 271 (1997): 149–56.

7. All translations are my own unless otherwise noted.

8. Mary Douglas, *Leviticus as Literature* (New York: Oxford University Press, 2000), 135 and 140. One could argue that the verses preceding this passage,

discussed below, impose such obligations on animals and human beings, but those obligations are not represented as part of the covenant.

9. See Leviticus 24:17–18. Similarly, in the next passage one word, *basar*, designates both living flesh and meat. These usages arise from a worldview that does not generally divide the animate from the inanimate or the metaphysical from the physical. See David Mevorach Seidenberg, *Kabbalah and Ecology: God's Image in the More-Than-Human World* (New York: Cambridge University Press, 2015), 354–56.

10. Commentaries debate whether humans and other animals all share the same food (Rashi, commentary to Genesis 1:29), or whether "the fruit of the tree" is especially designated for humans (Nachmanides, commentary to Genesis 1:29).

11. This may mean that any animal that takes a human life will be punished, but Nachmanides (commentary to Genesis 9:6) understands the phrase to mean that God will use animals to exact punishment from human beings. See Seidenberg, *Kabbalah and Ecology*, 155–57.

12. The term *b'heimah* (domesticated animal) does not appear in these verses. This may indicate that any relationship of domestication was annulled by the post-flood permission for humans to be predators.

13. Douglas, *Leviticus*, 136.

14. See, for example, Exodus 31:12–17, esp. 16, and Isaiah 58:13–14.

15. "Re-souled" translates *vayinafeish*, which is close to the word describing God's rest after creating, *vayinafash* (Exodus 31:17). This could suggest a higher level of covenant accessed only by human beings (though contrast it with Deuteronomy 5:14). These passages command rest for draft animals ("your ox and your donkey"); sheep and goats play a different role, as will be discussed shortly.

16. Many of the passages about animals mention not only the servant but also the stranger. If animals are included in the covenant, so are the non-Israelites who come to live among the people as immigrants and refugees. Ultimately, says Leviticus 25:23, we are all strangers and sojourners, *gerim v-toshavim*, in God's eyes.

17. Jacob Milgrom, *Leviticus 17–22* (New York: Random House, 2000), 1476–77.

18. Douglas, *Leviticus*, 137.

19. Ibid., 149.

20. Douglas writes, "Many religions are forced into casuistry to avoid contradiction between their affirmation of life and their act of taking life in sacrifice." Ibid., 68.

21. Milgrom, *Leviticus*, 1353, 1373, and 1474–77.

22. Douglas, *Leviticus*, 137.

23. Certain fat deposits called *cheilev*—the visceral fat, especially the omentum—were also regarded as inherently sacred (Leviticus 3:17, 7:23–7). The omentum is like a lattice surrounding the internal organs; it can contract over an injured internal organ to protect that organ while it heals. As an active organ, it differs radically from fat deposits that store energy.

24. David Mevorach Seidenberg, "Brit Taharah: Woman as Covenantal Body," *Sh'ma* 25, no. 486 (January 20, 1995), 5–6.

25. Seidenberg, *Kabbalah and Ecology*, 144–45.

26. Biblical scholars generally assume that the divine covenant is modeled on ancient Near Eastern suzerainty treaties between kings and vassal states. However, these chapters suggest that not only the divine covenant but even the relationships between king and people or between king and vassal state were modeled on a shepherd's relationship to the flock, and that the shepherding relationship was primary.

27. Though a few verses, such as 2 Samuel 7:8 and Amos 7:15, describe a shepherd going behind the flock, this portrays the way a shepherd may follow the flock without driving them.

28. Gary A. Rendsburg offers a very different and important interpretation: "Humans are unable to live up to the vegetarian ideal set forth at creation; God compromises and allows humanity to eat meat. But Israel wishes to adhere to that ideal, even in compromised fashion, and therefore Israel consumes only those animals that have not killed other animals.... Israel prohibits... the consumption of those animals that ingest blood, lest Israel consume blood 'through the back-door'... The vegetarian ideal comes first, and only secondarily were distinguishing characteristics noted." Gary A. Rendsburg, "The Vegetarian Ideal in the Bible," in *Food and Judaism*, ed. Leonard J. Greenspoon, Ronald A. Simkins, and Gerald Shapiro, (Omaha, NE: Creighton University Press, 2005), 327.

29. For further discussion, see David Mevorach Seidenberg, "Kashroots: An Eco-History of the Kosher Laws," Neohasid, September 2009, http://www.neohasid.org/torah/kashroots.

30. Proper animal husbandry almost requires the slaughter of most male animals. See Douglas, *Leviticus*, 95–96.

31. Douglas, *Leviticus*, 141 and 149.

32. *Chayah/b'heimah* may also be interpreted as predator/prey, but for our purposes, the contrast of wild/domesticated is more illuminating.

33. The prohibition on mating two different species fits as well (Leviticus 19:19), though it may also be thought of as taking care of animals on a species level. This may include a prohibition on neutering according to some scholars, though that is more likely a rabbinically derived law. See Ellen Goodfriend, "Leviticus 22:24:

A Prohibition of Gelding for the Land of Israel," in *Current Issues in Priestly and Related Literature*, ed. Roy E. Gane (Atlanta: SBL Press, 2015), 67–92.

34. The reason a goat kid is specified rather than lamb or calf may be because goats have a tendency to wander off from their flock and therefore show the mother-child relationship in greater relief.

35. Note also that although there is a different word for wild and domestic land animals, there is no such distinction for birds, which suggests that birds were never seen as fully domesticated.

36. Why does the verse say "days" instead of "your days"? Homiletically, the latter implies direct benefit to oneself, whereas the former implies benefit for all species affected by the commandment; more broadly, it implies sustainability.

37. In contrast with domestic animals, however, the *cheilev* fat of a wild animal may be used and even eaten.

38. Compare with Ezekiel 24:7, "for her blood was within her, she set it on bare rock, she did not pour it on the earth to be covered over with dirt," and with Job's plea in 16:18, "O earth, do not cover my blood, and may there be no [resting] place for my outcry." "Standing on the blood" as in, "Don't stand on your neighbor's blood" (Leviticus 19:16), may be read as the opposite of covering the blood.

39. It is also possible to explain this as a difference between Deuteronomy and Leviticus, rather than between domestic and wild animals (Douglas, *Leviticus*, 91–93), but here I am reading the Torah synoptically to understand its impact as a whole.

40. Milgrom discusses various interpretations in *Leviticus*, 1481–83; note especially *Midrash Yelamdenu*, 170, quoted in no. 5.

41. David Mevorach Seidenberg, "Genesis, Covenant, Shmitah, Jubilee and the Land Ethic," Neohasid, 2010, http://www.neohasid.org/torah/genesis-shmitah; and David Mevorach Seidenberg, "Shmita: The Purpose of Sinai," *Huffpost*, May 2, 2013, http://www.huffingtonpost.com/rabbi-david-seidenberg/shmita-the-purpose-of-sinai_b_3200588.html.

42. Rendsburg, "The Vegetarian Ideal," 328–29.

43. Hosea, however, being a committed farmer and no shepherd, makes only one passing reference to animal husbandry in 5:6, and a negative one at that.

44. *Exodus Rabbah* 2:2.

45. *Talmud Bavli* (Babylonian Talmud, henceforth *TB*) *Berakhot* 40a and *Gittin* 62a on feeding animals; *Chagigah* 14b and *Shabbat* 110b on neutering animals.

46. For more detail see *Maimonides, Mishneh Torah, Hilkhot Shmitah v-Yovel* 7.

47. *TB Bava Metzia* 32b.

48. *Sanhedrin* 59b, *Chullin* 102a, and *Pesachim* 22b.

49. *Genesis Rabbah* 34:12.

50. Rashi (attributed), commentary to verse cited above.

51. *Genesis Rabbah* 44:1.

52. See, for example, *TB Chullin* 113a–116a.

53. A parallel verse, Deuteronomy 14:21, suggests giving the meat to the *ger*, the stranger.

54. *Mekhilta Kaspa* 20, *Exodus Rabbah* 31:9, *Perek Shirah*, *Yalkut Shim'oni* 1:187, based on the verse, "And there will be a great cry in all the land of Egypt... and [yet] against all the children of Israel a dog will not sharpen [*yecherats*] its tongue" (Exodus 11:6–7).

55. The Midrash also imagines a covenant between God and the *dukhifat* or hoopoe (*TB Gittin* 68b, *Chullin* 63a), as well as one between Noah or God and the phoenix (*TB Sanhedrin* 108b, *Genesis Rabbah* 19:5). See Seidenberg, *Kabbalah and Ecology*, 345–46.

56. *Genesis Rabbah* 22:8. See note 35 on the inclusion of all birds in the same category as wild animals.

57. *TB Chullin* 87a, *Shabbat* 22a.

58. For example, *Pirkei D'Rabi Eliezer* chap. 24, *Genesis Rabbah* 63:13, as well as Torah commentary by Rashi, whose writing, though later, represents a rabbinic viewpoint uninflected by medieval philosophy. See Paul A. Kay and Bob Chodos, "Man the Hunter? Hunting, Ecology, and Gender in Judaism," *Journal for the Study of Religion, Nature and Culture, Ecotheology* 11, no. 4 (December 2006): 494–509.

59. *TB Avodah Zarah* 18b. Nevertheless, one rabbi is described as trapping deer to feed the hungry and then making a Torah scroll from their skins (*TB Bava Metzia* 85b). Note rabbinic lore that the mythical Leviathan, the ultimate wild animal, is destined to be served at a banquet for the righteous. However, only the archangel Gabriel can hunt Leviathan, only at the end of time, and only with divine assistance (*TB Bava Batra* 74b–75a). In the meantime, God takes him out to play with him every day, implying that God has a domesticating relationship with Leviathan (*TB Avodah Zarah* 3b).

60. The animal's body could be used for other purposes however, like fur for clothing, even if it was not slaughtered correctly. A wild animal's hide can be turned into parchment or *klaf* for writing a Torah scroll, and the hide may be obtained as a by-product of hunting (generally by non-Jews). In fact, deerskin Torahs were once common. Nevertheless, according to many scribes, it is forbidden to kill an animal for the sole purpose of obtaining *klaf* (Kevin Hale, personal correspondence, March 29, 2017). I am indebted to Kevin Hale and Linda Motzkin for my knowledge on this subject.

61. *Tanchuma*, Noah 10.
62. Seidenberg, *Kabbalah and Ecology*, 139–42.
63. *Pirkei D'Rabi Eiezer*, chap. 11.
64. *TB Chullin* 7a–b; *Pesikta Rabbati* 14; see "Animals as teachers, exemplars, and moral agents" in Seidenberg, *Kabbalah and Ecology*, 152–55.
65. *Genesis Rabbah* 33:3; *TB Bava Metzia* 85a; Seidenberg, *Kabbalah and Ecology*, 146. A recent effort to save an individual calf in Israel that is reminiscent of this story has led to an international vegan protest movement. See the website of the 269 movement, http://www.269life.com (accessed June 7, 2017).
66. Nahum N. Glatzer, "The Concept of Sacrifice in Post-Biblical Judaism," in *Essays in Jewish Thought* (Tuscaloosa: University of Alabama Press, 1976), 48–57.
67. *TB Pesachim* 49b. This statement appears in a section full of detractions against peasants (*am ha-aretz*). Although it suggests ordinary people should not eat meat, it also implies that people at higher spiritual levels should.
68. Traditional *halakha* places no limitations on the sourcing of these animals. As a result, a modern practice has evolved to use skins of fetal animals for Torah parchment because they are malleable and smooth. Such skins are readily available because pregnant animals are slaughtered worldwide in concentrated animal feeding operations; most of these animals' mothers would have died under awful conditions. See Shoshana Gugenheim, "Ethical Parchment Making," http://www.shoshanagugenheim.com/ethical-parchment-making (accessed March 27, 2017).
69. Commentary to Genesis 1:26, trans. Jeremy Cohen, part in *"Be Fertile and Increase, Fill the Earth and Master It": The Ancient and Medieval Career of a Biblical Text* (Ithaca, NY: Cornell University Press, 1989), 184–85, and part in "On Classical Judaism and Environmental Crisis," *Judaism and Environmental Ethics*, ed. Martin Yaffe (Lanham, MD: Lexington Books, 2001), 76–77. Contrary to other commentators, Saadyah also believed that humans were only temporarily banned from eating animals in Eden, until there would be enough of a population to cull from. See *"Be Fertile and Increase,"* 187.
70. *Hanivchar b'Emunot v'Dei`ot* (*Emunot v'Dei`ot*), trans. Yosef Kafich (Jerusalem: Makhon Sura, 1970), art. 4, introduction.
71. Maimonides, *The Guide for the Perplexed*, trans. Shlomo Pines (Chicago: University of Chicago Press, 1963), 3:12, 442.
72. Ibid., 3:13, 448, 452; also *Moreh N'vukhim*, trans. Yosef Kafich (Jerusalem: Mossad Harav Kook, 1977), 298 and 300–301. Maimonides's rejection of anthropocentrism was also a rejection of his position in earlier works. See, for example, *Mishnah `im Peyrush Harambam*, vol. 1 (Jerusalem: Mosad Harav Kook, 1963), *Hakdamah*, 21–2.
73. *Guide for the Perplexed*, 3:25, 504.

74. Ibid., 3:48 and 599.
75. Ibid., 600.
76. Ibid., 3:13, 452–53.
77. Ibid., 1:54, 124.
78. David Sears, *The Vision of Eden: Animal Welfare and Vegetarianism in Jewish Law and Mysticism* (CreateSpace, 2015), 95–98. Both wrote after the advent of Kabbalah and were inflected by it.
79. Genesis 4:4–8.
80. *Sefer ha-Ikkarim*, 3:15, http://www.daat.ac.il/daat/mahshevt/ikarim/c6-2.htm#3 (accessed March 28, 2017).
81. *Akeidat Yitzhak* (Lemberg/Lvov), 1868, Gate 41, 79b; quoted at length in Sears, *Vision of Eden*, 98. This ideal of ethical purity, which can also permeate modern veganism, can be strongly in tension with affirming or living closer to nature.
82. *Sefer Chasidim According to the Parma Manuscript*, ed. Yehudah Wistinetzki (Berlin: Itzkowski, 1891), §§1078–1080.
83. *Sefer Chasidim*, §1082, cf. §305. For other examples of this sensitivity see Seidenberg, *Kabbalah and Ecology*, 146.
84. *Sefer Bahir*, ed. Reuven Margaliot (Jerusalem: Mossad Harav Kook, 1994), §82, 168, 172.
85. *Bahir* §22, 119.
86. Ibid., §195. *Tikkunei Zohar* (published in the same volume cited for *Sefer Bahir*), §70, 133a, is a relatively early example from the fourteenth century that speaks about human reincarnation into animals.
87. Commentary to Genesis 1:29.
88. Ibid.
89. Commentary to Genesis 2:19.
90. Commentary to Deuteronomy 22:6–7.
91. One could say that here, too, Ramban is more worried about the impact on a human soul rather than the impact on other species, given that extinction was not imagined to be possible.
92. Moshe Cordovero, *Tomer D'vorah* (Jerusalem: Or Yikar, 1969), 19–20; and Moshe Cordovero, *The Palm Tree of Deborah*, trans. Louis Jacobs (New York: Sepher Hermon, 1974), 78, 83ff. Compare with *Tomer D'vorah*, 16; *The Palm Tree of Deborah*, 71.
93. *Tosefta Sanhedrin* 9:3 and *TB Sanhedrin* 45a, 52b, *Pesachim* 75a, and *Ketubot* 37b.
94. David Mevorach Seidenberg, "Building the Body of the Shekhinah: Re-enchantment and Redemption of the Natural World in Hasidic Thought," in *A New Hasidism: Branches*, ed. Arthur Green and Ariel Evan Mayse (Philadelphia:

Jewish Publication Society, forthcoming). The cosmology behind this view is that the first divine Creation shattered, and the second Creation, the one we inhabit, exists to reach out to the broken pieces and reintegrate the sparks of divinity they contain. Because of the importance and difficulty of this task, many Kabbalists taught that only one trained in Kabbalah should eat meat (Sears, *Vision of Eden*, 172).

95. Yaakov Yosef of Polnoye, *Ben Porat Yosef* (Pieterkov, Poland: Feivel Belchatovski, 1884), 74a.

96. See sources in Sears, *Vision of Eden*, 196–218.

97. More extremely, in the case of *shiluach ha-kein*, some Kabbalists saw a way to instrumentalize a covenantal connection between God and the mother bird. They understood that the purpose of chasing away the mother was to cause the bird anguish and thereby arouse God's anguish over Israel's exile. See Natan Slifkin, "Shiluach haKein: The Transformation of a Mitzvah" (Jerusalem, 2010), https://www.zootorah.com/RationalistJudaism/ShiluachHaKein.pdf (accessed September 2013), 17–18.

98. Abraham Isaac Kook, *Chazon Hatzimchonut v'Hashalom*, ed. David Cohen (Jerusalem: Nezer David, 1983), 23, online at https://he.wikisource.org/wiki/חזון_הצמחונות_והשלום; and *A Vision of Vegetarianism and Peace*, trans. Jonathan Rubenstein, 15, online at http://jewishveg.com/AVisionofVegetarianismandPeace.pdf (both accessed June 4, 2017). Some of his contemporaries interpreted *kisui ha-dam* instead as a kind of burial of the animal's soul. See Seidenberg, *Kabbalah and Ecology*, 147.

99. *Chazon Hatzimchonut*, 15, §8 (translation adapted).

100. Ibid., 21–2, §11 (adapted).

101. Abraham Isaac Kook, *Abraham Isaac Kook: The Lights of Penitence, the Moral Principles, Lights of Holiness, Essays, Letters, and Poems*, trans. Ben Zion Bokser (New York: Paulist Press, 1978), 221, or in Hebrew, Abraham Isaac Kook, *Orot Haqodesh*, 2 vols. (Jerusalem: Ha-agudah L'hotza'at Sifrei Hare'yah Kuk, 1937), vol. 2, 555.

102. Judging from PETA's 2003 "Holocaust on Your Plate" campaign, I do not think we can fault Kook for taking this position.

103. Rendsburg, "The Vegetarian Ideal," 320–23.

104. Both creation stories describe a vegan world (Rendsburg, "The Vegetarian Ideal," 321). However, they differ radically in how they have been applied to these issues.

105. Paul Shepard, *The Others: How Animals Made Us Human* (Washington, DC: Island Press, 1997), 4–5.

106. Even Jainism, which may present a premodern parallel to abolitionist veganism, allows using animals for dairy products (milking only after the calf has

nursed) and for plowing, though some Jainist sects discourage agriculture because of its inherent violence to plants and small animals.

107. Rabbi David Rosen makes this argument in "Is Any Meat Today Kosher?," in *Times of Israel*, March 16, 2017, http://blogs.timesofisrael.com/is-any-meat-today-kosher.

108. This would include larger operations like Kol Foods and Grow and Behold. Whether such a system would be accepted by vegans is another question. A protest at Urban Adamah's 2017 Purim party against the slaughter of chickens that are past egg laying—under the strictest humane conditions—highlighted this tension in the Jewish environmental community. Naomi Davis explicates the vegan perspective in "Why I Will Keep Protesting for Animal Rights at Urban Adamah", in *J.*, March 20, 2017, http://www.jweekly.com/2017/03/20/why-i-will-keep-protesting-for-animal-rights-at-urban-adamah.

109. A purist "vegan" alternative would be to run farm equipment on diesel engines fueled by vegetable oil. Neither ethical system can make good sense of indigenous hunting cultures, which can be sustainable and deeply respectful toward the animals they depend on, but covenantalism can be modified to fit such cultures.

9 Musar and Jewish Veganism

GEOFFREY D. CLAUSSEN

I am a rabbi, professor, and longtime vegetarian who committed myself to a vegan diet while I was immersed in research on the ideas and practices of the nineteenth-century Musar movement, a Lithuanian Jewish pietistic movement focused on the cultivation of moral virtue. My engagement with the literature of the movement and my adoption of practices that it recommended played and continues to play an important role in inspiring my veganism. This chapter explores some of the sources of that inspiration, focusing on approaches to loving-kindness, compassion, empathy, and self-restraint found in the writings of some of the most prominent figures in the early generations of the Musar movement. I give particular attention to the work of Rabbi Simchah Zissel Ziv of Kelm (1824–1898), founder of the first Musar movement yeshiva,[1] and I also consider some of the writings of Simchah Zissel's influential students Rabbi Natan Tzevi Finkel of Slobodka (1849–1927)[2] and Rabbi Yerucham Ha-Levi Levovitz of Mir (1873?–1936).[3]

DIVINE LOVE FOR ALL CREATURES AND THE PROHIBITION ON CAUSING SUFFERING

The Musar movement was characterized by its relentless efforts to encourage Jews to focus on the cultivation of virtues such as reverence for and fear of God, equanimity and self-restraint, humility and honesty, and generosity and loving-kindness. Its leaders sought to develop innovative practices of *musar* (moral discipline) that might help strengthen such virtues, rejecting the idea favored by the Lithuanian rabbinic elite that dedicating oneself solely to the intellectual study of Talmudic law was sufficient for guaranteeing a scholar's virtue. Musar movement leaders instead stressed the importance of other sorts of activities, including techniques of meditation, visualization, and emotionally charged chanting. They required students at Musar movement yeshivas not only to study Talmudic law but also to spend time contemplating biblical and rabbinic stories and developing "mental images" that would keep those stories and their key messages vivid in their imaginations, and they urged Jews to cultivate empathy and to seek out opportunities to perform deeds of loving-kindness far beyond the requirements of Jewish law.[4]

Musar movement rabbis were far more concerned with kindness to human beings than kindness to nonhuman animals. They clearly viewed humans as having a higher moral status than animals, and they followed the principle found in standard accounts of Jewish law that prohibits causing needless suffering to animals (*tza'ar ba'alei chayim*) but permits causing suffering to animals when justified by necessity. Their writings, however, also speak of the importance of treating all creatures with love and compassion and offer guided meditations to inspire the cultivation of such virtues.

The themes of love and compassion are particularly prominent in the writings of Simchah Zissel Ziv, who often speaks of the human obligation to strive toward an ideal of perfect, divine love. In one passage, he speaks of emulating divine love for all creatures by seeking to satisfy their needs and preventing needless suffering:

> The [fundamental] quality of God is that He loves all creatures; were it not so, they could not exist in the world. And we find that loving God's creatures is closeness to the Blessed One. . . . Our sages, in their holy way, have taught us (BT Sotah 14a): how can a person draw close to the Blessed One? By cleaving to [God's] attributes. And there are no character traits of the Blessed Lord more apparent to us than love of [God's] creatures. "You open up your hand and satisfy the desire of all that lives" (Psalms 145:16)—we see that every single creature receives pleasure and satisfaction for its desire, and this is simply God's love for [God's] creatures. And consequently we find that the prohibition on causing [needless] suffering to animals [*tza'ar ba'alei chayim*] comes from the Torah (BT Bava Metzia 32b).[5]

Simchah Zissel sees divine love as making life possible and satisfying the desires (or, as he would understand it, the needs) of all animals on Earth; in line with the Talmud's injunction to "cleave to God's attributes," he sees humans as required to emulate these qualities. While human beings cannot provide sustenance for all other creatures as God does, he indicates, we can emulate divine love by providing for animal needs in crucial ways, above all by not causing unnecessary suffering to God's creatures. The Talmud does not link this prohibition to any particular character trait, but Simchah Zissel sees it as a law that follows from the obligation to emulate divine love. Cultivating love must involve preventing the suffering of animals.

EMULATING NOAH'S CONSTANT CONCERN

Simchah Zissel did not issue any legal rulings on exactly how far the prohibition on causing needless suffering should extend. He did, however, point out that the prohibition applies to every animal species, which he explained in one of his discourses on the biblical character of Noah. Noah was commanded to preserve every species, he notes, each of which has significance for God's creation and deserves protection, such that "for each and every one of them [our sages] decreed that it is a Torah commandment to prevent [needless] suffering to animals."[6] One should learn from Noah that there is no species whose suffering can be ignored; one should also seek to be like Noah by being mindful of the needs of all species. Simchah Zissel builds on the midrashic tradition that Noah did not sleep during the year he spent on his ark, as he dedicated himself to caring for the needs of every species, feeding each one at the hour they needed to eat, even throughout the night. In Simchah Zissel's account, Noah possessed the equanimity that allowed him to be bothered by any need that might be unmet: "Behold, how anxious he was, for he habituated himself to the trait of equanimity, more than sufficiently."[7] We should all possess equanimity of this sort, in Simchah Zissel's view—not the sort of equanimity that allows us to feel calm and free from anxiety, but the sort that allows us to see the needs that exist in the world and to be anxious to respond to them.[8]

Simchah Zissel's student R. Natan Tzevi Finkel, founder of the Slobodka yeshiva, describes Noah as in fact successfully emulating the divine love that provides sustenance to all living beings. Building on midrashic tradition,[9] Finkel explains that Noah was like one who was

> appointed as Sustainer[10] of the world in [God's] place, for he was tested in terms of how he related to the animals, and how he discerned the needs and requirements of each one of them. Our sages have told that Noah did not let himself sleep during the whole twelve months, but rather would deliver the food that was fit for each one, at the set time.... Because of how Noah related to the animals, his character trait of loving-kindness and compassion was tested, and it was found to be like the character traits of the Holy Blessed One, and he was found to be fit to stand in [God's] place, to be the Sustainer of the world.[11]

As Finkel sees it, Noah met the test of being like God—neither slumbering nor sleeping, but acting with boundless love and compassion to meet the particular needs of every animal. Finkel asks his students to meditate on Noah's loving-kindness, holding a "mental image" of Noah before their eyes. After all, Finkel asks, "could we find a mental image of acting with loving-kindness that is more vivid than this—than serving animals with such great care for twelve months, not satisfying himself with the taste of sleep, sustaining them with great mercy and wisdom?"[12]

Finkel clearly sets the bar very high. Following a principle that was central to Simchah Zissel Ziv, he demands that human beings do all that they are capable of doing to meet such ideals of utter devotion, and he sees them as liable to punishment if they do not do so.[13] Finkel is guided in part by the midrash that points out that even Noah failed to do all that he was capable of in tending to the animals on his ark. According to the midrash, Noah was once late in feeding the lion on his ark, and the lion was justified in punishing him with a severe bite. Finkel understands the justice of this punishment in terms of the rabbinic tradition that the most righteous of people should be held to the strictest of standards. As he explains it, the most righteous have the ability to be people

> of true loving-kindness, focusing all of one's deeds, activities, movements, meditations, thoughts, innovations, and creations on the singular goal of loving-kindness. This is how a human being is obligated to resemble the Creator. But if one does not fulfill this obligation, one has damaged oneself, negating one's greatness and glory.... Even if one is immersed in loving-kindness and only loving-kindness day and night, and does not stop for even a moment ... but one finds any blemish at all within that loving-kindness, that is a punishable sin, and one will be punished for this with a bitter punishment.... [Thus, in the case of Noah] when a blemish was found within [Noah's] amazing loving-kindness, when his mind was distracted for a brief moment and he was late in feeding the lion, he was bitten.... The matter is amazing, showing how far the obligation of loving-kindness extends, even when it has not been [directly] commanded.[14]

Although I have little sympathy for praise for vicious punishments in response to momentary lapses of judgment, I agree with Finkel that "the matter is amazing." Even though none of us may ever be capable of reaching the saintly level of Noah as he is depicted here, I think that this story can inspire us to consider how far our loving-kindness can go and how we fail to tend appropriately to the legitimate needs of animals. While no human beings should forgo sleep entirely to tend to such needs, I think that there is power in challenging our complacency, even by meditating on incredible ideals, holding the image of Noah's constant wakefulness and loving-kindness before our eyes. Our responsibility to the animals in our care is such that, were we as alone as Noah was, we would be responsible to seek to act as he acted; called by hundreds of animals who have no one else to care for them, our responsibility to show loving-kindness would be never-ending.

"Once the other has called us, once we have fallen in love, we are enjoined to a life of never-ending responsibility," contemporary *musar* teacher Rabbi Ira Stone has written. "This love has taken away from us the ever-present luxury of infancy: the freedom to fall asleep at will. As adults, we must be wakeful and on guard; we must sleep with one eye open, as parents learn to do in the presence of their children." We should ideally be able to form communities, though, "so that the demands of infinite commitment, the demand of sleeplessness can be shared," for "without such a community the sleeplessness required by love would be unbearable."[15] Noah did not have a community and thus needed to stay awake all night; but his example can remind us of the constant need for our responsibility and care.

While in Noah's case the animals needed particular attention because the death of any of them would eliminate the species, we might be reminded of how our failures of compassion can still be very serious even when there is no such risk. This seems to have been the conclusion of R. Yerucham Ha-Levi Levovitz, who, like Finkel, marveled at Noah's compassion and God's judgment, and then added that God judges those who fail to respond to the pain of animals in other circumstances. As Levovitz points out, the story of Noah's punishment resembles a Talmudic story in which the editor of the Mishnah, Rabbi Judah the Patriarch, is punished for his own lack of attentiveness to the needs of animals (BT Bava Metzia 85a).[16] When a calf bound for slaughter escaped and, weeping, sought refuge with Judah, "[Judah] did not have compassion for it, but said to it: 'You were created for this.'"[17] For this, he was punished by God with thirteen years of suffering. Judah's suffering only ends when he protects a group of young rats who are about to be swept away by his maidservant, and he proclaims that "[God's] compassion is for all of [God's] works" (Psalms 145:9).[18] "If a person is lacking compassion for any of '[God's] works,' he is lacking in full righteousness" and is justly punished, Levovitz concludes, as Noah was.[19] Even the common act of slaughtering a calf so that humans may eat it is here presented as a failure to respond to the needs of animals and a failure of responsibility to protect those whom one can protect. Animals under the control of human beings deserve all the compassion that humans can offer them, even when they are hungry in the night, and especially when they are seeking to be saved from human brutality.

SHEPHERDS AND THE POWER OF EMPATHY

Simchah Zissel Ziv and his students taught, moreover, that the greatest human beings should be able to *empathize* with nonhuman animals: to seek to experience the world from their perspective and to feel their pain. Simchah Zissel saw Moses, in particular, as characterized by his empathy for others, building on traditions about how Moses empathetically identified with the Hebrew slaves in Egypt and also with the animals under his care when he worked as a shepherd in Midian. Simchah Zissel describes the disposition of seeing the needs of others, empathetically identifying with those in need, and responding with compassion as "sharing the burden of one's fellow" (*nosei be-ol im chaveiro*), and he sees this quality as the highest level of virtue demanded by the Torah.[20] In Simchah Zissel's understanding, Moses shared the burden of the slaves, for example, when he formed mental images of their suffering that remained before his eyes at all times, "until he felt their pain as if he himself was in such pain," and proceeded to act on their behalf.[21]

Simchah Zissel's reflections on Moses as a shepherd who feels the pain of his flock in this way build on the midrash that imagines God testing Moses and later David for their fitness to lead the people of Israel by testing their compassion for animals:

> "God tests the righteous" (Psalms 11:5). And how does [God] test them?—by shepherding flocks. [God] tested David with the flock and found him to be a good shepherd, as it is written: "[God] took him from the sheepfolds" (Ps. 78:70).... He would restrain the adults for the sake of the lambs, [first] bringing out the lambs to graze so that they could graze on the tender grass, and afterwards bringing out the old so that they could graze on the moderate grass, and afterwards bringing out the [strong] young so that they could eat the tough grass. The Holy Blessed One said: one who knows how to shepherd a flock, each according to their strength, let that one come and shepherd My people....
>
> And the Holy Blessed One also tested Moses, only by the flock. Our rabbis have said that when Moses our rabbi, peace be upon him, was shepherding the flock of Jethro in the wilderness, a kid escaped. He ran after it until he reached a shady place. When he reached the shady place, he happened upon a pool of water where the kid was standing, drinking. When Moses reached it he said, "I had not known that you had run away because of thirst. You must be tired." He placed it on his shoulder and walked back. The Holy Blessed One said: "You have shown compassion in guiding a flock belonging to a mortal; so, by your life, you should shepherd my flock, Israel."[22]

Simchah Zissel sees "sharing the burden" at work here. Though he admits that some might see this midrash as foolish, perhaps as a story only for children, he sees it as teaching the centrality of "sharing the burden" of all who are in need, including animals:

> Our forefathers—our father Jacob, peace be upon him, and David, and also our rabbi Moses the shepherd, peace be upon them—concerned themselves with livestock as shepherds for this reason: they wanted to habituate themselves even to share the burdens of animals, and all the more so to share the burdens of people of their generation.... My brothers and teachers, contemplate the wonders in this midrash, to learn such lofty teachings from one midrashic text. See the simple things that people scorn, as they are considered foolish in people's eyes. When these two great figures focused on this, training themselves in the character trait of "sharing the burden," they merited the kingship.[23]

It is clear from these texts and others that Simchah Zissel sees it as more important to relieve the burdens of human beings than the burdens of nonhuman animals; but he also sees empathy for animals as crucial. Working with animals can help one develop empathy, if such work is carried out in the proper spirit. Indeed, Simchah Zissel points out that the "lowly" task of being a shepherd helped Jacob, David, and Moses to turn away from the pride that inhibits empathy and to open themselves up to deeper compassion:

> In accordance with what has been explained above regarding the lofty matter of sharing the burden of one's fellow, we can understand why the great [leaders] of Israel chose to be shepherds. First, they chose lowly work, making a living in a humble manner. Second: humility leads to compassion, whereas pride means loving no one but oneself, not feeling the pain of the other, and not sharing one's fellow's burden. Therefore, they habituated themselves in the work of shepherding and in having compassion on the flock, leading them with gentleness and graciousness, as befit their fine manner.[24]

We are ordinarily inclined, as Simchah Zissel explains elsewhere, to focus on our own interests and to pay little attention to the needs of those we see as beneath us. But working with animals can help us pay attention to the needs even of those who cannot easily communicate their needs, who "do not know how to request or declare what they lack; and the physician (the herder) needs to seek out whether this way or that way would be good for them, and this requires much wise deliberation." Simchah Zissel thinks this is especially true with sheep or goats, whom he describes as "especially delicate, requiring a good deal of care, that one show compassion for them, and that one seek out what is good for them. Doing this places one at a high level."²⁵ Giving little attention to their own desires for honor and pleasure, and instead focusing on listening attentively and thoughtfully to the signals their flocks gave them, shaped Jacob, David, and Moses into the sorts of compassionate human beings who were also fit to lead the people of Israel.²⁶

Yerucham Ha-Levi Levovitz points out that the story of Moses's compassion as a shepherd should also be linked with the prohibition on causing needless suffering to animals (*tza'ar ba'alei chayim*). Moses's compassion allowed him to fully internalize the prohibition: "Such care for the flock, such caution not to cause suffering to animals in [even] this amount, is simply the force of his compassion in its fullness."²⁷ Moses refused to ignore "even the slightest suffering of an animal."²⁸ Natan Tzevi Finkel sees the story as revealing an obligation to discern and respond to the needs of every creature, and he connects Moses's understanding with the understanding that Rabbi Judah the Patriarch finally arrives at after his initial lack of compassion for the calf that had sought his protection:

> Our rabbi Moses, who followed the kid so that he could figure out why it ran away, after he found that it was tired and thirsty, he had compassion for it, and he placed it on his shoulder, and so it was revealed that he could understand and discern the needs of every creature. And so the Holy Blessed One found him fit to be the shepherd of Israel. And why did [God] test how [Moses and David] would relate to animals, in particular? It is because this reveals the loving-kindness and compassion that they possessed. So it is written regarding the Holy Blessed One: "His compassion is upon all of [God's] works" (Ps. 145:9), which includes all creatures, as in the story of Rabbi [Judah] and the calf and the young rats (BT Bava Metzia 85a). Moreover, it is written: "The eyes of all look to You expectantly, and You give them their nourishment promptly" (Ps. 145:15²⁹), as [God] is concerned for each [creature] in its own right, in accordance with its needs and promptly. Therefore, only a person who follows in the ways of God and who also has compassion for all creatures, and who knows how to determine and think deeply about the needs of each and every one of them, passes the test and is fit for the position of being a shepherd and leader.³⁰

Finkel makes clear that how one treats animals in one's care is the best guide to one's moral character, as it will reveal the depth of one's compassion.³¹

CONTEMPLATING MIDRASH AND OVERCOMING RATIONALIZATION

Of course, meditating on these midrashic narratives of compassion as they were explained by the Musar movement by no means guarantees a change in one's behavior toward animals. Even the Musar student who follows the instructions of Simchah Zissel Ziv to contemplate the midrash of Moses and the kid at length or the instructions of Natan Tzevi Finkel to hold a vivid image of Noah's compassion in one's mind, and even one who follows the Musar movement practices of discussing and journaling about how one's own behavior compares to these, can still easily rationalize a good deal of suffering inflicted on animals.[32] One can stress that Moses's compassion toward nonhuman animals was mere training for the more important task of showing compassion toward human beings. One can claim—as a commentator on Simchah Zissel's writings has—that "the prohibition of causing needless suffering to animals is not because the Holy Blessed One has compassion upon the soul of the animal, but rather only because good character traits are established in our souls through this."[33] One can also point out that according to the Torah's account, Moses helped institute a system in which humans were allowed to inflict substantial suffering on animals, especially by permitting the consumption of some forms of meat; and one can point out that Noah also sacrificed animals and also did not protest against the mass drowning of countless animals caused by the flood, even if he was fully dedicated to preserving the species on his ark.[34] One can also justify the suffering caused to these animals at the end of their lives with the comforting thought that their caretakers treated them with great compassion during the course of their lives.[35] One can easily empathize with one escaped kid, or with the particular animals on the ark, while overlooking the suffering of other animals who are not the focus of the stories.[36]

I think that a dedication to the practice of *musar* at its best, however, can help one to question these sorts of moves. Simchah Zissel warned his students to be wary of how one's self-interested inclination "deceives the human being with all sorts of cunning," seeking to rationalize one's moral failings.[37] Practitioners of *musar* today must also be mindful of how we may deceive ourselves and engage in rationalization of this sort. Meditating deeply on the principles discussed above and seeking to be as responsive as possible to "the needs of every creature" who depends on us can help us avoid our self-interested rationalizations.

Thus, for example, when one is tempted to dismiss compassion for animals as valuable only insofar as it trains us to be compassionate for human beings, meditating on Finkel's discussion of the divine concern "for each [creature] in its own right" can remind us of the dignity of each creature and the duties of compassion that are owed directly to it.[38] Or, for example, when one is tempted to defend one's desire to eat meat with reference to the meat eating permitted by the Torah, it can be valuable to think critically about why the Torah's authors gave this permission and to assess the morality of this permission in a way that takes seriously the value of preventing "even the slightest suffering of an animal."[39] So, too, when one is tempted to justify causing pain to an animal by pointing out that it has otherwise been treated with compassion throughout its life, I think it is important to question whether that pain is indeed necessary; it is essential to be careful not to act like Rabbi Judah when he sent the weeping calf to slaughter.[40] Calling that story to mind, and remembering to "think deeply about the needs of each and every creature," can help us to make more compassionate decisions about how we treat nonhuman animals.

We should be especially mindful of the danger that in our efforts to empathize with certain suffering animals, we will focus on them and be blind to the suffering of many others. This is a danger for all of us, including those of us who become vegetarians out of concern for animal suffering but ignore the suffering of animals who are tortured for their milk or eggs; or for those of us who commit to a vegan diet and, proud of our own commitments, fail to notice other ways we may be causing needless suffering in the world. It can be helpful to remind ourselves again and again of the obligation to take seriously the needs of all creatures, as these Musar teachers remind us with their telling of the stories of Rabbi Judah or Noah. As I suggested above, the story of Noah might especially remind us of the risks of exhaustion as we seek to help all creatures; at the same time, concerns about exhaustion should not serve as an excuse to ignore the many ways in which we can personally take greater responsibility for eliminating that suffering. Reflecting on these themes and meditating on these stories has certainly encouraged me in my own commitment to veganism, and my *musar* practice reminds me to always keep an open mind to other ways in which I can do better at reducing the suffering that we cause to our fellow creatures.

SHARING THE BURDEN OF THE ANIMAL

To be sure, empathy is an unreliable guide to morality, as we are prone to feel the pain of those to whom we are most attached and liable to ignore the pain of others, even when their pain is in fact far more serious and when there are many others.[41] We could imagine, for example, that Moses became attached to the one kid whom he lifted onto his shoulders but had limited empathy for the flocks of his neighbors or, all the more likely, the flocks of his enemies, even if those flocks were abundant and were treated cruelly. But the Musar teachers imagined Moses taking a more objective view, learning to have compassion as God has compassion—"compassion for all creatures," as Finkel put it, seeking "to determine and think deeply about the needs of each and every one of them."[42] I think that contemporary efforts to uncover and respond to the needs of animals can be deepened by empathy along these lines, informed by reasoned efforts to reduce bias and partiality. Contemporary empirical research indicates that empathy makes a difference in motivating human beings to help others; the efforts by Simchah Zissel and his students to promote the cultivation of empathy informed by reasoning may be one of the Musar movement's most valuable contributions to contemporary ethics.[43]

I think that we would do well, then, to adopt some of the Musar movement teachers' recommendations for empathetically considering the perspectives of others, guided by reasoning and our capacities to imagine the suffering of others, always seeking to respond compassionately. We may cultivate empathy not only by bringing to mind ideals of empathy associated with Moses or other figures described in the midrashic literature but also by bringing to mind concrete instances of animal suffering in the world around us, including instances of failures of empathy that lead to that suffering. Thus, when Simchah Zissel described how to understand the virtue of "sharing the burden," he urged his students to visualize a common case of animal abuse that could be eliminated through empathy:

> We can understand [the quality of "sharing the burden"] when we see a wagon driver steering a full wagon, when his horse does not want to go forward, and he beats it and beats it. If the wagon driver were himself to try to pull the burden with all his might, like the horse, then he would not be so cruel to the horse. But because he is not pulling along with the horse, he does not have a mental image which demands compassion for the horse, which is continually pulling with all its might. And this is what [our sages] hinted at: if you want to feel the pain of your fellow, stand next to him and pull his burden along with him, and then you will feel your fellow's pain.[44]

Those of us who live in the industrialized world no longer see images of cruel wagon drivers that remind us how to share the burden of animals in our care, but we are surrounded by comparable instances of cruelty that demand our empathy and compassion. In the contemporary West, where the vast majority of our interactions with land animals involve eating their bodies or drinking their milk, we are surrounded by animals who are confined in crowded cages, abused, and slaughtered in their youth so that such products can be sold for food at low prices.[45] The practice of *musar* today might especially focus on examples that were unknown in Simchah Zissel's days but are currently widespread, such as the case when a "spent" dairy cow is brought to a slaughterhouse, about which a contemporary *musar* teacher might say the following:

We can understand the quality of "sharing the burden" when we see a downed cow, having collapsed from fatigue, which cannot get up from the slaughter truck to go to the assembly line. The stockyard workers use their electric prods to try to get her out of the truck, and they beat her and kick her in the face, ribs, and back, but still she does not move; they tie a rope around her neck, tie the other end to a post in the ground, and drive the truck away, so that the cow is dragged along the floor of the truck and falls to the ground, landing with her hind legs and pelvis broken, lying for hours in the hot sun until a slaughterer finally comes to kill her. If the stockyard workers were to experience the perspective of this broken and exhausted cow, tortured all her life in an intensive production facility until being sent to slaughter, they would not be so cruel to her. But they do not have a mental image which demands compassion for her.[46]

Or we may understand the quality of "sharing the burden" when we consider the system in place for the slaughter of that cow and the slaughterhouse managers who have developed a process whereby cows are routinely "bled, skinned, and dismembered while conscious."[47] Or we might visualize an episode from earlier in the life of the cow, when she bellows in distress, as a dairy worker drags her newborn calf away so that her milk can be sold and the calf's flesh can be sold as veal.[48]

Or we may understand the quality of "sharing the burden" when we consider the factory farmers who engineer their broiler chickens so that their muscles and fat tissues grow faster than their bones, so that they can provide maximum meat even though they live in pain and struggle to walk and breathe during their short lives.[49] Or we may visualize the efforts of those who design systems for partially amputating the beaks of hens, causing severe pain for weeks, or for packing them into towers of battery cages in windowless rooms, or for grinding to death their male chicks who are not needed by the egg industry.[50] Or we may bring to mind the fishing company executives who design systems whereby fish and other sea creatures convulse in pain as they slowly die.[51]

In my home state of North Carolina, where the torture of pigs is especially widespread, we may visualize the workers who ram iron poles into the orifices of mother pigs, or who cut off pigs' legs while they are still conscious, or who bash the heads of runts who do not grow fast enough and are considered a drain on resources.[52] Workers are asked to heed the infamous counsel of the trade journal *Hog Farm Management*: "Forget the pig is an animal. Treat him just like a machine in a factory."[53] They do not have a mental image that demands compassion for the pigs; they are very far from sharing the burden of the animals and feeling their pain.

As has been well documented, contemporary factory farming offers countless other examples of cruelty.[54] The responsibility for the abuse of farmed animals clearly does not lie only with the workers who directly inflict it but with the supervisors who direct them, the executives who have overseen the creation of these systems, the investors who fund them, the marketers who market animal products, and the consumers who purchase these products.[55]

We might, then, understand the quality of "sharing the burden" when we see consumers who in theory care about the suffering of animals but who purchase food that is produced through the infliction of unbearable levels of suffering to animals. If we were to have mental images that demanded compassion for those animals, perhaps we would not purchase such products.

Images of the suffering caused by the animal agriculture industry are hard to bring to mind, though, when that industry ceaselessly advertises its products with nostalgic images of contented farm animals—cattle grazing under blue skies, chickens clucking contentedly in beautiful farmyards, and so on. "The power brokers of factory farming know that their business model depends on consumers not being able to see (or hear about) what they do," Jonathan Safran Foer notes.[56]

The Musar movement practice of meditating on other sorts of "mental images" can be an important antidote to such well-funded efforts to conjure up images of happiness and hide realities of violence from our gaze. We can do better than Simchah Zissel's wagon driver who was unable to bring the suffering of his horse to his mind, or Rabbi Judah, who was unable to take the weeping calf seriously. Just as Moses was able to visualize images of the suffering of the slaves in Egypt, despite the powerful interests that ignored that suffering, or perhaps just as Rabbi Judah eventually perceived the needs of the young rats in his home and stopped his maidservant from sweeping them away, we can keep in mind images of the violence toward animals that surrounds us and take action to prevent that violence, even if only by refusing to buy products that were produced in a way that caused unnecessary suffering to animals.

SELF-RESTRAINT BEFORE PLEASURE

It is difficult to make a case that the purchase and consumption of such products are "necessary." Rather, people generally purchase animal products because doing so is convenient or, above all, because doing so is pleasurable.[57] Thus, for example, meat eaters commonly justify meat eating on the grounds that animal flesh "tastes great" even though, as Elisa Aaltola has put it,

> it is a sign of very sloppy moral thinking to suggest that pain and suffering can be brushed aside on the basis of culinary pleasure. Can we not do better than this? Is it really true that the 30 or so days of misery that broiler birds have to face, the inability to walk properly, the breathing problems, the joint pains and the broken bones, can be justified by the fact that one day some human beings will be able to enjoy a five-minute meal of chicken wings?[58]

As one of the Musar movement's core concerns was to help people exercise self-restraint of their appetites, a contemporary engagement with *musar* can also help us cultivate a willingness to put aside the pleasures of eating animal products.

Simchah Zissel taught his students to break their appetites in a variety of ways, especially by asking them to meditate on the transient nature of the pleasures of appetite in comparison with the lasting nature of the pleasures of virtue. Although he considered it permissible to find some joy in eating and drinking, insofar as these activities are "the supporters for the tree of life in a person," he cautioned that the ultimate "tree of life," the Torah, is itself the essence of real and lasting joy.[59] Simchah Zissel counseled that appetitive desires often "interfere with one's clear view of what is good,"[60] that seeking after ephemeral pleasures is mere "vanity and striving after wind" (Ecclesiastes 1:14),[61] and that his chosen disciples should "share the burdens of their fellows without taking pleasure for themselves at all."[62] He urged his students to seek to break their own appetites, "not to go one day without restraining desire, for the essence of living as a human is to be in opposition to desire; if one does not do so, one is like one of the wild beasts of the forest."[63] One of his students reported that Simchah Zissel himself took so little pleasure in good tastes that he actually lost his sense of taste for a number of years.[64]

Even without going this far down the path of asceticism, one can learn from this model how to restrain the appetites that can lead to the cruel exploitation of animals. When we find ourselves desiring the pleasures of the meal of chicken wings, it can be helpful to remember the ephemeral nature of the pleasures of the brief meal; it can be helpful to see how our appetites can lead to rationalization, interfering with our clear view of what is good, unless we restrain them; it can be helpful to see how our appetites can be selfish, when we should be focused on sharing the burden of the other; and it can be helpful to remember how it is possible to control and break one's appetites. When our eating preferences cause suffering to other creatures, we should be able to restrain our desires to fulfill those preferences. Practices of *musar*, such as the practice of finding a way to restrain one's desires every day, can train us to do so.

SIMCHAH ZISSEL'S EXPLORATIONS OF VEGETARIANISM

Simchah Zissel does refer briefly in his writings to some period of time (of unknown length: a week? a month? a year?) when he committed to not eating meat. In one paean to the value of hosting guests in one's home, he reflects on how he was once hosted at another's home, and how grateful he was that his dietary commitment was honored by his hostess: "At that time, I did not want to eat meat... and she cooked good, meatless food for me, and I knew that I could rely upon her, that she would surely cook without meat as I desired."[65]

I imagine that this period of vegetarianism was an exercise in self-restraint on Simchah Zissel's part, a way of seeking to "restrain his desire" and be less like "one of the wild beasts of the forest." Perhaps it was also connected with his own consideration of how, if one is indeed like a beast oneself, slaughtering other beasts may be like murder. As he noted in another discourse:

> What can the world say regarding how they can be given permission to kill and eat beasts, and how they can be considered greater than the beast? Surely, it is only when one is differentiated through reason. But when the aim of one's reason is simply [to satisfy] appetite, everything follows that aim, and one is an animal, possessing great appetite, and one can find the strength to kill beasts for food and other purposes, or even to cause pain to human beings, or even to murder. Surely the world is uncompromising on these matters; how could they compromise on "murdering oneself"?...
>
> To what may this be compared? To a prayer group of the uneducated who see that they are disregarded among those who are honorable. What do they do? They build a House of Study for themselves, and there even the lowly can stand in the place of the great.... Thus, all the lowly build themselves synagogues for the wicked, and they say, "place knives in our hands, and a submissive beast in our hands; let us kill for meat, and slaughter the flock, and eat and take pleasure from our appetites all of our days, as if we were animals."
>
> No! You *are* like beasts! Why are you murdering every day, without interruption? What do you have against the beasts, that they are animals? You are animals!"[66]

We can see in these comments that Simchah Zissel clearly believed that human beings are in theory entitled to eat meat because they are on a higher level than nonhuman animals, distinguished by their capacities for overcoming their appetites with reason.[67] Insofar as one overcomes one's appetites—for instance, one's appetite for meat—then one may be entitled to eat meat. But if one does not overcome those appetites and is not guided by one's reason, then one is not entitled to eat meat. Those who desire meat the most may then be those who are least entitled to eat it; when they are so much like animals themselves, their own slaughter of animals is like murder, as they are killing their brothers and sisters.

Simchah Zissel clearly aspired to be part of the elite who would be fully human—"differentiated through reason"—and thereby permitted to eat meat. But he also believed that a great many human beings did not make use of their reason, and thus were less than fully human. "Many act without reasoning and contrary to reason," he notes at one point, "for they always proceed as if they are animals—and in this way, one truly becomes an animal."[68] Simchah Zissel certainly suspected himself at times of failing to act with reasoning; perhaps his exploration of vegetarianism, however brief, reflected his concern that for him, too, eating meat was participating in murder.

Today, we have access to a good deal more evidence than Simchah Zissel did about just how similar all human beings and nonhuman animals are; we can see how the capacities for emotion and reason among many nonhuman animals closely resemble those of humans; we have reason to be skeptical that any humans are able to be substantially "differentiated through reason" from animals. Simchah Zissel struggled with the question of how difficult it is to overcome one's animality and earn the right to be called superior to the species that he sometimes ate; I think we would be wise today to be even more skeptical of the idea that we can think of ourselves as superior to nonhuman animals in ways that justify causing them needless suffering.[69]

CONCLUSIONS

The relations between human beings and nonhuman animals in the contemporary West are vastly different than they were in the time of Simchah Zissel and his students. We now encounter land animals primarily as food that has been produced by factory farming, which involves unprecedented cruelty on an unprecedented scale. And we have new scientific knowledge that informs our understanding of these animals' intelligence and of their suffering. Still, I hope that Jews today, when evaluating their behavior toward animals, may be informed and inspired—as I have been—by some of the virtues, principles, and practices that the Musar movement's rabbis championed in the late nineteenth and early twentieth centuries. Many of us may benefit from Musar movement meditations on the divine ideal of concern for all creatures, on the commandment to prevent suffering, and on the compassion of figures like Noah and Moses; many of us may benefit from the counsel to engage in introspection regarding our own capacities for empathy and compassion and to create mental images that help us respond to the suffering of animals; and many of us may benefit from restraining our desires and from considering our animality. Engaging with these ideas and practices in our era of factory farming, though, may lead us to different conclusions than the Musar movement masters arrived at, such as committing to a vegan diet and boycotting the animal agriculture inustry.[70]

NOTES

1. I explore R. Simchah Zissel Ziv's life and thought at length in Geoffrey Claussen, *Sharing the Burden: Rabbi Simḥah Zissel Ziv and the Path of Musar* (Albany: SUNY Press, 2015). See also Tamar Ross, "Ha-Maḥshavah Ha-Iyunit Be-Khitve Mamshikhah Shel Rav Yisra'el Salanter Bitnu'at Ha-Musar" (Moral Philosophy in the Writings of Rabbi Israel Salanter's Disciples in the Musar Movement), Ph.D. thesis, Hebrew University, 1986. I have written one article that explores images of animals and animality in Simchah Zissel's thought (and the thought of his teacher, Rabbi Israel Salanter): Geoffrey Claussen, "Jewish Virtue Ethics and Compassion for Animals: A Model from the Musar Movement," *CrossCurrents* 61, no. 2 (2011): 208–16. The present chapter builds on the sources and ideas first presented in that article.

2. For background on R. Natan (Nosson) Tzevi Finkel, see Shlomo Tikochinski, "Yeshivot Ha-Musar Me-Lita Le-Eretz Yisra'el: Yeshivat Slabodka Ve-Shitatah Ha-Ḥinukhit, Aliyatah Ve-Hitbasesutah Be-Eretz Yisra'el Ha-Mandatorit," Ph.D. thesis, Hebrew University, 2009; Simcha Willig, "Gadlut Ha-Adam and the Greatness of Humanity: A Textual Analysis of Rabbi Nathan Tzvi Finkel's Psycho-Religious Educational Philosophy," Ph.D. thesis, New York University, 2016.

3. For background on R. Yerucham Ha-Levi Levovitz, see Ross, "Ha-Maḥshavah Ha-Iyunit," esp. 114–23 and 156–59; Ben-Tsiyon Klibansky, "Ha-Yeshivot Ha-Litayot Be-Mizraḥ Eiropah Bein Shetei Milḥamot Ha-Olam" (The Lithuanian Yeshivas in Eastern Europe between the Two World Wars), Ph.D. thesis, Tel Aviv University, 2009, 335–48; and Benjamin Brown, *Tenu'at Ha-Musar Ha-Lita'it: Ishim Ve-Ra'ayonot* (Moshav Ben-Shemen: Modan, 2014), chap. 10.

4. See my overview in Claussen, *Sharing the Burden*, 1–5. On the founding of the Musar movement, see Immanuel Etkes, *Rabbi Israel Salanter and the Mussar Movement: Seeking the Torah of Truth*, trans. Jonathan Chipman (Philadelphia:

Jewish Publication Society, 1993). An excellent Hebrew-language survey of the Musar movement is Brown, *Tenu'at Ha-Musar Ha-Lita'it*.

5. Simchah Zissel (Broida) Ziv, *Sefer Ḥokhmah u-Musar* (New York, 1957), 1:31. BT = Babylonian Talmud.

6. Simchah Zissel (Broida) Ziv, *Or Rasaz: Al Ḥamishah Ḥumshei Torah*, ed. Ḥayyim Shraga Levin (Jerusalem: Kefar Ḥabad, 1960), 1:72.

7. Ziv, *Ḥokhmah U-Musar*, 1957, 1:255, following Midrash Tanchuma Noah 9.

8. See Claussen, *Sharing the Burden*, 85.

9. Midrash Genesis Rabbah 30:6, 34:6; Midrash Tanchuma Noah 9.

10. Or "administrator" or "trustee" (in Hebrew, *parnas*).

11. Natan Tzevi Finkel, *Or Ha-Tzafun* (Jerusalem: Yeshivat Chevron, 1959), 2:8.

12. Ibid., 1:247. Finkel goes on to tell the story recorded in BT Sanhedrin 108b of how a phoenix observed just how busy Noah was—and had compassion on him.

13. See Claussen, *Sharing the Burden*, 116–24.

14. Finkel, *Or Ha-Tzafun*, 1:246.

15. Ira F. Stone, *A Responsible Life: The Spiritual Path of Mussar* (New York: Aviv Press, 2006), 22–23.

16. See also the version of the story of Rabbi Judah in Midrash Genesis Rabbah 33:3, where it is linked with the story of Noah.

17. This is the language in Yerucham Ha-Levi Levovitz, *Da'at Torah*, ed. Simchah Zissel Ha-Levi Levovitz (Jerusalem: n.p., 2001), 1:55.

18. The identity of the animals in question here is not certain, but Levovitz understands them to be rats. On the idea that they are young rats, see Aaron S. Gross, *The Question of the Animal and Religion: Theoretical Stakes, Practical Implications* (New York: Columbia University Press, 2014), 248–49, n. 83.

19. Levovitz, *Da'at Torah*, 1:55.

20. See Claussen, *Sharing the Burden*, 158–86. The phrase *nosei be-ol im chaveiro* comes from a list of the forty-eight virtues necessary for acquiring Torah in Mishnah Avot 6:6.

21. Ziv, *Ḥokhmah U-Musar*, 1957, 1:3.

22. Midrash Exodus Rabbah 2:2.

23. Ziv, *Ḥokhmah U-Musar*, 1957, 1:8–9.

24. Ibid., 1:6.

25. Simchah Zissel (Broida) Ziv, *Sefer Ḥokhmah u-Musar* (Jerusalem, 1964), 2:34.

26. I do not have the space within this paper to engage with presentations of the character of Jacob, but a relevant Musar movement source is Finkel's discussion of Jacob's equal regard for his sons and for his flock in Finkel, *Or ha-Tzafun*, 2:8–9.

27. Levovitz, *Da'at Torah*, 2:12.

28. Yerucham Ha-Levi Levovitz, *Sefer Da'at Ḥokhmah u-Musar* (Jerusalem: Me'orai Oros Hamussar, 2003), 1:28.
29. NJPS translation, modified thanks to a suggestion from Martin S. Cohen.
30. Finkel, *Or ha-Tzafun*, 2:7–8. I have built on these comments from Finkel and the preceding comments by Levovitz and Simchah Zissel, in Geoffrey Claussen, " 'I Will Be with Them': God at the Burning Bush as an Ideal of Compassion for All Creatures," in *Ehyeh Asher Ehyeh*, ed. David Birnbaum and Martin S. Cohen (New York: New Paradigm Matrix, 2019).
31. It is worth noting that a story has been told about the founder of the Musar movement, R. Simchah Zissel Ziv's teacher Rabbi Israel Salanter, that imagines Salanter also running after a lost animal and responding to it with compassion. See Shmuel Yosef Agnon, *Yamim Nora'im*, 3rd ed. (Jerusalem: Schocken, 1946), 297. The transformation of that story to include a motive of compassion for animals, however, arrives relatively late in its development. Compare to Louis Ginzberg, *Students, Scholars and Saints* (Philadelphia: Jewish Publication Society, 1928), 187–88. For further background on the story's development, see Gershon Kitzis, "Kol Mi-Bayit Ve-Kol Mi-Chutz," *Mabu'a* 18 (1983): 168–87.
32. For a discussion of how the Musar movement can easily rationalize violence, see Claussen, *Sharing the Burden*, 194–95; Geoffrey Claussen, "The Promise and Limits of R. Simḥah Zissel Ziv's Musar: A Response to Miller, Cooper, Pugh, and Peters," *Journal of Jewish Ethics* 3, no. 1 (2017): 165; and Jeffrey C. Pugh, "Whose Burden, Exactly, Are We Sharing?," *Journal of Jewish Ethics* 3, no. 1 (2017): 143–44. See also Geoffrey Claussen, "War, Musar, and the Construction of Humility in Modern Jewish Thought," *Interreligious Studies and Intercultural Theology* 2, no. 2 (2018). Regarding the Musar movement practices of introspection, conversation, and journaling, see Geoffrey Claussen, "The Practice of Musar," *Conservative Judaism* 63, no. 2 (2011): 11–15.
33. This summarizes an opinion from Yosef Sha'ul Ha-Levi Nathanson, *Sefer Divrei Sha'ul ve-Yosef Da'at: Sho'el U-Meshiv Mahadura Hamisha'ah* (Lemburg, 1879), brought as a caution regarding Simchah Zissel's words in *Beit Kelm: Emunah U-Middot* (Benei Berak: Siftei Ḥakhamim, Va'ad Le-Hafatzat Torah U-Musar, 2010), 571, n. 445. I also discuss this idea as framed by J. David Bleich in Claussen, "Jewish Virtue Ethics," 213–14.
34. The mass drowning is justified in the classical midrash, though, by the assumption that the animals were engaged in morally evil behavior just like their human counterparts. See Midrash Tanchuma Noah 5.
35. Katherine Wills Perlo, *Kinship and Killing: The Animal in World Religions* (New York: Columbia University Press, 2009), 46.

36. The general problem of how our intense empathy for particular individuals leads us to ignore others is discussed in Paul Bloom, *Against Empathy: The Case for Rational Compassion* (New York: Ecco Books, 2016). With reference to the midrash of Moses and the kid, see the comments by Misha Clebaner quoted in Geoffrey Claussen, "The Legacy of the Kelm School of Musar on Questions of Work, Wealth and Poverty," in *Wealth and Poverty in Jewish Tradition*, ed. Leonard J. Greenspoon (West Lafayette, IN: Purdue University Press, 2015), 176. For an example of misplaced compassion to animals in particular, with reference to the stories under discussion, see Perlo, *Kinship and Killing*, 65–66.

37. See Claussen, *Sharing the Burden*, 44. I discuss how Simchah Zissel himself was susceptible to rationalization of this sort in Claussen, "The Promise and Limits," 163–66.

38. See further Claussen, "Jewish Virtue Ethics," 214.

39. The theological orthodoxy of the Musar movement rabbis led them to assume divine authorship of the Torah and did not permit them to think critically about its authors' perspectives, but I think that *musar* at its best should embrace a historical-critical approach. I discuss this in Geoffrey Claussen, "The Kaddish, the Allegory of the Cave, and the Golden Calf: Meditations on Education and the Encounter with God," in *Kaddish*, ed. David Birnbaum and Martin S. Cohen (New York: New Paradigm Matrix, 2016), 318–31.

40. See the discussion of this story in Gross, *The Question of the Animal and Religion*, 164–71 and 176.

41. See Christian B. Miller, *Moral Character: An Empirical Theory* (Oxford: Oxford University Press, 2013), 126–27; and Bloom, *Against Empathy*.

42. See my discussion of empathy informed by reasoning and efforts to take an objective view in Claussen, *Sharing the Burden*, 83–84, 144, and 163–64.

43. Christian B. Miller, "How Contemporary Psychology Supports Central Elements of Simḥah Zissel's Picture of Character," *Journal of Jewish Ethics* 3, no. 1 (2017): 120–30. T. J. Kasperbauer brings important evidence to caution us that empathy does not appear to be "central" to motivating moral concern for nonhumans, but he does affirm the positive correlation between empathy and moral concern. See T. J. Kasperbauer, "Rejecting Empathy for Animal Ethics," *Ethical Theory and Moral Practice* 18, no. 4 (2015): 821.

44. Ziv, *Ḥokhmah U-Musar*, 1957, 1:14.

45. Gross, *The Question of the Animal and Religion*, 6 and 132; and David J. Wolfson and Mariann Sullivan, "Foxes in the Hen House: Animals, Agribusiness and the Law: A Modern American Fable," in *Animal Rights: Current Debates and New Directions*, ed. Martha Nussbaum and Cass R. Sunstein (Oxford: Oxford University Press, 2004), 206.

46. This example is based on the description by Elisa Aaltola, *Animal Suffering: Philosophy and Culture* (New York: Palgrave Macmillan, 2012), 39, drawing on video released in 2008 from a Humane Society of the United States investigation; and "Downed Cow: The True Story of One Anonymous Animal Born into the Meat Industry," PETA, http://www.peta.org/features/downed-cow-meat-industry (accessed August 12, 2016).

47. Jonathan Safran Foer, *Eating Animals* (New York: Back Bay Books, 2009), 230.

48. See Jeffrey Moussaieff Masson, *The Face on Your Plate: The Truth about Food* (New York: Norton, 2009), 79–92; and "Daisy Sour Cream and Cottage Cheese: Calves Torn from Their Mothers, Sick and Struggling to Breathe," PETA, http://investigations.peta.org/suffering-at-daisy-sour-cream-supplier (accessed August 12, 2016).

49. Foer, *Eating Animals*, 130.

50. Peter Singer, *Animal Liberation: The Definitive Classic of the Animal Movement*, updated edition (New York: Ecco Books, 2009), 98–119.

51. See Foer, *Eating Animals*, 190.

52. Ibid., 181–82 and 187.

53. John Byrnes, "Raising Pigs by the Calendar at Maplewood Farm," *Hog Farm Management* (September 1976): 30, quoted in Jim Mason and Peter Singer, *Animal Factories* (New York: Crown, 1980), 1.

54. Jonathan Safran Foer, in cataloging some instances of slaughterhouse abuse, writes that "I could have filled several books—an encyclopedia of cruelty—with worker testimonials" (Foer, *Eating Animals*, 252). For a particularly comprehensive work of investigative journalism on slaughterhouses, Foer recommends Gail A. Eisnitz, *Slaughterhouse: The Shocking Story of Greed, Neglect, and Inhumane Treatment Inside the U.S. Meat Industry* (Amherst, MA: Prometheus Books, 1997).

55. I do think that we are also obligated to show compassion toward those who cause such cruelty, and certainly for impoverished workers who take jobs that produce cruelty to provide for their own families. I am grateful to Jacob Ari Labendz for suggesting the importance of this point.

56. Foer, *Eating Animals*, 87.

57. David DeGrazia, *Animal Rights: A Very Short Introduction* (New York: Oxford University Press, 2002), 73–74.

58. Aaltola, *Animal Suffering*, 111. See, in this vein, Rosalind Hursthouse, "Applying Virtue Ethics to Our Treatment of the Other Animals," in *The Practice of Virtue: Classic and Contemporary Readings in Virtue Ethics*, ed. Jennifer Welchman (Indianapolis: Hackett, 2006), 142; and Foer, *Eating Animals*, 215.

59. *Kitvei Ha-Sabba Ve-Talmidav Mi-Kelm*, vol. 1 (Benei Berak: Siftei Ḥakhamim, Va'ad Le-Hafatzat Torah U-Musar, 1997), 15.

60. Ziv, *Hokhmah U-Musar*, 1964, 2:10.
61. *Kitvei Ha-Sabba Ve-Talmidav Mi-Kelm*, 1:12.
62. Ziv, *Hokhmah U-Musar*, 1957, 1:21.
63. Dov Katz, *Tenu'at Ha-Musar*, 2nd ed. (Tel Aviv: Avraham Tzioni, 1954), 2:159.
64. *Beit Kelm: Sefer ha-Zikaron* (Benei Berak: Siftei Hakhamim, Va'ad Le-Hafatzat Torah U-Musar, 2002), 179.
65. Ziv, *Hokhmah U-Musar*, 1964, 2:192. This may have been an experience of being hosted by his brother and sister-in-law, though when he refers to "my brother" in this passage, he may mean a colleague rather than his actual brother.
66. *Beit Kelm: Emunah U-Middot*, 594; emphasis added. Simchah Zissel appears to be building on the Talmudic dictum that "the uneducated [*am ha-aretz*] are forbidden to eat meat" (BT Pesachim 49b).
67. Ziv, *Hokhmah U-Musar*, 1964, 2:313.
68. *Beit Kelm: Emunah U-Middot*, 114, n. 140.
69. On Simchah Zissel's sense of the struggle to overcome animality, see Claussen, *Sharing the Burden*, 43–48, 71, 126–28, 148–49, 164, and 170–71; and Claussen, "Jewish Virtue Ethics."
70. It is worth noting that at least one contemporary rabbi whose intellectual lineage stems largely from Simchah Zissel's Kelm branch of the Musar movement, Rabbi Aryeh Carmell (whose teacher, Rabbi Eliyahu Eliezer Dessler, was a student at the Kelm Talmud Torah that Simchah Zissel founded), concluded that "it seems doubtful . . . whether the Torah would sanction 'factory farming,' which treats animals as machines, with apparent insensitivity to their natural needs and instincts." See Aryeh Carmell, *Masterplan: Judaism, Its Program, Meanings, Goals* (Jerusalem: Jerusalem Academy Publications, 1991), 69.

10 The Vegetarian Teachings of Rav Kook

RICHARD H. SCHWARTZ AND DAVID SEARS

Some of the strongest support for vegetarianism as a positive ideal in Torah literature may be found in the writings of Rabbi Abraham Isaac Hakohen Kook (1865–1935). An outstanding student of the Netziv of Volozhin and other Lithuanian *gedolim* (great sages), Rav Kook was first chief rabbi of the Yishuv, the prestate Jewish settlement in Palestine, and a revolutionary Orthodox Jewish thinker. He was a profound mystic, innovative *halakhist* (adjudicator of Jewish law), prolific writer and poet, and one of the foremost Torah scholars of modern times.

Rav Kook saw himself as a bridge between two worlds: the "old world" of Eastern Europe, Vilna, and the shtetl, and the new world in which once rigid religious, intellectual, and cultural boundaries were rapidly dissolving. He thus addressed diverse questions from a broad spectrum of Jews torn between perceived traditionalism and modernism and inspired many people to pursue spiritual, rather than materialistic goals.

Rav Kook also urged the Jewish religious community to become more involved in social questions and efforts to improve the world. He championed the return of the Jewish people to the land of ancient Israel, not only as an escape from persecution but also as the fulfillment of Jewish religious destiny, both personal and national. His boldly stated teachings on ethical vegetarianism are found primarily in *A Vision of Vegetarianism and Peace* (in Hebrew), edited by his dedicated disciple, Rabbi David Cohen (1887–1973), "the Nazir of Jerusalem."[1]

After careful scriptural analysis, Rav Kook contended that the Torah's permission to eat meat was only a temporary concession. He found it patently unthinkable that a merciful God would impose an eternal natural order in which animals would be killed for food.[2] He stated,

> It is impossible to imagine that the Master of all that transpires, Who has mercy upon all His creatures, would establish an eternal decree such as this in the creation that He pronounced "exceedingly good," that it should

be impossible for the human race to exist without violating its own moral instincts by shedding blood, be it even the blood of animals.[3]

Rav Kook inferred that the biblical text, "after all the desire of your soul you may eat meat (Deut. 12:20)" contained a concealed reproach.[4] He predicted that a day would come when people will detest eating animal flesh because of a moral loathing "and then it shall be said that 'because your soul does not long to eat meat, you will not eat meat.'"[5]

Along with permission to eat meat, Judaism mandates many laws and restrictions concerning the slaughter of animals and the preparation of meat, which compose the bulk of the *kashrut* laws. Rav Kook explained that the reprimand implied by these elaborate regulations is meant to raise the consciousness of the Jewish people—to lead Jews to think about what and how they are eating—with the aim of eventually guiding them back to the vegetarian regimen originally instituted by God in Genesis 1:29.[6]

This echoes the words of illustrious Torah commentator Rabbi Solomon Ephraim Lunchitz of Prague (1550–1619), the author of *K'li Yakar* (A Precious Vessel),

> What was the necessity for the entire procedure of ritual slaughter? For the sake of self-discipline. It is far more appropriate for man not to eat meat. Only if he has a strong desire for meat does the Torah permit it, and even this only after the trouble and inconvenience necessary to satisfy his desire. Perhaps because of the bother and annoyance of the whole procedure, he will be restrained from such a strong and uncontrollable desire for meat.[7]

Rav Kook understood the craving for meat as a manifestation of spiritual decline, rather than an inherent need. Like the medieval authorities, Rabbi Isaac Arama (1420–1494), author of *Akeidat Yitzchak* (The Binding of Isaac"), and Rabbi Joseph Albo (1380–1444), author of *Sefer ha-Ikkarim* (The Book of Fundamentals), he believed that in the messianic era all humanity would return to a vegetarian diet.[8] Rav Kook stated that in days of the Messiah, "higher knowledge (*da'at*) will spread even to animals."[9] This echoes Isaiah's prophecy:

> And the wolf shall dwell with the lamb, and the leopard shall lie down with the kid; and the calf and the young lion and the fatling together; and a little child shall lead them. And the cow and the bear shall feed; their young ones shall lie down together, and the lion shall eat straw like the ox.... They shall neither hurt nor destroy in all My holy mountain. (Isaiah 11:6–9)

According to the preeminent kabbalist Rabbi Isaac Luria (1534–1572), we may take this literally. Animals will attain levels of wisdom and understanding that are now exclusively associated with humans, and they will return to the Edenic vegetarian diet.[10] Rabbi Kook believed that antediluvian vegetarianism reflected and manifested a higher level of morality and that a virtue so precious could not be lost forever.[11] Therefore, in the messianic age, as in the time of the first generations following creation, humans and animals will no longer consume flesh.[12] Just as people will stop exploiting one another, so will animals lose their predatory instincts. Creatures will no longer kill one another to live. Rav Kook, indeed, asserted elsewhere that after the coming of the Messiah, the sacrificial offerings in the Third Holy Temple in Jerusalem would consist of vegetation alone![13]

KOOK'S CRITIQUE OF VEGETARIANISM AND RESPONSES

Despite Rav Kook's admiration for vegetarianism, he did not take an unequivocal position on how Jews should eat. He associated vegetarianism with the peace and harmony of the messianic age and understood the practice of vegetarianism to reflect a higher level of piety, especially for those inclined to it on ascetic grounds. Yet he also approached the widespread adoption of vegetarianism with caution, as he associated it primarily with the "end of days" and not present times. Recent critics of vegetarianism have used some of Rav Kook's other, more skeptical teachings and his personal practices to oppose the adoption of a more moral and ethically responsible diet.

We present eight of the most frequent objections to vegetarianism rooted in the writings and practices of Rav Kook and provide refutation from a provegetarian perspective. Our comments reflect our interpretations of Rav Kook's teachings and how they may be best applied in the present day. We do not claim to speak for him, nor do we insist that he would have agreed with all our conclusions. Nonetheless, he remains our guiding moral voice.

Rav Kook was not a Vegetarian.

Rav Kook ate a diet that was primarily vegetarian. It has been said that he ate small amounts of chicken on the Sabbath as a symbolic reminder that the messianic age had not yet arrived.[14] All the while, however, he maintained that vegetarianism represented the Jewish ideal. Moreover, he gave his blessing to his lead disciple, Rabbi David Cohen, to live devoutly as a vegetarian. As noted already, the *Nazir* compiled and edited two of Rav Kook's essays, which he published as *A Vision of Vegetarianism and Peace*.

Undoubtedly, we are closer today to the messianic age than ever before.[15] What the world is presently going through is nothing other than the "darkness before the dawn." Rav Kook's personal practices, viewed in isolation from other factors, thus do not constitute an insurmountable argument against vegetarianism. A century has passed, and we are living in a very different world. No one knows what Rav Kook's position on vegetarianism would be were he alive today.

Rav Kook did not allow his son Rabbi Zvi Yehuda Kook to become a vegetarian, and even encouraged him to study ritual slaughter.

A leading authority on Rav Kook, Rabbi Bezalel Naor, has recently mustered evidence showing that the former disapproved of his son's youthful desire to become a vegetarian because he believed that "poetic souls" were obliged to eat at least a modicum of meat under the prevailing conditions.[16] This appears to be consistent with Rav Kook's personal custom, even if one letter indicates that he was also concerned for his son's health.[17] The motivation behind Rav Kook's attitude apparently relates to the kabbalistic (Jewish mystical) doctrine of the "elevation of the holy sparks."[18] The ascent of the sparks contained in such foods can only be achieved if those of high spiritual attainment consume them and then use the energy derived therefrom for the study Torah and the performance of *mitzvot* (commandments).

As a centerpiece of Jewish mysticism, the argument based in the importance of "elevating the holy sparks" is unassailable. Yet most of us lack the qualifications to bring about this *tikkun* (spiritual rectification). The kabbalists indeed warn that the whole enterprise of eating is risky business. If one fails to elevate the transmigrated souls and holy sparks that are trapped in food, one may be harmed by them. This is especially true of meat. Many great Jewish mystics limited their consumption of flesh or avoided it entirely, as Rabbi Chaim Chizkiyahu Medini (1833–1903) explains in his masterwork, *S'dei Chemed* (A Desirable Field).[19] It would seem that ordinary people, lacking the requisite spiritual attainments, should practice even greater caution with regard to the holy sparks in meat.

What makes this a complicated matter is that Rav Kook seems to have taken contradictory positions. On one hand, he believed that vegetarianism was beneficial for more highly evolved individuals, closer to the messianic ideal. This view reflects in the works of the aforementioned medieval sages, Rabbi Isaac Arama and Rabbi Joseph Albo. The son of the *Nazir*, Rabbi Shear-Yashuv Cohen, the chief rabbi of Haifa and the president of the Ariel Institute, confirmed in a phone call to one of the authors that Rav Kook had approved of his father's vegetarianism because he knew the latter to have been a spiritually refined person and an accomplished Torah scholar. On the other hand, Rav Kook apparently considered eating meat to be the spiritual responsibility of people of this same caliber, like his own son, Rabbi Zvi Yehuda. This belief is shared by many kabbalists and Hasidim.

This apparent contradiction is not lost on Rabbi Naor, although he does not try to resolve it. The sources he presents address the issue of *shechitah* (ritual slaughter), but they go hand in hand with Rav Kook's views on the spiritual and ethical aspects of eating meat. In a letter dated 1909, Rav Kook wrote to his disciple Benjamin Menashe Levin:

> It goes against the clear emotions of the heart that a *talmid chakham* [a Torah scholar], a spiritual man, should be permanently engaged in the taking of animals' lives. Though *shechitah*—and, in general, the consumption of animals—remains a necessity in this world, nevertheless, it would be fitting that this work be done by men who have not yet evolved to the level of refinement of feeling. Educated ethicists, on the other hand, should be supervisors [*pekidim*] to ensure that the killing of the animals be not barbaric, and that there enter into this entire area of meat consumption an ethereal light which may one day illumine the world. This [light] is truly contained in the laws of *shechitah* and *tereifot* [unfit animals], as is well known to us.[20]

This states clearly that *shechitah* inherently goes against the grain of a spiritually evolved person's sensibilities. Yet in a series of letters written between 1916 and 1917 to his son studying in Switzerland, Rav Kook wrote,

> I am pleased that you agree to study *shechitah*. I accept that you delay the study until after the holidays of *Tishrei* [a month in the Jewish calendar]. These days do not afford the tranquility necessary for one starting this expertise, especially if he be a poetic soul.[21]

He also wrote:

> It is several letters now that I have forgotten to inquire whether you are practicing *shechitah*. How does the matter appear to you? How do you relate to this holy work? For sensitive, thinking people, it requires will power, strength of character blessed with patience.[22]

One might speculate that Rav Kook may have felt that to become an "educated ethicist," his son needed to gain knowledge through the hands-on experience of *shechitah*. That is, the elder Kook may have felt that his son needed to engage in such tasks for religious or emotional reasons. He may have felt that the young man could not be relied on to practice vegetarianism responsibly, especially while living away from home. Alternatively, it is entirely possible that Rav Kook was acting disingenuously for some reason. Whatever the truth may have been, it must be acknowledged that despite these ambiguous remarks about *shechitah*, Rav Kook clearly saw animal slaughter and the consumption of meat as moral concessions. Consider his concluding words in *A Vision of Vegetarianism and Peace*:

> At that time [in the messianic age] human beings will recognize their companions in creation: all the animals. They will understand how it is fitting from the standpoint of the purest ethical standard not to resort to moral concessions, to compromise the divine attribute of justice with that of mercy [by permitting the exploitation of animals by humans], for they will no longer need extenuating concessions, as in those matters of which the Talmud states: "The Torah speaks only of the evil inclination (*Talmud Bavli, Kiddushin*, 21b)." Rather, they will walk the path of absolute good. As the prophet declares, "I will make a covenant for them with the animals of the field, the birds of the air, and the creeping things of the ground; I also will banish the bow and sword, and war from the land (Hosea 2:20)."[23]

Rav Kook considered vegetarianism to be an ideal for the messianic age, when people will have a heightened spiritual awareness, but he argued that vegetarianism should not be widely adopted as a norm for human conduct before that time.

A pragmatic reply would be that as we grow increasingly aware of the devastating effects of animal-based diets and animal agriculture on human health and environmental sustainability, the strategy of waiting for the messianic age to adopt vegetarianism may be something the world can no longer afford. Many of the problems related to modern intensive livestock agriculture have become far worse since Rav Kook died in 1935. One can only wonder what his views would have been today if he were aware of the diseases, soaring medical costs, increasing environmental hazards, widespread hunger, cruel treatment of animals, and other negative effects associated with animal-centered diets and agriculture. Rav Kook did not address these practical issues, which no doubt seemed less urgent 100 years ago.

There is a spiritual reply, as well. In a booklet that summarizes many of Rav Kook's teachings, Joe Green, a Jewish vegetarian writer, concluded that by adopting the vegetarian diet that will be practiced during the messianic age, Jewish religious vegetarians are "pioneers" of that long-awaited time. They lead lives that reflect some of our loftiest religious ideals, and thus hasten the coming of the Messiah.[24]

More decisively, in recent times there have been a number of vegetarian chief rabbis, all of whom have ties to Rav Kook's school of thought, including Rabbi Shlomo Goren (1917–1994), the former Ashkenazi chief rabbi of Israel; Rabbi Shear Yashuv Cohen (1927–2016), the former Ashkenazi chief rabbi of Haifa; Rabbi Jonathan Sacks (b. 1948), the former chief rabbi of England; and Rabbi David Rosen (b. 1951), the former chief rabbi of Ireland. None of these men have advised "ordinary" Jews not to be vegetarians. On the contrary, by their word and example they have shown that vegetarianism is a legitimate Jewish option, even today.

Rav Kook asserted that at present, other societal issues, such as the enmity between nations and racial discrimination, should be of greater moral concern to humanity than the well-being of animals. Hence, he advocated that people first work on such societal issues before improving the lives of animals.

Vegetarian diets are not beneficial only to animals. They also improve human health, help the hungry through better sharing of food and other resources, put less stress on endangered ecosystems, conserve valuable resources, and in so doing reduce the potential for war and violence. As the Hasidic master Rabbi Nachman of Breslov (1772–1810) wryly observed, "The fighting doesn't begin until the food runs out."[25] In view of the many global threats related to today's livestock agriculture, which involves raising 70 billion farmed animals for slaughter worldwide on an annual basis, working to promote vegetarianism may be one of the most important actions one can take for the benefit of humanity and our imperiled planet.[26] Without a doubt, Rav Kook is correct in stating that there should be a hierarchy of moral concern. Judaism clearly rejects the moral equivalence of animals and humans. It could be argued on firm rabbinic grounds that the two spheres of concern are no longer mutually exclusive.

Moreover, compassion is "contagious." Showing kindness and sympathy toward anyone or anything tends to increase similar sentiments toward other living things. This concept is implied by Maimonides in the *Moreh Nevuchim* (The Guide of the Perplexed), wherein he discusses the Noachide Commandment of *eiver min ha-chai*, the prohibition of eating the limb of a living animal. He says this is prohibited "because such an act would produce cruelty and develop it."[27]

The author of *Sefer ha-Chinuch* (The Book of Education) echoes this idea as well.[28] This reflects the interpretation of the *Midrash Tanchuma* that Israel was given the laws of *shechitah* to refine their moral sensitivities.[29] Some authorities also understand this to be among the reasons behind the scriptural prohibition of [causing] *tza'ar ba'alei chayim* or "the suffering of animals."[30] This assumption is supported by scientific studies showing that those who abuse animals as children often go on to commit violent crimes as adults.[31] The converse is also true: compassion for animals leads to compassion for other humans. This is stated in *Sefer ha-Chinuch* with regard to the law proscribing muzzling an ox while it is treading grain and elsewhere.[32]

Often one hears comments that the Nazis were kind to their animals, yet were cruel to humans. The implication is that there is no correlation between how one treats animals and how one behaves toward humans. This contradicts and seeks to undermine the principle espoused by Maimonides and other authorities. Even if there were cases in which Nazis were nice to their dogs or cows, this would not invalidate the character of compassion for animals as a moral virtue. Rav Kook said that even in the worst of people one may find some admirable traits. The claim that Hitler was a vegetarian, moreover, is spurious. His biographers have pointed out that he enjoyed Bavarian sausage and he also ate pork, liver, and the flesh of hunted animals.[33] Hitler was indeed the antithesis of an ethical vegetarian. Even if we were to find that certain cruel and delusional people have nevertheless felt and exhibited sympathy for animals, what would this prove? In response to critics of vegetarianism who feel they must rely on "character assassination" through association, we acknowledge that one will always find some immoral or wrong-headed people among vegetarians, as among any group of people. Vegetarianism does not validate all of the opinions and habits of its adherents, nor is it the solution to all of the world's problems! When judged on its own merits, however, vegetarianism may rightfully be perceived as an ethical and social good.

Rav Kook criticized people who promoted vegetarianism in his own day and in our imperfect world, fearing they might use vegetarianism as an excuse to not involve themselves in other important societal issues.

Rav Kook was certainly correct in criticizing anyone who would be so deluded as to think such a thing. Yet many famous vegetarians have counted among the world's great humanitarians and demonstrated a deep commitment to improving conditions for people and animals. Some examples are Leo Tolstoy, George Bernard Shaw, Mahatma Gandhi, Leonardo da Vinci, Plutarch, Franz Kafka, Jane Goodall, Mary Shelley, Isaac Bashevis Singer, and S. Y. Agnon. That list should also include many religiously observant Jewish vegetarians, who are dedicated to upholding the Torah's commandments, whether they apply to our relationship with God, our fellow humans, or animals and nature. Just as the aforementioned examples of vegetarians committing heinous acts does not discredit vegetarianism, this list alone cannot prove its merits. However, it does demonstrate the weakness of the arguments that a concern for animals necessarily distracts from one's concern for humanity and that our ability to contribute significantly to betterment in both spheres is circumscribed.

Vegetarianism need not be a retreat from our responsibilities to humanity. Rather, it is an important means for improving the lot of the world's population. Only a very few vegetarians, people whom we would not dare to characterize as "ethical vegetarians," would suggest ignoring the well-being of humans so that greater attention can be given to improving conditions for animals. Such individuals are few and far between. Indeed, from our perspective, their main claim to fame would be in providing an "easy target" for those who seek to delegitimize ethical vegetarianism.

In reality, animal activists tend to be deeply concerned about the conditions of their fellow humans. An example comes to mind immediately. A belief prevailed throughout most of Western history that children did not possess rights as individuals. Many people continue to feel this way about animals today. Yet it was animal welfare advocates who spearheaded the drive to institute child labor laws and extirpate the shameful exploitation of children in the United States—all during a time when so many others saw nothing wrong with how children were being treated.[34] If we look at the human plight in the world today, no reasonable person, vegetarian or otherwise, could possibly think that all the problems affecting us have been solved. This does not constitute an argument against vegetarianism and, as we have argued, may suggest the urgency of adopting the practice.

Despite his strongly provegetarian stance, Rav Kook considered this diet to represent a spiritual rung that is presently too difficult for most human beings to attain.

As we have mentioned, there is a time-honored tradition of ascetic vegetarianism in Judaism, particularly among kabbalists. This type of vegetarianism is appropriate only to a spiritual elite. Contemporary vegetarians are not as restricted as their forebears (at least not in most modern Western societies). Virtually every supermarket offers an increasingly varied selection of vegetarian foods, some with the textures and tastes of animal products. Many of these products have a *hechsher*, a symbol indicating that they were produced according to the standards of *kashrut* under rabbinical supervision. Vegetarianism today thus does not require of its adherents as great of an ascetic and potentially dangerous sacrifice as it may have in the past.

Moreover, even if one feels that a completely vegetarian regime would be too restrictive for themself, it would still be extremely beneficial for them to reduce the amount of meat in their diet, perhaps restricting consumption to Shabbat, holidays, and special occasions. The health benefits alone of such "semi-vegetarianism" would be significant. This is consistent with the practices of many devout Jews today, who consider indulging in meat on ordinary weekdays to be a form of gluttony. Several authorities, including Don Isaac Abarbanel (1437–1509), Rabbi Ovadia Sforno (1470–1550), and Rabbi Samson Raphael Hirsch (1808–1888), have pointed out that the Torah's concession for humans to slaughter animals for food is dictated by need.[35]

The indigenous populations of places like the Himalayas or the Andes that have short growing seasons may have no recourse but to raise animals for food. Let us concede this. Yet what percentage of the world's population lives under such extreme conditions? According to the Worldwatch Institute, global meat consumption is highly concentrated, dominated by only a few nations. The United States and China, which account for 25 percent of the world's population, combine to consume 35 percent of the world's beef, over half of the world's poultry, and 65 percent of the world's pork. If Brazil and the European Union are included, this group consumes over 60 percent of the world's beef, over 70 percent of the world's poultry, and over 80 percent of the world's pork.[36] Most of us eat meat not because we must, but because we desire it, because we are accustomed to it, and despite the annual warnings of the American Dietetic Association, we do not seem to know better.

Rav Kook believed that when people take on austerities for which they are insufficiently prepared, their uncorrected evil traits will manifest themselves inevitably in other, possibly more harmful ways. He observed that a common psychological strategy for a corrupt person is to whitewash their self-image by finding an extremely idealistic cause to champion. He felt that these dangers apply to ethical vegetarianism. If the premature embrace of this lofty expression of compassion for animals should fail, he warned, it could lead to moral regression—even cannibalism.[37]

One would be hard pressed to find any religious Jewish vegetarians who advocate that the consumption of animal products be banned, based on *halakha* (Jewish religious law). The law is clear that animals *may* be slaughtered to serve any legitimate human need, especially for the purposes of consumption. As Jewish vegetarians, we fully acknowledge that we have a choice but insist that this choice not be made on the basis of desire alone but only after considering the contemporary reality of meat production and consumption and of how the related processes all too often impinge on basic Jewish teachings. Ethical vegetarianism belongs to the legal category of *lifnim meshurat ha-din*, going beyond the "letter of the law" to emulate the divine attribute of mercy and compassion and manifest more fully the spirit of the law. Should a person feel unable to persist in maintaining a vegetarian diet, they certainly have the option of returning to their former meat-inclusive diet.

As for the assertion that people deprived of the ability to eat meat might become cannibals, it has not been demonstrated that there have ever been cannibals who were formerly vegetarians. If anything, the opposite holds true: carnivores deprived of meat have been known to become cannibalistic.[38] In fact, as Rav Kook acknowledged, humans have a deeply ingrained ambivalence toward eating meat. We try to suppress our awareness of everything that went into the production of that meat: the suffering on factory farms and during transport, the pain of slaughtering, and so on. This is one of the reasons meat products are packaged and served the way they are. When one stops eating meat, such thoughts must no longer be suppressed.

Yet there is something to Rav Kook's equivocation. It must be admitted that vegetarianism may be used for self-serving psychological ends. Some may even use it as an outlet for their anger at social convention or at the human condition in general. Here, too, one must acknowledge that this can be true of any worthy cause, and all too often it is. It is unfair to single out vegetarianism for such criticism, and it is not a repudiation of vegetarianism.

According to Rav Kook, because people had fallen to an extremely low spiritual level, it was necessary that they be given an elevated image of themselves in comparison to animals. He feared that vegetarians might forget their human superiority and come to think of themselves as beasts.[39]

This argument was previously made by fourteenth-century Jewish philosopher Rabbi Joseph Albo. He acknowledges that once a person has come to realize and embrace the higher spiritual calling of human beings, the need to consume meat as a reminder of that higher calling falls away.[40] The reason we should concern ourselves with the plight of animals is precisely because we are human. If Jewish teachings regarding both people and animals were more widely known and put into practice, people would become aware of the sanctity of every person, created in the image of God, and the fact that our mandate to imitate God's attributes of compassion and justice dictates that we improve on conditions for animals. A vegetarian diet should only reinforce our humanness and thus elevate our moral sensitivities and standards.

If we look at the behavior of most animals and compare it to the behavior of humankind, animals might not fare so badly. Many years ago, the Bronx Zoo had a cage labeled "the world's most dangerous animal." Looking between the bars, all visitors could see was their reflections in a mirror. With very few exceptions (such as chimpanzees killing for sport and territory), animals kill only for food and survival, whereas humans also kill for power and even pleasure. Humans have the faculty of speech, but it is often used for evil, be it slander, *lashon hara* (badmouthing), profanity, or humiliation. This reflects in the words of our sages in the mishnaic discussion of the laws related to damages: "A human being is always considered dangerous [*mu'ad*, literally "forewarned"], whether inadvertently or intentionally, whether asleep or awake."[41]

Rabbi Shlomo Riskin of Efrat infers the human potential for great good or great evil from the biblical command that human beings have "dominion" over other creatures (Genesis 1:26).[42] He points out that *vi-yirdu*, from the Hebrew word for "to have dominion," can also mean "to descend." Thus, he observes, "The very ability to rise above our animal instincts can also cause us to sink to levels of depravity far below an animal's capacity." It may be argued that one way we may affirm our human moral superiority is by showing greater compassion for animals, rather than yielding to our own base instincts in wantonly and heartlessly exploiting the animal kingdom.

CONCLUSION

The present state of animal agriculture and the excessive consumption of meat in our society lead to violations of basic Jewish values and have disastrous consequences for human health and environmental sustainability. Rav Kook believed that vegetarianism is the diet most consistent with Jewish teachings, and none of his secondary concerns, expressed before the development and widespread expansion of factory farming and all of its attendant problems, should prevent Jews from adopting vegetarian diets. To do so is to act in anticipation of the time when "none shall hurt nor destroy in all of God's holy mountain" (Isaiah 11:9).

NOTES

An earlier version of this paper appeared on the website www.jewishveg.org.

1. Abraham Isaac Kook, *Ḥazon ha-tsimḥonut veha-shalom mi-veḥinah Toranit: orot mehama'amarim Afikim ba-Negev u-Ṭalele orot* [A Vision of Vegetarianism and Peace], comp. and ed. David Cohen (Jerusalem: Nezer David l'Torah ulemaḥshevet Yisrael, 1983).

2. Ibid., 1:4. See also David Sears, *The Vision of Eden: Animal Welfare and Vegetarianism in Jewish Law and Mysticism* (Spring Valley, NY: Orot, 2003), 338–39; and Nehama Leibowitz, *Studies in Deuteronomy* (Jerusalem: World Zionist Organization, 1980), 135–42.

3. Kook, *A Vision of Vegetarianism and Peace*, section 1. All translations, unless otherwise noted, are the authors'.

4. Kook, *A Vision of Vegetarianism and Peace*, section 1; see also Joe Green, "*Chalutzim* of the Messiah: The Text of a Lecture" (Johannesburg: n.p. 1971), 2.

5. Green, "*Chalutzim* of the Messiah," 2.

6. Abraham Isaac Kook, "Fragments of Light," in *Abraham Isaac Kook: The Lights of Penitence, the Moral Principles, Lights of Holiness, Essays, Letters, and Poems*, ed. and trans. Ben Zion (New York: NYU Press, 1995), 316–21.

7. Quoted in Abraham Chill, *The Mitzvot: The Commandments and Their Rationale* (New York: Bloch Publishing, 1974), 400. See Sears, *The Vision of Eden*, 184–85.

8. Kook, *A Vision of Vegetarianism and Peace*, 6:32. For additional information about rabbinical attitudes toward vegetarianism, see Alfred Cohen, "Vegetarianism from a Jewish Perspective," *Journal of Halacha and Contemporary Society* 1, no. 2 (Fall 1981): 38–63; and Roberta Kalechovsky (ed.), *Rabbis and Vegetarianism: An Evolving Tradition* (Marblehead, MA: Micah Publications, 1995).

9. Abraham Isaac Kook, *Olat Rayah*, vol. 1 (Jerusalem: Mosad Harav Kook and Agudah Lehotzoat Sifre Harayah Kook, 1939), 292.

10. Chaim Vital, *Sha'ar ha-Mitzvot* (*Kitvei Arizal*, Ashlag ed.) (Jerusalem: Kol Yehudah, 1986), *Ekev*, 42a.

11. Kook, *A Vision of Vegetarianism and Peace*, 6:32.

12. Ibid.

13. Kook, *Olat Rayah*, vol. 1, 292. This is based on the *midrashic* teaching that all of the sacrifices are to be abolished with the exception of the thanksgiving offering.

14. This is cited in the name of the late Rabbi Shear Yashuv Cohen of Haifa, son of Rav Kook's close disciple, the *Nazir*. See Moshe Nachmani, "The Rabbis of Religious Vegetarianism," Srugim website, May 7, 2014 (in Hebrew), https://bit.ly/2NanG25. We are grateful to Rabbi Channan Morrison for this reference.

15. See Babylonian Talmud, *Sanhedrin* 97a, which details the spiritual and social crises that are destined to precede the coming of the Moshiach. The Gemara also states that the final redemption will occur during the third 2,000-year period in the Jewish calendar, most of which has passed. Many great rabbis have understood the events of modern times to conform to these and other ancient Torah teachings about the coming of the Moshiach. These authorities include the Chofetz Chaim, the Baba Sali, the last Lubavitcher rebbe, and the eminent contemporary Torah authority

Rabbi Chaim Kanievsky (among many others). Yet this does not mean that we may leave all of the world's problems up to Moshiach to solve. No one in recent memory was as adamant as the Lubavitcher rebbe about the imminence of the coming of Moshiach, yet he cautioned that in the practical matters of life and in world affairs, we all must heed the laws of nature and common sense and act accordingly.

16. Bezalel Naor, "Rav Kook on *Shehitah* versus Vegetarianism" (2004), last modified March 14, 2013, http://orot.com/rav-kook-on-shehitah-versus-vegetarianism (accessed July 19, 2016). See also Tzvi Yehuda Kook, *Tzemach Tzvi: Letters of Rav Tzvi Yehuda Hakohen Kook* (Jerusalem: n.p., 1991), 110 and 138–39.

17. Abraham Isaac Kook, *Igrot Harayah*, vol. 1 (Jerusalem: Mossad Harav Kook, 1985), 82.

18. According to the Kabbalistic teachings of Rabbi Isaac Luria, there are "sparks" of the primordial, unitary Divine Light that have become dispersed throughout creation. It is the task of the Jewish people to redeem them by using the things of this world in a holy manner, especially by performing the commandments of the Torah.

19. Cited in translation in Sears, *The Vision of Eden*, 327–29.

20. Kook, *Igrot Harayah*, vol. 1, 230.

21. Ibid., 53.

22. Ibid., 79.

23. Kook, *A Vision of Vegetarianism and Peace*, conclusion.

24. Green, "*Chalutzim* of the Messiah," 1.

25. *Sefer ha-Midot, Inyan "Merivah,"* 1:60; see the Babylonian Talmud, *Bava Metzia*, 59a.

26. "Animals in Farming: Supporting 70 Billion Animals," World Animal Protection, https://www.worldanimalprotection.org/our-work/animals-farming-supporting-70-billion-animals (accessed January 10, 2018).

27. Moses Maimonides, *The Guide of the Perplexed*, trans. M. Friedländer, 4th ed. (New York: E. P. Dutton, 1904), 371, 3:48.

28. *Sefer ha-Chinuch, Mitzvah* (The Book of Education), trans. Charles Wengrov (Spring Valley, NY: Feldheim, 1992), 4:452.

29. *Tanchuma, Shemini*, 7, vol. 2 (Jerusalem: Eshkol, 1972), 523.

30. Sears, *The Vision of Eden*, 65–66.

31. Clifton P. Flynn, "Animal Abuse in Childhood and Later Support for Interpersonal Violence in Families," *Society and Animals* 7, no. 2 (December 1998): 161–72. It is possible, perhaps even likely, that this relationship is corollary rather than causative. Such studies may suggest more strongly that the abuse of animals among children can serve as an early indicator of underlying problems which can manifest later in life in violence against other humans. We submit, nonetheless,

that there is also ample evidence to suggest that how one behaves and how one trains oneself to behave can lead to changes in one's psychological and emotional makeup. How one chooses to act has consequences on the actor, especially over long periods of time.

32. *Sefer ha-Chinuch, Mitzvah*, 5:375.

33. Rynn Berry, *Hitler: Neither Vegetarian nor Animal Lover* (New York: Pythagorean Publishers, 2004).

34. The first anticruelty laws in the United States were enacted on behalf of animals. Within four years of the ASPCA's establishment in 1866, however, the group's founder, Henry Bergh, had enlisted Elbridge Gerry as the organization's counsel. The two men soon began protesting the maltreatment of children, leading to reform in this area, as well. "1870–1874: The Catalyst," NYSPCC, http://www.nyspcc.org/about-the-new-york-society-for-the-prevention-of-cruelty-to-ch ildren/history (accessed July 20, 2016). For a more contemporary example, see Mary Lou Randour with Howard Davidson, *A Common Bond: Maltreated Children and Animals in the Home: Guidelines for Practice and Policy* (American Humane Society, 2008), http://www.humanesociety.org/assets/pdfs/abuse/common_bond_08.pdf.

35. Sears, *The Vision of Eden*, 188–90.

36. These figures reflect data collected before 1998. Brian Halweil, "United States Leads World Meat Stampede," Worldwatch Issues Paper, July 2, 1998, https://www.worldwatch.org/node/1626.

37. Kook, *A Vision of Vegetarianism and Peace*, 6:9–11; and Rav Kook, *Ein Ayah, Berachot*, vol. 2 (Jerusalem: Machon al Shem HaRav Zvi Yehudah Hakohen Kook zt"l, 1990) 7:41 (187).

38. Sears, *The Vision of Eden*, 160–61, n. 7. The author states, "This apprehension is not borne out by studies of vegetarian societies or communities, such as those in the Far East. If anything, it appears that vegetarian societies are less prone to moral regression (much less cannibalism) than others. However, there are numerous precedents for societies with meat-based diets turning to cannibalism when unable to obtain sufficient meat from animals." Sears goes onto cite Louis Berman, *Vegetarianism and the Jewish Tradition* (New York: Ktav Publishing, 1982, 19–20); the latter cites Reay Tannahill, *Flesh and Blood: A History of the Cannibal Complex* (New York: Stein and Day, 1975) "and other sources."

39. Kook, *A Vision of Vegetarianism and Peace*, section 8, conclusion.

40. Joseph Albo, *Sefer ha-Ikkarim*, 3:15.

41. *Mishnah, Bava Kamma*, 2:6.

42. Shlomo Riskin, "We Can Master Sin," *Jewish News of Greater Phoenix* (October 16, 1998).

11 Relevant and Irrelevant Distinctions
Speciesism, Judaism, and Veganism

ALAN D. KRINSKY

How ought one to describe Cain's killing of his brother, Abel? As an act of jealousy and rage? As cold and calculated? An accident or in self-defense? A premeditated murder? An impulsive act? The Midrash suggests an answer we might otherwise never have considered: a human sacrifice.

Midrash Rabbah Genesis (22:8) points to Psalm 69: "And it shall please the Lord better than an ox or a bullock that has horns and hoofs" (69:32).[1] Any ox or bullock? Or a particular one? The Midrash draws our attention to the sacrifice of a bullock by Adam, the father of Cain and Abel; this sacrifice, this offering to God, set the precedent for Cain to offer up his brother. Rabbi Joseph Albo, however, directs our gaze instead to Abel's offering of his choicest animal as a gift to God. Whether father or brother set the precedent for Cain, whether we follow the Midrash or Rabbi Albo, what we have here is not merely a killing or even a murder. Rather, we seem to have a case of human sacrifice, the striking suggestion that Cain *schechted*, that he ritually slaughtered, his brother Abel as an offering to God.[2]

How we understand Abel's killing—and how Cain might have horribly misunderstood the difference between human sacrifice and animal sacrifice, indeed, between humans and animals altogether—will prove critical to understanding mainstream Judaism's take on one important argument for adopting veganism. This argument is that of speciesism.

Speciesism, a notion akin to racism or sexism, is prejudice or discrimination on the basis of one's species. First coined by psychologist Richard Ryder and then popularized by philosopher Peter Singer, speciesism can be defined briefly as the belief that humans are superior to other animals.[3] Opponents of speciesism find morally wrong such a claim of human exceptionalism—that human life is, in some absolute and essential sense, worth more than animal life. Rejecting speciesism logically entails rejecting the eating of animals and therefore embracing veganism as a moral commitment.

233

What do traditional Jewish texts and thinkers have to say about this matter? Do we find agreement with Ryder and Singer and others, who argue that the differences between humans and animals have no moral relevance, that these differences do not provide us with any right to kill and eat animals? Or is Judaism avowedly speciesist (though of course rejecting the negative moral evaluation and connotations of such a label)? Do we find in the sources an assertion of the notion that the differences between animals and humans are differences in kind and not just degree, that these differences have theological and moral and *halakhic* (Jewish legal) implications?

The discussion of these questions will unfold in five parts. I begin with a detailed elaboration of Rabbi Albo's account of Cain killing Abel. The second section presents Singer's articulation of speciesism, a nuanced and challenging argument based on a notion of equal consideration, rather than one of equality. Next I turn to what various Jewish sources have to say about differences between humans and animals, including whether animals have souls, whether animals and humans possess similar senses of potentiality and purpose, and whether animals were or are created in the image of God. The fourth part addresses the Jewish legal principle of *tza'ar ba'alei chayim*, a prohibition against causing unwarranted suffering to animals. The final section brings together these ideas to consider Singer's challenge. Do the traditional texts even anticipate, let alone refute, Singer's arguments? I offer an assessment and conclusions, addressing an intriguing question: does treating animals and humans equally result in better treatment of animals or worse treatment of humans?

RABBI ALBO'S ACCOUNT OF CAIN'S HUMAN SACRIFICE OF ABEL

The Spanish Jewish philosopher Rabbi Joseph Albo (c. 1380–1444) devotes the third volume of *Sefer ha-Ikkarim* (*The Book of Principles*) to revelation and to the troubling question of how divine law can appear to change. After all, if revelation issues from an eternal, unchanging God, why would there ever be a need for the laws of such a revelation to be altered? He offers a prime example of this phenomenon in the fact that eating meat was prohibited to Adam, yet permitted to his descendant Noah, and furthermore that not everything permitted as food for Noah was later allowed to the nation of Israel. How could this be? In the effort to answer this question, Rabbi Albo relates his account of Cain and Abel.

To start, why was Cain a tiller of the ground and Abel a raiser of animals? According to Rabbi Albo, Cain saw no essential difference between humans and animals: both ate plants, both drank, both died. The only, relatively unimportant difference, in Cain's mind, was the fact that humans worked the Earth to produce choicer plants for consumption. Cain therefore worked the Earth like his father, and Cain offered his gift to God to demonstrate human superiority over plants, not over animals. Indeed, Cain thought killing animals altogether forbidden, given the lack of any significant differences between animals and humans.

Abel, a shepherd, recognized more of a human superiority over animals, but only in terms of the ability to control and master them. He did not think humans could kill animals for human purposes but only for God, to show God's superiority over humans and animals, rather than to demonstrate human superiority over animals. Rabbi Albo sees the closeness of the brothers' attitudes in a textual clue. Genesis 4:4 tells us that Abel "also" brought a gift. Why *also*? To Rabbi Albo, this word indicates the similarity in the brothers' views in not seeing a great difference between humans and animals. In this Rabbi Albo also explains why Abel did not merit protection against being killed: his thinking was similar to that of his brother, and if anything, more likely to mislead others into misunderstanding the relationship between humans and animals.

Given Cain's beliefs and God's warm acceptance of Abel's animal offering, Rabbi Albo depicts Cain killing his brother not as an act of rage but as an act of reason, in accord with the law:

> For he still held the opinion that man is not superior to the animal. Therefore he said to himself, Since God favors Abel and his present, it is clear that it is permitted to kill animals, and hence it is just as lawful to kill Abel as any other animal.[4]

Cain did not imagine himself as committing a moral wrong in slaying his brother. Given his views on animals and humans, and given his brother's gift and God's response, Cain thought his act entirely lawful.

From this perspective, just as Abel offered an animal sacrifice to God, Cain offered a human sacrifice. To be clear, the import of Rabbi Albo's account is that the philosophical or theological error of failing to distinguish appropriately between animals and humans led to the first human sacrifice. We might reasonably infer that this same error, even in our days, leads to brutality against humans. Rabbi Albo explains that Cain's erroneous thinking continued into subsequent generations:

> But the opinion of Cain was widely prevalent among his descendants, and hence the earth was filled with violence on their account, their belief being that man has no superiority over the animal, and might is right. Therefore they were corrupt and lived like animals.[5]

He goes on to explain that these beliefs and animal behaviors served as the reason for God bringing the flood.

Noah emerged from the ark and offered to God an animal sacrifice because Noah "knew that man is superior by virtue of his reason and can know his Creator and serve Him better than the animals and can be thankful to God for this privilege."[6] However, this was not enough to establish the proper view as superior to those of Cain and his descendants. And therefore, according to Rabbi Albo, God immediately authorized the killing and eating of animals:

> The meaning is that as even Cain admitted that man is superior to the plants, since they are created for man, so all the animals are also for the sake of man, who is superior to them, and there is not the same spirit in all. For this reason He prohibited the shedding of human blood, giving as a reason that the spirit of man is not like the spirit of the animal, for in the image of God made He man, i.e. man has a rational form which is nobler than the spirit of the animal.[7]

Here God permitted eating all animals to remove Cain's beliefs from the world.

Why, centuries later, did the Torah place restrictions on eating animals? The old views no longer existed, and the meat of some animals "produce coarseness and ugliness of soul."[8] Returning to his initial concern over changes in divine law, Rabbi Albo concludes that "we may say, therefore, that there are matters in the divine law which are forbidden for a certain length of time, as God's wisdom decrees, and later are permitted in accordance with the same divine wisdom."[9] Rabbi Albo seems to be saying that God was concerned with the production of proper beliefs and attitudes; at different times, different rules regarding the consumption of animals might prove necessary to produce the same, correct opinions.

This is the general point Rabbi Albo seeks to establish—that divine law can change even when divine wisdom remains unchanging. In supporting this point, he shares something important about his understanding of the Torah's views on animals and human beings, their differences, and the dangers, including human sacrifice, of failing to understand these differences. As we learn next, some people view any differences between animals and humans as providing absolutely no justification for the latter to kill and eat the former.

SPECIESISM: A PRIMER

In his landmark and revolutionary book *Animal Liberation*, first published in 1975, Peter Singer offers the following definition of speciesism: "[a] prejudice or attitude of bias in favor of the interests of members of one's own species and against those of members of other species." He appears to have in mind here a particular and important notion of interests: "to use another for his or her own ends."[10] His concern goes well beyond attitudes and thoughts to actions in the physical world. Just as racism and sexism are much more than ideas—they affect the lives, health, and deaths of their victims—speciesism is about some beings using other beings for their own ends and claiming the right, justification, and even morality to do so based simply on belonging to a different species.

Of striking importance, perhaps, is the fact that Singer does not at all mention the notion of equality in his definition of speciesism. This is because he does not profess a general belief in the equality of humans and animals, or indeed of the equality of all humans. We are not all the same, neither as species nor as individuals. What matters to Singer is simply the *relevant* similarities, not any *irrelevant* differences.

Singer's concern, as per his definition, is interests. To have interests, in his reckoning and in the reckoning of his utilitarian forebears, is to have the possibility to suffer and to enjoy, to experience pain and pleasure. Singer finds these capacities (and only these) relevant in assessing our relationships as humans to animals. We can suffer, and they can suffer. Intelligence or the ability to reason do not matter at all in this regard. These are irrelevant characteristics, and this remains the case whether we are speaking about the human treatment of animals or the human treatment of other humans: "If a being suffers there can be no moral justification for refusing to take that suffering into consideration."[11] Just as the color of one's skin does not entitle some to enslave others, neither does the nature of one's species entitle one to abuse others, resulting in "the sacrifice of the most important interests of members of other species in order to promote the most trivial interests of our own species."[12]

Humans reveal themselves as speciesists "in their readiness to cause pain to animals when they would not cause a similar pain to humans for the same reason, . . . in their readiness to kill other animals when they would not kill human beings."[13] The logic works like this: if I would not cause pain to a human for a particular end, then I ought not to cause similar pain to an animal, which shares with the human the same ability to feel pain and the same interest in not experiencing such suffering.

Note that this is not a matter of animal rights, or of any rights. Singer does not identify animal rights as the source of moral obligation for how humans treat animals.[14] If not rights, then what? What could be the source of such moral responsibility? As we have seen, Singer begins with the relevant similarities between the human species and animal species and the common interest in avoiding pain. He asserts that these relevant similarities and common interests generate a moral obligation of what he calls equal consideration. This moral obligation is not diminished when the objects of our human consideration are animals rather than other humans. In the relevant respects, we are the same, and there are no moral grounds for treating differently those who are the same.

One might wonder whether Singer's principle of equal consideration entails treating humans and animals equally in all respects. Are human and animal lives equal in his view? If forced to choose between saving a puppy or a human child, does Singer think there's no difference? His response to such questions is at first comforting but soon thereafter disquieting. On one hand, he distinguishes between the equal consideration due to all beings who share the capacity to experience pleasure and pain and what we might call the unequal consideration we might apply to those beings who possess self-awareness or experience hope for the future. With two beings, one with self-awareness and one without, we ought to grant equal consideration in avoidance of causing pain, whereas we justly and nonarbitrarily would choose the life of the former over the latter. So we find ourselves relieved that Singer appears to recognize the value of human life over animal life.

Yet Singer quickly qualifies or clarifies what he means. In a situation pitting a severely intellectually disabled human against a particular animal, one following Singer's logic might choose to save the life of the latter over the former. Singer, remaining consistent, looks to the characteristics of the beings and not their membership in a species.

> It is not arbitrary to hold that the life of a self-aware being, capable of abstract thought, of planning for the future, of complex acts of communication, and so on, is more valuable than the life of a being without these capacities. To see the difference between the issues of inflicting pain and taking life, consider how we would choose within our own species. If we had to choose to save the life of the normal human being or an intellectually disabled human being, we would probably choose to save the life of a normal human being; but if we had to choose between preventing pain in the normal human being or the intellectually disabled one—imagine that both have received painful but superficial injuries, and we only have enough painkiller for one of them—it is not nearly so clear how we ought to choose.[15]

Singer applies the same logic when considering together humans and nonhumans:

> The same is true when we consider other species.... Normally this will mean that if we have to choose between the life of a human being and

the life of another animal we should choose to save the life of the human; but there may be special cases in which the reverse holds true, because the human being in question does not have the capacities of a normal human being. So this view is not speciesist, although it may appear to be at first glance.[16]

For those of us who would choose to save any human life over any animal life, or over any number of animal lives, Singer's position now appears horrifying—and indeed, his views have been the subject of controversy for decades. Nonetheless, he maintains a certain consistency. It is clear why veganism follows reasonably, if not inevitably, from his moral framework of speciesism. If we would not cause pain to another human and kill another human for food, then we ought not to do so to animals deserving of equal consideration. While respecting a gradualist approach of movement toward vegetarianism and veganism, Singer clearly finds veganism to be the logical outcome of a nonspeciesist commitment.[17]

THE DIVINE IMAGE, SOULS, AND DIFFERENCES BETWEEN HUMANS AND ANIMALS

In the opening chapter of the Bible, we learn that God created humans *b-tzelem Elohim*, in the image of God. This comes after several verses describing the creation of animals—in the seas, in the air, and on the land. The distinction is sharp. One might debate whether the "dominion" God grants to humans over the animals and the Earth is a power or a responsibility, free license or an obligation of stewardship. What the text leaves unambiguous is that humans are created in the divine image, whereas animals are not. This strongly indicates that humans and animals differ in kind, not just degree. However one characterizes this human resemblance of God—and over the centuries commentators have proposed various interpretations—we appear to have a distinction well beyond any evolutionary or genetic or biological characterization of differences among species. This is not a matter of the branching out of evolutionary trees, percentages of unshared DNA, or incompatibility in breeding and producing offspring. Even if one acknowledges that all life is sacred, the earliest verses of the Torah inform us that humans possess something not shared in any way with any other living beings on this Earth. And this is not the only difference.

What about souls? Do humans and animals differ in this regard as well? Do animals have souls? Here one must consider the language of the Torah and the discourses of later authorities. The first chapter of Genesis tells us that animals have a living soul, a *nefesh chayah* (Genesis 1:20, 1:24). What is this *nefesh*? Is it a soul in a spiritual sense? It might best be translated, here and in a number of other places, as a life force. We see later in Genesis and again in Leviticus and Deuteronomy, that the *nefesh* is associated with blood: "But flesh with its life [*b-nafsho*], which is its blood, you shall not eat" (Genesis 9:4), "For the life [*nefesh*] of the flesh is in the blood" (Leviticus 17:11), and "Only be sure that thou eat not the blood: for the blood is the life [*ha-nafesh*]; and thou mayst not eat the life [*ha-nefesh*] with the meat" (Deuteronomy 12:23). Of course, because animals and humans both have blood, they both possess this life force, this *nefesh chayah*.

Genesis chapter 2 informs us that human beings have a *nefesh chayah*, but not only that: "And the Lord God formed man of the dust of the ground, and breathed into his nostrils the breath of life [*nishmat chayim*]; and man became a living soul [*nefesh chayah*]" (Genesis 2:7). Although one might read this verse as sequential or causal—that receiving the breath of life led the human to become a living soul—we seem to be dealing with two different characteristics. Humans, like animals, possess a living soul, this animating life force, but nowhere does the Torah show God breathing life into animals. Indeed, as Rabbi Aryeh Kaplan points out, God created animals by speaking, and words are external, carried by sound waves, whereas a breath emerges from the inside. Of course, we cannot understand this on a literal level, but we can understand the Torah to be telling us that human life was created in a unique manner, that "the human soul came directly from God's innermost Essence."[18]

It appears that only humans have a *neshamah*, another kind of soul, this one linked to God and the spiritual realm. Indeed, as Rabbi Abraham ibn Ezra (1089–1167) suggests, the word *neshamah* might share a root with the word *shamayim*, the heavens. Genesis chapter 7 reports that "all in whose nostrils was the breath of life [*nishmat ruach chayim*], of all that was on the dry land, died" in the flood (Genesis 7:22). On one hand, this reference to a *neshamah* would appear to apply to all land animals, but on the other hand, as Rabbi ibn Ezra also notes, the previous verse ends specifically with a reference to humans. He understands the *neshamah* here as limited to humans. In addition, the phrasing is different, with the word *ruach* (spirit or wind) inserted.

In brief, the Torah text points to some sort of fundamental difference between the nature of animal and human souls. Certainly, a life force animates animals, but do they have souls like those of human beings? Beyond the language of the text, or building on the language of the text, the answer appears to be that they do not. As Rabbi Kaplan explains it, humans possess animal and spiritual souls, and these exist in tension, pulling us in opposite directions. He writes that the human being "shares physio-chemical life processes with animals, and on the physical plane is indistinguishable from them. We therefore speak of man having an 'animal soul' (*nefesh ha-bahamith*) which is contained in the blood, i.e. in the physio-chemical processes." This is the *nefesh*, but humans also possess *ruach* and *neshamah*, as hinted at by the expression *nishmat ruach chayim* we just saw. Rabbi Kaplan further explicates these notions: "Of these three levels of the soul, *neshamah* is therefore the highest and closest to God, while *nefesh* is that aspect of the soul residing in the body. *Ruach* stands between the two, binding man to his spiritual Source."[19] Whereas animals live definitively in one world, human beings have one foot, and even one soul, in each of two very different worlds.[20]

One additional dimension of this distinction is that only humans, not other animals, have a connection to immortality, to the eternal life of the nonmaterial realm or realms. The *nefesh*, the life force, comes to an end in our material world. This does not at all mean that animals (or plant life for that matter) are lacking in sanctity; after all, they are part of God's creation. Again, we find a difference in kind and not just degree between humans and other earthly species. It stands to reason that such a difference, between beings limited to the material world and beings with a share in the eternal spiritual world, might have practical consequences within the material world in how humans relate to other species.

Next let us consider another profound difference between humans and animals. As Rabbi Albo and others explain, animals are, in a sense, perfect in a way humans are not. Animals have their needs and possess their abilities from the start and never exhibit what modern writers might call "personal growth." Rabbi Natan Slifkin refers to the "Talmudic principle that 'an ox of one day old is called an ox'" and its implication that "an animal, although it grows, never essentially changes."[21] Humans, by contrast, are formed incomplete, with great potential and the possibility of realizing this potential toward becoming perfect. Such a metamorphosis is entirely unavailable to animals and sets the human species apart. Or at least should set humans apart. As Rabbi Slifkin notes, "If man does not fulfill his potential, he is no better than an animal (and quite possibly worse, since animals at least do what they are supposed to do)."[22]

Rabbi Albo describes this human potentiality as the "perfection of purpose," which he contrasts with the "perfection of existence." Some things are perfect, they are what they are, from the moment they come into existence; they have no further perfection to attain. He presents the example of a chair, which achieves its perfection of existence upon its manufacture, but its perfection of purpose only upon being sat on. Rabbi Albo also makes the fascinating observation that in the biblical account of creation, despite several uses of the phrase "that it was good," the Torah does not apply this word to the creation of humans:

The reason for the omission is in order to indicate that the good that is intended in the creation of man is not the perfection of existence merely, as in the other animals, but another nobler perfection, which can be attained only when he has actualized his potentialities.[23]

When combined with the belief in immortality, the opportunity of perfecting oneself surely becomes ever more meaningful.

Related to these ideas, Rabbi Albo notices another species distinction in the biblical use of the expressions "after its kind" and "after their kind." The text employs such phrases only in regard to animals and not to humans. Rabbi Albo infers from this language that animals, unlike humans, lack a certain individuality. Whether within species or across species, animals are all the same insomuch as "there is one general purpose including them all, and that is the perpetuation of the species, which is the perfection of existence."[24] Animals live a collective existence, with no potential for growth or perfection, and this fits with Maimonides's notion that God's providence extends over animal species and not individual animals.[25]

What, however, of scriptural statements to the effect that humans are no better than animals? For example, King Solomon tells us in Ecclesiastes that "the preeminence of the human being over the beast is nothing [*ayin*], because all is vanity" (Ecclesiastes 3:19; my translation). Here Rabbi Albo provides yet another ingenious, if perhaps strained, interpretation. He suggests that if Solomon meant to teach that humans have preeminence over animals, he could have written as such, without employing the word *nothing*. Rabbi Albo takes this "nothing" to be human potential. At the outset, potential is nothing in the sense that it has not been realized in whole or in part. Therefore, we should understand the verse to be telling us that this nothingness of potentiality itself figures as the human preeminence over animals. With no perfection of purpose and therefore no potentiality, animals do not possess this "nothing" instilled in human beings. Having this nothing, a nothing we should turn into something, is what makes humans greater than animals, according to the clever exegesis of Rabbi Albo.[26]

We have now seen, in a number of ways, how Jewish texts and authorities present or at least suggest some essential differences between humans and animals—differences in kind and not merely degree. Are these differences so great, so essential, that Singer's critique of speciesism ought not to apply? Before turning to this question, we must consider an important Jewish legal principle concerning the human treatment of animals.

TZA'AR BA'ALEI CHAYIM: LIMITS AND REASONS

Long before the notion of speciesism emerged, Judaism contained an important principle governing the human relationship with members of other species: *tza'ar ba'alei chayim*. Basically, this principle prohibits causing suffering to animals. Two dimensions of the prohibition are of concern in discussing veganism and speciesism: its limitations and the reasons offered for its existence.

First, the prohibition is not absolute. Although the term does not qualify the suffering, in practice we are forbidden to cause unnecessary suffering to animals. As one might quickly surmise, not everyone agrees as to how we ought to define *unnecessary*. Some might argue that if eating animals is unnecessary for human health, then killing animals for food should be prohibited. Even if one wants to argue that the Jewish ritual slaughter of animals is humane, surely no one can make a compelling argument that factory farming figures as a humane practice.

Whatever our notions of necessary and unnecessary might be, centuries of Jewish legal rulings suggest a much broader notion of necessary, to the extent that necessary might very well mean any human benefit. *Unnecessary* might not even be the best word; we might better think of the prohibition as being against unwarranted suffering to animals. So long as there is some human benefit, such suffering might not be considered unwarranted. This, for example, justifies conducting medical experiments on animals.

In an article on the topic of animal experimentation in Jewish law, Rabbi J. David Bleich offers numerous examples of authorities and rulings indicating rather broad exemptions to the prohibition. From the medieval luminaries, including Nachmanides and the Tosafot, to the sixteenth century's standard code of Jewish law, the *Shulchah Aruch*, and into the twentieth century, we find evidence of this expansive notion. Even in the Talmud, to honor a king as part of his funeral, permission is granted to cut the tendons of the horse he rode. In this case, the king's honor figures as a legitimate human purpose or need. According to Nachmanides, "slaughter and causing pain to animals is permissible for the need of man." Rabbi Moshe Isserles, the author of an Ashkenazi gloss on the *Shulchan Aruch*, allows causing suffering to animals for "healing or for any other legitimate purpose," in the words of Rabbi Bleich. Indeed, although there is not universal agreement among rabbinic authorities, Rabbi Bleich concludes that "the majority of rabbinic authorities regard financial gain as a legitimate 'need' or 'benefit' which, at least as a matter of law, may be fostered even at the expense of *tza'ar ba'alei chayim*."[27]

Rabbi David Sears, in his book *The Vision of Eden*, which presents a multitude of traditional Jewish sources on compassion for animals, acknowledges unambiguously that *tza'ar ba'alei chayim* has its limitations: "[It] does not apply to situations in which human beings are permitted to make use of animals, namely to serve legitimate human needs." It is not evident that Rabbi Sears believes the principle applies to any human needs, including trifling ones: "According to most authorities, this exemption extends to all other religiously sanctioned reasons for animal slaughter [i.e., in addition to providing meat for human consumption], such as to provide human beings with clothing or products for medical purposes, or to benefit us in any significant way."[28] In this way, Rabbi Sears associates "legitimate" with "significant," possibly excluding what most people would consider trivial needs or benefits.

The second and perhaps more relevant dimension of *tza'ar ba'alei chayim* is that of its reasons or justifications. How have Jewish thinkers conceptualized the prohibition? Can we uncover any evidence as to how Jewish authorities have thought of *tza'ar ba'alei chayim* in terms of our treatment of nonhuman species? We do not always know the reasons behind the *mitzvot*, the commandments, and knowing the reasons does not always change our obligation and practice, but insofar as we can speculate, what do we find in this case? We know the Torah prohibits Jews from causing unwarranted pain to animals, but why are Jews prohibited from causing such suffering?

The truth is that we do not find much in the way of explicit statements to the effect that the prohibition derives from any sort of responsibility to provide equal consideration to animals as members of other species. Rather, most commentators locate reasons for the prohibition in the effects produced in humans when humans cause suffering to animals. That is, the primary motivation for treating animals kindly appears to be one of shaping human sensitivities and character development and not for the sake of the animals themselves.

Even the many individual prohibitions of cruel treatment to animals—not muzzling an ox, helping unburden a donkey, shooing away the mother bird before taking its egg—do not necessarily amount to any sort of proof that humans ought to treat animals well for the sake of the animals. As Rabbi Bleich summarizes:

> Nor is it demonstrably certain that even these limited and particular duties are designed primarily for the purpose of promoting the welfare of animals. . . . In all likelihood, the rationale governing strictures against *tza'ar ba'alei chayyim* is concern for the moral welfare of the human agent rather than for the physical welfare of the animals; i.e., the underlying concern is the need to purge inclinations of cruelty and to develop compassion in human beings.[29]

He cites the example presented by the great medieval scholar Maimonides, who understood the prohibition against tearing a limb from a living animal and eating it as due to the unwelcome consequence of cruelty becoming habitual.

Rabbi Bleich further suggests that the human obligation to exercise compassion for animals derives from the fact that humans are created in the divine image, and Scripture tells us that God bestows compassion on animals. That is, we must be compassionate insomuch as we are like God and unlike animals.[30] As Rabbi Slifkin wittily and pointedly remarks, "We need to be kind to animals. But we must do it because *we* are humans, not because *they* are."[31]

As much as one might prefer otherwise, the reasons provided for *tza'ar ba'alei chayim* do not immediately strike one as resonant with Singer's arguments from speciesism, but seem to emerge from an entirely different foundation. Yet we must recall that Singer's argument proved not to be what we might have expected—an argument in favor of animal rights, or an argument about some abstract equality of animals and humans—but one rooted in a notion of equal consideration for shared interests. Do all of the explanations we have provided of human-animal differences or of qualifications to the principle of *tza'ar ba'alei chayim* have any impact on Singer's reasoning?

ASSESSMENT AND CONCLUSIONS

I presented Singer's arguments about and against speciesism. I reviewed numerous ways traditional Jewish thought distinguishes between humans and animals: animals not being created in the divine image, animals not possessing nonmaterial souls, animals not being immortal, and animals not having the capacity to grow toward perfection. I considered *tza'ar ba'alei chayim* and the various exceptions to this precept. Where do we stand? At first glance, the gulf would seem too great, that any coherent traditional Jewish approach would differentiate strongly between humans and animals, to the extent that speciesism could not serve as a persuasive Jewish argument in favor of veganism.

But as we learned, Singer's notion of speciesism proved to be anything but simplistic. No amateur philosopher, Singer no doubt anticipated possible objections and presented a carefully and logically argued position. Here's the challenge: could Singer acknowledge every one of the ways Jewish thinkers have distinguished humans from animals and nonetheless insist his arguments still stand, undefeated? Recall that Singer never asserts the equality of humans and animals. Indeed, he sees differences everywhere, within humans as well as between animal species. His argument concerns only the relevant interspecies similarities, those deserving of equal consideration. Perhaps he could argue that even if humans were created in the divine image and animals were not, even if humans have spiritual souls and animals do not, even if humans are immortal and animals are not, and even if humans are capable of growth and perfection and animals are not, nevertheless humans and animals share a capacity for pain and pleasure and share an interest to avoid suffering and therefore are deserving of equal consideration.

In other words, can, ought, or must Judaism recognize any sort of relevant, germane commonalities between humans and nonhuman animals, something shared and warranting equal consideration, such that the human killing and eating of animals for food must necessarily strike us as an immoral, discriminatory act? We might have thought the answer obvious, but is it? Is Singer not correct that humans and most (if not all) animals share the capacities to experience pain and pleasure? Perhaps all religiously observant Jews ought to adopt veganism in recognition of the compelling nature of these arguments against speciesism?

Even if we can admire Singer's reasoning and even if we cannot deny that humans and animals share a common interest in avoiding pain, is this the whole and sum of the matter? After all, the Torah, even if it presents veganism as an ideal rooted in the Garden of Eden, clearly permits the human consumption of animals. In addition, perhaps one could argue that the sorts of animal-human differences discussed here show demonstrably how animals and humans are different in kind and not merely degree, that the apparent shared interests should not matter. For instance, if a severely intellectually disabled human has an eternal soul, perhaps, *contra* Singer, there could never exist a situation in which Jewish law could or would favor saving an animal life over the human one. Also, although Judaism might incorporate utilitarian calculations in certain situations, most Jewish religious thinkers would reject the foundational principles of utilitarian philosophy and ethics. Judaism posits other values as higher than experiencing pleasure and avoiding pain and rejects the utilitarian goal of producing the most happiness for the most people as an essential element of our purpose in this world.

It is thus far from clear that Singer's arguments remain persuasive in a Jewish religious framework. Singer himself recognizes this. Concerning his criticism of using species membership to attribute a right to life to a human infant but not to a dog or chimpanzee or pig, he writes as follows in an endnote to his book: "I am here putting aside religious views, for example the doctrine that all and only human beings have immortal souls, or are made in the image of God. Historically these have been very important, and no doubt are partly responsible for the idea that human life has a special sanctity." He acknowledges the weakness or even failure of his argument in particular religious contexts. Singer's only maneuver at this point is to note that such religious views are not "reasoned" accounts of why all humans have souls and nonhumans do not—and then to propose that this belief itself "comes under suspicion as a form of speciesism."[32]

Without doubt, Judaism does place a special sanctity on human life. Sanctity on all life, yes, but a different and greater sanctity on human life. As Singer realizes, his arguments do not necessarily hold persuasive power over religious beliefs and commitments. Rabbi Sears is committed to expanding human compassion for animals and someone clearly supportive of those choosing veganism, and he writes, "One issue about which Judaism and the animal rights movement (or at least one trend within the animal rights movement) must disagree is the philosophical view that puts animals and humans on the same plane," a view he associates above all with Singer.[33] I think it is clear that no decisor of Jewish law would ever rule to save even a million healthy animal lives over a single human life, however compromised that individual's life might be. In this way, I suggest, Singer's argument against speciesism cannot truly find a home in traditional Judaism.

The concern for human sanctity is important, and one calling on us to return to the opening paragraphs of this chapter and to Rabbi Joseph Albo's account of Cain killing his brother. The lesson of this account is that we ought not to confuse human and animals and ignore the critical difference in sanctity, for such muddled thinking can all too easily lead to human sacrifice. Believing no essential difference separated humans and animals, and seeing his brother's offering favored by God, Cain reasoned that surely a human sacrifice would be prized all the more so.

We must ask: does treating animals and humans equally result in better treatment of animals or worse treatment of humans? If we turn animals into persons, do we end up turning people into animals? That is, if we see humans and animals as equal, will we treat animals with greater respect and increased kindness? Or will we treat humans the way we treat animals, with the same brutality we inflict on animals? In Rabbi Albo's view, Cain and his descendants demonstrated the latter outcome. From this perspective, human-animal equivalency does not enhance the value of animal life, but diminishes the value of human life.

In the end, there remain many good reasons—nutritional, ethical, and other—that a Jew, a religiously observant Jew, might adopt a vegan diet. One might present many quite cogent arguments, from Jewish perspectives, in support of veganism.[34] However, the evidence and arguments presented here suggest that the argument from speciesism does not figure as one of these.

NOTES

1. All biblical translations into English, unless otherwise noted, are from Koren Publishers Jerusalem and Harold Fisch, *The Koren Tanakh, New Edition of the Koren Jerusalem Bible, Personal Size*, bilingual ed. (Jerusalem: Koren Publishers, 2010).

2. Harry Freedman and Maurice Simons (eds.), *Midrash Rabbah*, 3rd ed., trans. Harry Freedman, 10 vols. (London: Soncino Press, 1961), vol. 1; Joseph Albo, *Sefer ha-Ikkarim: Book of Principles* (Philadelphia: Jewish Publication Society of America, 1946), vol. 3. My attention was first drawn to this interpretation by Rabbi Jonathan Sacks, "Violence and the Sacred (Tzav 5775)," website of Rabbi Jonathan Sacks, March 23, 2015, http://www.rabbisacks.org/violence-and-the-sacred-tzav-5775.

3. Richard Ryder, "Experiments on Animals," in *Animals, Men and Morals*, ed. Stanley Godlovitch, Roslind Godlovitch, and John Harris (London: Littlehampton Book Services, 1971), 41–82; Peter Singer, *Animal Liberation: The Definitive Classic of the Animal Movement*, reissue ed. (1975; New York: Harper Perennial Modern Classics, 2009).

4. Albo, *Sefer ha-Ikkarim*, vol. 3, 133.

5. Ibid., 135.

6. Ibid., 135–36.

7. Ibid., 136.

8. Ibid., 136–37.

9. Ibid., 137.

10. Singer, *Animal Liberation*, 6.

11. Ibid., 8.

12. Ibid., 9.

13. Ibid., 17.

14. Ibid., 8.

15. Ibid., 20–21.

16. Ibid., 20–21.

17. See ibid., chap. 4.

18. Aryeh Kaplan, *The Handbook of Jewish Thought* (Brooklyn: Moznaim Publishing, 1992), vol. 2, 355.

19. Ibid., 354–46.

20. See also Moshe Chayim Luzzatto, *Way of G-D: Derech Hashem*, 4th ed. (Jerusalem: Feldheim, 1983), chap. 1, part 3.

21. Natan Slifkin, *Man and Beast: Our Relationships with Animals in Jewish Law and Thought* (Brooklyn: Yashar Books, 2006), 72.

22. Ibid., 73.
23. Albo, *Sefer ha-Ikkarim*, vol. 3, 18–20.
24. Ibid., 21.
25. Kaplan, *The Handbook of Jewish Thought*, vol. 2, 288–89.
26. Albo, *Sefer ha-Ikkarim*, vol. 3, 22.
27. J. David Bleich, "Judaism and Animal Experimentation," in *Judaism and Environmental Ethics: A Reader*, ed. Martin D. Yaffe (Lanham, MD: Lexington Books, 2001), 344–49.
28. David Sears, *The Vision of Eden: Animal Welfare and Vegetarianism in Jewish Law and Mysticism* (Spring Valley, NY: Orot, 2003), 68–69.
29. Bleich, "Judaism and Animal Experimentation," 334–38.
30. Ibid., 334. See also Ze'ev Levy, "Ethical Issues of Animal Welfare in Jewish Thought," in *Judaism and Environmental Ethics: A Reader*, ed. Martin D. Yaffe (Lanham, MD: Lexington Books, 2001), 324–25.
31. Slifkin, *Man and Beast*, 158.
32. Singer, *Animal Liberation*, 258–59.
33. Sears, *The Vision of Eden*, 68; and Slifkin, *Man and Beast*, 157–58.
34. Sears, *The Vision of Eden*, 163–72. Sears presents nine reasons an observant Jew might choose vegetarianism (and presumably veganism).

12 A Morally Generative Tension
Conflicting Jewish Commitments to Humans and Animals

SHMULY YANKLOWITZ

The purpose of this chapter is to examine the Jewish philosophical underpinnings of animal welfare and rights. What is dignity, and how do we understand human and animal dignity differently? How are humans like and different from animals? Of what significance is an animal's sentience to ethical considerations? Should we introduce a language of differentiation between different types of sentient beings? What approaches have animal welfare activists and particularly Jewish activists used to protect animals from abuse?

Such questions are fundamental to a conversation about Jewish attitudes toward animals. I compare Jewish thinkers but start with a review of the secular history of animal welfare, rights, and legislation. We will see that Judaism has something noteworthy to contribute to the contemporary debate.

What we learn from various teachings is that there is ample room for the anthropocentric and egalitarian views in regard to the distinction between humans and animals and our moral obligations to each. Living with this paradox can allow humans to grow ethically, envisioning what may be ideal, while incrementally changing in pragmatic ways. The Jewish tradition embraces contradictory moral imperatives and even worldviews. Jews can learn from them and are obligated to wrestle with them, dialectically, to improve the world and Judaism.

MODERN SECULAR HISTORY

Historically and theologically, Judaism prioritizes ethics over theological dogma. How we apply our ethics—perceived as timeless—to the rapidly changing ecosystem of twenty-first-century life is of paramount concern. For example, highly industrialized agriculture has normalized the widespread availability of animals for consumption as meat, eggs, and dairy, increasing not just slaughter but cruelty. Do Jewish ethics allow this? Do secular ethics allow this? Well prior to our own time, Leo Tolstoy warned: "A man can live and be healthy without killing animals for food; therefore, if he eats meat, he participates in taking animal life merely for the sake of his appetite. And to act so is immoral."[1]

A teaching attributed to Mahatma Gandhi says, "The greatness of a nation and its moral progress can be measured by the way its animals are treated." Our relative callousness toward the mistreatment of other creatures, especially when carried out systemically and legally, shows our culture's relative lack of "moral progress." British common law, one of the foundations of the US legal system, derives from legal precedents established over centuries of judicial rulings, rather than statutory prescription.[2] One of common law's most widely emulated positions the world over has been its assumption that animals do not possess any rights akin to those attributed to humans.[3] Cases of abuse against animals were considered solely an infringement on the owners' rights to property. Such law does not recognize animals as having their own interests or at least does not attach legal significance to them.

One of the earliest challenges to such precedent came from Jeremy Bentham (1748–1832), who, skeptical of Sir William Blackstone (1723–1780), the foremost expert in common law in the eighteenth century, established utilitarianism (the moral ideology that actions are right if they reduce suffering or bring benefit to the majority). As he observed the abolition movement, Bentham began to question other abuses. In *An Introduction to the Principles of Morals and Legislation*, he asked "when the rest of the animal creation may acquire those rights which never could have been withholden from them but by the hand of tyranny. . . . The question is not, Can they reason? Can they talk? But, Can they suffer?"[4]

Blackstone's legal philosophy was the bedrock of early US jurisprudence on animals, until a major development after the Civil War. After witnessing the mistreatment of horses in Russia and encountering the Royal Society for the Prevention of Cruelty to Animals in England, Henry Bergh founded the American Society for the Prevention of Cruelty to Animals (ASPCA) in New York in 1866. To Bergh, it was simply a "moral question" that the "mute servants of mankind" such as horses needed protection.[5] The New York state legislature gave the ASPCA the authority to investigate animal cruelty and make arrests. Bergh helped close places where dog fighting (dog versus dog and dog versus rats) took place, and established an ambulance to evacuate disabled horses. By the time of Bergh's death in 1888, nearly every state had laws against animal cruelty.

Mark Twain (who may have quipped, "The more I know about people, the better I like my dog") was an early critic. He regarded any experimentation on animals as morally unacceptable and denounced the mistreatment of animals. "Of all the animals," he wrote, "man is the only one that is cruel. He is the only one that inflicts pain for the pleasure of doing it. It is a trait that is not known to the higher animals."[6] But Twain was in a very small minority.

Through much of the twentieth century, legal progress was minimal. Legislation limited the abuse that humans could visit on animals, but excluded many institutions and practices from criminality. The Federal Laboratory Animal Welfare Act of 1970 was motivated primarily by a desire to protect dog and cat owners from having their animals stolen and sold to laboratories.[7] In 1976, the law was amended to protect laboratory animals from egregious mistreatment while allowing animal experimentation to persist.

The prevailing attitude during most of the past century was technocratic:

> Some form of cost-benefit analysis should be performed to determine whether a particular use of animals is acceptable. The costs then considered consisted mainly of animal pain, distress, and death, whereas the benefits include the acquisition of new knowledge and the development of new medical therapies for humans.[8]

It was thought that if experiments on animals helped people live longer, aided in the development of penicillin and insulin, and helped create treatment for asthma, kidney disease, meningitis, and tuberculosis, then science in the service of human health was given primacy. The courts were reluctant to interfere. There were a few critics during the period of science's ascendancy.

The 1970s saw the start of the contemporary animal welfare and animal rights movements. Gerald Carson (1899–1989), a former advertising executive who later wrote social histories and served on the advisory board of *American Heritage* magazine, published *Men, Beasts, and Gods* in 1972. The book challenged the legality and moral validity of animal experiments. Carson noted that the air force used pregnant monkeys to conduct crash tests and declared the results "preliminary," so it could be repeated indefinitely. Carson sardonically noted, "How many pregnant women are expected to fly military aircraft has not yet been disclosed."[9]

Building on Carson's momentum and Bentham's utilitarianism, a true paradigm shift came when Peter Singer, now a professor at Princeton University, published *Animal Liberation* in 1975. Singer's thesis was as intellectually dynamic as it was morally rigorous. He questioned the validity of most animal experiments, dismissing them as "trivial and obvious," and asserted that millions of animals could be spared if these experiments were eliminated. "If possessing a higher degree of intelligence does not entitle one human to use another for his or her own ends," he wrote, "how can it entitle humans to exploit nonhumans for the same purpose?"[10] Like Bentham, Singer focuses on animal suffering, arguing that humans have a blind spot when they sanction the suffering of animals subjected to experimentation. He says that the enormity of animal suffering, in fact, outweighs the relatively minor advances to research commonly accrued through such practices. The resistance to new legal initiatives to curb animal abuse issued most strongly from animal entertainment industries—zoos, circuses, and aquariums—and human-benefit industries, such as slaughterhouses, dairy factory farms, and research labs.

In 1981, Alex Pacheco, a founder of People for the Ethical Treatment of Animals (PETA), began an undercover job at a federally funded laboratory, the Institute for Behavioral Research in Silver Spring, Maryland. He saw monkeys locked into cages with huge accumulations of urine and feces. The experiments, far from having any medical rationale, consisted of cutting the spinal nerve until a limb was disabled; then the monkeys were shocked until they made an attempt to use their disabled limb.[11] The monkeys were frequently unfed and experienced substantial pain from tight fetters and the experiments. Pacheco secretly documented the abuses, and PETA began a decade-long legal battle. The case culminated in the first arrest and conviction for abusive animal experiments, the rescue of animals from abusive experimental labs, and the strengthening of the Animal Welfare Act. It even led to a Supreme Court victory for animal welfare.

Organizations such as the Humane Society of the United States, the Nonhuman Rights Project, and the Animal Legal Defense Fund continue to propose legislation and pursue court cases on behalf of animals. Pending cases range from suits to prevent the mistreatment and killing of animals by private citizens and companies to requests for documentation guaranteeing that animals are treated fairly in city and state facilities and exhibitions, to cases against federal agencies such as the Food and Drug Administration and Department of Agriculture over their alleged failure to protect animals or their plans to kill them. Still, millions of animals are tortured and abused for entertainment, experimentation, or in the care of private individuals,[12] and that is not even considering the billions of animals subjected to cruelty and slaughter each year because of humans' skyrocketing appetite for animal products.[13] In fact, while there has been a growing number of vegans, vegetarians, and meat reductionists, the consumers of animal products are demanding more and demanding to get it cheaper.

Progress to limit animal abuse is slow, but the cause has certainly garnered more attention in recent years.[14] Even if animals do not become legal agents with rights that may be defended in courts of law, we should work to ensure that existing laws are enforced—as they have not been to date—and that more effective laws are passed. There must be comprehensive legal prohibitions against abusing animals with concomitant assurances of full transparency, enforcement, and accountability. Even humans without functioning nociception (pain reception) and cognition maintain their full rights because we consider such rights to be universal and self-evident. Although animals may not be moral agents, they may still be moral subjects deserving of moral and legal consideration for "animals are hardly strangers to our courts."[15]

Even if we may agree that humans and animals are fundamentally different, as I suspect most of us intuit, this does not license the instrumental use and zealous abuse of animals, as in slaughterhouses and other agriculture. An animal may not currently have the same legal rights as a human, but legal norms should be secured and defended. Our duty to animals should not be because they share our same capacity for cognition, reason, or communication. Rather, it should be because they experience pain. If one feels pain or has the capacity for pain (as all animals do because they have nervous systems), one has a right to be defended against that pain. Collectively, we are obliged to prevent needless pain, especially pain inflicted by humans.

JEWISH THOUGHT ON OBLIGATION

Bible and Early Rabbinic Thought

The Bible's creation story initiated the hierarchical system we have inherited. On each subsequent day, God creates something of seemingly greater significance than the day before, culminating with humans on the sixth day. This reflects an anthropocentric worldview, but the seventh day hints at the oneness of the universe. On Shabbat, all become equal. One may neither work the land nor use one's animal to do so. The creation story seems to say that we should value and mediate between conflicting anthropocentric (weekday) and egalitarian (Shabbat) models when considering the relationship between animals and humans.

Even if we decide that a hierarchy among human relationships is right or helpful, the ethics remain complicated. In traditional Jewish thought, the idea that humans may have an elevated status because we alone are created in *tzelem Elokim*, the image of God, does not make it necessarily simple to place human well-being over that of animals. Can one buy dog food if the same money could be used to feed person who is hungry? Should one rescue an abandoned cat, knowing that a homeless shelter needs money? Can one justify her time—and expend social capital—promoting veganism, when abused children need advocacy for foster placements and adoption? If one can give a little comfort to a human or prevent a hundred cows from torture and slaughter, should one prioritize the latter? Can one do both, even in the course of a life of limited time and resources?

Preventing animal suffering is so fundamental to the Torah that it is one of the seven *mitzvot*,[16] divine commandments, given to Noah and his sons after the flood. This was not only an instruction for Jews, but one of the few laws given to all peoples. Furthermore, the Torah teaches there are times where we must endanger ourselves by engaging with one's enemy to help animals, such as in Exodus 23:4–5.

> When you encounter your enemy's ox or ass wandering, you must take it back to him. When you see the ass of your enemy lying under its burden and would refrain from raising it, you must nevertheless raise it with him.[17]

By approaching an enemy, we make ourselves vulnerable to harm, but we do so because the animal needs our support. Deuteronomy places one's animals' needs before human needs: it is forbidden to sit down to one's own meal before one has fed one's pets and barnyard animals. As the Talmud says, " 'and I will give feed to your animals,' and only after that does the verse say 'and you shall eat and be satisfied.' "[18] Furthermore, "Rabbi Elazar HaKappar taught [in the Talmud]: It is forbidden for a person to buy an animal or bird unless he can feed it properly."[19]

The ideal of the compassionate person is explored repeatedly in ancient Judaic literature. Genesis 24:13–14 describes the search for a perfect wife for Isaac, who is imagined thus:

> Here I stand by the spring as the daughters of the townsmen come out to draw water; let the maiden to whom I say, "Please, lower your jar that I may drink," and who replies, "Drink, and I will also water your camels"— let her be the one whom You have decreed for Your servant Isaac. Thereby shall I know that You have dealt graciously with my master.[20]

In this unique moment—perhaps one of the first recorded in human history—Rebecca shows simultaneous compassion for humans and animals, expressing tenderness and mercy toward all in her actions. She demonstrates her virtue by attending to the needs of animals, even when she need not have done so. In so doing, she undertook an additional burden (never underestimate how much water camels need!). These holy attributes can separate the righteous from the wicked.

Other biblical moral exemplars cared for humans or animals. A rabbinic teaching distinguishes among the righteousness of Joseph, Noah, and Noah's sons.

> Two individuals are called righteous for having provided other creatures with food: Noah and Joseph . . . [The Torah calls Noah] "a righteous man (*tzaddik*)," because the term "righteous" specifically refers to one who provides food for God's creatures. Joseph sustained [his family and

all the people of Egypt]. Rav Achavah son of Rav Ze'ira said, "The sons of Noah... were all righteous because they showed compassion toward both animals and humans."[21]

Humans can demonstrate excellence of service to creation, and the creator, through an engaged commitment to other humans and animals.

In an elucidating *tosefta*, a Jewish law from an eponymously named compilation of laws dating from the time of the Mishnah, the rabbis taught that the lives of strangers have more weight in our moral obligations than animals do.[22] From an anthropocentric perspective—an approach that focuses on humans and their experiences, prioritizing human interests above all else—this makes sense. While animals may have value, it is usually understood on utilitarian or transactional terms: what can this animal do for me? How much is this animal worth? Even when an animal's concerns are recognized, it is considered fundamentally different to the concerns of humans, whose dignity is infinite and immeasurable. From a religious perspective, human dignity is understood as the sanctity of human life based on its rootedness within divinity.

Rabbinic commentary also preserves an opposing position. Rabbi Yose, a second-century sage, taught that caring for one's animals takes precedence over seeing to the welfare of strangers. In a world of limited resources, there are times when people ought to prioritize the lives of animals over the lives of humans. How shall we interpret and apply such a teaching? We know that the rabbis took animal welfare seriously. For example, they permitted their followers to violate rabbinically enacted prohibitions on the Sabbath to reduce any pain experienced by animals, because they believed that there was a biblical obligation to do so.[23] Yet Rabbi Yose's position is far more radical, given that the rabbis generally emphasized a distinction between humans and animals. It appears from his ruling that given limited resources, one is obligated to save the life of their own animal over the life of a human stranger (presumably due to one's relationship with the former). After all, few today would criticize a family that spends $1,000 on a medical procedure for their dog, knowing full well that they could save hundreds of children's lives in Africa by buying them mosquito nets to prevent malaria. An alternative interpretation is that Rabbi Yose may have been thinking about animals as property, rather than as independent beings, and therefore placed higher value on personal property than on the lives of strangers. Even according to this view, one's animals take precedence over human lives.

We also must examine our culpability in harming others. Is divine punishment the same for harming humans as it is for harming animals? Rabbi Yehudah HaChasid, a twelfth-century Jewish pietist in Germany, wrote:

> If one caused suffering to an animal without good cause, like putting too heavy a load upon an animal and beating it even though it could not walk, one must be brought to justice, because he caused an animal to suffer. Likewise, those who pull the ears of cats to make them scream are sinners. The sages expounded, "On that day, declares the Lord, I will strike every horse with panic and its rider with madness," (Zachariah 12:4) to mean that in the future God will require the humiliation of horses by their riders who strike them with boots.[24]

This *midrash* from the Babylonian Talmud concerns divine wrath for the abuse of animals:

> A calf was being taken to the slaughter, when it ran away, hid his head under Rabbi Judah the Prince's robes, and cried. He said, "Go. For this were you created." They [the angels] said, "Since he has no pity, let us bring suffering upon him." ... One day Rabbi's maidservant was sweeping the house, saw some young weasels lying there, and made to sweep them away. He said to her, "Let them be. It is written: 'And His mercy is over all His works'" (Ps. 145:9). They said, "Since he is compassionate, let us be compassionate to him."[25]

Here we see that God is willing to punish humans for the sake of animals and prioritize innocent animals over guilty humans in the divine scheme of justice.

Others suggest that we must differentiate between care for humans and care for animals by giving humans elevated treatment. But what is it that makes humans and animals fundamentally different? In what way can we distinguish between the worth of each?

Anthropocentrism

In today's Western zeitgeist, it is assumed that humans are the pinnacle of creation. What matters most is economic growth. But expansion is not always (indeed, rarely) what is best for the rest of life and the planet. We can return to some big questions: why was the world created? What role do humans have in achieving the ultimate purpose of the universe? For millennia, philosophers have debated the purpose of life. It has generally been assumed among Western philosophers that the purpose is for humans (to be happy, to thrive, to be holy, to redeem, etc.). Life—indeed, all of existence—is about human experience.

One of way of exploring whether humans are indeed the center of the universe is to inquire if we are similar to animals. Moses Maimonides (1135–1204), the Rambam, taught that with regard to pain, humans and other animals are the same:

> It is prohibited to kill an animal with its young on the same day, in order that people should be restrained and prevented from killing the two together in such a manner that the young is slain in the sight of the mother; for the pain of animals under such circumstances is great. There is no difference in this case between the pain of people and the pain of other living beings, since the love and the tenderness of the mother for her young ones is not produced by reasoning but by feeling, and this faculty exists not only in people but in most living creatures.[26]

Nonetheless, the Jewish tradition places great weight on human dignity (the sanctity of humans, since they are created in the image of God) in the Torah and Jewish law, both of which prioritize human life over animal life.[27] Whereas Singer dismisses human dignity and the sanctity of human life in his utilitarian calculations, Jewish ethics cannot do so and rarely take Singer's absolutist approach (where humans and animals are equated simply because neither has dignity and both experience pain fully).

How do we approach less severe cases, such as when a human is sick but not at risk of loss of life and an animal's life is at risk? Rabbi Samson Raphael Hirsch writes that animal pain is as profound as that of humans, and that animal vulnerability is even greater:

> There are probably no creatures that require more the protective Divine word against the presumption of man than the animals, which like man have sensations and instincts, but whose body and powers are nevertheless subservient to man. In relation to them man so easily forgets that injured animal muscle twitches just like human muscle, that the maltreated nerves of an animal sicken like human nerves, that the animal being is just as sensitive to cuts, blows, and beating as man. Thus, man becomes the torturer of the animal soul.[28]

Although there is ample textual evidence to support anthropocentrism, the opposite is true as well. Indeed, a humbler approach is to embrace the interconnectivity of all existence. Translating such a theology into moral imperatives will not be a simple matter, but such ambivalent moral deliberations is what is required of us.

Reincarnation

Although often considered to be relegated strictly to Eastern traditions, reincarnation (*gilgulim*) found its way into Jewish theology and left a permanent mark on Jewish thought. This perspective on existence may spiritually eliminate or mitigate the distinction between human and animal souls. Furthermore, a theology of reincarnation increases our responsibility for humanity in perpetuity. To act as ethical stewards of all creation, we are not bound by the temporal chains of mortality; reincarnation allows our souls to continue their work on the Earth. Many Kabbalists believed that humans return to this world not only in human forms but also in animal forms.

What moral lessons should we take from this esoteric theology? We can see reincarnation as a way of understanding how we should eat. Kabbalists have explained that we raise the sparks of the soul of an animal by consuming its flesh. In eating meat, one may be elevating the human soul trapped within the animal body, but it may be that this very act of consumption also causes one's own soul to eventually inhabit an animal. Rabbi Chaim Vital writes that in eating meat, a person risks eating an animal with an evil human soul; an act from which there may be no redemption.[29] Rabbi David Sears writes, "The status of a human may become exchanged with that of an animal, and vice versa."[30] He explains, "we must view these ill-fated creatures as we would our fellow human beings—even while rejecting the doctrine of the moral equivalence of all species."[31] Sears argues the interchangeability of souls as a reason for empathy and compassion.

The sixteenth-century kabbalist Rabbi Moshe Cordevero, the Ramak, taught that the reincarnation of human souls into animal bodies has deep roots as an ancient Jewish theology.[32] Some explain that a human can return to this world in animal form if that person acted like an animal in his or her life.[33] Furthermore, it is taught that reincarnation into animal form is so common that most animals alive today possess reincarnated human souls.[34]

How, then, does one maintain the health of one's soul while balancing the needs of the (present) body? If we believe souls continue after this life, we might heed the radical ethical implications of reincarnation theology. Perhaps the moral mandate to be compassionate to all creatures is based more in human self-interest than we might have thought. Reincarnation was an idea of a particular time and place but it can nonetheless help us envision a more moral way of living in the world, whether or not we accept the doctrine of reincarnation, which is far from common in Jewish thought.

Partnership

The idea of a Divinity "who teaches us by the beasts of the earth" (Job 35:11) promotes an understanding that animals were not placed here to be eaten but to be our teachers and partners. What if we reimagined our relationship to Creation from a hierarchical relationship to a partnered relationship?

The human relationship to animals need not be hierarchical. Multiple passages suggest that humans have much to learn from animals and that we engage with them to be helped by them. The Talmud, for example, offers a picture of natural morality, "If we had not received the Torah, we would have learned modesty from watching a cat, honesty from the ant, and fidelity from the dove."[35]

An earlier rabbinic folktale explains that the Israelites wanted to sing after achieving freedom by crossing the Red Sea. As slaves, however, they had forgotten how. They looked to the sky and saw birds chirping. From the birds, they once again learned to sing. The rabbis of the Mishnah also chose animals as models of virtue: "Judah the son of Teima would say, 'Be bold as a leopard, light as an eagle, fleeting as a deer and mighty as a lion to do the will of your Father in Heaven.'"[36] We learn even from the *Tanakh* that animals bring us closer to the divine: "The birds of heavens transmit the (human) voice" (Ecclesiastes 10:20).

Consider this related parable from the modern movement of Hasidism:

> After the death [of Rabbi Dov Ber ben Avraham of Mezeritch (1704–1772), also known as the Maggid], his disciples came together and talked about the things he had done. When it was Rabbi Schneur Zalman's turn, he asked them "Do you know why your master went to the pond every day at dawn and stayed there for a while before coming home again?" They did not know why. Rabbi Zalman continued, "He was learning the song with which the frogs praise God. It takes a very long time to learn that song."[37]

In ethos of ancient rabbinic Judaism, "there is nothing superfluous in the universe. Even flies, gnats, and mosquitoes are part of creation and, as such, serve a Divinely-appointed purpose."[38] Every creature has sanctity in such a religious teleology. Maimonides argues that the world does not exist for the sake of humans. Indeed, God cannot create something that does not exist as end in itself. Every divine creation has its unique telos:

> Now if the spheres exist for the sake of man, all the more is this the case for all the species of animals and of plants. However, if this opinion is carefully examined, as opinions ought to be carefully examined by intelligent men, the flaw becomes clear.... The correct view according to the beliefs of the Law—a view that corresponds likewise to the speculative views—is as follows: It should not be believed that all the beings exist for the sake of the existence of man. On the contrary, all the other beings too have been intended for their own sakes and not for the sake of something else.[39]

One of the weightiest Jewish religious imperatives is emulating God, *halakhta b-drakhav*, particularly divine humility. If humans are to cultivate humility, how are we to view our role within the universe? Entitled and central? Or interconnected with other beings with whom we share a destiny? From this perspective, we have a moral mandate to refrain from the hierarchical thinking that places humans above animals.

What we learn from these teachings on obligation is that according to well-established Jewish tradition, all of creation exists together in equal importance. But there is room for both the anthropocentric and egalitarian views. Living with this paradox allows humans to improve ethically, envisioning what is ideal, while incrementally changing in realistic ways. The tension between the ideal and the real seeds creative moral activity.

Rabbi Walter Wurzburger (1920–2002) writes about the plurality of Jewish ethics:

> The pluralism of Jewish ethics manifests itself in the readiness to operate with a number of independent ethical norms and principles such as concern for love, justice, truth, and peace. Since they frequently give rise to conflicting obligations, it becomes necessary to rely upon intuitive judgments to resolve the conflict. There is, however, another dimension to the pluralism of Jewish ethics: it is multi-tiered and comprises many strands. It contains not only objective components such as duties and obligations, but also numerous values and ideals possessing only subjective validity. Moreover, the pluralistic thrust of Jewish ethics makes it possible to recognize the legitimacy of many alternate ethical values and ideals.[40]

Jewish ethics offer not absolutes but a host of conflicting values that must be carefully navigated and balanced. At times, we will lean toward the utilitarian reduction of suffering. Other times, we will be compelled toward deontology to fulfill our moral duties. And at others, we will be guided by virtue ethics, the development of character through moral decision making. In any Jewish moral deliberation, we should be guided by empathy. Again and again, Jewish text reaffirms empathy as central to moral decision making.

CONCLUSION

Jewish law is unequivocal that we have obligations to animals, such as to avoid causing them unnecessary harm, and our tradition points to sacred opportunities to learn from them. It is also clear (with some minority disagreement) that we are more obligated to humans than to animals. But to what extent? There is no mathematical formula. The ethics may transcend logos. Rather, we must view this ethical dilemma dialectically. It is unclear where our infinite obligation to the needs of more than seven billion humans ends and where our moral duty begins to countless trillions of other animals that suffer, beings that coexist with us.[41] In the United States, more and more legislation is being passed to protect and grant rights to animals. Jews have tradition and a moral heritage that can aid in pushing for stronger legislation. Whether Jews have additional obligations to protect and care for animals is the moral frontier. Those inspired by Jewish tradition should see this as a unique moment calling for Jewish leadership. The Judaic ethos should be at the forefront of our collective discussions, as we navigate the muddy waters of dignity, sentience, sanctity, and rights. Furthermore, the pluralistic approach to ethics inherent to rabbinic Judaism should add an ambiguity that empowers us to act as moral agents, rather than paralyzes us. In our unique era, where our access to nutritious alternatives is so bountiful, little doubt is left that an ethical vegan diet should be viewed as most morally optimal for all who recognize the sanctity of all life.

NOTES

1. Leo Tolstoy, *Writings on Civil Disobedience and Nonviolence* (1886; New York: Bergman, 1967), 171.

2. "The Common Law and Civil Law Traditions," University of California, Berkeley, School of Law, https://www.law.berkeley.edu/library/robbins/CommonLawCivilLawTraditions.html (accessed March 1, 2016).

3. Anita Dichter, "Legal Definitions of Cruelty and Animal Rights," *Boston College Environmental Affairs Law Review* 7, no. 1 (September 1, 1978): 147–64.

4. Jeremy Bentham, *An Introduction to the Principles of Morals and Legislation* (Oxford: Oxford University Press, 1879), 311.

5. Marion Lane and Stephen Zawistowski, *Heritage of Care: The American Society for the Prevention of Cruelty to Animals* (Westport, CT: Praeger, 2008), 17.

6. Mark Twain, "Man's Place in the Animal World," in *Mark Twain's Book of Animals*, ed. Shelley Fisher Fishkin (Berkeley: University of California Press, 2011), 119.

7. Ibid.

8. Andrew N. Rowan, "Forum: The Benefits and Ethics of Animal Research," *Scientific American* (February 1997): 79.

9. Gerald Carson, *Men, Beasts, and Gods: A History of Cruelty and Kindness to Animals* (New York: Scribner's, 1972), 197.

10. Peter Singer, *Animal Liberation: Towards an End to Man's Inhumanity to Animals* (Wellingborough, UK: Thorsons, 1975).

11. Philip M. Boffey, "Animal in the Lab: Protests Accelerate, but Use Is Dropping," *New York Times,* October 27, 1981, http://www.nytimes.com/1981/10/27/science/animals-in-the-lab-protests-accelerate-but-use-is-dropping.html.

12. For information about contemporary animal abuse see, Animal Legal Defense Fund, "Current Cases," http://aldf.org/cases-campaigns/current-cases/. See also see Humane Society, "Our Work," http://www.humanesociety.org/work/; and Nonhuman Rights Project, https://www.nonhumanrights.org/ (all accessed on June 14, 2017).

13. Animal Equality, "Food," http://www.animalequality.net/food (accessed June 22, 2017).

14. Cara Feinberg, "Are Animals 'Things?,'" *Harvard Magazine*, March/April 2016, http://harvardmagazine.com/2016/03/are-animals-things.

15. Charles Siebert, "Should a Chimp Be Able to Sue Its Owner?," *New York Times Magazine*, April 23, 2014, https://www.nytimes.com/2014/04/27/magazine/the-rights-of-man-and-beast.html.

16. *Ever min ha-chai*, the prohibition against eating a limb from a living animal, is understood by many Torah commentators to be based in a concern for animal welfare.

17. New Jewish Publication Society of America Tanakh (NJPS) translation.

18. Babylonian Talmud, *Berachot* 40a on Deuteronomy 11:15.

19. Jerusalem Talmud, *Ketubot* 4:8.

20. NJPS translation.

21. *Midrash Tanchuma, Noah* 4.

22. *Tosefta Bava Metzia*, chap. 11:14.

23. See Babylonian Talmud, *Shabbat* 128b; *Hilchot Shabbat* 25:26; *Orach Chaim* 305:19–20.

24. *The Book of the Pious [Sefer Hasidim]*, section 44.

25. Babylonian Talmud, *Bava Metzia* 85a.

26. Moses Maimonides, *Guide for the Perplexed*, trans. Shlomo Pines, vol. 2 (Chicago: University of Chicago Press, 1963), 3:48.

27. Jewish law prohibiting causing pain to animals, *tza'ar ba'alei chayim*, has been waived when confronted with the needs of humans, *tzorech adam*. Now that human dietary needs can be fulfilled without using animals, this waiver must be reconsidered. Rav Eliyahu Klatzkin (1851–1932) wrote a legal *responsum* arguing that causing animal suffering is not permissible for mere human pleasure or for economic reasons, but only for human medical necessity. He brings many proofs in *Imrei Shefer* (Warsaw: Eliyahu ben Naftali Herz Klatzik, 1896), 59; available at http://www.hebrewbooks.org/664.

28. Samson Raphael Hirsch, *Horeb: A Philosophy of Jewish Laws and Observances*, trans. Isidor Grunfeld (London: Soncino Press, 1997), 60:415.

29. *Sha'ar Ha-Mitzvot, Eikev*, Ashlag edition, see 100b through 101b. Rav Vital also argues here than an *am haaretz* (unlearned Jew) is forbidden to eat meat because his *neshamah* (soul) is lacking sufficient *kedushah* (holiness) to refine the *siggim* (or spiritual dross) associated with the animal.

30. David Sears, *The Vision of Eden: Animal Welfare and Vegetarianism in Jewish Law and Mysticism* (CreateSpace, 2014), 84.

31. Ibid.

32. *Shiur Komah, Inyan Gilgul*, sec. 84.

33. *Sefer Hasidim*, sec. 169.

34. *Likkutei Halaakhos, Shechitah* 2:10–11, 3:2, 4:2.

35. Babylonian Talmud, *Eruvin* 100b.

36. *Ethics of the Fathers*, 5:20.

37. Martin Buber, *Tales of the Hasidim—The Early Masters* (New York: Schocken, 1947), 111.

38. *Bereshit Rabba* 10:7. Translation from Rabbi David Sears, *A Vision of Eden*, 199 (2003 edition).

39. Maimonides, *Guide for the Perplexed*, 3:13.

40. Walter Wurzburger, *Ethics of Responsibility: Pluralistic Approaches to Covenantal Ethics* (Philadelphia: Jewish Publication Society, 1994), 5

41. Indeed, our concern is not only for animal dignity (sanctity of beings that were chosen for life; for existence), but also due to sentience and the Jewish mandate to reduce suffering among all sentient beings.

13 Linking Judaism and Veganism in Darkness and in Light

SHERRY F. COLB

> For that which befalls the sons of men befalls beasts;
> even one thing befalls them;
> as the one dies, so dies the other; yea, they all have one breath;
> so that man has no preeminence above a beast;
> for all is vanity.
> All go to one place; all are dust.
> Who knows the spirit of men whether it goes upward;
> And the spirit of the beast whether it goes
> Downward to the earth?
> —Ecclesiastes 3:19–20

I am drawn to two powerful links between Judaism and veganism. One link is dark, having to do with the meaning of the designation "Jew" after the Holocaust and of the designation "animal" in a world that everywhere slaughters animals. The other is lighter, having to do with the connection between Judaism as a practice and veganism as a related and parallel practice. In the Torah story, darkness precedes light, and so it does in this reflection.

Being a Jew forms an integral part of what it is for me to be a vegan. I would not suggest that people of other faiths or who experience no connection to any religion or religious group are less equipped to be vegan than Jewish people are. I know and love many vegans. Some are Jews. Some have no religious affiliation; others are deeply religious people devoted to faiths other than Judaism. Sadly, few among Jews and few among other people whose commitments are to different religions or to no religion at all are vegan. Judaism is neither a necessary nor a sufficient condition for practicing veganism.

I would not suggest that being a religious Jew inclines a person toward ethical veganism. The Torah and religious texts contain teachings of great relevance to any ethical vegan, as I elaborate in greater detail in the "light" portion of this chapter. One important example is the injunction not to cause *tza'ar ba'alei chayim*, the pain of living beings or—to interpret the words literally—the pain of those who are owners of a life.[1] Yet the current system of animal agriculture arguably and profoundly violates Jewish rules about humane slaughter.[2]

I am a secular Jew who observes some Jewish traditions for cultural and personal reasons. My veganism and animal rights activism are "abolitionist." They aim to abolish animal exploitation.[3] Abolitionism acts as a counterpoint to approaches that seek to reform and regulate the use and consumption of animals and their "products." These latter "welfarist" approaches seek to improve the lot of animals in agriculture and render their treatment more "humane," rather than explicitly seeking to put an end to animal exploitation.[4] In my experience, abolitionism is more common among secular Jews than among religious ones. Perhaps because most Jewish religious injunctions regarding animals, beginning with those we find in the Bible, are welfarist, religious Jews tend to assume the acceptability and moral legitimacy of a system of animal exploitation. We see a version of this thinking in the requirement that if one comes upon a mother bird sitting on her eggs or her young, one may not take the mother with her young but must first shoo away the mother bird (Deuteronomy 22:6). A verse in Leviticus tells us not to slaughter a mother animal and her young on the same day (Leviticus 22:28). Still other Jewish laws require that we allow animal property to rest on the Sabbath (Exodus 20:10), that we not muzzle animals in the field (Deuteronomy 25:4), that we not tie strong to weak animals while they work (Deuteronomy 12:10), and that we slaughter animals in a specific (presumably more humane) fashion (Deuteronomy 12:21).[5]

DARKNESS

When I say that being a Jew feels intimately connected to being an ethical vegan, I mean to suggest something idiosyncratic about the link. For me, the experience of being a Jew resonates powerfully with the experience I would imagine of being an animal.

What Does It Mean to Be a Jew?

One is either born a Jew or becomes a Jew by choice. Under traditional Jewish law, being born of a Jewish mother confers Jewishness. So does conversion, an arduous process that requires a commitment by the convert to observe the tenets of their new faith.

Like religious converts to Judaism, most ethical vegans come to their way of living through a conversion process rather than by being born into it. Even my children, whom my husband and I have raised as vegans, were born consumers of animal products and "converted" several years after they were born, when we ourselves became vegan. The way my children and I are vegan—as converts— stands in strong contrast to how I am a Jew, as one born of parents who were Jews who survived the Holocaust.

For me, being a Jew is mostly an internal state that interacts with and reflects my dealings with the outside world, including my family's history. I am a Jew because I feel like a Jew, and I feel like a Jew because my grandparents and all but one of my aunts and uncles were murdered in the Holocaust because they were Jews. Knowing that if I had lived during the Holocaust, I would have likely been placed in a ghetto, a death camp, and then a gas chamber or shot in the killing fields of Eastern Europe makes me feel very much a Jew, regardless of what customs and traditions I do or do not uphold and regardless of how I project my Judaism into the world. My Jewishness is therefore an odd mix of descent and traumatic knowledge, neither of which has anything to do with how I behave on the Sabbath or holidays.

Admittedly, this does not sound like the most positive Jewish identification, and it certainly is not. The person who identifies as Jewish because they believe in the Jewish God, the commandments, and the miracle of Jewish survival over the millennia may have a more affirmative story to tell about their identity than I do about mine, as does the person who loves Jewish humor and culture and Jewish ways of being in the world and who identifies as Jewish for those reasons.[6]

To be sure, I also love Jewish humor and take part in some of the other distinctive ways that Jews find to be in the world, but my key connection, mediated through inheritance, is trauma.[7] One way of being a Jew, my way, is to have been brought into this world and told at a very young age that being "like me" triggered in others a genocidal wish to exterminate me and my kin. My way is a reactive way of being a Jew, and it seals my identity in fire. There is nothing that I could do or say that would make me stop experiencing myself as a Jewish person, any more than a person serving a life sentence in a prison cell could simply decide by dint of will to stop being a prisoner. Whatever else that person might be or aspire to become, they are also going to be a prisoner. The same could be said for a gay person or an African American—identity of this sort does not neatly come to an end at will.

For many vegans—including me—becoming vegan was a positive and life-affirming choice. Yet I became a vegan only after I fully absorbed the fact that animals became "animals" in much the same way that I became a Jew. More accurately, animals became "animals" in the way that those Jews who came before me and who perished before I arrived became Jews. For me, becoming vegan was the act of someone who had felt internally forced to be a "Jew" bearing witness to that force and then refusing to be a collaborator in the overwhelming majority of the population's choice to force animals to become "animals."

Becoming "Animals"

Today, most nonhuman animals in the world do not simply exist and live out their lives in the way that nature "designed" them to. They are not simply animals in the natural environment. Instead, people define and even design them—particularly the domesticated animals. People specifically designate animals as resources to be used to meet human needs and wants, whether for food, clothing, entertainment, scientific research, or companionship. The practice of pet ownership comes closest to allowing animals to just be who they are. Yet the breeding, selling (despite their mothers' cries), and killing of the "unwanted" majority of potential companions returns most members of even the higher-status companion animal group to the category that covers their brothers and sisters in other industries: "only animals." Furthermore, the long process of domestication, which has created "purpose-bred" animals who cannot live on their own and must depend on humans, their exploiters, for care and life itself, makes the lives and well-being of even companion animals precarious.

We can tell that animals have become "animals" by noticing that we casually name them for the purposes for which we have brought them into the world (or appropriated them from their prior environments), purposes for which they will almost certainly live painful lives and then die premature and terrifying deaths. We say that cows, chickens, pigs, and other such animals whom we farm primarily for their edible flesh and hormonal secretions are "farm animals." "Farm animals" sounds similar to the phrase that ethical vegans use to describe these beings, "farmed animals," but there is a crucial difference. The former treats the category of animals as naturally occurring and thus descriptively neutral: farm animals are animals who naturally live on a farm, where they belong.[8] "Farmed animals" refers to those animals whose unjust exploitation and abuse have taken a particular form. To say that a cow is a "farmed animal" is not to define the cow as such but to notice what we are doing to her. It is to make her ugly fate visible as something separate from her.

The linguistic distinction I am describing has an important parallel in human rights. Many people have begun to refer to "enslaved persons," when describing African Americans who had the grotesque misfortune to live under chattel slavery in this country.[9] To call the same people "slaves," as when Aristotle speaks of slaves in his natural hierarchy of beings in *Politics*, can sound too much like condoning and accepting their status as human property, as though "slaves" is just who they were.[10]

With respect to animals, our language, like our practices, has a long way to go. For example, in purchasing toy animals for children, one will come across many "farm animals" but will be unlikely to encounter a single "farmed animal." We thereby take the violence we routinely visit on these gentle, innocent beings, and we erase that violence from view and simultaneously neatly attribute what befalls them to their identity as creatures of the farm. Toy cows, for instance, all have distended udders, implying that it is normal for a female mammal to be lactating all the time. In truth, though, it is normal only because forced pregnancy (through violent inseminations) and the tearing away of nursing calves from their lactating mothers have become normalized practices.[11]

We see the same process in references to "zoo animals" rather than to the admittedly less catchy "captured free-living animals and their offspring whom humans have forced to live inside cages." The phrase "prison for animals as if they were guilty of a crime" would be more accurate than "zoological garden."

"Animalizing" occurs virtually everywhere. After my twelve-year-old daughter visited an open house at a veterinary school, she noted the oddity that a place for healing animals also provided animal meat as snacks. "It would be like a hospital serving human meat to its visitors," she remarked. Indeed, it would be, if only veterinarians truly were for animals what medical doctors are for humans. They (or many of them), however, are keepers of a mix of arguably incompatible missions: relieving and preventing their patients' suffering, while also inflicting great suffering on their experimental subjects to advance medical knowledge. One can only assume that veterinarians square that circle by using phrases that turn animals into "animals." Words like "laboratory rats" or "laboratory beagles" help distinguish between those animals who, for however long, are to be valued members of a human family with greater-than-market worth, and the living beings whose role in life is to face immobilization, mutilation, deliberate infection or poisoning, and then "sacrifice" (i.e., death) for the sake of someone else's knowledge.

Animals thus become "animals" when people breed them into the world, capture them, or purchase them to be harmed and killed for the sake of others. When we would consider it unethical to do something to a human, we can still comfortably do it to an animal whom we have defined as an "animal," so long as we can derive some human benefit from it.

Children seem to have the easiest time seeing through the magic of those words that turn animals into "animals" and thereby obscure the violence and the injustice of the violence that those living creatures experience. One can enjoy a sweet video of a child on YouTube who discovers with horror that the "octopus" on his plate is an actual octopus.[12] A friend of my daughter once said that she did not understand why it is murder to shoot humans but fine for the government to hire a contractor to shoot "excess" deer in a nearby neighborhood. "Why is that not murder, too?," she asked.

Becoming Jews

Nazis who experimented on and murdered Jews were able to do so partly because they came to understand Jews as *Untermenschen* (subhumans), associated with "vermin," the type of nonhuman animals whom we designate by their nuisance status rather than by anything intrinsic to themselves. Having made the subject a "Jew," experiments seemed (to those who performed them) like science rather than atrocity.[13] Often when people condemn the Holocaust, they use language that faults the Nazis for treating Jews as animals, not for treating Jews in a way that we should never treat any feeling being. Thus, people object to the fact that Jews traveled to the death camps in "cattle cars," typically without stopping to think that the term implies acceptance of the transportation of innocent cattle to bovine death camps.

Becoming a "Jew" during the Holocaust meant undergoing a process that was much like the process by which nonhuman animals become "animals." It is a process that happens *to* animals, *to* Jews.[14] Becoming someone whom people may persecute, harm, and even slaughter with impunity is a process over which the animals or Jews have no control. As an heir to this process of becoming a Jew, I accordingly did not have a moment when I decided that I would have a Jewish identity. I instead learned that I was a Jew virtually at the same time I learned what it had meant for my kin (and therefore for me, by traumatic inheritance) for others to make us "Jews."

When I first encountered footage of people torturing animals in the process of creating unnecessary products, the footage immediately triggered some of the same feelings I experienced when I viewed Holocaust footage and the same desire to look away. The pictures of what it meant to be a "Jew" were almost always stills, whereas the pictures of what it meant to be an "animal" were often moving pictures. But then the fictionalized movies about the Holocaust, in which viewers could watch people dying in gas chambers, came along to fill in the gap.

What makes moving pictures distinct from stills, as an emotional matter, is that a still implies that one is looking at a moment in time, while moving pictures feel far more eternal and ever-present. Watching documentary and fictionalized footage of the Holocaust led me to see myself and my family in ways that I had previously absorbed only through the stories I had heard from my mother about what the antisemites had done to "us." The stories, stills, and moving pictures eventually merged in my mind and became part of what I experience regularly. Though the Holocaust against the Jews (and gay people, Sinti and Roma, and other groups who endured the Nazis' program of extermination) is over, my own sense of trauma is ongoing. At some level, I do not regard myself as a valued human with rights but as subhuman "vermin," fit to be exterminated. I identify with the vermin, then, because others demoted me to their (designated) level and because I am intent on elevating them to what is in the present, in theory, my elevated status.

FROM DARKNESS TO LIGHT: *KASHRUT*

Most Jews who identify strongly as such probably do not derive their Jewish identity from a traumatic connection to the Holocaust. They associate Jewishness with the practice of religion or an affinity for the culture and associated practices. In keeping with this more affirmative and likely more common form of Jewish identity, let us turn to a positive practice that supports the connection between Judaism and veganism: the practice of observing *kashrut*. To be vegan or to keep kosher, one must pay close attention to what one eats. Ingredients are important; only some are permissible. Neither an observant Jew nor an ethical vegan can eat without some consciousness of what they are putting into their mouth. Yet this similarity does not resonate for me as the only link between Jewish identity and veganism, even in the context of *kashrut*. So I must turn to my own, idiosyncratic experience of *kashrut* before I explore its relevance to my veganism more generally.

When I was a child, my family was Orthodox. I bring this up only now, because it would have potentially confounded my earlier efforts to define myself as a "Jew" in the way that people sometimes call a death row inmate a "dead man," a phrase whose source lies wholly outside of the being it describes. Because I observed commandments, was there not a greater level of agency in my experience of being a Jew than there is in either a "dead man" or an "animal?" I acknowledge having some agency in my life as an Orthodox Jew, although I lived that way only until I left home for college, so it is difficult to separate my earlier Orthodoxy from having lived under my mother's roof.

Even as a child, when people asked me why I kept the Sabbath or why I kept kosher, I felt that the answer had little to do with what ordinary observant people say about observance. I kept *kashrut* and other *mitzvot* mostly out of habit and obligation. I know now, as an adult, that many people experience keeping kosher as a beautiful thing. They feel that it purifies their lives in positive ways; this was not my experience. I also failed to see the beauty in refraining from work on the

Sabbath. Rather than feeling like I could let go of my weeklong concerns and luxuriate in the day of rest, I felt an enormous sense of relief when the Sabbath ended and I could resume turning on lights, writing, watching television, taking buses, and otherwise conducting my life in the way that I did the rest of the week. The day of "rest" was for me a day of restrictions. Then, as now, my personal Jewish identity was not exactly life-affirming.

The Holocaust was the vehicle through which I forged my Jewish identity, including my former Orthodoxy. How so? My mother was my only parent from the time I was six years old, when my father (also a Holocaust survivor, as well as a Holocaust rescuer[15]) passed away. My mother's view of our religious observance was subtle, and she never expressly conveyed it to me, but I picked it up. She continued observing the commandments out of some combination of habit and fear of communal judgment. She had joyfully kept kosher and observed the Sabbath when she was a young girl, but then God betrayed her and took away almost everyone she held dear, so her relationship with God was irreparably altered.

Interestingly, the Holocaust never stopped my mother from believing in God, but she very much changed her view of the Almighty after she lost her parents and her four younger brothers in Europe. Once the war had ended, she no longer wanted to be religious, but my father persuaded her that they should be, for reasons I never learned but suspect had to do with not knowing how else to be. So she was religious, but she did not treasure being that way.

In attempting to understand her perspective for a moment, I believe she thought of God as a parent who had so utterly abused her that He had lost any claim on her. Yet out of habit and a respect for the wishes of her late husband, she continued to act as though she and her Father in heaven were still on speaking terms. She observed the *mitzvot*, the commandments, in the way an adult child acts civilly toward an estranged parent when circumstances forced them together. She went through the motions.

There was another element to my mother's observance. As she aged, she increasingly found comfort in the familiar. There was nothing more familiar to her than the *mitzvot* that she had kept almost all her life, with the exception of when she was "passing" as a non-Jew during the war and could not afford to observe Jewish laws publicly.

As an older person, then, my mother observed the commandments, at least in public. I used to tease her about being unwilling to openly violate the rules for fear of someone seeing her do it. I referred jokingly to the people who might catch her violating the Sabbath as "the Shabbos people." I should not have teased her, for this was unquestionably part of what motivated her to remain religious. She feared exile from a community, however frayed her ties to it, because she was so alone after my father passed away. Being religious was either a form without substance between her and her estranged God or a means of remaining connected to people with whom she had little other connection. Either way, because I perceived her observance as ultimately insincere, there was nothing to make me observant once I left home. The Holocaust kept me Jewish, but it was not enough to keep me religious.

Redeeming *Kashrut*

Kashrut, however, had much more to it than I initially realized when I was observing the kosher laws as a child. Like a fish living his life, unaware of the water, the kosher laws—and living in accordance with them—was all I had ever known before I left home. I slowly came to realize what these laws had to offer in the years that followed, when I no longer kept kosher but ate whatever I wanted. I stopped uttering blessings before eating; I no longer bothered looking at the ingredients on products that I purchased or asking waiters at (nonkosher) restaurants what I might order if I were avoiding (presumably nonkosher) meat. In the many years during which I no longer kept kosher, I became self-consciously oblivious to the nature of the foods I put into my mouth.

Every so often, though, during this lengthy period, I would forget that I "could" eat whatever I wanted, and I would notice with disgust that there were bits of pork or shrimp floating in the soup I had ordered; I would avoid those bits. When this happened, I wrote off the experience as an irrational remnant of the time during which I kept kosher. Like an adult who found herself aware with discomfort of stepping on sidewalk cracks, I internally mocked my own reluctance to partake in pork, shrimp, or some other blatantly nonkosher food as vestiges of meaningless childhood habits.

After reading a book about animals and their emotions, I began to become willingly conscious about food again, just as I had been (not-so-willingly) conscious about food when I observed *kashrut*.[16] My first step back into culinary awareness was a decision to stop consuming the meat of mammals. I then gave up all warm-blooded animals, including birds. Then came fish as well, and I finally stopped consuming dairy and eggs, once I absorbed the truth about the torments and death associated with these seemingly bloodless food products.[17]

I could not help but notice bemusedly, as I proceeded along these lines, that the closer I came to being vegan, the closer I came to keeping kosher again. With some notable exceptions, virtually all the rules of *kashrut* have something to do with avoiding some animal products.[18] As a vegan, there was something very familiar yet somewhat different about what I was doing. Like a friend of mine put it, veganism felt like "the new kosher" for me, and it was hard to dismiss the idea that perhaps the "old kosher" had meaningfully laid the groundwork for the "new kosher," in letter and spirit.

It is no accident, I believe, that the kosher laws so largely concern themselves with prohibiting various animal products and with regulating the way people slaughter even permissible animals and how people must prepare and consume their products. Jewish law seems to have tacitly integrated the knowledge that a meal consisting of animal products, unlike a feast of rice, beans, and fruit, necessarily involves taking something precious away from a sentient living being, a member of the group *ba'alei chayim*, literally owners of a life. This is comparable to animal rights philosopher Tom Regan's category of "subjects of a life," those to whom we owe moral consideration.[19]

Considering the rules of *kashrut* as a vegan, I noticed that they concern not only the consumption of meat (which most obviously raises moral concerns) but the consumption of dairy, too. If an observant Jew has recently consumed meat, they may not consume dairy for several hours. For most people who first consider conforming their eating habits to an ethical concern for animals, ovo-lacto vegetarianism seems like a worthy goal, and many wonder: what could be wrong with dairy and eggs? Yet as a formerly observant Jew who had become an "observant" vegan, I could think back to the regulation of dairy and egg consumption as a kind of proto-veganism. (Eggs are generally kosher unless they have a blood spot in them.) In the cases of dairy and eggs, the kosher rules seem to aim to make Jews conscious of the fact that consuming any animal product is a morally serious and even dangerous matter.[20] A *kashrut*-observing Jew cannot just eat animal products without thinking, as she can comfortably do with most non-animal-based foods. If she is not paying attention, she can easily make a mistake and commit a sin.

I do not want to overstate my point. The laws of *kashrut* do not prohibit the consumption of meat, dairy, or egg products. Although *kashrut* does prohibit the consumption of shellfish, it treats kosher fish as though they were vegetables. *Kashrut* does not regulate how people kill fish, even though it does regulate the method by which people slaughter warm-blooded (kosher) vertebrates.[21] Furthermore, by allowing the consumption of fish with dairy, *kashrut* appears to ignore the fact that the flesh of a fish is "meat." Once I came to understand the sentience of fish, I wondered why Jewish law did not mandate separation of fish and dairy, the way it did chicken and dairy.[22] I found it very odd that some kosher "vegetarian" restaurants serve the flesh of slaughtered fish.

If one believes that humans rather than God designed religious laws, perhaps this is unsurprising. We can expect humans to make compromises, and rules that prohibit some animal products but permit others represent a compromise between complete license and what I would now regard as a true commitment to the well-being of nonhuman animals through veganism. If one believes that religious law comes from God, one might surmise that God was attempting to make the consumption of animal products more cumbersome and onerous than the consumption of violence-free foods, as a means of motivating humans to come around to doing the right thing and foreswearing all products of violence.[23] Rav Albo (1380–1444) wrote along similar lines about the permission to eat animals and the permission to capture beautiful women in battle. Both represent a concession to human weakness, but the many laws surrounding the concession teach that it is better to refrain altogether from engaging in such conduct.[24]

The rabbis and communities who elaborated on the biblical laws regarding how Jews should eat seem clearly to have been struggling with the ethical implications of eating animals and their secretions. They accordingly reserved the most complex and demanding food-related injunctions for those engaged in the consumption of animal products. For ethical vegans, this reservation makes a great deal of sense, even though it does not go far enough.

Furthermore, consumption of animal products does not simply make life more complicated under Jewish law. The rules seem connected to the suffering that animals experience. The laws governing slaughter, for example, seem calculated to make the dying process less terrible for animals than it might otherwise be.[25] Sadly, modern slaughterhouses often make kosher slaughter worse rather than better for the animals, but that was almost certainly not its original goal.[26]

It is worth taking a close look at the biblical passage that commentators have interpreted as barring the consumption of meat and dairy together (or, in much contemporary practice, in close temporal proximity to each other).[27] Here, too, we find a concern for the ethical implications of consuming animal products.

The passage, which appears three times in the Torah, reads: "Do not cook a kid [a baby goat] in his mother's milk" (Exodus 23:19 and 34:26; Deuteronomy 14:21). The standard interpretation of this verse forbids consuming meat and dairy together.[28] But that is not the most natural reading. If one were interested in eating as much from the animal world as possible, one could point out that only one kind of animal is referenced, a goat, and one might note as well that the injunction says nothing about eating but only references cooking. Finally, one could observe that even when considering goats themselves, it may be acceptable to cook goat meat in goat milk, as long as the milk does not come from the mother of the specific goat whose flesh one is cooking.

Those religious scholars construing the meaning of the *mitzvot*, however, saw the fact that the injunction appears three times as evidence that one must expand on its meaning rather than interpret it as narrowly and literally as possible.[29] The conventional expansion meant that the passage would apply not only to goats but to all flesh (at least of warm-blooded animals, including those who do not lactate), that the injunction covered not only cooking but eating and using, and finally that not only milk from one specific source, that is, the mother of the source of the meat, would matter but that the prohibition concerned all milk from all kosher mammals.[30] As a result, Orthodox Jews today will wait six hours after eating the flesh of a mammal or bird before consuming dairy.[31] Jewish scholars thus chose to interpret the verse generously, to prohibit more than it literally appears to prohibit.

I would read the verse quite differently. As I have explained elsewhere, it seems mainly about relationships between animals rather than about when to eat select foods.[32] It says not to cook a baby in his mother's milk. It thus highlights the relationship between a mother and her baby and thereby reminds the reader that when they cook flesh, that flesh used to be a living being, perhaps a baby animal still nursing, when his or her life was cut short. The verse reminds us that if one is heating up milk, that milk came from a mother who was lactating to nourish her baby.

In prohibiting the flesh of a kid cooked in his mother's milk, then, it would seem that the Torah was deliberately reminding us that meat often comes from a baby and the milk we consume was originally the milk on which the baby would have nursed. Read in this way, the repeated verse calls attention to what we may casually think of as a tasty treat as being in truth the product of breaching a relationship between mothers (who produce milk following a pregnancy to nurse their young) and their infant children (who live on that milk).

Though the verse does not prohibit all flesh or dairy consumption, it seems logical to understand the verse as highly critical of both. In the absence of necessity, we might best understand this verse as telling us to stay away from foods that violate the sacred relationships between animals and their kin. Indeed, by focusing on the individual "kid" and his mother's milk, the text reminds us that animals are individual sentient beings with particular relationships and loves, not an undifferentiated mass of foodstuffs on which we might mindlessly dine.

Here's Your Damned Meat

The injunction against milk and flesh is only one of numerous biblical passages that we can readily understand as skeptical of the consumption of animal products. In Genesis, when God had just created the world, He told His creations what they could eat, and what He told them sounds like a vegan diet:

And God said, Behold, I have given you every herb bearing seed, which is upon the face of all the earth, and every tree, in the which is the fruit of a tree yielding seed; to you it shall be for meat. (Genesis 1:29–30)

In the original Hebrew, the word translated here as "meat" is actually "food." God was thus prescribing a vegan diet.

Notably, the obligation to eat a vegan diet comes right after humans learn that they have "dominion" over other animals (Genesis 1:26–28). Humans might thus naturally conclude that dominion entitles us to subjugate animals.[33] To avoid that inference, the verses immediately following the granting of dominion explicitly omit animal flesh and secretions from the approved menu.

Exodus contains another revealing story. After the Jews leave Egypt and are wandering in the desert, the Torah says that God supplied them with food called manna. Manna would fall from the sky each day, and people were expected to take as much as they needed for that day. Eventually, some complained about the absence of meat. They longed for the flesh pots of Egypt (Exodus 16:2–36; Numbers 11:1–35). Here are the relevant verses:

> And the mixt multitude that *was* among them fell a lusting: and the children of Israel also wept again, and said, Who shall give us flesh to eat? We remember the fish, which we did eat in Egypt freely. (Numbers 11:4–5)

Note three characteristics of the complaint. First, the complaining segment of the Israelite population was experiencing a "lusting," which has a negative connotation, a desire, it turns out, for flesh. Second, the negative connotation is reinforced by the complainers' ingratitude. The people yearning for animal flesh are those who value tasty treats over liberation from slavery. Third, unlike the kosher laws (which treat fish as something other than flesh), the complaining Israelites here understood that fish is flesh, though admittedly in their lusting for it.

As the story continues, we see Moses feeling despondent because he cannot satisfy the demands. In response, God turns angry, telling Moses to convey the following message to the flesh-lusting ingrates:

> say thou unto the people, Sanctify yourselves against tomorrow, and ye shall eat flesh: for ye have wept in the ears of the LORD, saying, Who shall give us flesh to eat? for it was well with us in Egypt: therefore the LORD will give you flesh, and ye shall eat. Ye shall not eat one day, nor two days, nor five days, neither ten days, nor twenty days; But even a whole month, until it come out at your nostrils, and it be loathsome unto you: because

that ye have despised the LORD which is among you, and have wept before him, saying, Why came we forth out of Egypt? (Numbers 11:18–20)

God was displeased with the ingratitude of the Israelites and was going to teach them a lesson, but note the nature of the lesson. The penalty for meat gluttony has an ironic justice to it: the satisfaction of that gluttony to the point of nausea. We learn that God carries out the punishment by smiting those Israelites who gathered the corpses of quails that God had brought forth from the sea "while the flesh was yet between their teeth, ere it was chewed." The passage continues by saying that "he called the name of that place Kibrothhattaavah: because there they buried the people that lusted" (Numbers 11:31–34). Notably, at a later point in the Bible, a passage describes the desire for meat in the same terms, as *ta'avah*, or lust, implying that God regards the craving for meat as something evil, potentially worthy of punishment by death (Deuteronomy 12:20).[34]

The commentator Rabbi Yosef Albo spoke in similar terms about the eating of meat:

> In the killing of animals there is cruelty, rage, and the accustoming oneself to the bad habit of shedding innocent blood, but the eating of the flesh of some animals produces besides, coarseness, ugliness and stupidity, as is stated in the Bible... But when the Torah was given to Israel... God prohibited certain animals which produce coarseness and ugliness of soul. Nay, even the animals that were permitted were merely a concession to human lust and desire, in the same way as the Israelites were permitted women taken in war. Thus the Rabbis say, commenting on the verse, "*because thy soul desireth to eat flesh*," There is a moral lesson in this expression, namely that one should not eat flesh unless he has an appetite for it. This shows clearly that the eating of flesh was permitted only because of necessity. For this reason it was forbidden at the time of creation.[35]

Rabbi Moses ben Nachman (also known as Ramban and Nachmanides, 1194–1270) also emphasized in his writing that:

> meat was not permitted to them until the time of the sons of Noah.... The reason for [this prohibition of eating meat] was that creatures possessing a moving soul have a certain superiority as regards their soul, resembling in a way those who possess the rational soul: they have the power of choice affecting their welfare and their food, and they flee from pain and death. And Scripture says: *Who knoweth the spirit of man whether it goeth upward, and the spirit of the beast whether it goes downward to the earth.*[36]

The permission to consume animals, in other words, was a concession to human weakness and had the regrettable effect of harming living beings with the desire to live.

We can understand the verses discussed here and the commentary cited, taken together, as commending veganism and condemning its opposite. Of course, the Torah has more in it than the stories and verses I have just discussed. Adam's son Abel was a shepherd, and God did eventually allow people to eat meat. Furthermore, animal sacrifice appears in the *Akedah*, the story of the binding of Isaac, and extensively in Leviticus.[37] Still, the verses I have discussed tell a story of ambivalence about the consumption of animals and a consciousness that moral danger lurks where people are indulging their "lust" for animals. Because of that danger, we have many regulations of animal consumption and very little to regulate the consumption of plant-based foods. As Maimonides (Rabbi Moses ben Maimon, also known as the Rambam, 1135–1204) said of our attitude toward other nonhuman beings,

> it should not be believed that all the beings exist for the sake of the existence of man. On the contrary, all the other beings too have been intended for their own sakes and not for the sake of something else.[38]

We arguably fulfill our best selves, then, when we consume a vegan diet, mindful as such a diet is of the inherent worth of our fellow earthlings, despite the fact that the Torah does not expressly require us to do so.

Why Not Just Require It?

The Torah makes me wonder why God did not simply require that we be vegan. Perhaps it is useful to think about this question in the context of a larger question that people have asked about God for millennia. If God is both good and omnipotent, then why does He permit people to behave badly in the world?

As a child in an Orthodox yeshiva, I learned the standard reply. Together with my questioning classmates, I learned that people's ability to do good exists only if people also have the opportunity (and temptation) to do evil. Unlike humans, we heard, angels are capable of doing only good deeds; therefore, they are more innocent than good, because they cannot do wrong. Humans, by contrast, have both the capacity and the inclination to do evil; as a result, when they overcome temptation and do what is right, they are truly good for doing so. To allow for there to be good in the world, then, God created both a good and an evil inclination in people, and people were free to choose between the two. It is through this choice that good (rather than mere innocence) can exist.[39] It is, then, the autonomy of the Israelites, living in the context and cultural setting in which they lived, that may explain why God permitted them to consume animals despite the evil of doing so.

When humans were in the Garden of Eden and God was announcing what people ought to do, God told people in clear language that despite their power over the rest of creation, they were to consume fruits, nuts and seeds, and other plant-based foods. Humans' power over animals, God made clear, does not amount to the rightful authority to slaughter and consume them. But then, as the Torah relates in subsequent chapters, people made terrible choices, despite the guidance they received from their divine ruler urging them toward better, more just alternatives. Only after God finds humans so despicably bad that He brings a flood to destroy them does He grant the survivors and their progeny permission to eat other animals.[40]

Perhaps the reluctantly granted permission to eat animal products reflects the view that a moral universe requires people to have choices. In this view, to be truly good, people need to have the option of doing bad deeds. The biblical figures proved themselves so invested in doing bad things that the options offered to them as permissible needed to include some bad deeds. This best explains, if one assumes some continuity of narrative, why God would expand a diet he prescribed for them in the Garden of Eden to include animal products, even though the best choice remained an animal-free diet.

If we treat the Torah as coming from a quasi-united source, as I learned it as a child, it does seem that the Torah contains strong hints and clues in various places indicating that consuming animals is wrong and that even the desire to consume animals is worthy of condemnation, as we saw in the story of the plague of the quail. The text also contains strong hints that people ought to be conscious of the relationships that animals have with one another before deciding to disrupt those relationships by consuming the animals in them, as we saw in the prohibition against cooking a young goat in his mother's milk.

Eating flesh necessarily means disrupting relationships between the creatures who previously wore that flesh on their bones. The Torah encourages mindfulness about that reality by enjoining some but not all slaughter, based on the relationships between the victims involved. It is up to us humans to take the next logical step, once we have become conscious of the harm we do when we consume animal products. We can understand the Torah as encouraging that step, one of which we are capable but must take of our own free will.

CONCLUSION

What, then, is one to take from my meditation on the connections between Judaism and veganism? There is, first, my own unique experience of the connection, one borne of inherited trauma from the Holocaust. This link draws me, as someone whose kin the Nazis defined and thus demoted as "Jews," to the "animals" over whom humans have exercised power by giving these sentient beings a debased status, a status that, once imposed, is almost impossible to see for the injustice that it is. That animals are "only animals" seems like a natural fact about these creatures, no more subject to contestation than the color of grass or the height of a tree.[41]

Being psychically at the receiving end of such a "magical" transformation (from Jew to "Jew") makes me especially open to those others who have seemingly eternally fallen victim to such magic—the animals whose flesh and secretions I used to eat. Like the "dead man walking" on death row, my Jewishness precedes my capacity to make choices and allows me a window into the world of the animals who, crowded by the millions into "cattle cars," elicit little outrage. I would not, however, give Nazis exclusive "credit" for inspiring my sensitivity to the plight of animals.

After all, my mother raised me as a religious Jew, and my upbringing exposed me to Torah, which itself provides (admittedly imperfect) wisdom about compassion toward animals. In urging us not to cook a kid in his mother's milk, in punishing a "lust" for flesh, and in pairing dominion over animals with an invitation to consume only vegan food, the Torah itself seems to aim at nudging us toward doing the right thing by our fellow creatures. The Torah tells us the ideal diet and also forces us in various places to be mindful of the harm we do when we consume animal products. Such mindfulness can give birth to ethical vegans.

The Torah seems to greatly value freedom of choice in moral matters, and through this commitment, we can understand why it contains no comprehensive ban on the consumption of animal products. Because people in biblical times may have found it nearly impossible to be vegan, given their cultural background, the Torah permitted them to consume animals and sacrifice them as well. But our context is different now, and we can make different choices. Interestingly, we who have become ethical vegans have done so without any law or rule requiring it of us; it was through mindfulness of the sort that one finds in the Torah that we came to practice nonviolence against animals as we have.

Perhaps one way I can meld the two "Jewish" and "vegan" identities that I bring to this chapter is by observing that for many of us who are Jews, vegans, or both, to be a Jew and to be a vegan are ways not only of "being" but of "doing" as well. In other words, Jewishness is not simply a status that one inherits (whether through blood or through trauma); it is a set of ways of conducting one's life, whether religious, cultural, or some combination of the two. Veganism is even more so not simply a status but a set of behaviors that couple an identification with nonviolence with an avoidance of violence in one's life. As a Jewish vegan, I feel infused with a consciousness about my own and my fellow earthlings' status—and the injustices that once did or continue to accompany those statuses. As a vegan Jew, I am struck by the consciousness that I must and do bring to the activities of daily life. For good or for ill, we all have choices we can make about what we will eat and how we will conduct our lives. Judaism teaches us that those choices can be holy or evil and that we will be responsible for painting the moral canvas of our own lives. Veganism teaches us that with all the choices we have, the most mindful is one of nonviolence toward all. Veganism makes us mindful of ourselves, of others, and of the injustices that we have experienced and that most of us have mindlessly visited on others. To fully embrace the "new kosher" is to bring an ethics of caring to our daily meals and the cloaks we wear on our backs. It is to become vegan.

NOTES

The author is extremely grateful for the tireless and expert research support of Margaret Ambrose, former Cornell Law School research librarian, and the outstanding editorial suggestions of Michael C. Dorf. The author also appreciates the summer research funding that helped support this project.

All translations of the Bible, unless otherwise noted, are from the Authorized Version.

1. The injunction against causing unnecessary pain to an animal emerges from Talmudic authority. A. Z. Zivotofsky, J. M. Regenstein, and D. Zivotofsky, "The Development of Religious Animal Welfare Code and its Relevance for Contemporary Civil Laws," *Journal of Animal and Natural Resource Law* 8 (2012): 71–75; Jeffrey Cohan, "The Prohibition on Causing Animals to Suffer: (Past) Time for It to Be Enforced," in *The Jewish Vegan*, ed. Shmuly Yanklowitz (Shamayim V'Aretz Institute, 2015), 57–62.

2. Shmuly Yanklowitz, "Is the Kosher Industry a Higher Standard?," in *The Jewish Vegan*, ed. Shmuly Yanklowitz (Shamayim V'Aretz Institute, 2015), 169–72.

3. *Animal Rights: The Abolitionist Approach*, owned by Gary Francione, http://www.abolitionistapproach.com (accessed June 22, 2016).

4. To be sure, many who seek welfare-related reforms also oppose animal agriculture as a whole. For simplicity, I refer to reform-seekers as "welfarist." For an excellent debate between proponents of the two positions, see "Debate: Vegan v. Vegan (Gary Francione vs. Bruce Friedrich)," YouTube, posted by TheVeganAtheist, July 27, 2013, https://www.youtube.com/watch?v=UJ1qFdR1cHA.

5. Prescription that mammals and fowl must be slaughtered in a specific fashion. Further elucidation is prescribed in Oral Law, the rabbinic tradition.

6. Roberta Rosenthal Kwall has claimed that the true foundation for Jewish identity, regardless of what an individual Jew may believe, is the Jewish religious tradition. Roberta Kwall, *The Myth of the Cultural Jew: Culture and Law in Jewish Tradition* (New York: Oxford University Press, 2015), 281. In response to her claim, I have proposed that forces other than connection to the Jewish tradition, including tribalism, shape Jewish identity for many. Sherry Colb, "A Review of Roberta Rosenthal Kwall's "The Myth of the Cultural Jew,'" *Dorf on Law* (blog), August 20, 2015, http://www.dorfonlaw.org/2015/08/a-review-of-roberta-rose nthal-kwals.html; previously published with footnotes as Sherry Colb, "The Reality of Richly Textured Judaism: A Review of the Myth of the Cultural Jew," *Balkinization* (blog), August 18, 2015, http://balkin.blogspot.com/2015/08/the-rea lity-of-richly-textured-judaism.html.

7. On generational Holocaust trauma, see Helen Epstein, *Children of the Holocaust* (New York: Penguin Books, 1988); and Eva Hoffman, *After Such Knowledge: Memory, History, and the Legacy of the Holocaust* (New York: Public Affairs, 2005).

8. Carol Adams has likened the ways in which "food animals" are portrayed—as "asking for" their fate—to the ways women are portrayed, in advertising, for example. Carol J. Adams, *The Sexual Politics of Meat* (London: Continuum, 2010).

9. Deborah White, "Revisiting *Ar'nt I a Woman?*," in *Ar'n't I a Woman?*, rev. ed. (New York: Norton, 1999), 8. White explains how if she had written *Ar'n't I a Woman?* in 1999 rather than 1985, she would have used the term "enslaved" rather than "slave."

10. The nature of slaves in the *Politics*: "[F]or the rule over the free differs from the rule over slaves, no less than that which is free by nature differs from that which is slave by nature." Aristotle, *Politics of Aristotle*, trans. Peter Simpson (Chapel Hill: University of North Carolina Press, 1997), 120.

11. Diana Stuart, Rebecca Schewe, and Ryan Gunderson, "Extending Social Theory to Farm Animals: Addressing Alienation in the Dairy Sector," *Sociologia Ruralis* 53, no. 2 (2013): 206–12; B. A. Ventura et al., "Views on Contentious Practices in Dairy Farming: The Case of Early Cow-Calf Separation," *Journal of Dairy Science* 96, no. 9 (2013); and A. J. Heinrichs et al., "The National Dairy Heifer Evaluation Project: A Profile of Heifer Management Practices in the United States," *Journal of Dairy Science* 77, no. 6 (1994): 1553.

12. This video seems to be the original, posted by the child's mother: "Luiz Antonio—A argumentação para não comer polvo," YouTube, posted by Flavia Cavalcanti, May 15, 2013, https://www.youtube.com/watch?v=NX4O6smZrLE.

13. Charles Patterson, *Eternal Treblinka: Our Treatment of Animals and the Holocaust* (New York: Lantern Books, 2002).

14. For a distinct but very interesting additional parallel drawn between Jews and animals (particularly kosher animals), see Gary A. Rendsburg, "The Vegetarian Ideal in the Bible," in *Food and Judaism*, ed. Leonard J. Greenspoon, Ronald A. Simkins, and Gerald Shapiro (Omaha, NE: Creighton University Press 2005), 326–28.

15. My father rescued 3,000 Jews from Eastern Europe: "As a Jew himself, rescuing others exposed my father to grave risks that he could have easily avoided... [b]ut like other people who rescued Jews at great risk and cost to their own safety, my father did not see how he could possibly have done otherwise." Sherry Colb, "Decoding 'Never Again'," *Rutgers Journal of Law and Religion* 16, no. 2 (2015): 256.

16. Jeffrey Moussaieff Masson and Susan McCarthy, *When Elephants Weep* (London: J. Cape, 1994).

17. For a detailed discussion of my evolution to veganism, see Sherry F. Colb, *Mind If I Order the Cheeseburger?* (New York: Lantern Books, 2013).

18. Notable exceptions include drinking wine touched by gentiles and using fermented grains or *chametz* during Passover. For a discussion on the origin of the prohibition against drinking wine touched by gentiles in Jewish law and the Avodah Zarah tractate in the Talmud, see Jordan Rosenblum, *Food and Identity in Early Rabbinic Judaism* (New York: Cambridge University Press, 2010), 81–83. For the prohibition against leavened (*chametz*) food during the Jewish holiday of Passover, see Deuteronomy 16:3–4.

19. Tom Regan, *Defending Animal Rights* (Chicago: University of Illinois Press, 2001), 42–44.

20. See the chapter by Richard Schwartz and David Sears in this volume (analyzing the dangers of animal consumption through the work of Rav Kook).

21. J. M. Regenstein, M. M. Chaudry, and C. E. Regenstein, "The Kosher and Halal Food Laws," *Comprehensive Reviews in Food Science and Food Safety* 2, no. 3 (2003): 122. They write, "The requirements of proper slaughtering and bleeding are applicable to land animals and birds. Fish and other creatures that live in water need not be ritually slaughtered."

22. Victoria Braithwaite, *Do Fish Feel Pain?* (New York: Oxford University Press, 2010); and Jonathan Balcombe, *What a Fish Knows: The Inner Lives of Our Underwater Cousins* (New York: Scientific American/Farrar, Straus, and Giroux, 2016).

23. Rabbi Abraham Isaac Hakohen Kook (1865–1935) makes this argument. Richard Schwartz, "The Vegetarian Teachings of Rav Kook," with editorial assistance from David Sears, Jewish Vegetarians of North America, http://www.jewishveg.com/schwartz/kook-expanded.html#_ednref6 (accessed July 1, 2016).

24. Quoted in David Sears, "Judaism and Vegetarianism," *The Vision of Eden: Animal Welfare and Vegetarianism in Jewish Law and Mysticism* (CreateSpace, 2014), chap. 6.

25. For contemporary issues related to this theme arising from the shackle-and-hoist method of slaughter, see J. E. Regenstein and C. E. Regenstein, "Looking in on Kosher Supervision of the Food Industry," *Judaism* 39 no. 4 (1990): 416–17.

26. Jonathan Safran Foer offers an account of video taken of cattle at Agroprocessors, the largest kosher slaughterhouse in the world, and expresses skepticism that it was an isolated incident: "their tracheas and esophagi systemically pulled from their cut throats, languishing for up to three minutes as a result of sloppy slaughter, and being shocked with electric prods in their faces... [w]e have no reason to believe that the kind of cruelty documented at Agroprocessors has been eliminated from the kosher industry. It can't be, so long as factory farming dominates." See Jonathan Safran Foer, *Eating Animals* (New York: Little Brown, 2009), 69.

27. Exodus 23:19 and 34:26; Deuteronomy 14:21; I. Grunfeld, *Jewish Dietary Laws* (London: Soncino Press, 1972), 123–25; and Aryeh Citron, "Meat and Milk," Chabad.org, http://www.chabad.org/library/article_cdo/aid/1149824/jewish/Meat-Milk.htm#footnote8a1149824 (accessed July 1, 2016)

28. Grunfeld, *Jewish Dietary Laws*, 123–25; Citron, "Meat and Milk."

29. The repetition of this expression has been interpreted in the Talmud to prohibit (1) boiling meat and milk together; (2) eating milk and meat together; or (3) benefiting from said mixture. A rabbinic decree expanded the prohibition to include any young animal of "clean" classification and not just a kid. Grunfeld, *Jewish Dietary Laws*, 116–23; Citron, "Meat and Milk."

30. Grunfeld, *Jewish Dietary Laws*, 116–23; Citron, "Meat and Milk."

31. Grunfeld, *Jewish Dietary Laws*, 123–25; Citron, "Meat and Milk."

32. See Sherry Colb, "Doesn't God Value Us More than the Other Animals?," in *Mind If I Order the Cheeseburger?* (New York: Lantern Books, 2013), 112–29.

33. Critical scholars have interpreted "dominion" to mean something more akin to stewardship or even service, rather than domination. Matthew Scully, *Dominion: The Power of Man, the Suffering of Animals, and the Call to Mercy* (New York: St. Martin's Press, 2002); and Norm Phelps, *The Dominion of Love: Animal Rights According to the Bible* (New York: Lantern Books, 2002). See also discussion of stewardship by Adrienne Krone, chapter 6 in this volume.

34. Nehama Leibowitz comments, "The wording of the above dispensation is odd indeed [referring to the permission to eat meat]. But how grudgingly is such permission granted! If you cannot resist the temptation and must eat meat, then

do so—seems to be the tenor of this barely tolerated dispensation." See *Studies in Devarim (Deuteronomy)*, trans. Aryeh Newman (Jerusalem: World Zionist Organization, 1980), 135–36.

35. Rabbi Yosef Albo, *Sefer ha-Ikkarim: Book of Principles*, ed. and trans. Isaac Husik (Philadelphia: Jewish Publication Society of America, 1946), vol. 3, chap. 15, 129–37; emphasis added.

36. Ramban (Nachmanides), *Commentary on the Torah: Genesis*, vol. 1, trans. Charles B. Chavel (New York: Shilo Publishing House, 1971), 57.

37. Note that according to Maimonides, the Torah required animal sacrifice because God was accommodating the Israelites' needs at the time and not because it was ideal. See Samson Raphael Hirsch, *Horeb: A Philosophy of Jewish Laws and Observances*, trans. I. Grunfeld (London: Soncino Press, 1962), 2:328–31.

38. Moses Maimonides, *The Guide of the Perplexed*, trans. Shlomo Pines (Chicago: University of Chicago Press, 1969), 452.

39. There are many examples of theodicy in the Old Testament, including the Book of Job, the Book of Ruth, and Lamentations; see Antti Laato and Johannes Cornelis de Moor, *Theodicy in the World of the Bible* (Boston: Brill Academic Publishers, 2003).

40. "God blessed Noah and his sons and said unto them . . . [e]very moving thing that liveth shall be meat for you; even as the green herb have I given you all things" (Genesis 9:1–3). For a similar analysis of postflood permission to eat animals as a compromise due to humans' revealed flaws, see Gary A. Rendsburg, "The Vegetarian Ideal in the Bible," in *Food and Judaism*, ed. Leonard J. Greenspoon, Ronald A. Simkins, and Gerald Shapiro (Omaha, NE: Creighton University Press, 2005), 322–23.

41. Aaron S. Gross, *The Question of the Animal and Religion: Theoretical Stakes, Practical Implications* (New York: Columbia University Press, 2014), chap. 5.

14 Jewish Veganism as an Embodied Practice
A Vegan Agenda for Cultural Jews

JACOB ARI LABENDZ

I have been Jewish my entire life and a vegan since 2012. When I finally adopted a relatively animal-product-free lifestyle, I knew that I would enjoy the benefits of living in accordance with my own political and moral commitments. What I could not have expected is how profoundly it would enrich my Jewishness and my sense of self as a Jew.

For many years I have struggled with both Judaism and Jewishness. I am an atheist and no longer consider myself a member of the Jewish religion (narrowly considered). I reject most forms of nationalism, including political Zionism, and have been a public critic of the State of Israel. At the same time, I remain culturally, intellectually, and politically Jewish. My holidays are Jewish holidays. My birth family, to which I still belong, is a Jewish family that welcomes non-Jews lovingly into Jewish spaces and moments. When I walk my dog, I often hear myself singing Jewish songs in my head and sometimes, embarrassingly, aloud.

Years of devout Jewish practice, participation, learning, and questioning have shaped me. Perhaps that is why I choose to wrestle—not unlike my biblical namesake—to maintain a Jewish center, to feel enmeshed in Jewish frameworks of meaning-making, wherein there exists for each part of life a Jewish reference. I miss how Jewishness once offered an ample anchor for my sense of self—even if I am happy with who I have become since then. I recall feeling fully connected to *Yiddishkeit* and "the Jewish people"—marked too often by the marginalization of people of color and non-Ashkenazim and the exclusion of non-Jews—as a day-school student, a Jewish summer camper, a participant on Jewish travel programs, on a gap year in Israel, and during my first semesters as an undergraduate at Brandeis University. In those years, I experienced Jewishness as a thread running through and defining almost every aspect of my life. It transcended the categories through which I saw myself and served as a unifying theme for self- and community-construction. With this in mind, I have chosen to use the word *transcendent* to describe the type of Jewishness that I have lost and whose pleasures I seek to recover.

The not-so-recent changes in how I experience myself and my place in the world do not have to pose a problem—certainly not an ethical one. But they feel wrong to me. I carry burdens of loss and disorientation as I move through Jewish spaces that I can no longer call my own but where I must venture uncomfortably to feel like myself and enjoy what I love about Jewishness. My growing networks of likeminded friends and colleagues and the rise of new Jewish dissident movements suggest that I am not alone. Studies of US Jews have long confirmed such trends and have provoked a wide range of institutional responses.[1] My coconspirators and I know that we must drive our own processes of self- and communal transformation if we are to succeed. I seek a type of Jewishness that does dominate my life to the exclusion of other aspects—that would be impossible for me now—but one that nonetheless playfully and powerfully transcends my divided and ever-evolving self.

Adopting a vegan lifestyle has helped me rebuild my weakening Jewish center and find Jewish transcendence. This may come as a surprise, as it has also prevented me from participating in many rituals and Jewish cultural practices. I forgo the boiled eggs at the Passover Seder and I may never purchase *tefillin* (phylacteries) again— even if I cherish the pair I inherited from my namesake. What sort of Ashkenazi boy can feel more Jewish without Bubby's—now Mom's—chicken soup? This apparent contradiction inspired me to delve into Jewish veganism, which I believe holds a key to addressing the crisis faced by many cultural and secular Jews who share my feelings of loss and alienation and my commitment to renaissance.

In the coming pages, I identify this crisis as a failure of cultural Judaism to provide a sufficient framework for Jewish self-understanding and community formation. I explain how Jewish veganism can offer a partial response to this crisis and embark on a series of meditations on that theme. By Jewish veganism I mean veganism embraced as an expression of Jewishness and Jewishness enriched and transformed by veganism. For the purposes of this chapter, I ask readers to assume that veganism, broadly defined, is ethically preferable to nonveganism. Although I believe that most people should approximate an animal-product-free lifestyle— especially city dwellers in the industrialized, urban North—I will not make that case here, nor will I evaluate the reasons that usually motivate such choices. In the conclusion, nonetheless, I offer advice for promoting Jewish veganism from a progressive perspective.

THE CRISIS OF SECULAR OR CULTURAL JUDAISM

James Loeffler, a historian of modern Jewry, recently pronounced the death of Jewish culture.[2] He did not mean that Jews have stopped engaging in culture. We can, to be sure, point to an efflorescence of Jewish cultural production in recent decades and to the emergence of thriving Jewish subcommunities around the world. Loeffler argued, rather, that for well-integrated, secular, American Jews (like me), no amount of cultural production can replace the holistic (or transcendent) Jewish experiences once and still offered by religion and nationalism, the type found in relatively closed communities bound by Jewish languages like Hebrew, Yiddish, and Ladino. The success of Jews in the United States has offered Jews unprecedented opportunities to shed their status as outsiders. It has left *us* free not to be *we* and that has changed *us*.

This opportunity has come at a price, one often gravely felt. For many cultural and secular Jews, Jewishness—understood broadly—no longer serves as a totalizing axis for identity construction. It no longer offers life-holistic experiences. We struggle to rebuild and maintain our Jewish selves with collages of artifacts, events, tastes, and tales, but the center will not hold. Our cultural and secular Judaism, no matter how dear, is often only episodic Judaism and only fully accessible in major Jewish urban centers.

Almost daily, I mourn the loss of my former Jewish self, despite working professionally in Jewish studies and engaging as an activist in Jewish spheres. What—or rather, who—is to become of me . . . of us? What about individuals who seek deeply felt Jewish experiences but cannot call on years of Jewish education and practice as I can? Jewish veganism offers a partial solution to this problem. As I came to understand why this has been so for myself, I began to wonder how to recognize, seek out, and embellish additional means by which cultural and secular Jews may construct fuller and more transcendent Jewish selves.

RELIGIOUS AND ETHNIC JUDAISM AS TECHNOLOGIES OF THE SELF

Modern religious Judaism, as a system of behaviors, symbols, concepts, and beliefs, empowers practitioners to experience their whole lives as sanctified by Jewishness. Traditionally observant Jews vest (or believe they should vest) every moment, movement, and decision with Jewish meaning. They accomplish this by performing repetitive and predictable actions and by turning for instruction to a corpus of texts, which they interpret using sanctioned hermeneutics and with deference to chosen authorities. Knowing that Jews have participated in this system and have transformed it for millennia lends a certain authenticity to this lifestyle and burdens it with the weight of history. *Halakha*, Jewish religious law, thus functions as a cultural technology for those striving to experience Jewishness transcendentally and imminently—even if the phenomenology of such experiences can suggest movement in the opposite direction: from belief or being to action and becoming.[3]

I have described an ideal system. Even traditionally observant Jews experience doubt and alienation. Observant Judaism, however, has the capacity to accommodate this as well. Many years ago, as a devout high school student, I confessed to my teacher, Hirsch Jacobson, that I no longer felt moved by prayer and that I saw no point in going through the motions. A pupil of Abraham Joshua Heschel, Mr. Jacobson explained that through *keva*, repetition, I would achieve the appropriate *kavanah*, intention.[4] I would come to understand why we pray by praying. Adherence to the system thus produces the experiences and dispositions that retroactively—or perhaps reciprocally—provide the very reasons for participation.

The idea that behavior precedes meaning can be difficult to comprehend or accept. We like to believe that we act with intention and that our behaviors reflect our values and beliefs. (Some scholars of religion attribute this expectation to the influence of Protestantism, which can even condition how Jews understand Judaism.[5]) Sigmund Freud may have convinced us that we do not have full access to our deeper selves, but he did not fundamentally challenge the idea that some sort of selfhood precedes action.

Contemporary scholars have developed these ideas further by situating the self—if we may speak of such a thing—in biological, narrative (or non-narrative[6]), and social contexts. Jonathan Haidt, a social psychologist, argues that "moral intuitions arise automatically and almost instantaneously, long before moral reasoning has a chance to get started and those first intuitions tend to drive our later reasoning."[7] He later continues:

> religion is (probably) an evolutionary adaptation for binding groups together and helping them to create communities with a shared morality. . . . People bind themselves into political teams that share moral narratives. Once they accept a particular narrative, they become blind to alternative moral worlds.[8]

Elsewhere Haidt elaborates on the semi-automatic nature of moral decision making:

> My claim is that moral judgement is very much like aesthetic judgement . . . I think whatever is true of aesthetic judgement is true of moral judgment, except that in our moral lives we do need to justify, whereas we don't generally ask others for justifications of aesthetic judgments.[9]

This means that we account for our moral judgments (and actions) primarily in hindsight, and that we may thus consider our attempts to justify those judgments to be subsequent actions. We are bound to established systems of metaphors and signification and to the shifting "moral narratives" of our communities.[10]

However, this does not necessarily render the individual powerless. Saba Mahmood, an anthropologist who has studied women's piety movements in Egypt, compares the cultivation of religious devotion and personal submission with how musicians master their instruments. It requires rigorous and regular embodied practice. Rightly considered, she explains, one cannot separate musical faculty from the daily exercises that musicians must perform. Pianists become and remain pianists because they practice and play the piano; not the other way around. The very act of practicing—of moving one's body—helps produce a change in subjectivity and selfhood.[11] It follows, then, that by observing Jewish laws, we produce and change ourselves as Jews: through *keva* we achieve *kavanah*.

Elias Sacks, a scholar of religion, finds these ideas reflected in the philosophies of Moses Mendelssohn (1729–1786), popularly considered the first figure of the *Haskalah*, the Jewish Enlightenment. Sacks uses Mendelssohn to reintroduce belief as a motivating and fundamental factor for such subject-forming practices. To do so, he explicates Mendelssohn's defense of the enduring value of Jewish religious law as commensurable with the values of the Enlightenment, whose philosophers sought universal truths and celebrated the power of human reason. (In later decades, this led some Jewish thinkers and movements to reconsider *halakha* and transform Jewish practice.) According to Sacks, Mendelssohn believed that:

> a specific type of subject is produced by the recurring performance of actions grounded in divinely sanctioned rules, since such performances generate frequent opportunities for reflecting on God that endow practitioners with a constellation of dispositions crucial to engaged citizenship. At the same time, Mendelssohn's reasoning suggests that we cannot understand this process of subject formation engendered by practice without carefully considering the beliefs of the practitioners. In his model, the formation of subjects by practice depends on the prior existence of beliefs.... Moreover, in this model, the formation of subjects by practice not only depends on, but also results in, the existence of beliefs. The type of subjects that Mendelssohn takes to be produced by religious practice is, to a significant extent, a believing subject.[12]

This question of belief and its role in the production of subjectivities pertains fundamentally to the issues under consideration here—even if Haidt might ask us to focus more on some preconscious sense of belonging.

Faith and practice reinforce and perhaps even constitute one another. I simultaneously lost my faith in God and stopped practicing Judaism as a religion in my early twenties. For some time, I believed I would always be able to step back into religious practice on an occasional basis, whenever I pleased. I even anticipated that I would continue to derive from it the same spiritual rewards that I had in the past. At first, I could; but this is no longer true. As Mr. Jacobson explained, actions produce and sustain intentions, and I am out of practice. I have lost my religious center. I am now little more than a well-educated tourist in the synagogue. Lately I have found myself stammering through liturgical passages I thought I would never forget. At such moments, I experience what religious studies scholar Lee H. Yearley has called "spiritual regret"—that feeling of loss that one may encounter when confronted with the finitude of one's own existence and thus one's inability, due to circumstance or choice, to enjoy "the varieties of human flourishing" offered by traditions not one's own or willfully abandoned.[13]

Jewish Ethnic Self-Understanding and Practices

Jewishness is a complex phenomenon that exceeds the religious sphere. It encompasses a multifaceted, even fractious ethnic component. This provided fodder for the emergence of modern Jewish nationalism in the nineteenth century, a movement that reached its zenith in the second half of the twentieth. Jews can thus sometimes struggle in their attempts to accommodate the prevailing Western demand to distinguish ethnonational identification from religious affiliation.[14] For many of us, Jewish experience and practice cannot be broken down easily into such neat categories.

Having said that, I turn to the recent history of Jewish ethnic identification in the United States to explore why this way of thinking about Jewishness has faced challenges in recent decades and why it no longer offers the secure refuge it once did to nonbelieving Jews like me. I also must distinguish ethnic and national Jewishness—the belief that Jews around the world compose some sort of coherent people with its own history and perhaps even inalienable political rights—from the sort of cultural Judaism to which I am attracted, which celebrates Jewish traditions, histories, and communities without making such strong, exclusive, and political claims about belonging, unity, and identity. To that end, when describing myself carefully, I much prefer to use the adjective *Jewish* rather than the noun *Jew*.[15]

The founder of Reconstructionist Judaism, Rabbi Mordecai Kaplan, characterized Judaism as a civilization, though one heavily defined by its religion.[16] In the 1940s, he began with success to promote the concept of "Jewish peoplehood" as a way for American Jews to express their ethnic ties to one another and their support for Jewish settlement in Palestine and, later, the nascent State of Israel, without falling prey to non-Jewish accusations of dual loyalties or un-Americanness.[17] The antisemitism and related anti-Bolshevism of the early Cold War years, indeed, threatened the integration of Jews into the fabric of US society.[18] Other Jews reacted differently to the complementary forces of antisemitism and US liberal universalism by attempting to recast Judaism strictly as a religion: one of America's three great faiths, alongside Protestantism and Catholicism[19] (the latter a relative newcomer to white American normalcy as well).[20]

For most phenotypically white American Jews, the 1950s and early 1960s were marked by suburbanization, upward mobility, increased affluence, and growing acceptance into white society. Jewish life, for all but the most devout or politically active, came to center around synagogues seldom visited by most of their members. During these years, the trend among US Jews tended toward the pursuit of comfort and conformity, and in many cases also toward conservatism (in part as a refutation of the antisemitic trope of Judeo-Bolshevism). This holds true even if a very significant number American Jews also supported the movement for civil rights to one extent or another. The early postwar decades thus witnessed a decline in religious observance and other markers of Jewishness among Jews who felt free to choose the measure and means of their own Jewish engagement. As historian Hasia Diner explains, "In the suburbs the Jews de-emphasized their ethnic distinctiveness."[21] She argues that although many Jews continued to center their lives on various expressions of Jewishness:

> for an increasing number of others, Jewishness became a matter of minor significance, a mere fact of parentage, perhaps a curiosity, but devoid of personal meaning and making no difference in how they led their lives.[22]

For many white Jews, suburbanization and acculturation went hand in hand.

Support for Jewish nationalism and even Zionism, in the context just described, did not disappear. Yet it often assumed the more tempered, critical, and sometimes hesitant face that Noam Pianko, a scholar of religion and Judaic studies, has associated with Kaplan's construction of "Jewish peoplehood." At that time, the State of Israel did not yet function as fully as it would in later decades as a publicly uniting factor for many US Jews, even if most Jewish communities shared a deep and abiding concern for the welfare of Israel and its Jewish citizens.

The postwar changes in the character of American Jewry inspired anxiety and feelings of loss in some. Others waxed nostalgic either for "the old country" or for New York's Lower East Side. The performance of this memory, as historian Steven Zipperstein has shown with reference to *Fiddler on the Roof* (1964), however, also often served to demonstrate Jewish distance from such old worlds and to confirm the place of white Jews in white America.[23]

Beginning in the early 1960s, however, and culminating after the 1967 and 1973 Arab-Israeli Wars, there emerged an ethnic current in American Jewish culture, part and parcel of a broader "white ethnic revival."[24] The impetuses behind this transformation were manifold: the politics of civil rights, the emergence of Black Power and new tensions between white Jews and African Americans (including Black Jews),[25] the aforementioned Middle Eastern wars, concern for Jews in the Soviet Union and elsewhere, and the status of Jews and the State of Israel as sites of symbolic (and in the case of Israel, also armed) conflict in the Cold War. Pianko has recently argued that powerful Jewish organizations and leaders began assuming and insisting on positions of uncritical support for Israel, which would have been anathema in earlier decades, to distance the Jewish community from currents of dissent then perceived as "un-American." They worried in particular about instances when activists framed dissent as a Jewish imperative.[26]

Intergenerational divisions within the US Jewish community, reflective of the divergent life experiences of the war and postwar generations, contributed to the rise of a new ethnic consciousness among Jews as well. During these years, many young Jews began asserting new ethnonational identities as Jewish Americans (alongside Irish and Italian Americans). Their concerns included "Jewish continuity"; the prevention of intermarriage; the development of spiritually resonant forms of Jewish practice, culture, and education; and the establishment of a public Jewish politics, often featuring outspoken identification with the State of Israel.

This revolution transformed what it meant to be Jewish both inside and outside of the synagogue. During the 1960s and 1970s, Judaism emerged as "civic religion," as Jews used religious symbols to fight for Soviet Jewry and the State of Israel.[27] They also suffused their private religious practices with political meanings.[28] They demanded more forthrightly that the world remember the Holocaust and drew from that tragedy new lessons in support of Israel and for Jewish national survival. Scholars have recently pointed to the profound depth of Holocaust consciousness and politicization even before 1967, but the late 1960s remain transformational.[29]

This cultural and political turn led to the embellishment of religious practice, alongside other forms of Jewish congress and cultural production. One might point to the emergence of *Havurot*—"relatively small clusters of individuals and families which met regularly for self-directed study and worship," first associated with the Reconstructionist movement[30]—the expansion of the Jewish camping movement, and the increasing importance of Jewish community centers and federations. This meant that for decades, US Jews, even those who did not adhere strongly to the Jewish religion, could experience Jewishness as a life-transcending, ethnic, and national phenomenon supported by increasingly well-funded institutions. Much of this depended on identifying with Jewish communities in distant and seemingly dangerous lands. The particularities of Cold War politics regarding Jews and Zionism, as well as America's ethnic turn, helped make this type of ethnocentrism seem commensurate with liberal and even progressive American values.[31]

In recent decades, the potential for Jewish Americans to cultivate and maintain transcendent Jewish selves through ethnonationalism—including Zionism—has diminished. Jews—white-identified, Ashkenazi Jews in particular—find nearly complete acceptance in mainstream US society. (I am setting aside the recent antisemitic turn in US politics and culture, the implications of which have yet to be seen.) Television audiences are expected to understand complex jokes about Jewish culture and history—some even told by non-Jews like Stephen Colbert.[32] In the pilot episode of the hit TV show *Blackish*, the conceit that demonstrated that the son of an affluent black man had lost touch with his ethnic roots and had become too white was that the child wanted to have a bar mitzvah.[33] The use of Jewishness to signal whiteness points to a major cultural transformation—one with significant consequences for what it means to be Jewish in North America today.

Not only has the antisemitism that helped motivate Jewish solidarity significantly abated (despite its recent and disquieting public reassertion), but many Jews—as part of a broader trend—have come to think about ethnic groups and nations in general as cultural constructs and often dangerous ones at that. We consider identity to be illusory, fractured, and polysemic. Some scholars argue that we should focus on processes of "identification"—how we perceive and categorize our world—rather than insisting that the "identities" we impose on people and things have objective reality.[34] This can make it difficult to speak about "the Jews" and believe oneself to be a part of that or any other people.[35] Scholars and activists have also raised significant challenges to the tendency within the US Jewish community (and in Israel) to perceive the Ashkenazi experience as normative. The possibilities for advancing a singular Jewish nationalist or ethnic option have been further diminished by the increasing porousness of Jewish spaces and the success of intercultural and interfaith families in our own communities, which I embrace.

We also have trouble thinking in terms of *we*, due to the contentious intracommunal conflict regarding Israel (including the distancing of millennials from that state), the end of the Soviet Jewry crisis that had united us, and the fading of the Holocaust from memory into history.[36] What I am describing represents an intensification of the processes which divided and fractured the American Jewish community in 1970s—a time when, according to Jewish studies scholar Michael Staub, "that collectivity known as a Jewish people also came closer to an end."[37]

I have lost my Jewish ethnonationalist center. In fact, I find most forms of nationalism deeply problematic. Despite being a product of the ethnoreligious renaissance of the last century, I am now little more than a well-educated tourist—at best, a visiting scholar—in the Jewish community center. Without religion and without nationalism to structure my Jewishness and bind me to a community, I have felt adrift. Perhaps I should have expected this. Legal scholar Roberta Rosenthal Kwall argues for the inseparability of Jewish culture from *halakha*, which she presents as mutually constitutive and dialectically related. Absent some relationship to Jewish religious law, she maintains, Jewish cultural identification can be difficult if not impossible to uphold (especially across generations).[38]

THE REWARDS OF SECULAR JEWISH VEGANISM

By thinking about veganism on Jewish terms and as a Jewish practice, secular and cultural Jews can experience their own Jewishness as transcendent, because veganism transcends daily life. Inhabiting a world dominated by consumers of animal products, vegans make constant choices about what we purchase, consume, and tolerate. We explain our decisions to others and attempt to teach them our values. We debate these among ourselves as well and trade strategies for balancing veganism with our other commitments and our desire to participate fully in society. As an embodied and therefore intimate practice, veganism influences who we are and who we feel ourselves to be. We are far more how we eat than what we eat.[39]

To state the obvious, veganism resembles *kashrut*. That is why it works so well as an embodied cultural technology for crafting transcendent Jewish identities. Jews who keep kosher use their consumption choices to construct ethnic and ethical selves, to demarcate events and spaces as Jewish, and to participate in a community of similarly minded individuals. Like vegans, they make choices on a regular basis about how strictly to adhere to their commitments and how to behave in different settings. Do we insult or embarrass well-meaning hosts by refusing to eat their foods? Some people maintain strictly vegan homes but are less picky when dining out. I make rare and careful exceptions to taste local foods when traveling abroad.

This type of veganism reminds me of how my family practiced *kashrut* when I was a boy. Some called us hypocrites for maintaining stricter standards at home than we did "out in the world." I have endured similar challenges from vegan allies and meat-eating antagonists, when they find out that on rare occasions, some form of animal product makes its way into my diet or that I promote eating insects and some bivalves.[40] What such critics fail to see, however, is that this willingness to compromise and reconsider one's practices can reflect a determination to remain mindful of one's values. Many of us experience such negotiations not as weakness or ambivalence but as a reflection of our lived commitment to a system of ethical consumption, one that is contextually dependent and demands constant choices and reevaluation.

David Rakoff, a Canadian Jewish essayist who lived in New York City, wrote that non-Jews can never enjoy bacon as deeply as Jews can.[41] For many of us, it tastes (or tasted) of transgression (and bacon!). Whether or not we subscribe to this notion, it suggests that Jews who are accustomed to keeping kosher experience the consumption of nonkosher foods as a Jewish event. From a certain perspective, then, we might say that only practicing Jews can eat *treif* foods, because only they use that category to think about what they consume. This feeling can diminish over time if one does not maintain a kosher lifestyle. The same applies to vegans. Many of us experience the exceptions we make—whether well considered or thoughtless—as part of being vegan. After all, to think of food as nonvegan implies that one perceives food through a vegan lens. Making room for such allowances (and failures) can even help novices overcome the challenges of adopting and maintaining a vegan (or kosher) lifestyle. Annual Christmas visits to Chinese restaurants may reinforce, rather than undermine, Jewish and vegan practices.[42]

Veganism and *kashrut* thus function similarly as embodied and consumption-oriented technologies of self-construction. Many secular and cultural Jews, however, find it difficult to maintain a kosher lifestyle (in the absence of veganism). They may not see the point, or they may take issue with aspects of *kashrut*. For example, they may not want to manifest in their foodways a fundamental separation between themselves and their non-Jewish friends and relatives. This pertains especially to the prohibition against drinking wine touched by non-Jews, which is not technically a matter of *kashrut* but is commonly spoken about on those terms.

Yet *kashrut* can be powerfully compelling. The last Jewish religious practice I relinquished was maintaining a kosher home. I loved purchasing kosher meat and separating meat and dairy products because it made my home feel like my own—and like my parents'. One day, however, I began to perceive that I was purchasing my Jewishness on the cheap. Could a mainstay of my identity really consist of paying extra for meat products and denying myself delicious meat and dairy combinations at home? My friends, both Jewish and non-Jewish, thought I was eccentric. Learning about the terrible conditions for laborers and animals in kosher food processing plants made it even harder for me to derive any personal satisfaction from consuming kosher meat.[43]

I still lost something meaningful when I stopped maintaining a kosher kitchen. My home felt less like my own. I imagined myself packed away like so many sets of redundant dishes. Changing who I was at home by transforming my house also led to changes in who I felt I was in the world. A poet of the Russian Jewish *Haskalah*, Judah Leib Gordon, introduced the motto: "Be a (hu)man in your goings-out and a Jew in your tent." Little do critics understand that this was "a call not for the bifurcation of Jewish identity, but for its integration."[44] We need our metaphorical Jewish tents to be the very humans we seek to be out in the world.

We require intentions, practices, and spaces to remain Jewish, but we cannot have these things if they do not feel authentic—which is to say that authenticity has far more to do with how things make us feel than with the history of those things. If keeping kosher has stopped providing me with a feeling of Jewish authenticity, then I am thankful that learning to think about my veganism on Jewish terms has helped fill that gap. Surprisingly, it has mattered little that I based my initial decision not to consume animal products on concerns that I did not think about on specifically Jewish terms. My newfound dietary laws feel comfortable to me because I grew up keeping kosher; because my parents raised me to use consumption choices and foodways to define myself. Going vegan has thus felt like coming home.

Going vegan also feels Jewish because I have intentionally cultivated an appreciation for how veganism *can* reflect Jewish values. Whether or not I have maintained a spiritual relationship with Judaism, I still tend to see things through a Jewish lens. I involuntarily recall Jewish texts, prayers, songs, sayings, and customs throughout the day. It is part of what it feels like to be me. When I consider the values that led me to veganism, I often hear them articulated in Jewish terms. My desire for social justice is a demand for *tzedek* (justice). I defend the welfare of animals so as not to contribute to *tza'ar ba'alei chayim* (the suffering of living beings), and I take care of the environment out of a commitment to *tikkun olam* (repairing the world). I conserve resources to avoid being a *ba'al tashchit* (wasteful person), and I feel obligated to stand for justice as a Jew because of *ma'arit ayin* (public perception). Perhaps a well-developed, vegan Jewish language will inspire even those without a robust Jewish background to learn more about veganism and Judaism.

Upon further reflection, I am not sure I can trace my adoption of a vegan lifestyle to a root cause. Did Jewish values—or what my community considered Jewish values—predispose me to the politics that inspired my veganism, or have I imposed veganism on Jewishness and a Jewish language on veganism? Elias Sacks argues that Mendelssohn believed that:

> Insofar as Jewish practice leads adherents to privilege actions over specific sets of words and thereby discourages fixed verbal formulas, Jewish practice discourages the rise of creedal statements that might prevent individuals from revising their beliefs, and thus secures conceptual flexibility in light of the dynamic nature of philosophical history.[45]

I grant that I am taking considerable liberties with Sacks's work, not to mention Mendelssohn's. Yet there is something suggestive about the conceptual malleability of both veganism and Judaism as embodied ethical practices, especially in combination. Veganism, like Judaism, directs the focus of its practitioners to moral thought and invites them to rethink their practices and invest them with new and current meanings. I thus do not feel compelled to dwell on origins or think in terms of authenticity when considering Jewish veganism; to decide between the proverbial and now taboo chicken and egg. This tension, indeed, may be the very stuff of my Jewish veganism. Everything within me exists in relationship to everything else. That said, if I became vegetarian in 2011 on terms that had little overtly to do with being Jewish, it was my coeditor, Rabbi Dr. Shmuly Yanklowitz, who inspired my transition to a vegan lifestyle. He invited me into a Jewish space, free from coercion, to evaluate my principles and behaviors. At least autobiographically, my veganism is truly Jewish veganism.

VEGANISM AND JEWISH VALUES

Having reached this point, I must be clear that I do not believe that one can or should present veganism as a Jewish imperative. The Jewish tradition is manifold and meat intensive. The prominence of animal products in Jewish food cultures from around the world, alongside the extensive laws for how such food may be prepared and consumed, make it difficult—I would say impossible—to argue that "authentic" Judaism forbids or even eschews the consumption or use of animal products. Even if we were to ignore these facts or proclaim such traditions to have been the product, divine or otherwise, of bygone, more primitive times, I would still feel uncomfortable making normative claims about what Judaism is or is not, should or should not be. Judaism may indeed impose a general and limiting framework for constructing ethical and behavioral systems, along with a set of supporting texts and traditions from which to draw. Yet from an anthropological perspective, Judaism is nothing more and nothing less than what we Jews do as Jews and how we narrate and experience those behaviors. This includes our relationship to the texts we consider holy and our interpretational hermeneutics. We must acknowledge that we cannot speak of Jewish values as if they existed outside of a particular context and community.

I therefore consider it disingenuous and harmful to argue that Judaism presents a clear and unassailable imperative to adopt a vegan lifestyle. That is simply not true, and we do not need it to be true to produce and promote a meaningful and lasting Jewish vegan culture. Rather, we should be wary of the temptation we may feel to use our interpretations of Judaism as a cudgel with which to bully others into adopting a vegan lifestyle—or to make any other choices. It is rude, epistemologically unsound, and ultimately ineffective.[46] Avoiding this common pitfall will also position us to refute as irrelevant the arguments of those who seek to portray veganism as somehow antithetical to traditional Judaism. It is not.[47]

We lead and advocate best when we teach rather than instruct; when we invite rather than command. Having something so wonderful as Jewish veganism to offer makes this simple. What we should be doing is working to create a meaningful, compelling, and diverse Jewish vegan culture. Judaism and veganism can be mutually enriching. We can use our tradition to develop a resonant language for contemplating and expressing the worldly values which motivate and sustain our veganism. Incorporating ethical food choices into Judaism infuses a system already of limitless meaning with even more meaning. At once, we can find new avenues for expressing Jewish values and introduce Jewishness into new spheres of life.

THE REINVENTION OF TRADITION

Vegans have an opportunity, perhaps even a moral imperative, to invent new Jewish foodways and cleanse our rituals of animal products. The extent to which we do so, in some cases, will reflect our relationship to *halakha*. Those who feel bound by traditional interpretations of *halakha* may not see it as an option to produce vegan Torah scrolls, *shofars*, *mezuzot*, and *tefillin*. I hope that this does not dissuade them from embracing veganism in other areas of their lives and from working to remove animal products from other spheres of Jewish culture and practice. Perhaps the unique use of animal products in cases deemed nonnegotiable will lead more traditionally observant Jews to see the use of animal products as something reserved for only the most sacred moments and rituals—an inversion of our values that highlights their importance; a meaningful meeting of the most holy and profane. (I cannot help but think about cases in the Torah where the sacred exceeds the bounds of the ethical, such as the ambivalence one may discern in the text regarding child sacrifice and necromancy, spiritual practices the Torah absolutely forbids but also acknowledges as powerful.[48])

We need not all adopt the same standards to develop a shared language and moral struggle. Our goal should be to make wrestling with the morality of animal product use central to what it means to be Jewish. Even if we make an exception for *halakhic* imperatives, we are still left with culinary and ritual practices that feature and foreground meat, dairy, and eggs. Egg challah, the Passover shank bone, herring, *kibbeh*, blintzes, and *shakshuka* are the very tastes, smells, and sights of Judaism for many. What shall we do about our holidays? We feel pressure not to "ruin" *yom-tov* meals by eliminating traditional dishes. It can take a long time not to miss these foods; fear of such loss can deter people from going vegan. What a shame! Perhaps some will make exceptions for themselves on holidays.[49] This might even help them reduce their consumption of animal products throughout the year. Others may want to consider adopting stricter standards on *Shabbat* and festivals as a way to honor and sanctify them.

To alleviate these problems for future generations, we must reinvent Jewish culinary and ritual traditions. We must self-consciously produce new Jewish cuisines. This goes well beyond finding meatless replacements for nonvegan dishes, which often fall disappointingly short of their targets. We should instead mine the culinary traditions of Jewish communities from around the world for vegan foods with which to mark our holidays. We can honor the other cultures in which our own is enmeshed by incorporating their culinary riches into our traditions. Together, we can change the tastes, sights, and smells of Judaism for the next generation. Our children will never miss foods they never taste. They will not associate with "home" delicacies never served in our houses. I would much prefer for the next generation of Jews to inherit our most cherished values, rather than a taste for foods that we may well have loved but that violate our principles. I envision them enticing their own children with newly traditional vegan dishes (which we invented) at holiday and other celebrations. Together, we can develop a global and globally responsible Jewish food culture.

Rituals can be trickier to reinvent. They tell stories, produce emotions, and serve didactic purposes. They connect us to previous generations in ways sometimes more dramatic than culinary fashion. However free we may feel to transform our rituals to accommodate our values, I hope we will do so in ways that preserve their original aesthetics and content and that offer opportunities for us to recall our inherited traditions and the reasons we modified them. We should also be mindful to invent new rituals that feel like rituals. This will help them become the traditions of the future.

Elsewhere, I suggested replacing the boiled eggs eaten on Passover with edible flowers. Not only can the latter similarly symbolize spring and the life cycle of birth, mourning, and renewal, they also have a unique quality to them. They stand out and can therefore become something we look forward to all year. In time, Passover may simply not be Passover without the edible flowers and the annual debates about who brought the most beautiful or tasty arrangement. I also suggested placing a scorched, wooden egg on the Seder plate, to replace and yet still recall the traditional roasted egg. Because the original item evokes the idea of sacrifice, my family chose to use hollow wooden eggs, into which we placed notes indicating the sacrifices that we intended to make in the coming year. We can thus forgo without forgetting the egg.[50]

Our greatest challenge might be the loss of unified sets of rituals and foods. (Readers may not have found my egg replacements in good taste!) Most Jews and Jewish communities will not join us in cleansing our traditions of animal products. We will also disagree about which traditions may be changed and how to change those we can. For this, I can offer only minor consolation. Jewish traditions and practices have always been manifold and varied, and they have never stopped evolving. (The Talmud teaches, "These and these are the ways of the living God."[51]) The illusion of timeless uniformity provides a false sense of authenticity at best. At worst, it enables those who would resist ethical progress to use our love of Judaism against us; to turn our commitment to preserving our heritage into a reason for abandoning the imperative to improve on it and maintain its relevance.

JEWISH VEGANISM AND ADVOCACY

There is a political side to this as well, which will resonate for Jews who have centered their Jewish identities around themes of social justice. This relates to the concept and history of Judaism as a "civic religion." As Jewish vegans, we have an exceptional opportunity to advocate for veganism, animal welfare, the environment, and food justice within our communities. Our success will depend on our ability to frame veganism as a Jewish possibility, rooted in our traditions and reflecting our most precious values.

In addition to the concerns I raised about the dangers of presenting veganism as the only form of authentic Judaism, I would also counsel that we be sure to occupy ourselves as much, if not more, with cultural production than with criticism of contemporary norms. Our goal should be to introduce a new Jewish language to facilitate cultural transformation and to be the agents of dynamic innovation. We must remain mindful of the sacrifices we ask of our communities and offer some compensatory vision of the future, especially for people who are not swayed, as we are, about the injustice of animal-product consumption. Criticism alone will not do. Let us offer our innovations as gifts and praise small steps when taken. Relatively minor institutional changes, such as when synagogues commit to not serving veal or promise to provide vegan options, make it more likely that individuals and households will see change as possible, positive, and Jewish.

We also have a unique opportunity to use our voices as Jewish vegans to intervene into contemporary politics, well beyond our communities' porous boundaries. We should participate in multiconfessional and ecumenical projects. As the heirs to an ancient tradition to which newer faiths and cultures may trace their roots, we can add voices of perceived authenticity to our collective struggle. We can show the world that people of all faiths and backgrounds have found a common cause in veganism.

As Jewish vegans, we also have the responsibility to stand against those who would misuse our values—to the extent that I may assume consensus—in the service of less noble causes. I have in mind the manipulation of animal-welfare politics to stigmatize and marginalize minority communities. This happens when activists project the widespread cruelty to animals, which is endemic to our society as a whole, on Jews and Muslims. It manifests in attempts to ban ritual slaughter—*kosher* and *halal*—rather than outlawing industrial animal agriculture or meat production in general. The laws in question tend to demand that animals be "stunned" before slaughter to minimize the pain they endure—a procedure many Jewish and Muslim authorities prohibit. I would welcome more restrictive laws, but not when they target ethnic and religious minorities. To focus on stunning is a choice. Not only do these laws contribute to ongoing patterns of exclusion and marginalization, particularly in Europe, they also enable majority populations to avoid considering the morality of their own mainstream practices. The perception of Jews as a people long oppressed will help us stand against efforts to misuse veganism to discriminate, alienate, and oppress.[52]

VEGAN ADVOCACY AND ISRAEL

As Jews, we are also members of a transnational community. We can thus contribute to making veganism a truly global phenomenon. This brings me to Israel and Israeli culture. The State of Israel is home to an incredibly dynamic and growing vegan community. Without reservation, I congratulate my Israeli and Palestinian allies. I look forward to witnessing the spread of their influence through a globalizing culture. I hope to collaborate with them, across oceans and continents, in the project of building more ethical global communities.

Liberal Zionists and others commonly marshal the phenomenon of Israeli veganism, alongside the state's treatment of its LGBTQIA citizens, to portray Israeli society as progressive.[53] In some ways and in some sectors, it is exceptionally so. Critics nonetheless consider this type of praise to be a distraction from the fundamental issues facing Israeli society: endemic racism, ethnic violence, the occupation of the West Bank, the siege of Gaza, and the disparities of income, resources, and opportunities enjoyed by Palestinian and Jewish citizens, not to mention the painful disparities among Jewish Israelis. Some characterize any attempt to highlight the progressive aspects of Israeli society as a part of a broad effort to cast Palestinians and other Arabs into false moral relief and thereby justify the perpetuation of an untenable and unethical status quo. Some ask how Jewish Israeli vegans can have so much compassion for animals and apparently so little for their fellow human beings. Others refuse to partner with Israeli organizations or at least with a specific set of them.[54] The relatively new vegan Birthright trips to Israel, discussed in this volume, have fallen prey to such criticism as well.[55]

Must Jewish vegans who do not reside in Israel or the West Bank respond to this, and if so, what should that response be? This question presumes—falsely— that Jewish vegans hold similar opinions on contemporary politics and Jewish nationalism. We do not, just as we do not agree on matters of religion. Taking into account the divisiveness of such debates, one Jewish vegan listserv in which I participate has adopted a policy of avoiding discussions of Israeli-Palestinian politics. That was a pragmatic decision designed to facilitate and focus our internal communication. It is by no means a tenable strategy for Jewish vegans to maintain in general, especially when engaging with the public and with a wide range of organizations. Feminist forms of veganism and vegan activists of color, in particular, have urged vegans to see their practice as part of a broader, intersectional struggle against all oppression and hierarchy.

I suggest that we celebrate Israeli veganism as a major and hopefully enduring contribution to contemporary Jewish culture. Yet we should also remember that to advocate for veganism is to fight for a more just society and, for some, to sacrifice dearly for its achievement. We take radical strides on behalf of animals. We literally embody our commitment to their lives and to preserving the environment through our consumption choices. *Kal ve chomer*, how much more so, should we fight alongside and for Palestinians in their struggle for justice and equality? Saryta Rodríguez joined many others in criticizing vegan activist Gary Yourofsky for failing to promote a veganism of "boundless inclusiveness," a phrase she borrows from Will Tuttle. Rodríguez explains that Yourofsky "showed a shocking level of disregard and even contempt for Palestinians, Black people and others in his video 'Palestinians, Blacks and Other Hypocrites,' (2015)."[56] This matters because of Yourofsky's prominent role in launching the movement for veganism in Israel, of which he boasted in the aforementioned video.[57]

Should not Jewish veganism predispose us to advocate for all who are oppressed, excluded, and underserved? As Mendelssohn argued (per Sacks), Jewish religious practice—and here, Jewish veganism—should "endow practitioners with a constellation of dispositions crucial to engaged citizenship." If we sense that portrayals of Israeli Jewish veganism are being used to draw attention from the pursuit of justice for Palestinians (or for other communities), we must protest. There can be no excuse for ignoring injustice. It is simply insufficient to note that the vegan movements in Israel and Palestine have been, to some extent, spheres where Arabs and Jews have come together.⁵⁷ Palestinians and Jews have always found such opportunities but this has yet to yield a just, sustainable, and equitable future for all.

I freely admit that my politics and even my veganism—if I may still call it that—includes a strong degree of speciesism.⁵⁹ It was, indeed, my concern for humanity that led me to veganism. I therefore cannot stand in solidarity with anyone who would champion animal welfare without first—or also—rallying behind their fellow human beings. To ignore persecution in the name of other political and cultural passions is to exercise the very privilege on which human oppression turns. This is not the place for me to delve more deeply into Middle Eastern politics or questions of nationalism. I will thus not take a stance here regarding the solutions I support and the strategies I trust to achieve them. I will instead simply offer the hope that for all readers, compassion yields compassion. Let our diets and the steps we take daily to accommodate them transform us and be a constant reminder to fight against every injustice. Such can be the moral dividend of an intentional and embodied practice of Jewish veganism.

CONCLUSION

As a boy, when I would misbehave, my mother would admonish me with the words, "Is that a Torah way to act?" The Jewish religion offers practitioners a means for constructing an ethical (and ethnic) framework for living in the world. This is not to suggest that observant Jews conduct themselves ethically all of the time or even at all. I am concerned, rather, with how Jewish people, skeptical of nationalism and without religion, might still experience Jewishness as a transcendent factor of their lives—among others. I see in Jewish veganism one such opportunity and have found in it a key to identifying others. Jewish veganism, like *kashrut*, may be considered an embodied practice of community and self-construction.

Pianko has shown the concept of "Jewish peoplehood" with which most US Jews are familiar to have been a recent innovation and a response to specific postwar contexts. Looking to the future, he suggests adopting a language of "Judihood," which acknowledges not only the fissures of identification and practice among Jews but also the permeability of our communal boundaries and the flexibility of categories once believed to have been firmly established.⁶⁰ He writes of Jewish interconnected "neighborhoods," many of them virtual, where Jewish people come together for specific purposes and to which they belong on terms less complete, exclusionary, and lasting than those conveyed by the idea of "peoplehood." Jewish veganism may be one such neighborhood. It has functioned so for me.⁶¹

Jewish veganism has offered me opportunities for self-actualization and community formation, and so I explore it. It has strengthened my veganism and led me to activism, and so I cherish it. I encourage fellow secular and cultural Jews to do the same. I also hope that my exposition of how Jewish veganism works for me will inspire others to apply my methods to finding even more opportunities for making cultural and secular Judaism more fulfilling and, as I have called it here, "transcendent." What other practices and "technologies" are available to us? What other frameworks and qualities, aside from embodiment, will help us achieve our desired results? May we work together to build a stronger and more diverse Jewish vegan community, to seek justice, and to support each other as we do.

NOTES

I benefited from suggestions offered by participants in the 2017 meeting of the Society for Jewish Ethics. I also thank Alan Lenovitz, Anna Elena Torres, Elias Sacks, Katie Light Soloway, Megan Kramer, Mira Sucharov, Sandra Fox, Sarah Chandler, and Shmuly Yanklowitz. All errors are my own.

1. Pew Research Center, "A Portrait of Jewish Americans: Findings from a Pew Research Center Survey of U.S. Jews," October 1, 2013, http://www.pewforum.org/2013/10/01/jewish-american-beliefs-attitudes-culture-survey. The National Jewish Population Survey of 1990 drove a great deal of Jewish communal innovation, which culminated in the launch of the Birthright program. Sydney Goldstein, "Profile of American Jewry: Insights from the 1990 National Jewish Population Survey," *America Jewish Yearbook* (1992): 77–173. On the links to Birthright, see Leonard Saxe and Barry Chazan, *Tend Days of Birthright Israel* (Waltham, MA: Brandeis University Press, 2008), 26–30; Shaul Kelner, *Tours that Bind: Diaspora, Pilgrimage, and Israeli Birthright Tourism* (New York: NYU Press, 2010), 39–44.

2. James Loeffler, "The Death of Jewish Culture," *Mosaic Magazine*, May 4, 2014, http://mosaicmagazine.com/essay/2014/05/the-death-of-jewish-culture.

3. I am indebted to Joshua Schwartz for drawing my attention to this consideration.

4. Abraham Joshua Heschel, *Man's Quest for God* (New York: Charles Scribner's Sons, 1954), 67–68.

5. Leora Batnitzky, *How Judaism Became a Religion: An Introduction to Modern Jewish Thought* (Princeton, NJ: Princeton University Press, 2011); Jonathan Z. Smith, *Relating Religion: Essays in the Study of Religion* (Chicago: University of Chicago Press, 2004), 179–96. My thanks to Elias Sacks for pointing me to this scholarship.

6. Galen Strawson, "Against Narrativity," *Ratio* n.s. 17, no. 4 (December 2004): 428–52.

7. Jonathan Haidt, *The Righteous Mind: Why Good People Are Divided by Politics and Religion* (New York: Pantheon, 2012), xx.

8. Ibid., xxii–xxiii.

9. Jonathan Haidt, interviewed by Tamler Sommers, *The Believer*, August 2005, http://www.believermag.com/issues/200508/?read=interview_haidt.

10. Haidt, *The Righteous Mind*; Jonathan Haidt and David F. Bjorklund, "Social Intuitionists Answer Six Questions about Moral Psychology," in *Moral Psychology, Volume 2: The Cognitive Science of Morality: Intuition and Diversity*, ed. Walter Sinnott-Armstrong (Cambridge, MA: MIT Press, 2008), 181–217.

11. Saba Mahmood, "Feminist Theory, Embodiment, and the Docile Agent: Some Reflections on the Egyptian Islamic Revival," *Cultural Anthropology* 16, no. 2 (2001): 210–12; Saba Mahmood, *Politics of Piety: The Islamic Revival and the Feminist Subject* (Princeton, NJ: Princeton University Press, 2005).

12. Elias Sacks, *Moses Mendelssohn's Living Script: Philosophy, Practice, History, Judaism* (Bloomington: Indiana University Press, 2016), 231.

13. Lee H. Yearley, "Conflicts among Ideals of Human Flourishing," in *Prospects for a Common Morality*, ed. Gene Outka and John P. Reeder Jr. (Princeton, NJ: Princeton University Press, 1993), 233–53; see 245 for quote. I am grateful to Alan Lenovitz for drawing my attention to this concept.

14. It matters little that non-Jews fail at this as well. Consider, for example, the place of Catholicism in Polish nationalism. Of consequence here is the common faith in the paradigm of ethnic and religious division, especially in liberal circles.

15. See Mark Oppenheimer, "Reclaiming 'Jew'," *New York Times*, April 22, 2017, https://www.nytimes.com/2017/04/22/opinion/reclaiming-jew.html. See also Cynthia M. Baker *Jew*, Key Words in Jewish Studies (New Brunswick, NJ: Rutgers University Press, 2017).

16. Mordecai M. Kaplan, *Judaism as a Civilization: Towards a Reconstruction of American-Jewish Life* (Philadelphia: Jewish Publication Society of America, 2010).

17. Noam Pianko, *Jewish Peoplehood: An American Innovation* (New Brunswick, NJ: Rutgers University Press, 2015), 39–56.

18. On the history of Jews in the United States, see Hasia Diner, *The Jews of the United States, 1654 to 2000* (Berkeley: University of California Press, 2004). For a closer look at patterns of Jewish identification and politics, see Michael E. Staub, *Torn at the Roots: The Crisis of Jewish Liberalism in Postwar America* (New York: Columbia University Press, 2002); and Pianko, *Jewish Peoplehood*. I have based the present discussion on these volumes.

19. Will Herberg, *Protestant, Catholic, Jew: An Essay in American Religious Sociology* (Garden City, NY: Doubleday, 1955).

20. On whiteness in the United States, see David R. Roediger, *Working Toward Whiteness: How America's Immigrants Became White: The Strange Journey from Ellis Island to the Suburbs* (New York: Basic Books, 2005). On Jewishness and whiteness see Eric L. Goldstein, *The Price of Whiteness: Jews, Race, and American Identity* (Princeton, NJ: Princeton University Press, 2006); Karen Brodkin, *How Jews Became White Folks: And What That Says about Race in America* (New Brunswick, NJ: Rutgers University Press, 1998).

21. Diner, *The Jews of the United States*, 288.

22. Ibid., 306.

23. Steven J. Zipperstein, *Imagining Russian Jewry: Memory, History, Identity* (Seattle: University of Washington Press, 1999), 15–41.

24. Matthew Frye Jacobson, *Roots Too: White Ethnic Revival in Post-Civil Rights America* (Cambridge, MA: Harvard University Press, 2008). I am grateful to Sandra Fox for referring me to this book.

25. "Black and Jewish in America," panel discussion moderated by Jane Anne Gordon and featuring April Baskin, MaNishtana, and Rebecca Pierce, organized by the Center for Judaic and Holocaust Studies and the Africana Studies Program at Youngstown State University, Youngstown, OH, February 19, 2018.

26. Noam Pianko, "The End of Dissent: Israel and the Politics of the Radical Left, 1967–1977," paper presented at the Association for Jewish Studies Conference, Washington, DC, December 2017.

27. Gal Beckerman, *When They Come for Us, We'll Be Gone: The Epic Struggle to Save Soviet Jewry* (Boston: Houghton Mifflin Harcourt, 2010).

28. Shaul Kelner, "Ritualized Protest and Redemptive Politics: Cultural Consequences of the American Mobilization to Free Soviet Jewry," *Jewish Social Studies: History, Culture, Society*, n.s. 14, no. 3 (Spring/Summer 2008): 1–37.

29. Atina Grossmann, "Shadows of War and Holocaust: Jews, German Jews, and the Sixties in the United States, Reflections and Memories," *Journal of Modern Jewish Studies* 13, no. 1 (March 2014): 99–114; Hasia Diner, *We Remember with Reverence and Love: American Jews and the Myth of Silence after the Holocaust, 1945–1962* (New York: NYU Press, 2009); Norman G. Finkelstein, *The Holocaust Industry: Reflections on the Exploitation of Jewish Suffering* (New York: Verso, 2000); Peter Novick, *The Holocaust in American Life* (Boston: Houghton Mifflin, 1999).

30. Bernard Reisman, "A Perspective on the Havurah Movement," *Sh'ma: A Journal of Jewish Ideas* 9, no. 176 (September 7, 1979): 124.

31. Shaul Kelner, "The American Soviet Jewry Movement's Uneventful 1968: Cold War Liberalism, Human Interest and the Politics of the Long Haul," *American Jewish History* (January 2018): 5–35; Nathan Perl-Rosenthal, "The Liberal American Jewish Psyche in Crisis: Can Zionism and U.S. Liberalism

Coexist under Netanyahu?," *Tablet*, April 2, 2015, http://tabletmag.com/jewish-news-and-politics/189933/liberal-jewish-psyche-crisis.

32. Comedy Central offers a collection of Jewish jokes featured on the *Colbert Report*: http://www.cc.com/video-clips/m3zujh/the-colbert-report-5-x-five---colbert-on-religion---judaism.

33. *Blackish*, "Pilot," directed by James Griffiths, written by Kenya Barris, ABC, September 24, 2014.

34. Benedict Anderson, *Imagined Communities: Reflections on the Origin and Spread of Nationalism*, rev. ed. (1983; New York: Verso, 2006); Rogers Brubaker, *Ethnicity without Groups* (Cambridge, MA: Harvard University Press, 2004).

35. For Jewish responses to this challenge, see Caryn Aviv and David Shneer, *New Jews: The End of the Jewish Diaspora* (New York: NYU Press, 2005); Shaul Magid, *American-Post Judaism: Identity and Renewal in a Postethnic Society* (Bloomington: Indiana University Press, 2013).

36. Pew Research Center, "A Portrait of Jewish Americans"; Dov Waxman, *Trouble in the Tribe: The American Jewish Conflict over Israel* (Princeton, NJ: Princeton University Press, 2016). My thanks to Mira Sucharov for calling my attention to this book.

37. Staub, *Torn at the Roots*, 308.

38. Roberta Rosenthal Kwall, *The Myth of the Cultural Jew: Culture and Law in Jewish Tradition* (New York: Oxford University Press, 2015).

39. I owe inspiration to Alan Lenovitz, *The Gluten Lie: And Other Myths about What You Eat* (New York: Regan Arts, 2015).

40. Diana Fleischman, "The Ethical Case for Eating Oysters and Mussels," *Sentientist*, May 20, 2013, https://sentientist.org/2013/05/20/the-ethical-case-for-eating-oysters-and-mussels.

41. David Rakoff, "Dark Meat," in *Half Empty* (New York: Doubleday, 2010), 81–96.

42. On the American Jewish affinity for Chinese food (especially on Christmas), see Marc Tracy, "Why Eating Chinese Food on Christmas Is a Sacred Tradition for American Jews," *Tablet*, December 25, 2012, http://www.tabletmag.com/jewish-life-and-religion/53569/jewish-christmas.

43. I have in mind, among other things, the 2008 scandal at the Agriprocessors facility in Iowa. See Aaron Gross, *The Question of the Animal and Religion: Theoretical Stakes, Practical Implications* (New York: Columbia University Press, 2015).

44. Michael Stanislawski, *For Whom Do I Toil?: Judah Leib Gordon and the Crisis of Russian Jewry* (Oxford: Oxford University Press, 1988), 52; cited in Peter Kivisto and Giuseppe Sciortino, *Solidarity, Justice, and Incorporation. Thinking through the Civic Sphere* (Oxford: Oxford University Press, 2015), 193, n. 5.

45. Sacks, *Moses Mendelssohn's Living Script*, 224–25.

46. Some vegan Jews—those who invest their own understanding of Judaism with divine authority—may not be bothered by this objection. They have a right to believe and teach what they like. I suggest, however, that they are fighting a losing battle when they attempt to portray the deep and manifold Jewish traditions of animal-product consumption as somehow inauthentic or un-Jewish. One could even argue against this sort of activism by pointing to the *halakhic* imperatives not to cause hardships for the community and not to interpret Jewish law in such a way as to create sinners out of most Jews.

47. See chapter 10 in this volume, as well as Kobi Nahshoni, "Rabbi Lior: Vegetarianism Not Right for our Times, Jewish World, *Ynet News*, March 18, 2010, http://www.ynetnews.com/articles/0,7340,L-3864255,00.html; Richard Schwartz, "Eighteen Reasons Why Jews Think They Should Not Be Vegetarians (and Why They are Wrong)," *Society of Ethical and Religious Vegetarians*, n.d., http://serv-online.org/Schwartz-eighteen-reasons.htm; Steven Plaut, "Judaism and Eating Meat: Letter to a Vegan Animal Rights Activist," *Jewish Press*, December 26, 2013, http://www.jewishpress.com/indepth/opinions/judaism-and-eating-meat-letter-to-a-vegan-animal-rights-activist/2013/12/26/.

48. I have in mind the binding of Isaac, referenecs to Moloch, and King Saul's visit to the Witch of Endor, as well as the prohibitions and curses found in the book of Deuteronomy.

49. For one such movement, see "Four Questions: Aaron Potek, Yeshiva Chovevei Torah Rabbinic Students and Founder of MOOSHY," Jew Hungry (blog), September 7, 2011, http://jewhungrytheblog.com/four-questions-aaron-potek-yeshiva-chovevei-torah-rabbinic-student-and-founder-of-mooshy. See also chapter 10 in this volume.

50. Jacob Ari Labendz, "New Traditions for a Vegan Passover," March 29, 2015, http://jewschool.com/2015/03/36590/new-traditions-vegan-passover.

51. Babylonian Talmud, Eruvin 13b.

52. Jacob Ari Labendz, "Move to Ban Kosher Slaughter Not Really about the Animals," *Forward*, June 20, 2014, http://forward.com/articles/200067/move-to-ban-kosher-slaughter-really-not-about-the. See also Robin Judd, *Contested Rituals: Circumcision, Kosher Butchering, and Jewish Political Life in Germany, 1843–1933* (Ithaca, NY: Cornell University Press, 2007).

53. Tamara Zieve, "Israeli Veganism: Introducing the Land of Soy Milk and Date Honey to the World," *Jerusalem Post*, March 26, 2017, http://www.jpost.com/Diaspora/Israeli-Veganism-Introducing-the-land-of-soy-milk-and-date-honey-to-Berlin-485246; more thoughtfully, Frederick Hertz, "Pinkwashing: Is it Really so Black and White?," *+972*, June 10, 2017, https://972mag.com/pinkwashing-is-it-really-so-black-and-white/128004.

54. Aeyal Gross, "Vegans for (and against) the Occupation," *Haaretz*, November 14, 2013, http://www.haaretz.com/opinion/.premium-1.557912; Haggai Matar, "Can Animal Rights Take Precedence over Human Rights?," *+972*, November 12, 2013, https://972mag.com/promoting-animal-rights-at-the-expense-of-human-rights/81628/; Shawndeez Davari Jadalizadeh, "What's Wrong with the Israeli Animal Rights Movement, 269?," *Vegan Feminist Network*, October 28, 2015, http://veganfeministnetwork.com/269life/. For a scholarly perspective on this phenomenon and the attendant debates, see Erica Weiss, " 'There Are No Chickens in Suicide Vests': The Decoupling of Human Rights and Animal Rights in Israel," *Journal of the Royal Anthropological Institute* n.s. 22 (2016): 688–706; Esther Alloun, " 'That's the Beauty of It, It's Very Simple!' Animal Rights and Settler Colonialism in Palestine-Israel," *Settler Colonial Studies* (2017), doi: 10.1080/2201473X.2017.1414138. I thank Limor Chen for these references.

55. Julia Tanenbaum, "Apartheid Isn't Vegan: Renouncing Vegan Birthright," Collectively Free, September 22, 2017, http://www.collectivelyfree.org/renouncing-vegan-birthright.

56. Saryta Rodríguez, "Move to Berkeley! and Other Follies," in *Veganism in an Oppressed World: A Vegans of Color Community Project*, ed. Julia Feliz Brueck (Sanctuary Publishers, 2017), 97. See also Unnatural Vegan, "Misanthropy Is Not Okay (A Response to Gary Yourofsky)," YouTube, May 27, 2015, https://www.youtube.com/watch?v=NU-xuTW-eos.

57. Gary Yourofsky, "Palestinians, Blacks and Other Hypocrites," YouTube, May 16, 2015, https://www.youtube.com/watch?v=pqhUIns86cA&t=167s.

58. "Jews and Arabs March Together for Veganism and Animal Rights," *The Vegan Woman*, July 28, 2015, http://www.theveganwoman.com/jews-and-arabs-march-together-for-veganism-and-animal-rights.

59. On the difficulty of separating concerns for humans and nonhuman animals in discussions of veganism see chapter 10.

60. Pianko, *Jewish Peoplehood*, 134. See also Magid, *American Post-Judaism*.

61. Noam Pianko, "The Future of Peoplehood: From Nationhood to Neighborhood," *E-Jewish Philanthropy*, October 30, 2013. http://ejewishphilanthropy.com/the-future-of-peoplehood-from-nationhood-to-neighborhood.

# REPORT
Jewish Vegan and Vegetarian Movements in North America

SARAH CHANDLER AND JEFFREY COHAN

A BRIEF HISTORY OF THE JEWISH VEG MOVEMENT

1970s: The Beginning

The contemporary North American Jewish veg movement can trace its roots to 1975, when activists founded Jewish Vegetarians of North America as a nonprofit organization (JVNA; renamed Jewish Veg in 2015).

JVNA's first president, Jonathan Wolf, had just attended the World Vegetarian Conference in Maine. He came to the realization that the ideal Jewish diet was indeed a vegetarian diet; today the movement promotes veganism.

The initial planning meeting was held in the home of Richard Schwartz, a contributor to this volume. Schwartz remains a leader of Jewish Veg, currently serving as president emeritus, and a vigorous advocate for vegan and ecological causes within the Jewish community.

Publishing and Conferences

With help from Wolf, Schwartz wrote a comprehensive book on Jewish vegetarianism. Titled *Judaism and Vegetarianism* (1982), the book has been in print for more than thirty years and has been published in three updated editions. To date, it remains the most complete and authoritative book ever written on the subject.

Another major contributor to Jewish vegetarian thought and publishing has been Roberta Kalechofsky. She released an edited volume titled *Jews and Animal Rights: Classical and Contemporary Responses* (1992). She later published *Rabbis and Vegetarianism: An Evolving Tradition* (1995), followed by *Vegetarian Judaism: A Guide for Everyone* (1998).[1] In conversation with Jeffrey Cohan, Kalechofsky credited Richard Schwartz with first influencing her thinking on Jewish vegetarianism.

Charles Stahler and Debra Wasserman, JVNA members who went on to create the highly respected Vegetarian Resource Group, were instrumental in planning JVNA conferences and distributing literature in the late 1970s and early 1980s. In the mid-1980s, Israel and Eva Mossman assumed the mantle of JVNA and published its newsletter, which kept people informed about Jewish vegetarian events and included book reviews and recipes, much like the *Jewish Vegetarian* magazine in the United Kingdom.

The Eco-Jewish Value of Not Eating Meat: Teva Learning Center

In 1993, Camp Isabella Freedman partnered with Surprise Lake Camp to launch the Teva Learning Center, an experiential learning retreat for Jewish elementary school students that "integrates ecology, Jewish spirituality, and environmental activism." Teva's educational programs take place primarily in the fall, usually for four days. In addition to daily hikes, lessons in earth science, and Jewish ecospirituality activities, Teva students follow a vegetarian diet for the duration of the program. For most, it is the longest they have ever gone without eating the flesh of animals. The youngsters learn about the devastating environmental impacts of global meat consumption, as well as the Jewish value of compassion for animals. Even those educators who are not vegan or vegetarian promote the importance of meat reduction as an essential component of a sustainable lifestyle.

Twenty-First Century: Podcasts and a Documentary

In 2002, Schwartz assumed the presidency of JVNA. A tireless advocate and educator, he has written 150 articles and created 25 podcasts about the intersection of Judaism and vegetarianism and has given hundreds of interviews and lectures. For his efforts, he has been inducted into the North American Vegetarian Society's Hall of Fame.

The most impressive achievement of Schwartz's tenure was the 2007 production of *A Sacred Duty*, an hour-long documentary film directed by Lionel Friedberg. JVNA and its successor, Jewish Veg, have distributed more than 35,000 copies in DVD format. Thousands have watched the film on YouTube. All these accomplishments occurred while JVNA functioned as an all-volunteer organization.

The First Professional Jewish Vegetarians

In 2012, JVNA took a leap forward by hiring its first professional staff member, Jeffrey Cohan. The organization built a new website, created a formal board of directors, and assembled impressive advisory and rabbinic councils. Among the members of the first board of directors was Alex Hershaft, a Holocaust survivor and prominent figure in the animal rights movement. Today, Hershaft is one of the most moving and popular presenters in the organization's speakers' bureau.

In recent years, JVNA forged a partnership with Hillel International, the organization that provides for Jewish life on more than 500 college campuses. Through Hillel, JVNA/Jewish Veg brought Israeli vegan leader and restaurateur Ori Shavit to the United States for two national speaking tours, which reached thousands of Jewish college students. JVNA also established the Veg Pledge program, in which enrollees receive online resources and even a mentor to help them transition to a vegan diet.

In October 2015, at JVNA's fortieth anniversary celebration in New York, the organization announced that it was changing its name to Jewish Veg to reflect the transformation of the organization from one that was confined to the margins of the US Jewish community to one that had been embraced by major international Jewish organizations like Hillel. The name change also reflected a reorientation of the organization's mission, which is to promote veganism as the Jewish ideal and the ultimate personal objective, while also supporting conscious reductions in the consumption of animal products. Jewish Veg now has full-time employees and a part-time video editor.

In 2017, Jewish Veg recruited seventy-five rabbis—who broadly represent the full spectrum of Jewish observance—to sign a statement urging all Jews to transition to plant-based diets. A video version of the statement—featuring interviews with former chief rabbi of Ireland David Rosen and prominent Conservative Rabbi David Wolpe—has garnered more than 100,000 views. Jewish Veg has plans to reissue the statement with more than 100 rabbis. Also in 2017, Jewish Veg created the first-ever vegan Birthright trip, with a second trip scheduled for 2018. This is yet another example of veganism entering the mainstream of Jewish institutional life.

THE ROLE OF MEAT REDUCTION IN JEWISH FOOD AND FARMING EDUCATION

Contemporary Jewish vegan and vegetarian movements exist within a broader culture of Jews learning to think more critically about food consumption and production. The organization Hazon was founded in 2000 to build a sustainable Jewish community around the values of environmental protection and fitness through bike riding. During its inaugural cross-country bike ride, a visit to a kosher slaughterhouse compelled two of their participants to adopt a vegan lifestyle. In 2004, Hazon expanded its mission to include projects related to food sustainability and Jewish agricultural education.

In an email response to questions submitted in the preparation of this report, Hazon's founder and CEO Nigel Savage reflected:

> I think that I have a deeper understanding now of mixed use farming. On the one hand, I understand that—for instance—not eating meat, but drinking milk and eating cheese, is quite inconsistent. And on the other hand, I feel that we all live and die and that humans have been omnivores for several hundred millennia—or more. So my preference now is that a) I do eat meat but b) far less frequently than when I was a kid or in my twenties and c) I want to eat meat from animals that I feel have lived good animal-like lives.

On the question of "Is there a role for people who are meat reductionists to be vegan some of the time?" Savage added:

> I'm personally a gradualist—I think it's good to eat more healthily and [be aware of the food we eat] more of the time, but wouldn't a hard core vegan raise an eyebrow at someone who is vegan except for when they eat meat?

As the North American movement for community farming has had its resurgence, so has the world of Jewish farming. The Adamah Environmental Fellowship, based at Isabella Freedman in Connecticut, was founded in 2005, and its sibling organization, Urban Adamah in Berkeley, California, was founded in 2010. Both cultivate organic vegetables and raise animals as part of an educational program.

In 2006, Hazon (which has since merged with Isabella Freedman) hosted their first annual Jewish food conference at Isabella Freedman. As part of this program, they chose to have a public educational *shechitah* (slaughter in accordance with traditional Jewish practices) of a goat. In a now-infamous poll taken during the Shabbat meal when meat from this goat was served, the participants were asked: "Who usually eats meat but chose not to eat meat today after witnessing this slaughter? Who usually doesn't eat meat but is now choosing to eat this meat?" To many people's surprise, each question brought about more than a few hands raised.

Since their founding, both Adamah and Urban Adamah include annual educational slaughter programs, for the benefit of their participants and as part of the overall sustainability of the farm. Noah Weinberg (24) commented on his time at Adamah in spring 2016:

> Remember the experiences with the animals: witnessing the birth of, feeding, and snuggling with the beautiful baby goats and burying the one who died... taking eggs from the beautiful majestic chickens squawking and pecking at you, burying the found dead chickens in the compost, and holding the cone [for securing chickens' necks] during *shechita*, marveling

at the decision to put a knife to an animal's throat. This is why you don't eat animal products. This is also why you also respect those who do who are connected to the realness of life and death and pain and emotion of animal agriculture, who are deeply involved with those animals as a part of a farm ecosystem that provides for their welfare to [the] highest extent possible, and utilize their natural behavior as a key part of that ecological farm system. And this is why you see no place in this world for industrial animal agriculture as it exists today, even in its slightly adjusted "humane" and "sustainable" versions. (personal communication, November 3, 2016)[2]

Bonnie Wolf (34), who was an Adamah fellow in 2010, reflected:

I've always been an animal lover, so my original reason for becoming a vegetarian as a kid was that I didn't like the idea of killing animals for food. Over time, I started to understand the environmental and health reasons as well. So if eating meat is not necessary (and actually causes harm in most cases), why do it? But then, during my Adamah experience, I came to learn about the inextricable link between dairy/eggs and meat. So I started to wonder—should I become a vegan? Or should I start eating meat, eggs and dairy in a more conscious, responsible way? The easiest and most comfortable answer for me would be to become vegan, but then that leads to my question [of whether it is possible to produce large amounts of vegetables without manure or chemical fertilizers]. If we need the manure, we need to raise animals, right? So then I start thinking about the global consequences of all of this. Is it reasonable to promote veganism? or should I be focusing my efforts on changing the animal-based food system for the better? (personal communication, November 11, 2016)

Each of the Hazon conferences includes sessions on the topic of ethical, sustainable, or humane meat consumption, concepts that are anathema to many vegans and vegetarians. Most conferences, including regional ones, have also included sessions on the health and environmental impacts of plant-based diets. Many conferences have looked carefully at small-scale, ethically raised animal agriculture, such as back yard chickens or "boutique" kosher meat companies such as Grow and Behold. There is even a stand-alone initiative, MOOSHY (meat only on Shabbat, happy occasions, and yom tov [holidays]), to encourage meat reduction among Jews.[3]

In his postscript to "Jewish Environmentalism in North America," Rabbi Dr. David Seidenberg connects performative, educational *shechitah* with other Jewish ethical consumption projects:

Concurrent with the farming movement there has been a movement to bring shechitah, kosher slaughter, back to the small farm, using humanely- and sustainably-raised animals. The growth of shechitah operations was sparked largely by the Adva Dairy (an outgrowth of Adamah founded by Aitan Mizrahi in 2006), which needed to make use of its male animals. Also, there is widespread interest in a kosher certification (or certifications) that would guarantee that food is produced in an ethical manner. Efforts towards this have been led by Magen Tzedek within the Conservative movement and Uri L'Tzedek among the Orthodox—however, thus far workers rights have been emphasized, rather than ecology/sustainability, though there is some acknowledgment of ecological issues.[4]

It was not until the 2014 food conference, "Poultry, Pollinators and Policy," that Hazon's flagship conference included sessions that addressed the welfare of animals.[5] In 2015, Paul Shapiro, the vice president for farm animal protection of the Humane Society of the United States, offered the keynote address for the Hazon-Philadelphia Jewish Food Festival, along with Sarah Chandler, with moderation by Nigel Savage. By December 2015, Hazon had unveiled their new agenda, which for the first time explicitly mentioned animal welfare as a core value of its seven-year plan, as well as the new Hazon Seal of Sustainability food audit.

NEW JEWISH ANIMAL WELFARE ORGANIZATIONS

In recent years, two new Jewish organizations have arrived on the North American scene. The Shamayim V'Aretz Institute (SVA), founded in 2013, defines itself as a collective of Jewish animal welfare advocates. The Jewish Initiative for Animals (JIFA), launched in 2016, has focused much of its efforts on helping Jewish orga- nizations create food policies that take the safeguarding of animal welfare as a Jewish value. SVA and JIFA are supportive of Jewish veganism and vegetarianism and support suffering reduction efforts that appeal to Jewish omnivores.

SVA, founded by modern Orthodox Rabbi Dr. Shmuly Yanklowitz, has convened leadership conferences on both coasts to bring together Jewish activists. The SVA website, annual retreat, and electronic discussion list provide resources, training, networking, and a platform for community building to Jewish vegans from across the religious spectrum. SVA's fourth conference, held in 2017, brought together college students, rabbis, community leaders, and Jewish representa- tives of seven animal advocacy groups. In addition to the London-based Jewish Vegetarian Society, Jewish Veg, SVA, and JIFA, the following secular organiza- tions had one or more attendees: Humane Society of the United States (HSUS), the American Society for the Prevention of Cruelty to Animals (ASPCA), Factory Farming Awareness Coalition (FFAC), and People for the Ethical Treatment of Animals (PETA).

JIFA is a project of Farm Forward, a national nonprofit committed to ending factory farming through its mission to implement "innovative strategies to promote conscientious food choices, reduce farmed animal suffering, and advance sustainable agriculture." Farm Forward founder and CEO Dr. Aaron Gross, also a professor of religious studies at the University of San Diego, hired a three-person team to run JIFA that included Sarah Chandler, a Jewish food and farm educator; Melissa Hoffman, who holds a master's in animals and public policy from Tufts University School of Veterinary Medicine; and Yadidya Greenberg, a *shochet* (Jewish slaughterer) who is passionate about animal welfare issues. Working closely with Hazon and the Humane Society of the United States, JIFA has rallied Jewish support for national animal protection campaigns, supported the development of the animal welfare component of the new Hazon Seal of Sustainability, and helped synagogues, camps, and Hillel groups shift their food sourcing to better align with Jewish commitments to animal welfare.

Today JIFA advises dozens of institutions that are making public commitments to the Jewish value of avoiding *tza'ar ba'alei chayim* (the suffering of animals) by reducing meat consumption, promoting plant-based foods, and purchasing higher-welfare animal products. JIFA is also advising Jewish communal farms on how to develop educational programming featuring animals. In 2017, they published the groundbreaking Ark Project, a new curriculum for b'nai mitzvah youths to take part in service learning with animals. It is the most comprehensive animal-focused Jewish educational curriculum ever developed.

COLLABORATION AND POINTS OF TENSION

Although Jewish Veg, SVA, and JIFA have overlapping missions, they also disagree about whether animal advocates should be involved in endorsing higher-welfare animal products, especially when the available supply of these products is so limited. Of the three groups, Jewish Veg comes closest to promoting abolitionism, advocating for veganism and eschewing messaging that endorses animal products even when they are produced in less cruel systems. As such, Jewish Veg has sought to discourage educational *shechitah* presentations of the type that JIFA (and Hazon) have sometimes supported. In 2014 there was a particularly heated clash around these *shechitah* presentations. Protests by JVNA, in collaboration with United Poultry Concerns,[6] led to the cancellation of a public *shechitah* event in which Urban Adamah had planned to slaughter several birds.[7] Urban Adamah subsequently slaughtered the birds without using the occasion for educational purposes, despite offers from JVNA to transfer the birds to a sanctuary.[8]

A practice that has raised concerns from all groups is *kapparot*, a ritual of repentance at the Jewish New Year that involves waving a chicken in circles around one's head. Many within the Jewish community, even those not typically associated with activism on behalf of animals, oppose this practice. In fall 2016, JIFA's humane education specialist, Melissa Hoffman, coauthored a piece in the *Forward* with JIFA kosher meat and animal welfare specialist Yadidya Greenberg in which they countered:

> While Kapparot originated in a society where factory farms did not exist, today the overwhelming majority of the chickens you see in these ceremonies—likely upwards of 99%—are bred and raised in the same conditions as the chickens Americans eat on a daily basis. Criticism of Kapparot can and should open up discussion about a much larger question: are we going to spend another year tolerating the suffering we collectively support on factory farms?[9]

Instead of targeting the people performing the ritual, Hoffman and Greenberg sought to direct critical attention to the factory farming industry. Jewish Veg and SVA have adopted similar positions: on one hand, urging the abandonment or modification of *kapparot*, and on the other hand, declining to support active disruptions of the ritual, instead using the perennial issue of *kapparot* to provoke discussions of more fundamental matters related to animal welfare and rights.

Jewish Veg, SVA, and JIFA are poised to create fundamental and desperately needed changes in the North American Jewish community in the years ahead. They have strong relationships with key Jewish leaders in major cities, as well as in each of the major movements. Furthermore, they are working in close partnership with the leading national and international animal welfare and animal rights groups. Public Jewish communal support for animal compassion is on the rise.

NOTES

1. For a more comprehensive list of Jewish vegan and vegetarian publications, see note 25 in the introduction to this volume.

2. For more on the experiences of participants in such programs, see chapter 6.

3. "Four Questions: Aaron Potek, Yeshiva Chovevei Torah Rabbinic Students and Founder of MOOSHY," *Jew Hungry* (blog), September 7, 2011, http://jewhungrytheblog.com/four-questions-aaron-potek-yeshiva-chovevei-torah-rabbinic-student-and-founder-of-mooshy.

4. David Seidenberg, "Jewish Environmentalism in North America," David Seidenberg, November 2011, http://neohasid.org/ecohasid/jewish_enviro_history/.
5. Sarah Chandler, a coauthor of this report, organized that meeting.
6. "Jewish Organization Opposes Slaughter of Hens, Pleads for Mercy, Urges Protest," Jewish Veg, May 1, 2014, https://www.jewishveg.org/press-release-jewish-organization-urges-mercy-hens.
7. "JVNA Commends, Thanks Urban Adamah for Canceling Chicken-Slaughter Workshop," Jewish Veg, May 1, 2014, https://www.jewishveg.org/press-release-jvna-applauds-cancellation-chicken-slaughter.
8. Andy Altman-Ohr, "In Private, Urban Adamah Slaughters 15 Chickens at Center of Ethical Debate," *Jewish News of Northern California*, May 23, 2014, http://www.jweekly.com/2014/05/23/urban-adamah-slaughters-chickens-in-private.
9. Melissa Hoffman and Yadidya Greenberg, "We Need to Talk about Kapparot," *Scribe*: The *Forward*'s Contributor Network, October 6, 2016, http://forward.com/scribe/351506/we-need-to-talk-about-kapparot. See also Jay Michaelson, "Why This Hasid Was Right to Flip the Bird to Kapprot Protester," *Forward*, September 21, 2015, http://forward.com/opinion/spirituality/321311/why-hasid-was-right-to-flip-the-bird-at-anti-kapparot-protester.

AFTERWORD

AARON S. GROSS

This book starts with a basic fact of modern and contemporary Jewish life: that a significant minority of Jews identify themselves as vegan or vegetarian. It is equally concerned with a second fact: that many of these Jews are, it seems increasingly, connecting their commitment to plant-based diets to their practice of Judaism or their Jewish identity. Just what does this blending of Judaisms and various forms of veganism and vegetarianism mean? Is the relationship between plant-based dietary commitments and Jewish traditions an organic one? Obviously there are Jewish vegans and vegetarians, but is their veganism and vegetarianism Jewish? In sum, is there a phenomenon best characterized as *Jewish* veg'ism (I'll use veg'ism to refer to the spectrum of plant-based diets that run from vegan to ovo-lacto vegetarian)? This fundamental question, in addition to being directly engaged by some of the chapters of this volume, hovers behind the entire book.

The answer to this question of Jewish veg'ism depends on what one understands Jewish traditions to be in the first place. Some interpretations of Judaism will answer in the negative, stubbornly insisting that Judaism is inherently a carnivorous tradition. That said, I think the chapters that constitute this volume give us reason to believe that the better answer—and here I mean "better answer" in terms of descriptive adequacy rather than a moral judgment—is affirmative. This is so in part because the recent history of Jews linking Judaism and veg'ism documented in this volume—and the ongoing efforts to build on these historical associations also documented here—is simply too extensive to be seen as external to Judaism.

That said, the intelligibility of Jewish veg'ism is not only a product of the recent efforts of Jews who embrace it but also emanates from the fact that so much of the historical work of Judaism has consisted in explaining the exploitation of domesticated animals—a phenomenon, we all quickly forget, that characterizes only the last 10,000 years or so of the more than 200,000 years of human history. The most basic question of Jewish veg'ism, in some respects, is whether biblical and rabbinic explanations of human domination over and predation on other species are normative justifications (God wants humans to be dominating predators) or whether stories like the ninth chapter of Genesis, in which the nonviolence of Eden is replaced with a world in which humans eat animals and animals "fear and dread" humans, are instead descriptive of our broken world (a world God wants to see transformed). In telling a story in which humans become apex predators is the Torah endorsing or critiquing this reality? To see Jewish veg'ism as an authentic part of the Jewish past and the Jewish present is to bet that there has always been an element of critique in classical Jewish discussions of eating animals.

It is true that historically most Jewish communities have eaten animals and animal products when they could obtain them. The fact is so mundane, so strong a part of Jewish memory and self-conception, that it hardly seems a fact at all. It is, or has often been, unthought, like the breathing of air and the drinking of water. For many Jews, it is as if consuming the flesh, eggs, and milk of domesticated animals is just what people do, and Jews are no different in this regard; thus a critique of these dietary traditions seems unrelated to Judaism. Alternatively, it may seem as if the affirmation of eating animals and their products that most contemporary Jews participate in is so secure, so obviously embraced by Judaism, that no further thought needs to be given to it.

Yet the threshold of the unthought is where the real power of thought begins. The still mostly unthought possibility of a someday widely adopted practice of Jewish veg'ism may well be a crucial source of the renewal of Jewish thought as such. The very fact that despite its growing appeal, so many Jews will undoubtedly find the notion of Jewish veg'ism uncomfortable or worse signals that we are digging close to a power line. It suggests the way at least some of the streams of human life we call Jewish are built on a disavowal of another Jewish and human possibility that has been with us since the very beginning—that today, the often unthought possibility of a widespread embrace of veg'ism has, when we take the time to think about it, haunted Jewish traditions all along.

Far from being unrelated to the textual and social traditions commonly understood as Jewish—the Tanakh, rabbinic texts, kosher practice, communal meals, and so on—the practice of veg'ism is a human possibility that, through its rejection and endorsement, has helped build the tents of Jacob. The rejection of veg'ism as well as its embrace—that is, more fundamentally, seeing the question of Jewish veg'ism as a question that matters in some ultimate sense—has in fact been constitutive of Jewish traditions.

Within the capacious borders of its rabbinic and social corpus, there are both Jewish justifications of human predation and Jewish rejections of it. Indeed, the rejections and the embrace point to how eating animals and their products is charged with meaning, which is the deeper reality that both advocates and critics of Jewish veg'ism implicitly acknowledge. I am not insisting that historical Judaism demands veg'ism any more than I am insisting that historical Judaism demands eating meat; instead, I am insisting simply that Judaism offers a vehicle for discerning an ultimate question in our decisions to eat or eschew animal-based foods, and for this reason, there are distinctively Jewish ways to eat meat and, by the same token, distinctly Jewish ways to reject eating meat.

Jewish veg'ism is cast in the pages of this volume as a conclusion reached because of its resonance with Jewish values—and this is certainly fair—but at another level, Jewish veg'ism is the inversion of the world we Jews actually live in and have helped build along with our co-religionists: a world where humans are valued in relation to their wealth rather that their character, where the vulnerable—human or nonhuman animals—are ruthlessly exploited, and in which violence, slavery, and war are regular features (however much we may want to paint them as aberrations). Jewish veg'ism says *no* to these dark but widespread features of civilization and brings that *no* into daily life by rejecting one of the most visible ritual enactments of the dominant culture: consuming the muscle tissue of domesticated animals. Nobel Prize laureate Isaac Bashevis Singer is one of the few Jewish vegetarians to explicitly articulate this: "This is my protest against the conduct of the world. To be a vegetarian is to disagree—to disagree with the course of things today . . . starvation, cruelty—we must make a statement against these things. Vegetarianism is my statement. And I think it's a strong one."[1]

So if I am correct that Jewish veg'ism (or at least the ethical form of veg'ism I am privileging here) is largely a rejection of the unjust civilization we Jews dwell in and partially built, is it not precisely foreign to Judaism? The answer might be *yes* but for the fact that Judaism has wound within itself certain tensions and, in an alchemy hard to fathom, makes these very tensions the most essential stuff of Judaism. With good reason, the introduction to this volume features a quote from Genesis worth repeating here at its end:

> Behold I give to you all the vegetation that sprouts seed which is upon the face of all the earth, and every tree in which the fruit of the tree sprouts seed, for you it shall be as food. And to all the animals of the earth and to all the birds of the sky and to all that creeps on the earth, in which there is life, [I give] all the green vegetation for food. (Genesis 1:29–30)

In one of our oldest sacred texts, Genesis, we—Jewish vegan, vegetarian, and omnivore alike—tell the story of a world originally created to be vegan that ends up filled with meat-eating, injustice, and war. Yet Genesis 1:29–30 does not so much give a dietary recommendation for all time as it functions to articulate a tension between, on one hand, human violence to and domination over animal creation (Genesis 1:26–28 in which humans are given dominion) and, on the other, a lesser violence and greater benevolence (Genesis 1:29–30 in which humans, and it seems animals, are commanded to be vegan). This tension constantly repeats itself in Judaism's textual corpus.[2] In this sense, I think veg'ism, at least to the extent that it is a statement against bloodshed and violence, is, as a matter of fact rather than moral judgment, an organic part of Judaism.

Let us assume for a moment that this organic connection between veg'ism and one of the generative tensions of Judaism is simply a descriptive fact. Where would this conclusion leave us today as Jewish veg'ism mobilizes itself in an era when most Jews insist on eating animals? Following Jacques Derrida, I suggest it leaves us in the midst of

> an unequal struggle, a war (whose inequality could one day be reversed) being waged between, on the one hand, those who violate not only animal life but even and also this sentiment of compassion, and, on the other hand, those who appeal for an irrefutable testimony to this pity.... This war is probably ageless but it is passing through a critical phase.[3]

And this war—the tension itself—is what we have known as Judaism, not only the side in the war that happens to be ascendant or that appears most morally defensible. Taking a stand for or against human predation and domination of animal life can claim historical continuity with the Jewish past. The only truly un-Jewish position, in the sense of lacking continuity with Judaism's textual and social history, would be the claim that these questions are unimportant.[4]

While I have argued so far, wearing my scholar of religious studies cap, that Jewish veg'ism can claim historical connection with one of the generative tensions of Judaism's sacred texts and traditions, this is perhaps less important than the question of what the Jewish future will bring—and the ethicoreligious question of what the Jewish future *should* bring.

In closing, I speak as a Jew rather than as a scholar, to suggest that in an age when the consumption of animal products has congealed into the monstrously destructive system that now dominates animal agriculture globally, the question of Jewish veg'ism has become more urgent than ever. The dominant factory farm system has brought into being forms of *tza'ar ba'alei chayim* (suffering of living beings) inconceivable in Judaism's classical period—egg production that involves the immediate killing of hundreds of millions of male chicks, genetic "improvements" that turn animals' very bodies into cages of misery, and birds that cannot fly or even reproduce without artificial insemination. The stakes of Jewish veg'ism cut to the heart of Jewish traditions, for if the system of animal production that is ubiquitous among Jews today and spreading globally from its birthplace in the United States is truly compatible with Jewish law and ethics—if the suffering we humans routinely inflict on billions of animals each year is acceptable, as the complacency of most of us Jews with our present food system would suggest—what is Judaism? Jonathan Safran Foer, in his deeply (but not explicitly) Jewish book *Eating Animals*, asks a parallel question:

> The global implications of the growth of the factory farm, especially given the problems of food-borne illness, antimicrobial resistance, and potential pandemics, are genuinely terrifying. . . . If the world followed America's lead, it would consume over 165 billion chickens annually (even if the world population didn't increase). And then what? Two hundred billion? Five hundred? Will the cages stack higher or grow smaller or both? On what date will we accept the loss of antibiotics as a tool to prevent human suffering? How many days of the week will our grandchildren be ill? Where does it end?[5]

Perhaps the beginning of the end emerges in the hope Jewish veg'ism offers—the hope for at least a rejection of factory farming and, in its fullest expression, the rejection of all exploitation of the vulnerable by those with power.

I do not mean to invoke hope naively, as if all stories must end with hope. The truth is, anyone working toward a wider embrace of veg'ism has more reasons for frustration than celebration. But true hope, the messianic hope of Jewish traditions, begins precisely at the moment when hope seems most implausible. Abraham Joshua Heschel, who embodied just this kind of hope, liked to describe himself as an optimist against his better judgment. Vegetarians and vegans today are a seemingly hopelessly small minority, Jewish or otherwise. But if Judaism's texts teach us anything it is that a hopeless minority, even a rabble of slaves, may bend the long arc of history.

NOTES

1. Singer as cited in Steven Rosen, *Food for the Spirit: Vegetarianism and the World Religions* (New York: Bala Books, 1987), preface.

2. For discussion, see Aaron S. Gross, *The Question of the Animal and Religion: Theoretical Stakes, Practical Implications* (New York: Columbia University Press, 2014), chap. 6.

3. Jacques Derrida, *The Animal That Therefore I Am*, trans. David Wills, ed. Marie-Louise Mallet, Perspectives in Continental Philosophy (New York: Fordham University Press, 2008), 28–29.

4. For discussion, see Aaron S. Gross, "Jewish Animal Ethics," in *The Oxford Handbook of Jewish Ethics and Morality*, ed. Elliot Dorff and Jonathan Crane (Oxford: Oxford University Press, 2013).

5. Jonathan Safran Foer, *Eating Animals* (New York: Little, Brown, 2009), 143.

CONTRIBUTORS

Irad Ben Isaak is a doctoral researcher at the Institute of Cultural Studies at the Humboldt University of Berlin. His dissertation project explores the genre of Bildungsroman in Yiddish modern literature. Irad holds an MA in Yiddish literature from Tel Aviv University. His thesis examined the figure of the Yiddish poet and cultural activist Melech Ravitch, focusing on his vegetarian poetry and ideology. Growing up in Tel Aviv, Irad developed a strong criticism of common food practices after taking a wrong turn at the Carmel Market and finding himself at the slaughterhouses' back street.

Beth A. Berkowitz is Ingeborg Rennert Professor of Jewish Studies in the Department of Religion at Barnard College. She is the author of *Execution and Invention: Death Penalty Discourse in Early Rabbinic and Christian Cultures* (Oxford University Press, 2006), *Defining Jewish Difference: From Antiquity to the Present* (Cambridge University Press, 2012), and *Animals and Animality in the Babylonian Talmud* (Cambridge University Press, 2018). She is coeditor of *Religious Studies and Rabbinics: A Conversation* (Routledge, 2017). Beth is a life-long vegetarian and enjoys the companionship of her dog and volunteering at Sean Casey Animal Rescue near her home in Brooklyn.

Sarah Chandler is a Brooklyn-based Jewish educator, artist, activist, and poet. She holds an MA in Jewish education and an MA in Hebrew Bible from the Jewish Theological Seminary and a certificate in nonprofit management and Jewish communal leadership from Columbia University. She teaches, writes, and consults on issues related to Judaism, Earth-based spiritual practice, the environment, mindfulness, food values, and farming. Sarah previously served as the director of Earth Based Spiritual Practice for Hazon's Adamah Farm, where she was responsible for Food, Farm, and Forest Jewish Educational Programming. Recently, she was the chief compassion officer at the Jewish Initiative for Animals, where she supported institutions in establishing meaningful food policies rooted in Jewish ethics and animal welfare. Ordained as a Kohenet (Hebrew Priestess) in 2015, she is studying as a shamanic healer apprentice at the Wisdom School of SOPHIA and kabbalistic imaginal dream work at the School of Images.

Geoffrey D. Claussen is the Lori and Eric Sklut Scholar in Jewish Studies and associate professor of religious studies at Elon University. He was ordained as a rabbi at the Jewish Theological Seminary in 2007 and earned his PhD in Jewish thought there in 2011. Geoff became a vegetarian as a high school student in 1993 and became a vegan in 2010. He is the past president of the Society of Jewish Ethics, and he is the author of *Sharing the Burden: Rabbi Simḥah Zissel Ziv and the Path of Musar* (SUNY Press, 2015) and *Modern Musar: Contested Virtues in Jewish Thought* (Jewish Publication Society, forthcoming).

Jeffrey Cohan is the executive director of Jewish Veg and the author of "The Beet-Eating Heeb," a blog about the theology of veganism. Jeffrey became a vegetarian in 2007 and a vegan in 2011, after studying the Torah's instructions about dietary choices. An experienced public speaker, he worked in print and broadcast journalism before starting a second career in Jewish communal service. Jeffrey was the director of community relations for the Jewish Federation of Greater Pittsburgh from 2005 to 2012, before taking the helm of Jewish Veg, then known as Jewish Vegetarians of North America. Jeffrey earned a BA from the University of California at Berkeley and a master's of public management from Carnegie Mellon University.

Sherry F. Colb is C.S. Wong Professor of Law at Cornell Law School. She earned her JD from Harvard Law School. She has written about Jewish veganism in *Decoding Never Again*, which discusses the connections—and the sensitivity with which one must discuss connections—between Jewish identity, the Holocaust, and the plight of nonhuman animals. Her most recent book, *Beating Hearts: Abortion and Animal Rights* (coauthored with Michael C. Dorf), takes on the relationship between the pro-life view of abortion and the animal rights view of animal consumption.

Michael Croland is the author of *Oy Oy Oy Gevalt! Jews and Punk* (Praeger, 2016) and *Punk Rock Hora: Adventures in Jew-Punk Land* (Kindle Direct Publishing, 2019). He has written about Jews and punk for the *Forward, JTA, New Voices,* and *Jewcy*, among others. From 2005 to 2010, he ran a Jewish/vegan blog called "heebnvegan" (heebnvegan.blogspot.com). For more information about Michael and his books, visit OyOyOyGevalt.com.

Victoria (Veta) Greenstone is a former graduate fellow in the Forensic Linguistics Program in the Comparative Literature and Languages Department at Hofstra University. She holds a master's in forensic linguistics from Hofstra University. Apart from exploring sociocultural aspects of veganism, Veta's academic interests include investigating complex concepts in legal contexts. Her thesis explored the definition of legal personhood in the US courtroom through an examination of fetal, corporate, and animal rights cases. She currently works as an English teacher in northern Israel.

Aaron S. Gross is a historian of religions who focuses on modern and contemporary Jewish thought and ethics. Thematically his work centers on the study of animals and religion and food and religion. He is active in the leadership of the Society for Jewish Ethics and the American Academy of Religion's Animals and Religion Group, and founded and serves as CEO of the nonprofit advocacy organization Farm Forward. His book *The Question of the Animal and Religion: Theoretical Stakes, Practical Implications* (Columbia University Press, 2015) makes a case for elevating the category of the animal in the study of religion through an investigation into recent, high-profile scandals involving one of the largest kosher slaughterhouses in the world in Postville, Iowa.

Alan D. Krinsky is a writer and healthcare analyst. He earned his MPH from Brown University and his PhD in history and the history of science from the University of Wisconsin, Madison, with a dissertation titled *Let Them Eat Horsemeat!: Science, Philanthropy, State, and the Search for Complete Nutrition in Nineteenth-Century France*. He has taught courses on culture and food and on critical thinking. Alan's essays have been published in *The Forward*, *Conversations*, *Jewish Action*, South Africa's *Jewish Life*, *Jewish Press*, the *Rhode Island Jewish Voice and Herald*, *Huffington Post*, and *Providence Journal*. He is writing a book considering the compatibility or incompatibility of Judaism and Libertarianism. Despite the arguments he makes in his chapter, Alan is indeed a vegan.

Adrienne Krone is assistant professor of religious studies and director of Jewish Life at Allegheny College. She holds a doctorate in American religion from Duke University. Her research focuses on religious food and farming movements in North America. Her manuscript, "American Manna: Religious Responses to the American Industrial Food System," is an examination of the religious complexity that pervades contemporary Jewish and Christian food reform movements. Her current project is an ethnographic and historical study of the Jewish community farming movement in North America.

Jacob Ari Labendz is the Clayman Assistant Professor of Judaic and Holocaust Studies and the director of the Center for Judaic and Holocaust Studies at Youngstown State University. He holds a PhD in history from Washington University in St. Louis. He is on the advisory committee of the Shamayim V'Aretz Institute. When he is not advocating for Jewish veganism, Jacob writes about the history of Jews in and from Central Europe in the twentieth century and on contemporary antisemitism. Jacob is the editor of a collection of articles titled *Jewish Property after 1945: Cultures and Economies of Ownership, Loss, Recovery, and Transfer* (Routledge, 2018).

Hadas Marcus is an associate fellow at the Oxford Centre for Animal Ethics at St. Stephens House at Oxford University, under the direction of theologian Andrew Linzey, a prominent voice for animal protection and vegetarianism. Hadas is an active member of the Research Forum on the Human-Animal Bond under the auspices of the Tel Aviv University Porter School of Environmental Studies. A long-experienced instructor of English for academic purposes at Tel Aviv University and Oranim College of Education, Hadas spends much of her time writing articles and presenting papers at international conferences related to environmental humanities, animal welfare, and ecocriticism.

Richard H. Schwartz is president emeritus of Jewish Veg, formerly known as Jewish Vegetarians of North America (JVNA), and president of the Society of Ethical and Religious Vegetarians. He is the author of *Judaism and Vegetarianism*, *Judaism and Global Survival*, *Who Stole My Religion? Revitalizing Judaism and Applying Jewish Values to Help Heal our Imperiled Planet*, and *Mathematics and Global Survival*, as well as more than 250 articles and 25 podcasts at JewishVeg.org/schwartz. In 1987, he was selected as Jewish Vegetarian of the Year by JVNA and in 2005, he was inaugurated into the North American Vegetarian Society's Hall of Fame. He is a patron of the International Jewish Vegetarian Society and is the associate producer of a JVNA-sponsored documentary, *A Sacred Duty: Applying Jewish Values to Help Heal the World* (www.asacredduty.com), produced by Lionel Friedberg. He is spearheading a campaign to stress that a major shift toward plant-based diets is an essential part of shifting our imperiled planet onto a sustainable path.

Rabbi David Sears is the author of more than a dozen books on Jewish thought, including *The Vision of Eden: Animal Welfare and Vegetarianism in Jewish Law and Mysticism* (Orot 2003; revised 2015). A skilled visual artist, he has written and illustrated a number of Jewish children's books and also works as an abstract painter. Since 1997, Rabbi Sears has directed the Breslov Center of New York, an outreach organization founded by Rabbi Elazar Mordechai Kenig of Tzefat, Israel. He has been a vegetarian for many years.

David Mevorach Seidenberg is the author of *Kabbalah and Ecology: God's Image in the More-Than-Human World* (Cambridge University Press, 2015). David earned a doctorate from the Jewish Theological Seminary and ordination from both JTS and Rabbi Zalman Schachter-Shalomi. He studied physics at Dartmouth College and social ecology with Murray Bookchin. David teaches in communities and universities throughout North America, in Europe, and in Israel. His website, www.neohasid.org, is a well-loved source for eco-Torah, *nigunim* (Hasidic songs), and new liturgy. His research interests include Talmud, Maimonides, and Hasidic thought. He teaches about embodied Torah and dance, and leads Earth-centered rituals. David's writing can be found in the *Encyclopedia of Religion and Nature*, *The Forward*, *Tikkun*, and *The Jewish Journal*.

Shlomi Shmuel is a student of medicine and biomedical engineering at the Technion—Israel Institute of Technology. As part of being a vegan, he wishes to investigate different aspects of the vegan diet and spread the ideal of veganism using scientific methods. He is a former squadron commander in the Israel Defense Forces and is an amateur runner.

Nick Underwood holds a PhD in history from the University of Colorado, Boulder. When not reading Yiddish cookbooks and German recipes, he writes on Yiddish culture in France. Nick's first book project is titled *Yiddish Paris: Nation and Community in Interwar France*. His articles have been published by *Jewish Social Studies*, *French Politics, Culture and Society*, *Urban History*, and *East European Jewish Affairs*.

Rabbi Dr. Shmuly Yanklowitz is the president and dean of the Valley Beit Midrash (Jewish learning and leadership), the founder and president of Uri L'Tzedek (Orthodox social justice), the founder and CEO of the Shamayim V'Aretz Institute (Jewish animal welfare), and the author of ten books on Jewish ethics. *Newsweek* named Rav Shmuly one of the top fifty rabbis in the United States and the *Forward* named him one of the fifty most influential Jews.

INDEX

activism/advocacy, xiv, xv, 38, 72–73, 74, 182, 316
  intersectional forms of, xiv–xv, 122
  animal rights, 17, 30, 70–71, 72, 253, 268, 313–22
  vegan, ix, xii, xiii, xiv, xv, xvi, xix, xxin15–16, 71, 80, 30, 308, 315–22
  vegetarian, ix, xii, xiii, xv, xvi, 30, 39–40, 71
Adamah (organization), 125-27, 318-20
  Urban Adamah, 194n108, 318, 321
Agnon, S. Y., 76–77, 213n31, 224
Albo, Rabbi Joseph, xviii, 178, 179, 183, 184, 218, 220, 227, 233, 234–35, 236, 241–42, 247, 248n2, 277, 280
ancient Israelites, xvii, 162, 163, 164, 165, 167, 169, 170, 174, 184, 185, 190n54, 193, 199–202, 217, 234, 261, 278–81, 281, 288n37
  and animal sacrifice/slaughter, 167–68, 169, 170, 171–72
  domestication of animals, 169
  ecological concerns of, 169–70
  farming practices of, 169–70
  rules regarding meat consumption, 169, 170
anthropocentrism. *See* speciesism
animal agriculture, xi, xvii, 63, 118, 119, 120, 123, 127, 185, 194n108, 207, 211, 222, 223, 228, 229, 251, 254, 255, 268, 270, 305, 319, 328–29, 333
  in ancient Israel, xi, 169, 184
  and animal welfare, 68, 78, 185
  baleful consequences of, 67, 68, 87, 106, 124, 185, 328–29
  as practiced by modern Jews, 124–25
  progressive visions of, 185–86, 194n109, 328–29
  sustainable models of, 124, 125, 126, 169, 185–86, 268, 321
Animal Liberation, 3, 5, 19n11, 71, 236–37, 253. *See also* Singer, Peter
animal liberation movement, 6, 107
animals
  artistic renderings of, 68, 70–91
  as beings with souls, 164, 165, 166, 169, 171, 172, 175, 179, 180, 181, 182, 193n94, 203, 234, 239–41, 245, 246–47, 259–60, 280
  and capacity to think, reason, and act morally, 5, 6, 9, 11, 51–52, 59–62, 64, 72, 75, 104, 140, 164, 175, 201, 210, 219, 227–28, 237, 251, 255, 275, 276, 277, 278
  compassion fatigue, 203
  compassion towards, xviii, 4, 58–59, 68, 91, 96, 99, 104–5,

123, 131, 173, 175, 176, 181, 183, 186, 196, 197, 199, 201–3, 204, 205, 206–7, 210–11, 213n31, 223–24, 226–27, 228, 243–44, 245, 247, 256–57, 260, 283, 306, 307, 316, 319, 322, 328
cruelty towards, 59–60, 63, 67–68, 70, 72, 73, 78–79, 91, 104, 120, 131, 141, 185, 203, 205–7, 210, 215, 230n30, 231, 244, 245, 251, 252, 253, 254–55, 270–73, 280, 287n26, 305, 325, 328
as distinct from humans, 168, 176, 233, 255
domesticated vs. wild, 163, 170–73, 177–78, 183, 188n32, 189n35, 189n37, 189n39, 190nn59–60
empathy for, xvii, 4, 70, 71, 72, 89, 178, 195, 196, 199–201, 204, 205, 211, 260, 262, 273
ethical concern for, ix, x, 175–76, 251, 276
experimentation on, 69, 70, 140, 243, 252, 253–54, 270, 271, 272.
exploitation of, 96, 140, 161, 162, 164, 208, 222, 228, 253, 268, 270–71, 325, 327, 329
hunting of, 72, 148, 163, 171–72, 175, 184, 190nn59–60, 194n109
inherent worth of, xviii, 171, 177, 199, 203, 261, 261
as metaphors, xvi, 74, 76, 77, 87
moral status of, 195, 223
ownership of, 5
naming of, xviii

slaughter of, xviii, 17, 18, 30, 55, 56, 57, 58, 59, 60, 61, 62, 63, 64, 67, 70, 71, 76, 78, 80–86, 101, 102, 104–5, 106–7, 146, 166, 167, 170, 172, 174, 188n28, 190n59, 191n68, 194n108, 199, 205–7, 209, 210, 216n70, 223, 227, 251, 254, 255, 267, 268, 270, 287nn25–26 (see also *kashrut*)
as superior to humans, 228, 252
animal rights, x, xiv, xxin13, xxiiin25, 5, 6, 18, 30, 31, 67, 70, 72, 73, 74, 78, 80, 97, 98–99, 107, 140, 148, 161–63, 163, 170–72, 175–76, 182–83, 186n3, 194n108, 196, 199, 225, 237–38, 245, 246, 247, 251, 252, 253, 255, 263, 276, 284n4, 316–17, 322, 332
humans' rights vis-a-vis animals, 141, 177–78, 180–81, 234, 251–52, 264n27, 268, 270, 279, 280–81
legislation to protect, 231n33, 263
and punk rock/punk ethos, 99
See also Singer, Peter
animal sacrifice, xi, 169
animal suffering, xvi, xvii, 3–21, 102, 131, 136, 139, 140, 144–50, 161, 162, 195–96, 202
anticruelty legislation, 231
and biblical redactors, 13
human responses to, 4, 6, 7
in comparison to human suffering, 138–39, 141–42
and Jewish values, 102
obligation to prevent, 14, 199, 203, 211, 237–39, 243–45, 256, 264n27

and rabbinic teachings, 14–15, 174
and religiosity, 144, 148
and the Talmud, 15
and veganism, 137, 243
and Western religion, 6–7
animal welfare, x, xi, xiv, xvi, xviii, xx, 14, 67–91, 95, 98, 103, 104–5, 123, 126, 132, 142–43, 144–48, 161, 171, 182, 185–86, 222, 225, 227, 244–45, 251, 253–55, 257, 268, 281, 300, 304, 305, 307, 319, 320, 321–22, 331
antisemitism, 23, 24, 25, 26, 27, 30, 31, 34, 38, 39, 73, 87, 273, 294, 295, 297, 334
Ashkenazic Jewry, 74, 117, 129, 180
ASPCA, 231n33, 252, 321

Bekoff, Marc, 6
Bentham, Jeremy, 5, 6, 72, 252, 253–54. *See also* utilitarianism
Biale, David, xii
Bialik, Mayim, ix, 128

Cahan, Rabbi Joshua, 16
cannibalism, 73, 226, 227, 231n37
cattle
 as food, 6, 80
 as living animals, x, 6, 57, 59, 63, 64, 67, 68, 71, 73, 75, 87, 89, 89f, 91, 103, 104, 106–7, 167, 169, 170, 173, 183, 205–6, 207, 218, 224, 270, 271, 272, 287n26
 as slaughtered animals, 86
Chagall, Marc, 33, 71, 72, 80–81, 86–88, 88f, 89f

chickens
 as food, 53, 57, 80, 104, 105, 120, 208, 219, 329
 as living animals, 60, 61, 63, 64, 67, 73, 75, 76, 78, 79, 86f, 87, 89, 90f, 91, 107, 120, 126, 197, 206, 207, 270, 276, 290, 318–19
Christianity, ix, xii, 7, 8, 73, 144, 148, 162, 179, 292, 295
cookbooks, 34, 36, 39
 bilingual (Yiddish and English), 29
 kosher cookbooks, 108
 vegan and vegetarian, ix, 26–27, 29, 31–32, 33, 87, 95, 96, 108–12
covenantalism, 162–86
 definition of, 163–64
 as a basis for ecological ethics, 163
 and treatment of animals, 163
 and veganism, 163, 184, 185
cultural Judaism/Jews, xii, 290, 294, 298–99, 308
dairy consumption, 35, 36, 55, 63, 73, 102, 129n2, 150, 193–94, 251, 254, 275, 276, 277, 278, 299, 302, 319

Derrida, Jacques, 68, 328
de Waal, Frans, 6
Der idisher hoyz-doktor (The Yiddish House Doctor), 28
diaspora, the, 105, 106
Diaspora nationalism, 24-25, 31, 34, 41n10, 45n47
domesticated animals, 89, 163, 183, 186

in biblical literature, 163, 165,
167, 170–72, 181, 184, 187n12,
188n32, 189n37, 270, 325, 327
in modern literature, 71
dominionism, 7, 103, 131, 144, 148,
161–62, 163, 164–65, 167–68,
174, 184, 228, 239, 279, 283,
287n33, 328
Dubnow, Simon, 28, 45n47
Dylan, Bob, 69

Eating Animals. See Foer, Jonathan
Safran
ecocriticism, xvi, 68, 70, 71–72
environmentalism, xiv, 68, 185,
194n108, 222, 228, 316, 319.
See also under Judaism; veganism
(general); veganism (Jewish);
vegetarianism (general); and
vegetarianism (Jewish)
Eternal Treblinka, Paterson, Charles,
54, 74, 105

factory farming, 67, 69, 70, 80, 101,
105, 124, 126–27, 140, 148, 185,
205–6, 207, 210, 211, 216n70, 227,
228, 243, 254, 287n26, 321, 322,
328, 329
boycotts of, 207, 211
complicity of consumers in, 207
propaganda for, 207
Farm Forward (organization), 321
feminism, xiv, 5, 6, 19n10
Foer, Jonathan Safran, ix, 70, 71–72,
80, 207, 215n54, 287n, 329
Folksgezund (Popular Health), 28
food studies, x

foodways, x
American, 119–20
in ancient Israel, xi
among European Jews in interwar
period, 23–29, 31–39
Jewish, ix–x, 300, 302–4
and national identity, 25–26
among secular and cultural Jews,
299
Freud, Sigmund, 6, 292

Gandhi, Mahatma, 26, 32, 67, 224,
252
Ginger–The Vegetarian Community
Center in Jerusalem, xxn1
Gnessin, Uri Nisan, 25
Greenberg, Yadidya, 321-22
Gross, Aaron, xvi, xix, 13, 17, 321,
Goodall, Jane, 6

halakha, xii, xvii, 16, 74, 103, 119,
150, 154n31, 217, 226, 234, 244,
261, 276, 291, 293, 298, 302,
312n46
and animal products (e.g., shofars,
tefillin), 176, 191n68
and human-animal relationships,
176
and *kavod la-dam* ("respecting the
blood"), 175
and meat consumption, 226
and treatment of animals, 181, 254
halal, 305
Haredim. See ultra-Orthodox Judaism
hasidism, 87, 261
and concern for animals, 179–80,
182

and meat consumption, 221
and veganism, xi, 132
and vegetarianism, xi, 223
Haskalah (Jewish Enlightenment), 293, 299
Hazon, 317, 318-21
Hebrew, xvii, 38, 58, 73, 78, 102, 134, 135, 137–39, 141–43, 151, 167, 279, 291
Heschel, Abraham Joshua, 292, 329
Hillel (campus organization), 317, 321
Hitler, Adolf, 26, 34, 43, 48, 224
Hoffman, Melissa, 321-22, 323n9
Holocaust, the, x, xviii, 54, 69, 74, 77, 79, 87, 97, 105, 266, 269, 272–73, 275, 282–83, 296, 297, 316
   as metaphor for animal slaughter, 74, 87, 106
human-animal relationship, the, xviii, 68, 70, 71, 75–76, 87, 118, 120, 124, 128, 131, 133, 141, 149, 161, 163, 168, 175, 184–85, 186, 201, 222, 227–28, 235, 259, 263, 328
   in ancient Israel, 68, 168–69, 170
   as conceived of by Judaism, 163, 167, 239–47, 255, 261–62
   in rabbinic teachings, 173–77, 178, 257
   in the Torah, 173, 184, 236, 239–41, 260–61, 325–26
humans and animals
   distinctions between, 75, 167, 168, 175, 176, 180, 209–10, 211, 233–35, 237, 238, 239–42, 245–46, 251, 255, 258–59, 260
human obligations to animals, 199, 203, 237–38, 239, 255–57, 263
Humane Society, the, 215n46, 231n33, 254, 320, 321

Hyman, Paula, 24, 41n11

intersectionality, xiv, 121
Islam, 7
Israel (modern) xi, 68, 70, 133, 149, 154n31, 188n28, 191n65, 217, 289, 294, 295, 296, 297
   animal welfare organizations, 157n51
   conflict with Palestinians, 305–6
   creation of, 183
   cuisine and foodways of, 105, 107
   influence on global Jewish vegan and vegetarian practices, xiii–xiv
   religiosity in, 135–36
   veganism in, ix, xiii–xiv, xv, 69–70, 71, 92n1, 132, 152–53nn6, 305–6, 317
   vegetarianism in, xiii–xiv, xv, 53, 77–78, 79, 106, 132, 152–53nn6, 223

Jainism, 131, 193-94n106
Jewishness, ix, xiii, xvi, xix, 26, 39, 40, 95, 269, 273–75, 294
   in contemporary America, 100
   definitions of, 118
   and *kashrut*, 300
   and punk rock/punk ethos, 95, 99–100, 109
   and social justice, 304
   and veganism, x, xvii, xviii, 268
   and vegetarianism, 26, 27, 29, 31, 38
Jewish Initiative for Animals (JIFA, organization), xix, 320–22

Jewish punks, 97, 102
  and animal welfare, 102–7, 111
  and comic shtick, 103, 104, 105, 106, 108, 110
  and cookbooks, 109–121
  and Jewish identity, 100, 102, 103
  maverick spirit of, 101, 102, 110, 111
  and social justice, 95, 101
  and *tikkun olam*, 97–98, 111, 112
  and veganism and vegetarianism, 95, 97, 100–112
Jewish Vegan, The, 21, xxiin24, 117, 123, 128, 129n1, 130n26, 130n48, 130n49, 284n1, 284n2. *See also* Yanklowitz, Shmuly
Jewish Vegetarian Society, xxn1, xxiin25, 320, 334
Jewish Vegetarians of North America (JVNA and JewishVeg), 315–17, 321-22, 323n7
Judaism, xvii, xviii, 5, 7, 13, 53, 58, 71, 97, 98, 99–100, 101, 110, 111, 118–19, 124, 125, 126, 127, 128, 161, 261, 281, 291–92, 293, 294, 295, 296
  and animal products, 132
  and animal slaughter (see also *kashrut*), 174, 175, 176, 177, 179–80, 181–82, 204, 218, 226, 243–45, 251, 258, 268, 272, 282, 284n5, 321–22
  and animal suffering, 17, 20n29, 185, 199, 243, 263
  and dominion over animals (*see* dominionism)
  and ecological/environmental issues, 119, 123–24, 126, 300, 317, 318
  and ethical treatment of animals, 59, 68, 69, 91, 99, 123, 131, 164–65, 174–76, 177–78, 179, 184, 243–45, 251, 256–58, 263, 283, 284, 320, 328
  and ethics/values, xviii, 98, 131, 251, 263
  and exploitation of animals, 69, 268, 329
  and hunting animals, 175
  and individualism, 100
  and meat consumption, 31, 128, 132–33, 164–65, 166, 174, 176, 178, 183, 203, 243, 277–78, 301, 302, 326–27
  postethnic Judaism, xvii, 118–19, 122, 127, 128
  and punk music/ethos, xvi, 97–98, 110
  and race, xv
  and radical politics, 99
  tradition of questioning in, 101
  and veg'ism, 325–30
  and veganism, ix, xi, xiii, xv, xviii, 69, 73, 117, 122, 123, 127–28, 132, 133, 161, 178, 182, 233, 245, 246, 247, 255, 267, 268, 281, 282–83, 301–2, 312n46, 325
  and vegetarianism, ix, xi, xiii, 103, 124, 132, 161, 178–79, 225, 316, 325
Judaism and Vegetarianism, xxiin25, 71, 111, 123, 315. *See also* Schwartz, Richard

Kabbalism, 259–60
  and concern for animals, 179–82

Index

and humans reincarnated as
animals, 259–60
Kafka, Franz, 51, 72, 77, 224
Kalechovsky, Roberta, xxii–xxiiin25,
71, 123, 315
Kant, Imannuel, 140
Kaplan, Mordecai, 294–5
kapparot (repentance ceremony), 322
kashrut
and animal suffering, 277
in interwar Poland, 29–30
laws against, 25, 29, 30, 31, 34, 35,
37, 39, 41-2n12, 47n76
laws and practices, xi, 24, 25, 26,
41, 46n68, 55, 63, 73, 107, 108,
110, 111, 119, 125, 126, 131,
145, 148, 150, 169, 171, 175,
184, 218, 225, 273, 274–77,
278, 279, 284, 286n14, 287n29,
298, 299, 300, 301, 305, 307,
317, 319, 320, 322, 326
and ritual slaughter (*shechitah*),
30, 35, 70, 74–75, 87, 89, 125,
126, 174, 176, 181–82, 183,
218, 220, 221, 243, 276, 277,
286n21, 287n25, 305, 317,
318–19, 320, 321
and veganism, 119, 298
Kenig, Leo, 28–29
Keret, Etgar, 79–80
Kipnis, Menakhem, 29
Kook, Abraham Isaac, xvii–xviii,
71, 133, 182–84, 185, 193n102,
217–31, 286n23
attitude towards animal slaughter,
183, 220, 221, 222
compassion toward animals, 183
and meat consumption, 183, 184,
219, 220, 221, 222

messianic vision of, 183, 185, 217,
218–19, 220
and *shechitah*, 221–22
and veganism, 184, 185
Kwall, Roberta Rosenthall, xi, 285n6,
298

Ladino, 291
LGBT[QIA] Jews/Israeli Citizens,
110, 305
locavorism, 119–21

Magid, Shaul, xvii, 118–19, 122, 127,
128
Maimonides (Rambam), 181, 186n1,
224, 242, 245, 288n37
on animal slaughter, 177
on the obligation to prevent cruelty
to animals, 223, 245, 258–59
respect for animals, 177–78,
191n72, 261, 281
and veganism, 179
masorti (traditional Judaism), 136,
154n31
meat consumption, xviii, 51, 63, 69,
71, 73, 102, 117, 126, 136, 140,
141, 142, 143, 161, 169, 176, 185,
207, 236, 244, 270, 277, 281, 304,
312, 316, 317, 327, 328
arguments against, 208–9, 251–52
in art and literature, 76, 77, 78–80,
107, 108
in the bible, xi, 188n28, 279–80,
281
in contemporary society, 205
ethical forms of, 319–20

as forbidden (or discouraged) by
Judaism, 165, 166, 185, 191n69,
217–18, 223, 234, 240, 278–81,
287–88n34, 282, 301, 326
as part of Jewish life, 302–3
justifications for, 207–8, 260
as permitted by Judaism, xi, 104–5,
132–33, 164–65, 167, 180, 184,
188n28, 191n69, 203, 217, 218,
220, 234, 236, 243, 246, 281,
282, 283, 287–88n34, 326
pleasures of, 207–8
rationales/justifications for, xi, 73,
108, 207–8, 209–10, 219, 223,
226
terrible consequences of, 222
vegan/vegetarian alternatives to
(e.g., soy franks, veggie burgers,
etc.), 79–80, 105, 117, 128, 225
Yiddish terms for, 62
meat reduction/restriction, 86, 161,
185, 225–26, 254, 298–99, 303,
316, 317, 318, 319, 321
Mendelssohn, Moses, 293, 300, 301,
306
Messianic era
and veganism, 133, 183, 185
and vegetarianism, xi, 218–19, 220,
222
See also Kabbalah; Kook, Abraham
Isaac
Mishnah, the, 5, 9, 10, 11, 12–13, 14,
20n22, 199, 228, 257, 261
mitzvot (commandments), 124, 175,
176, 180, 181, 220, 244, 256, 273,
274, 277–78
Mizrahim, xiv
Moskowitz, Chandra, 108-111
Muslims, ix, xii, 305,

Musar movement, xvii, 195–211
and compassion for animals, 195,
196, 197–98, 199–207
as moral example for modern Jews,
210–11
and veganism, 211
See also Ziv, Simchah Zissel

Nachman of Breslov, Rabbi, 223
Nachman, Moshe ben (Ramban)
(Nachmonides), 180–81, 187n11,
243, 280–81
Nazis, xvi, 23, 24–25, 27, 30, 35–40,
46-7n74, 82, 105, 108, 272–73,
283
treatment of animals, 224
NewKosher Cookbook, 108, 111, 112
non-Jews, 14–15, 286n18
Nussbaum, Martha, 6

Orthodox Judaism, ix, xiv, 16, 35, 53,
71, 73, 78, 81, 98, 126, 136, 150,
217, 273, 274, 278, 281, 320
ovo-lacto vegetarianism, 276, 325
Oz, Amos, 77–79, 92–93n19

Palestine (mandate), xvii, 24, 182–83,
217, 294
Palestinians, ix, xxin16, 305, 306–7
Passover, 32, 101, 109, 110, 127–28,
129n2, 286n18, 290, 302, 303–4
Seders for vegans and vegetarians,
117–18
pescatarianism, 76, 139, 140, 142,
143, 151

PETA (People for the Ethical Treatment of Animals), 102, 105, 107, 193n102, 254, 321
pigs
  as food, 80, 104, 224, 226, 275, 299
  as living animals, 5, 57, 63–64, 104, 206–7, 246, 270
  as metaphors, 105
pikuach nefesh (saving a life), 98–99, 123
Pissarro, Camille, 89, 90f, 91f
Poland, xvi, xvii, 23, 24–25, 27-28, 29–31, 34, 35, 37, 39–40, 46n68, 49–50
Portman, Natalie ix, 78, 80, 99, 106
Post Punk Kitchen, 109–10
purity (ethical, spiritual, etc,), 20n23, 132, 133, 162, 179, 192n81

race/racism, xiv, xv, 121, 233, 237, 305,
Ramones, 95, 102
Rashi, 17, 174, 187n10, 190n58
Ravitch, Melech, 49–64
  biography of, 49
  path to vegetarianism, 49, 50–53, 56, 57
  personal concern for animals, 53–56
  poetry and essays by, 49, 50, 51, 53–54, 57–64
Reconstructionist Judaism, 150, 294, 296
Reform Judaism, 136, 150, 154n29
restaurants, 25, 53, 80, 275, 299
  vegan, 69, 109
  vegetarian, 27, 33–34, 39, 87, 277

Rosh Hashanah, 110

Sacred Duty, A (film), 316,
Sabbath, the, 219, 269, 273–74
  and animal labor, 7, 164, 257, 268
  cooking on, 33
Savage, Nigel, 318, 320
Schwartz, Richard, xvii, xxiin25, 71, 111, 123-24, 315-16
Schweitzer, Albert, 67, 131–32, 149
secularism, 32, 49–50, 62, 69, 74, 99, 142, 144, 172, 251–52, 293–94
  in Israel, 132, 136
  and Yiddish, 53, 62
secular Jews, 25, 34, 63, 100, 136, 141, 150, 289, 291
  and veganism, ix, xviii–xix, 268, 290, 298–99, 308
  who promote animal welfare, 71
Sephardim, xiv
Sforim, Mendele Mocher, 71, 76
Shamayim V'Aretz Institute, ix, xix, xx, xxn1, xxiin25, 320
Singer, Isaac Bashevis, xvi, 49, 71, 72, 73–76, 105, 224, 327
Singer, Peter, xviii, 3, 6, 236–39
  critiques of, 6, 7
  and veganism, 239
  See also *Animal Liberation*
Soutine, Chaim, 72, 80–82, 83–86f
speciesism, 68, 71, 140, 204, 236–39, 242–43, 258, 307
  and Judaism, xviii, 161, 177, 179, 196, 223, 233, 234, 245–46, 247, 251, 255, 257, 258–59, 262

tikkun olam, 96, 97–98, 99, 100, 111, 112, 220, 251, 300
Tolstoy, Leo, 32, 78, 224, 251–52
Torah, the, x, xi, xvii, 23, 103, 185, 190n58, 282
 and animal consumption, 166
 animal husbandry in, 168
 and animal rights, 170, 171
 and animal sacrifice, 166–68, 169, 233, 235–36
 and animals' moral standing, 164
 and animal slaughter, 166, 168, 171–72
 and animal welfare, 11, 161, 169, 199, 200
 and compassion for animals, 200, 211
 and dominion over animals, 7, 103, 131, 144, 148, 161–62, 63, 164–65, 167–68, 174, 184, 228, 239, 279, 283, 287n33, 325–26, 328
 and meat eating, xviii, 184, 203, 236
 taboo against consuming blood, xi, 165, 166, 171, 174, 240
 treatment of animals in, xvii, 5, 8, 9–10, 163, 165, 170–71, 172–73, 184, 197–204, 224, 235, 239–42, 256–57
 and veganism, 172, 184, 328
treif (nonkosher), 174, 275, 299
Twain, Mark, 252–53
tza'ar ba'alei chayim (suffering of living creatures), 16, 53, 103, 123, 131, 174, 196, 202, 223, 234, 243–45, 264n27, 267–68, 300, 321, 328. *See also* animal suffering

ultra-Orthodox Judaism, ix, 136, 150
utilitarianism, 5, 6, 68, 69, 72, 237, 246, 252, 253, 257, 259, 262. *See also* Singer, Peter

veganism (general), 63, 68, 69, 70, 71, 72, 91, 106, 119, 121, 122, 124, 127, 129n2, 133, 140, 142, 143, 149, 151, 161, 163, 178, 179, 182, 183, 185, 186, 195, 203, 239, 254, 283–84, 290, 298, 299, 305, 306–7, 316, 318, 319, 321, 325–29
 abolitionist veganism, 185, 186, 193, 268, 321
 among African Americans and People of Color, xiv, xv
 and animal rights, 162
 compatibility with Judaism, xi, xvii, xviii, 118, 121, 122, 123–24, 161, 267, 273, 275–76, 277–79, 282, 283, 301–2, 304, 307, 325, 326, 327, 328
 definition of, 117–18
 and environmental concerns, xiv, 118, 125, 133, 300
 and ethical considerations, 70, 102, 125, 133, 225, 247, 263, 290
 as a growing movement, 71, 80, 92n1
 and health, xiv, 95, 98, 102, 125, 133, 247
 hostility towards, 121
 and Jewish values, 99, 300
 and Jewishness, 126, 290, 300
 and *kashrut*, 111, 273, 290, 299
 paths toward, 69, 78, 117, 120–21, 122, 125, 126, 149, 211, 239, 268–69, 275–76

popularity of among Jews, 235
and punk rock/punk ethos, 95,
    96–97, 101, 109–12
and secular Judaism, 298, 299, 308
and spiritual concerns, 179
stereotypes about, 149
veganism (Jewish), ix, x, xi, xxn1,
    xxiin23, 118–19, 122, 123, 127,
    128, 277, 283, 290, 291, 298, 300,
    301, 304, 305, 307, 308, 322n1,
    325, 327
    arguments on behalf of, xii
    artistic expressions of, 111–12
    authenticity of, xii
    communities based on, xii, xvii,
        xix, 122, 124–25, 127, 307–8
    definition of, ix, 122
    and the environment, 98, 111, 124,
        126, 127, 128, 133
    and ethics, 111, 124, 273, 289
    and *halakha*, 111, 301
    and health, 111, 123, 126, 318
    as an import from non-Jewish
        cultures, xii
    paths toward, 100–101, 124, 317
    increasing popularity of, ix
    and progressive causes, 306–7
    and punk rock/punk ethos, 95, 99,
        100, 101, 102, 108–10
    resistance to, 4
Veganism in an Oppressive World, xv
*Vegetarian Judaism: A Guide for
    Everyone*, xxiin25, 71, 123, 315. See
    also Kalechovsky, Roberta
vegetarianism (general), xvi, 25, 28,
    51–52, 56, 70, 71, 77, 120, 123,
    131, 140, 142, 143, 149, 151, 161,
    178, 184, 195, 210, 227, 231, 239,
    254, 301, 316, 325–29

arguments against, 56–57
artistic expressions of, xiii, xvi, 49,
    51, 53–54, 55, 57–64, 70–91,
    103–8, 110, 111–12
compatibility with Judaism, xi,
    xvii, 25, 26, 28, 99, 107, 219,
    325, 326, 327, 328
criticism of, 92–93n19, 224
and ecological/environmental
    concerns, 55, 63, 123, 223, 319
and ethics, 53–56, 70, 74, 123,
    133, 203, 218, 219, 224,
    226–27, 319
in Europe, 26, 28, 63
financial benefits of, 39–40
flexibility within, 298–99
as a gesture of defiance, 327
and health and wellness, xiv, 24,
    27–28, 29, 31–32, 36, 37, 38,
    39, 43, 45n43, 54, 63, 95, 102,
    121–22, 123, 220, 222, 223,
    225–226, 228, 243, 251–52,
    319
as a movement, xvi, 26, 29, 31
partial-vegetarianism, 225–26
paths toward, 29, 53, 62–63,
    74, 78, 79, 119–20, 125, 149,
    208–9, 319
as a political tool, 26
and punk rock/punk ethos, 95, 97,
    98, 99, 101–8, 111–12
and the Yiddish press, 28
vegetarianism (Jewish), ix–x, 26, 123,
    224, 315, 317, 325, 327
    authenticity of, xii
    and the environment, 98, 126
    and family conflict, 25
    and gender, 24, 27
    and health, 24, 98, 123, 126

historiography of, 26
in interwar Europe, 23, 25, 27
movements based on, 23, 29
and pacifism, 23
paths toward, 23, 24
and politics, 25, 27
popularity of, ix
and punk rock/punk ethos, xvi, 99, 101, 102, 103–8
in the United States, 24
various forms of, xiv

Yanklowitz, Shmuly, xviii, xix, 123, 301, 320
Yiddish, 33, 44n36, 45n47, 49–50, 51, 53, 59, 61, 63, 73, 74, 87, 89, 289, 291
periodicals, 16, 27
vegetarian cookbooks, 29, 87
vegetarianism-related writings, 28–29, 39, 55, 57, 61, 62, 64, 76
Yiddishism, 24, 31
See also Ravitch, Melech; Sforim, Mendele Mocher; Singer, Isaac Bashevis
YIVO, 28, 45n47
Yom Kippur, 110

Zionism, 289, 294, 295, 296–97
Ziv, Simchah Zissel, 195, 196–97, 198, 199–202, 203, 205, 207, 208–9